Civil Society and Social Capital in Post-Communist Eastern Europe

This book presents a selection of recent research on the general theme of civil society and social capital. In particular, it brings together in one volume a selection of articles that have helped to take the debate forward on the relation between social capital and democratisation and on the role and political strength or weakness of civil society in post-communist countries. The authors range in their approaches from detailed examinations of the extent and character of social capital in different societies in post-communist Eastern Europe, to studies of civil society in particular countries of the region and case studies of different civil society groups including environmental groups, local interest groups, pensioners' groups, car drivers' groups and trade unions. The newly written introduction provides a critical review of the wider body of literature on the theme, placing the selected articles in a broader context, and identifying ways forward for future research.

This book is a compilation of articles published in *Europe-Asia Studies*.

Terry Cox is Professor of Central and East European Studies at the University of Glasgow, UK, and Editor of the journal *Europe-Asia Studies*. His recent research has focused on the politics and sociology of post-communist transformations in East Central Europe, including work on civil society and the politics of interest representation.

Routledge Europe-Asia Studies Series

A series edited by Terry Cox
University of Glasgow

The **Routledge Europe-Asia Studies Series** focuses on the history and current political, social and economic affairs of the countries of the former 'communist bloc' of the Soviet Union, Eastern Europe and Asia. As well as providing contemporary analyses it explores the economic, political and social transformation of these countries and the changing character of their relationships with the rest of Europe and Asia.

Civil Society and Social Capital in Post-Communist Eastern Europe

Edited by
Terry Cox

Routledge
Taylor & Francis Group

LONDON AND NEW YORK

University *of* Glasgow

First published 2014
by Routledge
2 Park Square, Milton Park, Abingdon, Oxfordshire OX14 4RN

and by Routledge
711 Third Avenue, New York, NY 10017

First issued in paperback 2015

Routledge is an imprint of the Taylor & Francis Group, an informa business

British Library Cataloguing in Publication Data
A catalogue record for this book is available from the British Library

ISBN 13: 978-1-138-95366-6 (pbk)
ISBN 13: 978-0-415-71719-9 (hbk)

Typeset in Times New Roman
by Taylor & Francis Books

Publisher's Note
The publisher accepts responsibility for any inconsistencies that may have arisen during the conversion of this book from journal articles to book chapters, namely the possible inclusion of journal terminology.

Disclaimer
Every effort has been made to contact copyright holders for their permission to reprint material in this book. The publishers would be grateful to hear from any copyright holder who is not here acknowledged and will undertake to rectify any errors or omissions in future editions of this book.

Contents

Citation Information

The chapters in this book were originally published in *Europe-Asia Studies*, various issues. When citing this material, please use the original page numbering for each article, as follows:

Chapter 7
Civil Society, Trade Unions and Post-Soviet Democratisation: Evidence from Russia and Ukraine
Paul Kubicek
Europe-Asia Studies, volume 54, issue 4 (2002) pp. 603-624

Chapter 8
Driving at Democracy in Russia: Protest Activities of St Petersburg Car Drivers' Associations
Markku Lonkila
Europe-Asia Studies, volume 63, issue 2 (March 2011) pp. 291-309

Chapter 9
Making a Difference? NGOs and Civil Society Development in Russia
Jo Crotty
Europe-Asia Studies, volume 61, issue 1 (January 2009) pp. 85-108

Please direct any queries you may have about the citations to
clsuk.permissions@cengage.com

Notes on Contributors

Martin Åberg is Professor of History at Karlstad University. His previous publications include *Social capital and democratisation. Roots of trust in post-communist Poland and Ukraine* (co-author, 2003) and *Swedish and German Liberalism. From factions to parties 1860–1920* (2011). His current research interests include migration, social capital, and political parties. *Email*: martin.aberg@kau.se

Babken V. Babajanian is a Research Fellow at the Overseas Development Institute, London. His research interests include international and comparative dimensions of social policy, poverty reduction strategies, social exclusion, decentralisation, and civil society. He has consulted extensively for the World Bank, the UK Department of International Development (DFID), UNICEF, ADB and GIZ. His notable publications on post-Soviet countries include articles in *Development in Practice, Post-Soviet Affairs*, and *Communist and Post-Communist Studies. Email*: b.babajanian@odi.org.uk.

Jo Crotty is Professor of Strategy and Corporate Social Responsibility at the University of Salford. Her publications include articles in *Environment and Planning C: Government and Policy, Non-profit and Voluntary Sector Quarterly, Progress in Development Studies, Europe-Asia Studies, Organization Studies*, and *Communist and Post Communist Studies. Email*: j.crotty@salford.ac.uk,

Terry Cox is Professor of Central and East European Studies at the University of Glasgow, UK. His recent publications include edited books *Challenging Communism in Eastern Europe: 1956 and its Legacy* (Routledge 2008), *Reinventing Poland: Economic and Political Transformation and Changing National Identity* (Routledge 2008) and *Reflections on 1989 in Eastern Europe* (Routledge 2012), as well as articles in *Perspectives on European Politics and Societies* and *Journal of Agrarian Change. Email*: Terry.Cox@glasgow.ac.uk.

Kathleen M. Dowley is an Associate Professor of Political Science at SUNY New Paltz, where she is also the Coordinator of the Women's, Gender, and Sexuality Studies Program. Her research and writings focus on ethnopolitics and democratic governance in Europe and Eurasia, including publications in the *International Journal of Public Opinion, Comparative Political Studies*, and *Communist and Post-Communist Studies. Email*: dowleyk@newpaltz.edu.

Seán Hanley is Senior Lecturer in East European Politics at University College London. His research interests include the development of new anti-establishment parties, the political representation of older people in post-communist states, and the comparative politics of the right in Central and Eastern Europe. He is author of *The New Right in the New Europe: Czech transformation and right-wing politics, 1989-2006* (Routledge 2007). *Email*: s.hanley@ucl.ac.uk

Paul Kubicek is Professor of Political Science and Director of International Studies at Oakland University. His larger research project on post-communist trade unions was published as *Organized Labor in Post-Communist States: From Solidarity to Infirmity* (University of Pittsburgh Press). *Email*: kubicek@oakland.edu.

Markku Lonkila is a Professor of Sociology at the University of Jyväskylä. His publications include several articles in international journals and the monograph *Networks in the Russian Market Economy* (Palgrave Macmillan, 2011).
Email: markku.lonkila@jyu.fi

Tsveta Petrova is a Fellow at the Harriman Institute at Columbia University. Her articles have appeared in *Comparative Political Studies, Europe-Asia Studies*, and most recently, in the *Journal of Democracy*. Her book, *Exporting Revolution: The New Role of Eastern Europe in Democracy Promotion*, is under contract with Cambridge University Press. *Email*: tap25@cornell.edu

Brian D. Silver is Professor of Political Science at Michigan State University (East Lansing, Michigan). His career specialty is the politics and demography of Eurasia. He has published widely on public opinion and population change with a special focus on ethnicity, both in Eurasia, in Europe broadly, and in the United States. *Email*: bSilver@msu.edu

Anders Uhlin is Professor of Political Science at Lund University, Sweden. His main research interests include civil society and democratisation, focusing specifically on Post-Communist Europe and Southeast Asia as well as a global context. He is the author of *Post-Soviet Civil Society: Democratisation in Russia and the Baltic States* (Routledge 2006) and *Legitimacy Beyond the State? Re-examining the Democratic Credentials of Transnational Actors* (Palgrave 2010, co-edited) as well as articles in journals such as *Democratization, Europe-Asia Studies, Global Governance, International Political Science Review*, and *Third World Quarterly*.
Email: anders.uhlin@svet.lu.se

Introduction: Transformation, Post-socialist Legacies and the Problem of Civil Society

TERRY COX

In the literature on social transformation and the political transitions from communist rule in Eastern Europe the predominant view has been that while formal democracy has been established in much of the region, in the shape of the new constitutional and institutional arrangements of liberal democracy, democratic consolidation depends further on the embedding of these institutions into society and the active involvement of citizens in the political process. According to Agh (1998, p. 9), the 'minimum democracy' of new democratic institutions 'should be, in fact, only the start of the democratization process, and its logic immediately moves beyond minimum procedures in any extension of that process'. This logic requires that citizens should have effective mechanisms 'for pressing claims on the state' (Parrott 1997, p. 6). However, in order to ensure the capacity of citizens to press claims, consolidation also requires that social groups should have means of influencing decision makers more directly than in the processed and amalgamated forms of party programmes.

Crucial to democratic consolidation therefore, is the question of the relations between state and civil society. According to Linz and Stepan, 'the conditions must exist for the development of a free and lively civil society' which can act as 'that arena of the polity where self-organizing groups, movements, and individuals, relatively autonomous from the state, attempt to articulate values, create associations and solidarities, and advance their interests' (Linz & Stepan 1996, p. 7).

In this way, the predominant view of post-communist democratic transitions has placed enormous responsibilities on civil society as the basis for democratic consolidation. As Encarnación has noted, 'according to the prevailing conventional wisdom, a strong civil society lies behind successful democracies while a weak civil society is the root of failed or flawed democracies. This axiom ... also permeates policy debates within the international aid community about the most effective way to fortify fragile and fledgling democracies' (Encarnación 2003, p. 3).

In view of this high level of expectations on civil society, and as a further step in the reasoning, it has become necessary therefore to specify those characteristics of civil society that are important in providing a basis for democratic consolidation. On this point a further assumption has been introduced that successful democratization not only requires a civil society in which groups 'articulate values, create associations and solidarities, and advance their interests', as Linz and Stepan had suggested, but that civil society, following Tocqueville, should be sustained by widely shared values and a rich associational life. And since such characteristics were observed to be only weakly developed in Eastern Europe, it has been argued that democratic consolidation has remained incomplete. A major factor underlying the weakness of associational life was seen to be the absence of appropriate forms of social capital to sustain high levels of trust and cooperation between the wide range of different individuals and groups with differing outlooks and interests that are typical of complex and heterogeneous modern societies.

Social capital and civil society

Perhaps the most important influence on discussions of social capital and its role in providing a basis for the development of a rich associational life has been the work of Robert Putnam. According to Putnam, social capital takes the form of 'trust, norms and networks that can improve the efficiency of society by facilitating coordinated actions' and this enables and supports interaction between governments and citizens (Putnam 1993, p. 167). The stock of social capital in a society is therefore seen as a crucial basis for economic and political transformation and development. A high level of trust encourages engagement in reciprocal exchange relations and thus enables the formation of the networks on which civil society is based. In turn this facilitates the formation of interest groups, associations and political parties and fosters trust in government and formal political institutions (Putnam 1993, pp.170–176).

Thus, for Putnam, as Babajanian notes in this collection, 'interpersonal trust is the key variable that facilitates societal cooperation. The definition of trust used by Putnam stems from game theoretical assumptions, in which trust is an assessment by an individual of whether or not the behaviour of other individuals is trustworthy. This holds that overlapping positive expectations about other individuals' actions can lead to cooperation and collective action' (Babajanian 2008, p. 39).

However, not all forms of social capital are seen as having such a positive effect on community relations and, as Åberg notes in this collection, a distinction is made between positive or communitarian social capital on the one hand, and negative or non-communitarian social capital on the other hand. The negative form of social capital exists in the context of 'particularistic networks and informal connections' and gives rise to related phenomena 'such as clientelism and corruption' (Åberg 2000, p.14). For Putnam, negative social capital is generated in such networks because 'sanctions that support norms of reciprocity against threats of opportunism are less likely to be imposed upwards and less likely to be acceded to, if imposed' (Putnam 1993, p. 174).

Thus, a distinction is made between different kinds of social capital, not all of which have a positive influence. Positive or 'communitarian social capital' is often described as 'bridging social capital' in that it connects groups and individuals in a wider society, and is therefore seen as a positive support for a strong civil society. It is contrasted with 'bonding social capital' or 'non-communitarian social capital' that is characteristic of more close-knit local and kinship networks, which is seen as a barrier to the development of democratisation and a strong civil society.

In recent years this conceptualisation has informed the strategies of a number of leading international agencies concerned with aid, development and democracy promotion, including for example USAID as well as the World Bank. Reviewing the literature on these strategies Encarnación (2003, p. 17) has commented that 'numerous academics and policy experts have come to view civil society as the ideal vehicle to dislodge authoritarian, corrupt and incompetent governments, to fortify civil liberties and human rights, to promote good governance and economic prosperity, to improve health and general well-being, to deter nationalism and ethnic conflict and to consolidate fledgling and fragile democratic institutions and practices'.

Analyses linking social capital and a strong civil society to democratisation attracted much attention in the comparative literature that emerged in response to the fall of authoritarian regimes in southern Europe and Latin America from the 1970s onwards. Many contributors to this research argued that a strong civil society was an important precondition for successful democratisation, and in particular, as argued by Linz and Stepan (1996) and Diamond (1994), for the consolidation of democracy following the initial post-authoritarian constitutional and institutional changes. As Diamond suggested, an active civil society was most important 'for consolidating democracy than for initiating it' (1994, p. 5).

However, at the same time as such ideas have been very influential, they have also prompted much debate and the predominant approach has been criticised from a number of different angles, in relation both to its understanding of the role of social capital and to its discussion of the weakness of civil society. With regard to social capital, it has been suggested that seeing it as basis for the vitality of community or civic life involves a circular argument. For example, according to Portes (1998, p. 5), it involves 'equating social capital with the resources acquired through it' and therefore it 'can easily lead to tautological statements'. As further noted by Haynes (2009, p. 10), 'untangling the causes, effects, correlations and conjunctions is a difficult undertaking when dealing with networks and complex interdependencies'.

There are also problems concerning the different types of relations and networks that are brought together under the heading of social capital, and what the political implications are for the possession of different types of social capital. A number of authors have questioned whether an active involvement in associational life actually produces experiences where people are socialised into democratic practices and attitudes (Newton 1997; Cohen 1999). As Bermeo has commented, 'the idea that a dense associational landscape is more likely to be a democratic one appears highly questionable' (2000, p. 239).

A further problem concerns the question, for example raised by Levi (1996), of whether social trust can form the basis for communitarian social capital in situations where societies are divided along ethnic, religious or other cultural lines so that different groups and associations are in conflict over basic issues that potentially undermine the establishment of stable democracy with broad agreement over the political rules of the game.

This in turn relates to a problem raised more generally with regard to civil society. For example, as Foley and Edwards (1996, p. 41) have suggested, there seems to be a paradox in Putnam's views on how shared values and trust can necessarily provide a basis for democratic politics in situations where people are divided by different interests:

> Putnam's preoccupation here is a familiar one. In order to foster a genuine spirit of 'wider cooperation', his argument suggests, such associations must not be 'polarized' or 'politicized'. They must 'bridge' social and political divisions and thus, presumably, be autonomous from political forces. These caveats echo a long tradition of 'pluralist' analysis. Yet how can such associations shape political participation and 'civic engagement' without engaging in specifically political issues and without representing compelling social interests?

Other writers have questioned the historical evidence for whether there was a close relationship between strong associational life and democratisation in Western Europe and North America. For example, a collection of articles edited by Skocpol and Fiorina (1999) has suggested a more nuanced version of the past relationship between civil society and democratisation in the USA, and Tarrow (1996) has questioned Putnam's focus on the role of civil society in northern Italy. Others have described examples of countries where a strong associational life formed the context in which authoritarian rule emerged, as in Weimar Germany where, according to Berman (1997), conflicts of outlook and interest between equally strong social movements enabled the Nazis to take power. Taking more recent examples, Encarnación (2003) has examined the contrasts between Brazil in recent decades, where the context of a relatively strong civil society did not provide the foundation for clear democratic consolidation while post-Franco Spain achieved a more secure democratic consolidation on the basis of a weaker civil society.

Underlying many of these criticisms is the argument that the dominant approach ignores the significance of social movements and political institutions in providing a basis for building trust across a society and promoting civil society. For example in his critique of Putnam's work on Italy, Tarrow questions the significance accorded the legacy of a civic culture as providing the main basis for the greater robustness of democratic politics in the north of the country compared with the south, and draws attention instead to the roles of both Catholic political parties and of the labour movement and left parties in promoting active civic organisations and improving governance (Tarrow 1996). Similarly, Encarnación, questions 'the widespread assumption that social capital is the product of face-to-face interaction that civil society provides ordinary citizens' and contends instead that it is more likely 'the product of the constitution and performance of political institutions' (2003, p. 40).

Eastern Europe and the weakness of civil society

Following the end of communist rule in Eastern Europe, it was the conventional wisdom discussed above that formed the basis for both the analysis of democratisation and the development of strategies of democracy-promotion throughout the region. It has generally been argued the state socialist system bequeathed a legacy of negative forms of social capital and that civil society in the countries of the region is therefore politically weak and passive. Drawing on Putnam, empirical research on the topic has identified the best indicators of the strength of civil society and a rich associational life as measures of levels of membership and participation in civic associations and interest groups.

Using both large-scale international comparative survey data and a range of different single-country studies, research has found evidence of much lower participation rates in civic associations, NGOs and interest groups in Eastern Europe than in Western Europe and North America (Howard 2003; Bernhard & Karakoç 2007). Furthermore, Bernhard & Karakoç (2007, pp. 561–562) found that 'the legacy of the antecedent form of dictatorship ... and how long it endured were critical factors in explaining the lower levels of activity in posttransition civil societies'. Such evidence has been taken as confirmation of the widespread view in the literature concerning the influence of post-socialist legacies on the insufficiency of communitarian or bridging social capital and the 'weakness' of civil society in Eastern Europe. This draws for example on the influential work of Ken Jowitt who has argued that a significant characteristic of East European societies under the communist regimes was a 'Leninist culture' characterised by low levels of trust and a suspicion of politics (Jowitt 1992). Communist rule, along with centralised bureaucratic management of the economy and the central role of the Communist Party in all aspects of policy making and implementation, also entailed top-down mobilisation of the population into front organisations that took the form of trade unions and public associations but which were set up by the state and ruling Party. The outcome was a popular reticence towards engagement in associational life that persisted after the change of regime and encouraged a continuing suspicion of involvement in civic groups and associations.

In response, a critical literature has also emerged concerning civil society in Eastern Europe. First, a number of authors have argued that while the research on membership densities and participation rates within NGOs and civic associations has been informative on those questions specifically, it does not offer direct evidence about the political strength or weakness of civil society that could be provided by examination of the activities and relationships of associations and interest groups as institutions of representative democracy. Following such criticisms some research has gone on to develop approaches using such direct indices. For example Fink-Hafner (1997; 1998) and Cox and Vass (2000; 2007) conducted national level surveys of interest group leaders in Slovenia and Hungary respectively to gather information on the strategies of interest groups, opportunities to exert influence and leaders' estimations of their success in influencing policy or decision making. Taking a different approach Petrova and Tarrow explored the dynamics of 'transactional activism' between different social actors in a local-level case study in Hungary. They examined mobilisation around a local protest about the building of a road through a residential area which took on a further dynamic as grassroots protesters built links with NGOs and lawyers became involved in pressure politics at Hungarian state and EU levels, building links that would help facilitate further campaigns and raise awareness about contradictions between transport policy and nature conservation law at EU level (Petrova & Tarrow 2007, p. 83).

Secondly, it has been argued, there is a tendency in this literature to assume that generalisations can be made across all of formerly communist Eastern Europe, which ignores the possibility that different historical legacies and different post-communist political arrangements may have different outcomes in terms of the political strength or weakness of civil society (Ekiert & Foa 2011). Thirdly, it has been argued that research should focus more clearly on civil society in the wider context of contentious politics and the relationship between civil society and political institutions (Kopecký 2005; Mansfeldova 2006; Fink-Hafner 2011; Cox & Gallai 2007).

In the context of this on-going debate, important contributions have been made by the essays collected in this volume which were all originally published in *Europe-Asia Studies* during the period from 2000 to 2013. In different ways they have taken up issues raised in the general debate and have offered critical views on existing conceptual approaches or have developed empirical research on different countries in Eastern Europe to shed light on particular issues in the debate. The contributions have ranged from studies focusing on the concept of social capital and on the evidence concerning trust, community relationship and democracy, which form the next section below, to articles focusing on the position of civic associations, NGOs and interest groups, their activities and outlooks, and their political activities and relationships, which form the following section.

Social capital, trust and community relationships

The problems of circular argument and a lack of political focus that have been raised in the general critical literature on social capital are also key concerns when it comes to putting the concept of social capital into operation in research on Eastern Europe. As noted by Martin Åberg, Putnam attempts to resolve the problem of the variety of types of social capital by categorising them under the headings of communitarian and non-communitarian social capital, where the former fosters relations of trust vertically to societal level institutions, including the institutions of democratic government such as parliaments and parties, while the latter works against the generation of society-level trust by confining it to relations and networks within communities and family or friendship groups. However, drawing on social survey research on Donetsk and L'viv in Ukraine, Åberg raises the question of why a prevalence of non-communitarian forms of social capital, as seen in the continuing strength of particularistic networks and informal connections, should be seen as part of a vicious circle and a barrier to demo-cratisation. From his analysis of the Ukrainian survey data, he concludes that although the evidence confirms that 'people have little trust in formal institutions and formal organisations', this does not mean that people in Ukraine 'do not solve practical pro-blems of the kind mediated by Western-style civic networks, interest organisations and political parties', but that 'people have an uncanny capacity for practical problem sol-ving' through networks based on non-communitarian social capital (Åberg 2000, p. 307). Further, he argues that not all non-communitarian social capital is necessarily negative in relation to democratisation and the reasons why it remains prevalent after the collapse of the institutions of state socialism may have more to do with the inef-fectiveness of the new post-socialist institutions to meet peoples' needs (2000, p. 312). For Åberg, 'Putnam's "virtuous" and "vicious circles" are far from representing deter-ministic outcomes [and] it is important to note that institutional design and state poli-cies are also very much part of the problem' (p. 313).

The question of the role of social capital in divided societies is also significant in the case of Eastern Europe. Kathleen Dowley and Brian Silver explore this question in relation to Eastern Europe through an analysis of data on 20 former Soviet and East European societies in the World Values Surveys from 1995 to 1998 and the Freedom House annual rankings of societies in terms of political rights and civil liberties. First, for the post-communist countries of the region overall, they found that there was no positive correlation between the aggregate stock of social capital and the level of democratisation, either when they used data from expert evaluations of democracy or from survey evidence of peoples' confidence in democratic institutions. Secondly, in ethnically divided societies, while participation in groups and associations was posi-tively related to support for democratic institutions in the majority or titular ethnic group, it was negative, especially among the more mobilised and engaged members of groups. As Dowley and Silver note, this does not mean 'that ethnically plural societies cannot democratise but that it is more difficult for them to do so if the majority ethnic groups are exclusive in their post-communist nation-building project, or if a past his-tory of injustice against minority populations mobilises them during periods of uncer-tainty in a way that makes the national unity condition impossible to satisfy' (Dowley & Silver 2002, p. 525). Thus, as with the question of the effectiveness of new democratic institutions in meeting the needs of the population discussed by Åberg, so with the ethnic inclusiveness of the new institutions as discussed by Dowley and Silver, it would seem that social capital cannot be seen simply as a basis for democratisation but that democratic institutions at nation state level affect the degree of trust that enables or inhibits democratic development.

As with the question of what factors enable institutional change towards democratisation at national level, so with the promotion of community participation at local level, scholars have found that the approach that sees cultural factors such as a lack of trust and weak communitarian or bridging social capital do not offer an adequate explanation. In a study of community-driven development programmes aimed at encouraging community participation in Armenia, Babken Babajanian found that 'the governance environment plays a key role in affecting the nature and forms of community participation' (Babajanian 2008, p. 37). In his study of seven communities in rural Armenia, Babajanian found on the one hand that people did not feel they were able to participate and influence policy decisions affecting their community and they distrusted the 'possibility of achieving beneficial outcomes through democratic forms of participation and collective action' (p. 50). However, on the other hand he 'found strong networks of mutual support based on trust and reciprocity in all of the studied villages ... both within smaller groups , such as kinship and friendship networks, and between different groups within a community'. Thus, he argues, 'endowments of social capital may not necessarily translate into community participation' (p. 52). His conclusion therefore is that 'institutionalising participation requires concerted action, which would go beyond the scope of individual projects, sectoral interventions and policy reforms. It requires a change in political systems that reproduce unequal power relations' (p. 55).

Civil society organisations and their political relations

Focusing more specifically on civil society and the groups that make it up and represent its interests, the studies reported in this collection present a more complex and nuanced picture, with evidence of greater variation between different countries, than the conventional view of a general weakness of civil society across Eastern Europe. Such variation can be observed not only between countries, for example between the countries of the former Soviet Union and formerly communist-ruled Eastern Europe, but also within countries such as Russia where civil society has been characterised conventionally as uniformly weak.

Among the studies collected in this volume, the firmest conclusions concerning evidence of political strengths of civil society are those focusing on Eastern Europe rather than the former Soviet Union. Exploring the politics of interest representation at national level, Seán Hanley provides a comparative overview of the range of organisations representing pensioners' interests in the Czech Republic and Slovenia. He finds that both countries have witnessed the emergence of 'sizeable membership-based pensioners' interest organisations integrated into national interest representation systems' (Hanley 2013, p. 161). In both countries these include newly established associations set up since the fall of the old regimes and successor organisations to those originally set up under communist rule, groups connected to trade unions and independent associations, as well as some charities and NGOs providing support and services but not seeking to represent pensioners politically. Furthermore membership density is relatively high by European standards, although they are less well endowed with resources than their West European counterparts. In terms of tactics, their leaderships have sought to represent the interests of pensioners politically at elite level by lobbying and consultation with policy makers. In discussing the reasons for the relative strength of interest representation in this sector Hanley draws attention to the broader political context in which it has occurred, including 'the galvanising effects of early fears over the social impact of transition, post-communist governments' need for interlocutors to legitimise and inform their policies, and the diffusion of new paradigms of population ageing as new policy sectors requiring stakeholder consultation and participation' (p. 161).

A further dimension to the question of the strength or weakness of civil society is added by Tsveta Petrova's local-level study of the participation of groups from civil society in local governance. Exploring questions about the weakness of local governments, and drawing on survey data on municipalities across Bulgaria as well as interviews with policy actors in six municipalities, Petrova argues that local policy makers have been able to improve governance and increase their administrative capacities and their authority by drawing on strengths provided by cooperation with NGOs and civic groups. 'Despite the weak institutionalisation of state-society cooperation, the passivity of many municipalities, and their preference for working primarily with political actors, there is evidence of widespread and diverse cooperation between local authorities and societal actors in Bulgaria' (Petrova 2011, p. 104). Examples included the use of the capacity and authority of civic actors to improve policy making, drawing on the expertise of civic groups in identifying priorities; developing projects, securing external funding, managing policy implementation, and mobilising public interest and support. At the same time, such cooperation was also a source of support for civic groups in achieving more effective representation of their members' interests. Developing further on the theme of the positive effects of building networks and improving communication both vertically and horizontally with other policy actors, a theme she explored in her work with Tarrow discussed above (Petrova & Tarrow 2007), Petrova argues, that 'horizontal and vertical communication networks' are important in creating a dynamic situation for the strengthening of civil society in that they 'raise public awareness and help make civil society groups more professional, organised and strategic in their planning and activism' (p. 83).

Compared with these studies of the Czech Republic, Slovenia and Bulgaria, a more nuanced picture emerges from Anders Uhlin's research on Latvia. The results of two surveys conducted by Uhlin, one a survey of public attitudes towards civil society organisations and the extent of trust, tolerance and support for democracy in the population, and the other a survey of activists in civil society groups, offers some support for the conventional view of weaknesses in civil society, but also suggests a cautious approach to generalising too broadly for all countries in Eastern Europe. On the one hand, Uhlin found that 'civil society in Latvia is weak when measured on the individual level', as reflected in relatively low levels of membership and participation in civil society organisations, a finding consistent with Howard's conclusions. On the other hand, he found a greater strength at the organisational level, as reflected in 'a relatively large number of civil society organisations covering a broad spectrum of issue areas', and although many groups only had small membership numbers, they demonstrated professionalism in the activities they pursued and were 'perceived as relatively autonomous from the state' (Uhlin 2010, p. 131). However, despite a degree of organisational strength, a further significant finding, underlying the complexity of assessing questions of the strength and weakness of civil society, was that most of the activities of the civil society groups was non-political in character, and did not seek to 'influence political decision-making or to act as a check against the abuse of state power' (p. 131).

Further variation in Russia is highlighted by two different studies, one focusing on car drivers' organisations in St Petersburg, and the other on environmental groups in Samara. In his study of St Petersburg car drivers' associations, Markku Lonkila compares the structures and membership characteristics of two quite different organisations, with different histories and outlooks, that were active in representing the interests of car drivers in the city in different ways. On the one hand, a recently formed and locally based organisation called 'St. Petersburg: Freedom of Choice' was formed as a protest group to mobilise for the political rights of car drivers, including the right to drive imported cars with right-hand drive, and also more broadly to defend drivers against false accusations from corrupt traffic police. On the other hand, a city district branch of the All-Russian Society of Car Drivers is an organisation that was originally formed in the 1970s to help drivers deal with typically Soviet problems such as the short supply of spare parts and repair services in the state managed economy, and continues to operate as a source of support for car drivers, especially in the provision of secure parking facilities. In focusing on these two different groups, Lonkila makes the point that much research seeking to apply western-based concepts and criteria for the strength of civil society 'runs the risk of leading to "deficit studies" of Russia which often end up describing Russia mostly in terms of what it is lacking in comparison to the "West"', and he calls instead for a 'more balanced approach [which] also pays attention to the particular features of Russian forms of joint action and organising' (Lonkila 2011, p. 190).

However, in her in-depth study of environmental groups in Samara *oblast'* Jo Crotty found a situation where civil society groups were politically weak. Based on observation of the groups' activities and interviews with leading people in each group, she found that the Samara environmental movement 'was devoid of professional organisations that are politically adversarial' and was dominated by apolitical grass roots organisations with a narrow membership base and focusing on local issues, and politically subservient 'marionette' organisations that are allied to and sometimes formed by government bodies, and 'failed to embody a public political dimension' (Crotty 2009, p. 101). Thus, at least as far as Samara was concerned, there was no evidence to support some previous research on Russia that environmental groups were more active and adversarial than groups in other issue areas (Henry 2002). Crotty's research suggests a pattern for her chosen area of provincial Russia that conforms quite closely to the conventional view of a weak civil society. However, the underlying reasons for this weakness, she found, do not lie only in the post-Soviet legacy of 'forced volunteering' and a consequent reliance on personal networks, but also in the contemporary Russian problems of 'economic issues that disillusionment that have dominated Russian society since transition' (p. 102).

A further dimension to the question of the significance of the wider political context for the extent of the strength or weakness of civil society is introduced by Paul Kubicek in his discussion of the role of trade unions in post-Soviet democratisation in Russia and Ukraine. He points out the puzzling absence in most of the literature on civil society of the role and significance of trade unions, noting especially the surprising nature of this omission in view of their central importance historically in the emergence of democracies in Western countries. The explanation, he suggests, is that trade unions do not fit very neatly into the liberal understanding of the composition of civil society that has stressed the importance of generalised trust and the achievement of consensus as a basis for democratic consolidation. In this context unions tend to be seen as too particularistic in the representation of their members' interests and insufficiently civic-minded to promote compromise, and in the context specifically of post-communist transition, they have been seen as either ambivalent or opposed to the neo-liberal policy agenda. However, Kubicek argues, 'one can profit from "unpacking" the notion of civil society and looking more carefully at its constituent parts. ... [T]angible groups and interests must be taken into account ... [and] once one accepts the need to subject the various parts of civil society to scrutiny, the consideration of trade unions becomes obvious, particularly when one takes into account the importance of political economy in post-communist transformation' (Kubicek 2002, p. 606). Exploring this argument in a discussion of Russia and Ukraine, Kubicek shows how the weakening of the influence of trade unions has weakened potential sources of opposition to the emergence of an 'oligarchic corporatism' and a 'dependent democratisation' as key features of transformation in those countries (p. 619). Thus, rather than seeking explanations in the survival of attitudes of lack of social trust and an insufficient stock of social capital, 'the weakness of civil society and the rise of an oligarchy in both countries, bemoaned by would-be democratisers, is in part the very result of policies pursued by yesterday's "reformers". Despite rhetoric about the importance of civil society, one can see that many of the most basic policies of the post-Soviet period have helped undermine a key actor in civil society, trade unions' (p. 621).

Conclusion

A clear impression that emerges from the studies collected in this volume is that while civil societies in the countries of Eastern Europe to some extent share a common legacy from their years of communist rule, this legacy contains different elements and combines in different ways with other aspects of the economic, political and cultural make-up of each society and with their differing experiences of post-communist transformation. As a result, the different countries each display differing degrees of political strength or weakness in their civil societies, reflecting in part the different ways they have combined elements of the historical legacy with their post-communist experiences. In the words of Ekiert and Foa (2011) therefore, they are 'recombinant civil societies'. Their legacies do not simply involve low levels of social trust and an aversion to civic engagement stemming from their experience of 'forced volunteering' and the reliance on personal networks of communist times. These aspects may be present in most societies of the region but they are more evident for example in Latvia as described by Uhlin than in Bulgaria as described by Petrova, or the Czech Republic and Slovenia as described by Hanley. Even within one country, in Russia, they are more evident in Samara as described by Crotty than in St Petersburg as described by Lonkila.

Moreover, it is far from evident that the kind of social capital that is based on personal networks and shared community values, rather than more generalised societal values, necessarily acts as a barrier to civic engagement and support for democratisation. Rather, as shown by Åberg, Babajanian and Dowley & Silver in different ways, the extent to which different kinds of social capital, including 'communitarian' or 'bonding' social capital, enable or undermine support for democratisation in a society also depends on the broader political context in which they occur.

This in turn supports the arguments made strongly by Kubicek, but also finding resonance in the studies by Hanley, Petrova and Lonkila, that research needs to focus on the interconnectedness between states and the economic and social policies they pursue and civil society. The state or political society provides a context and helps shape the opportunity structures within which civil society organisations can operate and develop. As Petrova & Tarrow have argued, the dominant approach has sought to 'to frame activism as a property of individuals or of individual civil society organizations' (2007, p. 79), and has focused on explaining the weakness or strength of civil society mainly as the outcome of membership size and density. In contrast, much of the research collected here shows the insights to be gained from a focus on the relations between civil society groups and power holders and on the dynamics of their transactions. This enables an understanding of the strength or weakness of civil society as shaped by the rules of the game of the political system in which it exists and the definitions of the political sphere that are imposed by the elites who exercise power.

If this conclusion is followed through, it supports the development of a new research agenda in place of the hitherto dominant approach that has linked effective bridging social capital to the strength of civil society and has seen an already strong civil society as the precondition for democratic consolidation. Instead it calls for more research to explore that aspect of the activity groups in civil society that focuses on inter-relations between political and civil society and on what Petrova & Tarrow call the 'transactional activism' of civil society organisations. This, it can be suggested, would comprise three main aspects, all of which have been explored to some extent in the existing literature, but which have rarely been considered together as part of the same project, and have not so far been carried out on a comparative basis as parts of the same project. These are, first, an exploration of the institutional infrastructure and context that may either enable or impede the pursuit of advocacy and interest representation by civil society groups; detailed analysis of the relations between interest groups and associations, and between them and other political actors such as parties, movements, consultants, lobbyists and with policy makers. Secondly, it would involve studies over time of the dynamics of civil society development, including the extent to which the vitality of a civil society is path dependent and shaped by legacies from previous periods, and the processes through which civic activists gain experience and relations between citizens and decision makers take place in either conflicting or shared understandings. Thirdly, it would explore the interconnectedness of state or political society and civil society in the way in which state or political society provide a context and help shape the opportunity structures within which civil society organisations can operate and develop. This would involve both the influence of political society in shaping the activities of civil society and the translation of civil society values and expertise into the broader political arena. (For further discussion, see Cox 2013).

References

Ágh, A. (1998) *The Politics of Central Europe* (London: Sage).
Berman, S. (1997) 'Civil Society and the Collapse of the Weimar Republic', *World Politics,* 49, 3.
Bernhard, M. & Karakoç (2007) 'Civil Society and the Legacies of Dictatorship', *World Politics,* 59, 4.

Bermeo, N. (2000) 'Civil Society After Democracy: Some Conclusions', in Bermeo, N. & Nord, P. (eds) (2000) *Civil Society Before Democracy: Lessons From Nineteenth Century Europe* (Lanham: Rowman & Littlefield).

Cohen, J. (1999) 'Trust, Voluntary Associations and Workable Democracy', in Warren, M. (ed.) (1999) *Democracy and Trust*, (Cambridge: Cambridge University Press).

Cox, T. (2007) 'Democratisation and State-Society Relations in East Central Europe: the case of Hungary', *Journal of Communist Studies and Transition Politics*, 23, 2.

Cox, T. (2012) 'Interest Representation and State-Society Relations in East Central Europe', *Aleksanteri Papers* 2.

Cox, T. & Gallai, S. (2009) 'Policy Actors and Policy Making in Contemporary Hungary', in Staronova, K. & Vass, L. (eds) (2009) *Public Policy and Administration: Challenges and Synergies*, (NISPAcee, Bratislava).

Cox, T. & Vass, L. (2000) 'Government-Interest Group Relations in Hungarian Politics Since 1989', *Europe-Asia Studies*, 52, 6.

Cox, T. & Vass, L. (2007) 'State and Organised Interests in Post-Communist Hungarian Politics', *Perspectives on European Politics and Societies*, 8, 2.

Diamond, L. (1994) 'Rethinking Civil Society: Toward Democratic Consolidation', *Journal of Democracy*, 5.

Ekiert, G. & Foa, R. (2011) 'Civil Society Weakness in PostCommunist Europe: A Preliminary Assessment', *Carlo Alberto Notebooks*, 198.

Encarnación, O. (2003) The Myth of Civil Society: Social Capital and Democratic Consolidation in Spain and Brazil, (New York: Palgrave MacMillan).

Fink-Hafner, D. (1998) 'Organized Interests in the Policy-making Process in Slovenia', *Journal of European Public Policy*, 5, 2.

Fink-Hafner, D. (1997) 'Interest Organisations in the Policy Making Process', in Danica Fink-Hafner & John R. Robbins (eds) (1997) *Making a New Nation: The Formation of Slovenia* (Aldershot: Dartmouth).

Fink-Hafner, D. (2011) 'Interest Representation in Post-Communist Parliaments Over Two Decades', *Legislative Studies*, 17, 2.

Fiorina, M. (1999) 'Extreme Voices: A Dark Side of Civic Engagement', in T. Skocpol, T. & Fiorina, M. (eds) (1999) *Civic Engagement in American Democracy*, (Washington DC: Brookings Institution Press).

Foley, M. & Edwards, B. (1996) 'The Paradox of Civil Society', *Journal of Democracy*, 7, 3.

Haynes, P. (2009) 'Before Going Any Further With Social Capital: Eight Criticisms to Address', *Ingenio Working Paper Series*, 2.

Howard, M. (2003) The *Weakness of Civil Society in Post-Communist Europe* (Cambridge, Cambridge University Press).

Jowitt, K. (1992) 'The Leninist Legacy' in Banac, I. (ed.)(1992) *Eastern Europe in Revolution* (Ithaca NY Cornell University Press).

Kopecký, P. (2005) 'Civil Society, Uncivil Society and Contentious Politics', inKopecký, P. & Mudde, C. (eds) (2005) *Contentious Politics in Post-Communist Europe* (London, Routledge).

Kubik, J. (2005) 'How to Study Civil Society: The State of the Art and What to do Next', *East European Politics and Societies*, 19, 1.

Levi, M. (1996) 'Social and Unsocial Capital: A Review of Robert Putnam's making Democracy Work', *Politics and Society*, 24.

Linz, Juan & Stepan, Alfred.(1996) *Problems of Democratic Transition and Consolidation: Southern Europe, South America, and Post-Communist Europe* (Baltimore, MD, Johns Hopkins University Press).

Mansfeldova, Z. (2006) 'Political and Administrative Accountability in the Czech Republic' in Pleines, H. (ed.) (2006) *Participation of Civil Society in New Modes of Governance. The Case of the New EU Member States. Part 2: Questions of Accountability*, Bremen.

Newton, K. (1997) 'Social Capital and Democracy', *American Behavioral Scientist*, 40.

Parrott, Bruce. (1997) 'Perspectives on Post-Communist Democratization', in Dawisha, Karen & Parrot, Bruce (eds)(1997) *The Consolidation of Democracy in East-Central Europe* (Cambridge, Cambridge University Press),

Petrova, T. & Tarrow, S. (2007) 'Transactional and Participatory Activism in the Emerging European Polity', Comparative Political Studies 40, 1.

Portes, A. (1998) 'Social Capital, its Origins and Application in Contemporary Sociology', *Annual Review of Sociology*, 24.

Putnam, R. (1993) *Making Democracy Work: Civic Traditions in Modern Italy*, (Princeton, University of Princeton Press).

Putnam, R. (1995) 'Bowling Alone: America's Declining Social Capital', *Journal of Democracy*, 6, 1.

Tarrow, S. (1996) 'Making Social Science Work Across Space and Time: A Critical Reflection on Robert Putnam's Making Democracy Work', *American Political Science Review*, 90.

Putnam's Social Capital Theory Goes East: A Case Study of Western Ukraine and L'viv

MARTIN ÅBERG

THE NEGATIVE OR NON-COMMUNITARIAN SOCIAL CAPITAL of post-socialist societies has attracted considerable attention in the literature on the transition to market economy and democracy in these countries,[1] not least following the publication of Putnam's *Making Democracy Work* (1993).[2] Interpreted as a legacy of and a reaction to inadequate and inefficient state socialist institutional arrangements, particularistic networks and informal connections and related phenomena such as clientelism and corruption continue to represent a salient feature of society after the downfall of communism. Thus, notwithstanding the great differences between different countries, non-communitarian social capital serves as a pertinent illustration of the path-dependent nature of the transition. This problem is at the heart of most current research on 'civil society' in East-Central and Eastern Europe.[3] However, in the attempts to test Putnam's theory explicitly in the analysis of post-socialist polities—most notably former East Germany—attention has been directed more towards his equilibrium thesis of 'virtuous' and 'vicious' circles. While stressing Putnam's neglect of factors such as institutional design and third-party enforcement,[4] the focus in current analyses has been less on the issue of social capital as such and the micro-sociological underpinnings of non-communitarian social capital. The latter is the topic of this article.

Therefore, rather than asking ourselves 'what is the importance of social capital to successful democratisation', the proper question to pose in our case should be 'exactly what is it in the nature of social capital in post-socialist societies that makes people less inclined to invest trust in formal democratic institutions?' Putnam's own reply is that 'sanctions that support norms of reciprocity against threat of opportunism are less likely to be imposed upwards and less likely to be acceded to, if imposed' in the kind of particularistic and vertical networks from which negative social capital breeds.[5] Contrary to Putnam's argument, though, we hold that lack of trust in formal institutions is not due primarily to difficulties in implementing sanctions in social networks. Although Putnam was right in focusing on the exchange relations that constitute the backbone of these networks, the important point is actually that communitarian and non-communitarian social capital draw on two different modes of reducing social transaction costs. It is this difference rather than the problem of sanctions that accounts for the difficulties of transforming non-communitarian social capital into trust in formal institutions. In addition, as non-communitarian social capital in many respects continues to represent a more efficient tool for practical problem solving than do formal institutions, these two features also shed light on the reasons why institutional design and third party enforcement are crucial aspects of building democracy.

Although the aim here is not to provide the basis for empirical generalisations or general theoretical statements, neither to refute nor confirm Putnam's theory, an alternative explanation is outlined. In line with the scheme Lijphart once proposed, a case study approach is used for hypothesis-generating purposes,[6] suggesting that, contrary to Putnam's interpretation, communitarian and non-communitarian social capital and networks respectively draw on two different modes of reducing social transaction costs. It is argued that above all the difference between modes of reducing social transaction costs explains why non-communitarian social capital cannot automatically be transformed into trust in formal institutions. This is illustrated by analysing the concepts of 'exchange' and 'social transaction costs' both theoretically and empirically with the help of the various approaches underpinning Putnam's account, most notably those of Coleman, Homans, Mauss and Lévi-Strauss.

For these purposes western Ukraine and the city of L'viv during the first years of independent statehood are analysed using survey data, focus group discussions and in-depth interviews.[7] Consistent with the single-case study approach, local context is stressed in the analysis.[8] Local context and to some extent differences in historical background account for several important regional differences between western Ukraine and other parts of the country with respect to social capital. On crucial dimensions comparisons are made with the city of Donets'k in eastern Ukraine, although probing of the hypothesis must be conducted more extensively and among more cases in the future, including in countries with a non-Soviet background. At the same time L'viv can be argued to constitute a particularly strong case for analysing non-communitarian social capital, as the city and the surrounding region have often been regarded as a positive exception compared with the rest of Ukraine in this respect. I will begin with a brief review of Putnam's theory and its critics and continue with an analysis of the political culture and social capital of western Ukraine and L'viv. The last two sections of the article address the question of the relationship between non-communitarian social capital, trust and formal institutions.

Putnam's social capital theory and democratisation in post-Soviet Ukraine

On the one hand it can be argued that democracy has already emerged victorious from the shambles left by the Soviet Union. The NIS-countries west of the Urals—Belarus being the primary exception—have undoubtedly liberalised, free elections have been held, and constitutional reforms promoting democracy have gained impetus. On the other hand such new institutional arrangements have not yet stabilised into durable paths in terms of political behaviour. Among the reasons most often cited as an explanation are that institutional reforms have so far been insufficient, most notably so in the case of Russia and Ukraine. In addition, economic hardships in connection with the transition to a market economy as well as the lingering habits of Soviet totalitarianism, including political culture—i.e. what is conventionally understood as lack of civic traditions—are included in this array of negative circumstances. In part accounting for this lack is a specific, negative or non-communitarian social capital, promoting clientelism and non-legal practices at all levels of society. Importantly, some have also identified long-term historical factors that could be seen as indirectly contributing to the persistence of the latter kind of practices. For example, Huntington suggested a lack of democratic potential in parts of Eastern Europe, ultimately deriving from the relative incompatibility of democratic ideas and institutions with orthodox culture (Huntington 1993, basically a re-interpretation of the argument in his more optimistic (1991) 'third wave' analysis).[9] New forms of authoritarianism would therefore be a plausible outcome of history, should the logic of current processes be analogous to that underpinning Pipes' claim, i.e. that communist dictatorship in the growing Soviet empire was actually moulded by the pre-revolutionary institutions of tsarist Russia.[10] Indeed, if we add the lessons from Putnam's Italian study and the role of social capital in democratisation to this picture, democratisation seems ultimately predestined to failure in Russia and Ukraine regardless of structural factors and institutional reform.

Putnam's argument, we remember, is that social capital is decisive to the efficacy of formal institutions, and specifically of institutions for collective bargaining and collective action in democratic polities. One of the comments most commonly made by Putnam's critics, to be sure, is that institutional performance as such does not tell us very much about degree of democratic behaviour.[11] From one point of view this is of course true, but on the other hand institutional performance can also be considered a crucial aspect of the 'responsiveness' of polities as analysed by Dahl in his classic interpretation of democracy as 'polyarchy' (1971).[12] That is, 'trust' deriving from social capital serves as a form of lubrication in the political system. Trust enhances 'responsiveness' in democracies, i.e. smoothens the interactive process by which the elected government responds to the demands of the citizens. Hence it is important to the performance of democratic decision making and its ability to secure and keep its legitimacy as a political system. In this respect trust is an integral part of the process by which people become 'convinced' of the advantages to be gained from sticking to democratic practices.

What, then, can Putnam's social capital theory teach us about 'trust' and the modes of political behaviour in transitional cultures? The concept of social capital itself is not entirely free from ambiguity and Putnam uses it in a number of meanings. Accordingly it is defined as 'features of social organisation, such as trust, norms, and networks, that can improve the efficiency of society by facilitating coordinated actions'.[13] The bottom line of the argument, though, is that social capital should be seen as the quality of people being connected through reciprocal exchange relations. This relational property of society leads to the formation of 'networks of civic engagement', including interest organisations and political parties, and increasingly fosters trust in the institutions represented by the state. Looked at the other way round, social capital makes it possible for institutions to perform efficiently.[14]

Although the social capital theory was less categorically summarised in earlier versions of the model (Putnam et al., 1983),[15] Putnam also makes an important distinction between what he calls 'virtuous circles' and 'vicious circles'. In cases of high levels of social capital and trust, social capital tends to regenerate itself increasingly, while the reverse holds for societies that start out from a low level of social capital.[16] As transitional phases as such are extremely volatile situations during which the entire social system is put under enormous stress, this would further strengthen the impression of post-socialist countries such as Ukraine being caught in a 'vicious circle' of a particularistic and authoritarian political culture.

Obviously this argument is too one-sided. Culture is not an a-historical category and path-dependencies are not irreversible. Indeed, Huntington himself was careful to stress this too when first outlining his argument on democratic 'waves' and the 'clash of civilisations'.[17] Neither society nor culture can be regarded as static phenomena. Therefore they cannot be interpreted as exercising a categorically 'negative' or 'positive' influence on democratisation and with social capital and negative social capital respectively as forever given. The historical traditions Putnam identified in the case of northern Italy were certainly somehow important to the shaping of a modern democratic political culture. The precise patterns, though, in terms of causes and effects from a historical point of view, were equally certainly not as straightforward as Putnam held them to be. One important example to the contrary is that north Italian culture proved susceptible to fascism in the 1920s rather than being inclined towards democracy.[18]

Similarly, important aspects of culture have provoked different responses in terms of political culture in Ukraine, depending on both period and context. In Ukraine attempts at nation building, the revival of national culture, including traditional religious life, and democratisation move hand in hand in contemporary society, at least in certain regions such as western Ukraine. While this also holds historically as far as the connection between nationalism and political activism goes, in a longer perspective religion and the clergy, though, have tended to play a more ambiguous role. For a number of historically specific reasons the relations between nationalism, political behaviour and religion as an expression of culture are different today than they were during the 'first wave' of Ukrainian nationalism one century ago. In the 1860s anti-clericalism was initially part of Galician Ukrainophilism (national populism).[19] During the closing years of the Soviet Union, however, revival of religious culture and political dissent were more unanimously and intimately connected phenomena in L'viv and western Ukraine.[20]

Importantly, considerations of this kind have implications for Putnam's argument about 'social equilibrium' and 'virtuous' and 'vicious circles'. Not surprisingly, when putting Putnam's social equilibrium hypothesis to the test, Cusack found strong evidence that it does not hold up to empirical scrutiny. That is, if we choose, in the words of Cusack (1997), to study a large number of separate cases, according to the hypothesis one of three mutually exclusive patterns would eventually dominate.

(1) as in the case of Italy, a bimodal situation with one mode characterised by high levels of social capital, and the other low levels. Or one would find in situation (2) and (3) either uniformly high levels of social capital or uniformly low levels of social capital. There should not be a pattern where high and low as well as mixed levels exist.[21]

Studying local government in post-1989 Germany, Cusack demonstrated that this was not the case. Concluding from this, Cusack admitted the importance of social capital but argued that the results also indicated the crucial importance of institutional design for democratic efficacy.[22] A similar pattern has also been demonstrated by several studies of Western countries, for instance in Patrick Ireland's investigation of political mobilisation among immigrant groups in France and Switzerland. According to Ireland's 'institutional channelling model', formal institutions and hence institutional design are crucial to explain the manner in which immigrant groups can and do take part in the democratic decision-making process.[23] Indirectly this also highlights the importance of the state as one of the crucial mechanisms for enforcing institutions and institutional behaviour.

Political culture and historical legacies, institutions, state agency and structural factors, such as level of socioeconomic development, do, as most people would agree, mutually intervene to produce specific outcomes in terms of polities and without following the deterministic pattern suggested by Putnam's theory. Rather, even in seemingly extremely path-dependent cases such as Ukraine and Russia, the outcome of transition is as likely to be new types of democracies—compared with Western standards—as outright authoritarianism. It is, to be sure, beyond the scope of this article to outline the possible relations between all the above factors. Importantly, however, so far very little if anything has been written relating directly to the crucial question of what it is, exactly, in the non-communitarian social capital of former socialist states that impedes the building of trust in formal, democratic institutions. In line with Putnam's own research design, we will begin by outlining some relevant regional differences in Ukraine, including the historical dimension of the problem. In particular the importance of the post-war period is stressed, as this was a crucial phase from a social capital perspective. As a second step the nature of non-communitarian social capital in the post-socialist context will be investigated more closely.

Political culture: the case of western Ukraine

Ukrainian regional differences in political culture have been analysed by, among others, Szporluk, Pirie, Hrytsak & Susak, Wilson, Jackson and Meyer. There exist contrasts in several respects, both between the 'Right Bank' and the 'Left Bank' and between the western and eastern areas of Ukraine and the south, in particular Crimea. Such differences include variations in level of identification with independent statehood and attitudes to regional autonomy, but also level of civic activities including a higher level of public interest in political affairs in L'viv and western Ukraine compared with other regions of the country.[24] Although distrust in politicians and government institutions is generally a widespread phenomenon in Ukrainian politics, to some extent this is less marked in western Ukraine (see below). Admittedly there is a historical dimension to this. Large areas of Ukraine—i.e. what is commonly referred to as the 'Right Bank' (of the Dnepr)—were never part of the tsarist empire and therefore neither became Russified nor were influenced by habits of Russian patrimonialism, serfdom and communal ownership based on the institution of the *mir*. Instead, from 1569 the Right Bank for 200 years belonged to the dominion of the Polish Commonwealth. Later—from 1772—among these lands Galicia was part of the Habsburg Empire up to 1918. Whereas eastern Orthodoxy had a profound impact in large parts of the country, the western areas remained more influenced by Roman Catholicism, among other things symbolised by the emergence of the Greek Catholic (Uniate) Church.

However, while the importance of deeply rooted differences in historical tradition surely play a part in political culture, the analogies with today's situation should not be stretched too far. For one thing we may ask ourselves precisely about the extent to which regional traditions of the above kind match the characteristics typical of communitarian social capital á la Putnam in crucial dimensions such as trust and reciprocity. Secondly—and more importantly—it is a question of how successful such traits were in surviving the changes imposed on Ukrainian society during the Soviet period. In the first case, in Galicia the same semi-feudal manorial system of production typical of pre-partition Poland—and thus yet another although presumably more lenient form of authoritarianism—continued as the dominant form of social organisation under Austrian rule after 1772. In the second case, after the final Soviet take-over in 1944–45, and with it the implementation of state socialist institutions, the social structure in Galicia did for obvious reasons change dramatically. Equally important, therefore, are the post-war changes in the region.

For the purpose of illustrating a number of differences in terms of political behaviour in relation to formal institutions in more detail, L'viv can be contrasted with Donets'k in eastern Ukraine, a city which is in many respects an opposite world compared to L'viv. This approach, then, would be consistent with the notion that agency and the social meaning actors attribute to behaviour tend to become coloured by differences in local setting.[25] While L'viv is the regional centre of the historically more Western-oriented but also less industrialised and more rural part of the country, Donets'k lies in a heavily industrialised and urbanised but also 'Sovietised' part of Ukraine. While contemporary L'viv is relatively homogeneous from an ethnic point of view, the composition of the population in Donets'k is mixed, hence also leading to a more 'blurred' sense of identity among its residents.[26] Importantly, considering L'viv, most of these changes occurred in connection with the war and during the post-war period. Before World War II Polish Lwów was the historical city of Poles and Jews, only to a lesser extent a city of ethnic Ukrainians.[27] After the Nazi Holocaust and the Soviet mass expulsion of Poles, beginning in 1945, L'vov/L'viv became a Soviet-Ukrainian city, a transformation which, among other things, involved migration of large numbers of Ukrainians to the city from the surrounding country-side.

Circumstances such as these have undoubtedly had an impact on political culture in contemporary western Ukraine, albeit the pattern is complicated and difficult to analyse. Nevertheless, as Szporluk pointed out during the initial stage of the transition process (1992), and thereby in a sense echoing the early 20th century radical Ievhen Chykalenko on the role of Galicia, 'the city and *oblast*' of L'viv clearly represent an "anomaly" if a republic average is taken as a norm ... it may be setting the pace and providing a model for the Western region' in the political sphere. In this case possible reasons explaining the landslide victory of Rukh in the western districts of Ukraine in the 1990 March election to the Ukrainian Supreme Soviet were being analysed. Concluding from the historical, demographic and cultural characteristics of the city and the surrounding region, the pattern indicated what could perhaps be considered

TABLE 1
INTEREST IN POLITICS, L'VIV AND DONETS'K, 1994

City of interview	Very interested	Interested	Not very interested	Not interested at all	Totals
L'viv	8.7	38.5	34.6	18.2	100.0
Donets'k	6.1	33.4	40.9	19.6	100.0

Note: $n = 821$. Valid cases = 818 (L'viv 390, Donets'k 428).
Source: 1994 survey on Identity Formation and Social Issues in East and West Ukraine, by courtesy of the Institute for Historical Research, L'viv State University.

a higher degree of social capital, or in any case a higher level of political awareness compared with the rest of Ukraine at the time.[28]

For such reasons both L'viv and Donets'k represent highly interesting cases and surveys have been conducted by the University of Michigan and L'viv State University in the two cities, addressing problems of 'social identity' and 'social issues'. Yet, drawing on the 1994 survey and re-interpreting the results, its main findings are still—despite the differences between the two cities—considerably less encouraging from a social capital perspective than could have been expected judging from the degree of political activism in L'viv five years earlier. The survey, for instance, concluded that 52.8% of the respondents in L'viv and no less than 60.5% of the Donets'k sample were either little interested or indifferent to politics (see Table 1). In addition people in both cities generally shared a low level of trust in mass media, politicians, government officials and similar categories of key players. Variations existed between L'viv and Donets'k in these respects as well. Nonetheless, measured on a scale from 1 to 10, the results of the survey—as analysed elsewhere— usually indicated only a slightly positive view on mass media and indifferent or negative views on politicians and government officials.[29]

At the same time, the overwhelming majority of the samples declared that they would vote in the coming parliamentary election that year. Previous experience of different modes of political and civic agency, though, was scant. Among other things, the respondents in the survey were asked about which modes of action they resorted to for 'resolving social problems'. The alternatives included whether they had ever (i) contacted a 'central newspaper, magazine or television'; (ii) a 'deputy or any other public official'; (iii) 'signed a petition'; (iv) joined a 'social organisation' or 'initiative group' other than the Communist Party or Komsomol; (v) 'participated in a rally or demonstration'. In addition the respondents were asked to indicate the rate of such experiences. Indeed, a category such as 'social problems' may include almost anything, but nevertheless the results of the survey give some indication of the practical experience of a number of selected key post-Soviet institutions for practical problem solving. Among the most important of the above alternatives, from a social capital perspective, would be alternatives (ii) and, most notably, (iv). The latter, about joining organisations, would in a sense equal membership in 19th century mutual aid societies and modern interest organisations as studied by Putnam. Important in this respect is above all repeated or routine experience of agency, not isolated instances of encounters with formal institutions, and also the political context of agency (Table 2).

TABLE 2

MULTIPLE EXPERIENCE OF DIFFERENT MODES OF POLITICAL AND CIVIC AGENCY, L'VIV AND DONETS'K, 1994

City of interview	Contact— mass media	Contact— officials	Signed petition	Joined organisation	Participated in demonstration
L'viv	4.3	14.3	12.5	6.4	40.0
Donets'k	2.6	6.8	4.4	2.8	12.6

Note: $n = 821$. Valid cases ranging between 389 and 391 for L'viv and 428 and 429 for Donets'k.
Source: 1994 survey on Identity Formation and Social Issues in East and West Ukraine, by courtesy of the Institute for Historical Research, L'viv State University.

While most people in both L'viv and Donets'k had no experience of any of the above-mentioned types of action, the proportion of respondents who actually had more than one experience of contacting public officials and joining organisations was considerably larger in L'viv than in Donets'k. The same holds for contacts with mass media as well, and in particular experience of participation in demonstrations. To some extent, though, the relatively high rate of such experiences as revealed by the L'viv sample is most probably reflecting public mobilisation during the mass rallies in the city during the summer of 1988, or the demonstrations in connection with the 1990 election. That is, they represent events occurring during a rather specific period more than they reflect any permanent political activism among the citizens. As no time limit was imposed in the questionnaire, this is the reason why such an explanation is plausible.

In the former case the demonstrations were triggered above all by three sets of circumstances. One was the growing impatience with the slow pace of reforms in Ukraine during *perestroika*. Another factor was the impact on public opinion of the Chernobyl disaster two years earlier. This catastrophe and its consequences provided a strong case for illustrating the impotence of the regime. Third, the Chernobyl disaster also triggered the formation of what Kuzio has called new 'informal groups' in society, not least in L'viv, and such organised opposition was important for political mobilisation at the time.[30] Similarly, as the erosion of state socialist institutions had accelerated dramatically two years later, events in connection with the 1990 election were, in a sense, atypical as well. Finally, while Kyiv and L'viv were the centres of national awakening and political opposition in the late 1980s, in the case of L'viv proximity to Poland and the impression made on public opinion in both instances by reforms in Poland[31] probably encouraged public dissent even more. Consequently, in the case of L'viv, experience of 'signing petitions' and 'participating in demonstrations' to a great extent reflects the rather specific situation shortly before the dissolution of the Soviet Union.

In addition, 'social organisations' may mean almost anything in its contemporary Ukrainan context. Anything from chess clubs to political parties may be classified as *hromads'ki ob'ednannia*.[32] Since 'hromada' means 'community' or 'assembly', this would certainly seem—in a very superficial manner—to relate to what Putnam described as 'civic networks' and interest organisations in the case of northern Italy. But generally speaking there is ample reason to agree with Kubicek's more negative conclusions on the issue of interest organisations in Ukraine. For one thing, there are great difficulties in actually identifying and defining political interests and interest groups with any degree of precision. As Kubicek notes with particular reference to privatisation and state ownership, what is best described as a 'surreal' situation has therefore developed,[33] opening the way to clientelism and a wide array of informal as well as illegal practices.

On the elite level of society this probably indicates the same pattern as in Levitas' & Strzalkowski's (1990), or Pickvance's (1996) analyses.[34] Although similar data are lacking in the case of L'viv, they have suggested, with particular reference to post-socialist cities such as Budapest and Moscow, that non-communitarian social capital is often being used for purposes of 'asset conversion'; 'individuals with strong backgrounds of participation in Communist Party organisations were highly likely to jettison their party identification and to redeploy their resources (finance, networks, etc.) to take advantage of whatever economic opportunities emerged'.[35] From a political point of view, circumstances such as these led to slightly paradoxical results in Ukraine, as in connection with the 1998 parliamentary elections in which the reformed Communists returned as the largest faction in Ukrainian politics. While rates of voting turnout were at high levels—above 70.0% on average and closer to 80.0% in L'viv *oblast'*—opinion polls indicated that a majority of people (66.0%) voted for leaders for whom they shared no or only slight trust.[36] Further probing of the 1994 survey data as well as interview material demonstrates the relation between lack of trust, non-communitarian social capital and above all post-war changes in western Ukraine.

Political behaviour, formal institutions and 'trust'

Focusing on the rate of experience of different types of political and civic agency, two examples will be discussed, the first of which relates to experience of joining organisations. In this case we can observe what is most probably an effect not of long-term historical legacies but rather of post-war demographic patterns, urbanisa-tion and the impact of state socialist institutions on civic behaviour, although with some differences if L'viv and Donets'k are compared. The eastern regions of the country were already more urbanised before World War II, while western Ukraine to this day has kept much of its rural character. Importantly, this had consequences for the post-war development. Following the virtual eradication of the pre-war urban community, including expulsion of the Polish population from L'viv, the subsequent re-urbanisation of the city from the late 1940s onwards to a great extent took the shape of extensive migration of ethnic Ukrainians from the surrounding rural areas and villages. The same migration pattern holds well into the late 20th century. For instance, 47.0% of the L'viv respondents in the 1994 survey were born in villages, compared with 29.8% of the Donets'k respondents. Therefore, should the 'continuity hypothesis' about a historically transmitted mode of civic behaviour among western Ukrainians in L'viv hold up to scrutiny, such traditions could be expected to be found not least among migrant groups arriving from the countryside. Among other things, it is likely that we would be able to observe marked differences between 'villagers' and 'urbanites' in the local population, possibly implying a rural–urban continuum in

TABLE 3
URBAN/RURAL ORIGIN AND EXPERIENCE OF JOINING ORGANISATIONS , 1994

Place of birth	No	Once	More than once	Totals
L'viv				
Large city	89.2	4.1	6.8	100.0
Medium-sized city	92.8	3.6	3.6	100.0
Small city	96.6	3.4	–	100.0
Village	91.2	1.1	7.7	100.0
Donets'k				
Large city	95.2	1.9	2.9	100.0
Medium-sized city	97.9	–	2.1	100.0
Small city	97.6	–	2.4	100.0
Village	93.6	3.2	3.2	100.0

Note: L'viv: $n = 391$. Valid cases $= 388$. Donets'k. $n = 430$. Valid cases $= 421$.

Source: 1994 survey on Identity Formation and Social Issues in East and West Ukraine, by courtesy of the Institute for Historical Research, L'viv State University.

terms of political culture and social capital. By the logic of this hypothesis, locals with a rural background would by force of tradition have been more active in civic activities following Ukrainian independence. By and large this is not the case.

When we examine joining organisations we find that the proportion of 'villagers' in L'viv having one or more than one such experience was, to begin with, higher than for 'villagers' in Donets'k. The same kind of difference between L'viv and Donets'k holds, however, and is in fact even more marked, if we compare people born, for instance, in large cities as well. In addition, if we examine the L'viv sample specifically, we can also see that 'villagers' in L'viv were somewhat less active in organisational life than 'urbanites' although there is a slight difference in favour of the former group when only multiple experience of joining organisations is considered (see Table 3). In other words, at least in this respect the 'rural' segment of the population in L'viv does not seem to have differed from the rest of the local community. While this by no means refutes the possibility of long-term historical legacies having an impact on other aspects of political and civic behaviour, it nevertheless implies that such interpretations should be reformulated. Indeed, that historical traditions—with or without connection to the rural–urban dimension—seem to play a part in yet other respects is illustrated by our next example.

In this case we can see how variations in religious affiliation were tied to variations in organisational experience in L'viv (Table 4). Among the types of affiliations that were clearly identifiable in the 1994 survey, people belonging to the Ukrainian Orthodox Church of the Kievan Patriarchate and the Greek Catholic Church had the greatest experience of joining organisations (6.0% and 9.4% respectively had more than one experience of joining organisations). However, compared with the average rate of multiple experience among the entire L'viv sample (6.4%),[37] only the Greek Catholics stand out as a relatively more active group in the local community. The same holds if both single and multiple experience of joining organisations are added, although in this case with a slightly higher rate for the Ukrainian Orthodox Church (Kievan Patriarchate). In addition, respondents associating with Ukrainian Orthodoxy

TABLE 4
RELIGIOUS AFFILIATION AND EXPERIENCE OF JOINING ORGANISATIONS, L'VIV, 1994

Religious affiliation	No	Once	More than once	Totals
Ukrainian Orthodox (Kievan Patriarchate)	90.0	4.0	6.0	100.0
Ukrainian Orthodox (Moscow Patriarchate)	100.0	–	–	100.0
Ukrainian Autocephalous Church	97.8	–	2.2	100.0
Russian Orthodox	92.3	7.7	–	100.0
Greek Catholic	87.4	3.1	9.4	100.0
Roman Catholic	100.0	–	–	100.0
Judaism	100.0	–	–	100.0
Other	88.9	–	11.1	100.0

Note: $n = 391$. Valid cases = 286.
Source: 1994 survey on Identity Formation and Social Issues in East and West Ukraine, by courtesy of the Institute for Historical Research, L'viv State University.

of the Moscow Patriarchate, as well as members of the Roman Catholic Church and Judaism, did not account for any organisational affiliations at all. The point, however, is that, particularly in the case of Greek Catholicism—part and parcel of traditional west Ukrainian culture—religious life was related to a potentially richer experience of civic networks and organisations. To some extent this was the case with the Ukrainian Autocephalous Orthodox Church as well, although this is less clear from the 1994 survey. In both cases we are dealing with churches that re-emerged during *perestroika*, and the latter church especially had close links with Rukh in the closing days of Soviet Ukraine, according to Kuzio.[38]

Nevertheless, despite the obvious differences in political culture between L'viv and Donets'k, it should be stressed that the overall experience of various types of civic activities of the kind Putnam highlighted was and still is at a low level in both cities. In L'viv democratisation and the building of a Western-style 'civic culture' have not proceeded with the speed occasionally envisaged early on during transition. The generally low levels of interest in politics and the low levels of public trust in mass media, politicians and government officials revealed by the L'viv-Donets'k survey and in connection with the last election more than anything else indicate lack of any more widely dispersed communitarian social capital.

All of this is, of course, far from surprising. To some extent it is simply due to the time factor, i.e. inexperience of collective and democratic action due to the short time span since independence. To some considerable extent, however, the situation also reflects the fact that the political culture of Ukraine is still shaped by the empirically less tangible effects of decades of experience of Soviet state institutions. It is from that perspective that variables previously analysed most notably by Pirie—post-war patterns of urbanisation, industrialisation, ethnic inter-marriage and linguistic

Russification[39]—have intervened to produce regional differences from the effects of state socialist institutions, whereas long-term historical and cultural differences exercise a more indirect influence. As changes of the former kind were of a different nature in western Ukraine after 1945 they most probably had a different impact on the local and regional social fabric compared with those in Donets'k.

As previously noted, rural migration to L'viv was intense during the first post-war years. Yet it was mostly ethnic Ukrainians who moved to the city, leaving the ethnic composition of the population relatively homogeneous, although—as the official Soviet account of the *oblast'* put it—'help' and 'qualified experts' from all over the Union quickly arrived to help rebuild society.[40] Unlike Donets'k, though, 'Ukrainisation' of L'viv rather than 'Russification' is the proper word, as the proportion of Ukrainians among the population started to increase from the late 1950s, from 60.0% in 1959 to 79.1% in 1989.[41] This roughly matches the results of the 1994 survey, when, in the crucial dimension of language usage, 77.5% of the respondents claimed Ukrainian as their native language. In Donets'k, however, the population is mixed and multiethnic, including a bias in favour of Russian speaking Ukrainians and people claiming both Russian and Ukrainian as mother tongues. The family pattern in L'viv as well is more homogeneous than in Donets'k, something which also relates to Pirie's findings on the contrasts between the western and eastern parts of the country.[42] Adding to these differences is the lower degree of urbanisation in the west, including L'viv *oblast'*. According to 1990 figures the level of urbanisation in L'viv was at that time 64.1% compared with 91.3% in Donets'k.[43]

Importantly, urbanisation and industrialisation went hand in hand. As Hoffman's investigation of Moscow or Kotkin's analysis of Magnitogorsk in the inter-war period have demonstrated,[44] these processes should not be interpreted only from an economic perspective. State policies for rapid urbanisation and industrialisation had a deep and profound impact on the social organisation and culture of local society at large and were at the heart of the notion we usually associate with the concept of 'socialist cities'. The same was the case in pre-war Soviet Ukraine, and the same policy was also implemented in L'viv by the end of the war. By directive 755/213 from the Supreme Soviet, issued on 13 April 1945, it was declared that L'viv should be transformed into a modern industrial centre of western Ukraine, including allocation of light manufacturing and food industry. Yet, in comparison with Donets'k, these processes did not reach equally deep in L'viv. Plans rapidly became bogged down when confronted with realities[45] and L'viv never became the same mono-cultural type of city as Donets'k in terms of the local economy, or the specific type of social organisation associated with the expansion of heavy industry.[46]

Rather, what the previous data suggest is that post-war changes, although dramatic, in other respects did not have the same profound effects on the social fabric of society as in the eastern parts of the country. Indeed, as already noted, the entire pre-war community of L'viv was shifted after the war. But at the same time other aspects of the migration pattern, as well as the pace of urbanisation and industrialisation, and cultural aspects such as language usage, indicate that state policies vis-à-vis the new Soviet Ukrainian region partly failed to re-mould local society. At the same time, though, the building of state socialist institutions had other effects of relevance from a social capital perspective.

Following Kaminski (1992), typical characteristics of state socialist-type polities (Kaminski uses the expression 'Soviet-type polities') can be summarised as: (i) central planning instead of the market as regulator of the economy; (ii) 'dictatorship of the revolutionary vanguard' instead of government through an elected parliament and 'legal guarantees of individual liberties'; (iii) one-party rule instead of a plurality of competing political parties; (iv) moral and political unity on the basis of the nation instead of pluralism and competing ideologies; (v) state ownership and state management instead of private property, and; (vi) a top-down rather than bottom-up practice of policy making and administration.[47] By promotion of the rigidity of this system, compartmentalisation, large-scale corruption and clientelism among the members of the *nomenklatura* became an intrinsic feature of Soviet politics at the same time as a war of merciless repression was waged against all forms of dissent from below. Add to these features the Potemkin-like nature of state socialist institutions and the fact that little if anything in terms of practical matters ever worked really smoothly, and it comes as no surprise that generations of Ukrainians share a certain suspicion towards authorities and formal institutions, regardless of regional belonging. As 'Zenoviy', a street vendor in L'viv put it in 1996 when commenting on the fall of the Soviet Union:

If the Soviet Union had had a market economy, competition, then maybe it wouldn't have fallen apart. Well, thank God that it was the kind of economy where the Soviet Union fell apart, you see? If there was a market economy, then we would have [normal] ties, there would be competition, enterprises would produce competitive goods, they would be sold, and there would be jobs. And you guys know this perfectly well, and the people who ruled us—they completed evening or correspondence courses, they didn't go to regular universities, they got their credits in a way that you know well—[by bribing professors] with a bottle [of vodka] or with money. And then he comes with his diploma, with an education, without [real] knowledge. These are the kind of men who ruled us. What kind of new technologies could there be if he earned only 150 Soviet rubles [per month]—did he want to think for this money? Then, if a person invented something, how many co-authors [who had nothing to do with this invention] would he have? So this person was desperate, he didn't even want to think. This is why everything fell apart.[48]

Concluding that people have little trust in formal institutions and formal organisations, though, should not automatically lead us to conclude that people in Ukraine and in L'viv do not solve practical problems of the kind mediated by Western-style civic networks, interest organisations and political parties. If anything certain can be said of the East-Central European societies it is, indeed, that people reveal a sometimes almost uncanny capacity for practical problem solving and successfully going about their business. Consequently, the kind of non-communitarian social capital fostered by the experience of state socialist institutions has features that are not in all respects entirely negative. The problem, from our perspective, is why the kind of exchange relations this social capital is built from do not facilitate collective agency and trust in a situation in which non-authoritarian and less vertical formal institutions are attempted.

Non-communitarian social capital

Let us reconsider the above picture. Once more: the very essence of Putnam's social capital theory is that people, in a first step, build trust in each other by being involved in horizontal and reciprocal exchange relations. In a very basic sense 'trust' means that the actors can calculate the effects and responses provoked by their behaviour among other actors. 'Trust' means that people 'know' that the people they are involved with will 'honour the agreement' between them of their own choosing. Importantly, this considerably lowers the transaction costs involved in gaining access to the public good. 'I trust you, because I trust her and she assures me that she trusts you'. One of Putnam's illustrations for this is by referring to Hume's discussion of public-spiritedness and the conclusion that everyone would really be better off if only they co-operated.[49]

However, complex large-scale societies cannot be efficiently administered purely by means of personal contacts and direct links between the members of society. If for no other reason, this is impossible from a practical point of view, although it is correct, as for instance Granovetter but also Putnam himself have stressed, that we often tend to underestimate the importance of informal social organisation in modern societies.[50] In a second step, therefore, accumulated trust based on such relations as above makes the members of society inclined to form organisational ties for collective action. Putnam's most important historical example of this, apart from his analogies with the medieval guilds, were the mutual aid societies of 19th century northern Italy and the subsequent rise of modern interest organisations. In a third and final step the learning process also makes the individual actors more susceptible to the institutions represented by the state. Consequently trust serves the purpose of reducing the effects of the 'free rider' problem, as enforcement of institutions purely by the state is not enough to ensure efficient institutional performance.[51] Trust serves to lubricate the political system and it enhances the 'responsiveness' of democratic polities. Needless to say, none of these conditions was characteristic of state socialist societies.

Considering social capital and trust, the crucial thing is what happens between the first and second steps in Putnam's model, i.e. the transformation leading from direct involvement in exchange relationships to social capital in terms of accumulated trust in impersonal institutional arrangements. Although the connection between the first and second steps of this process may seem self-evident, nevertheless the logic underpinning it depends, if not entirely, then at any rate heavily on Putnam's perception of exchange relations. Importantly, communitarian social capital is seen as being built from horizontal networks of exchange relations, while non-communitarian social capital is the result of particularistic and vertical exchange relations of the kind we may find not only in southern Italy but also in the former socialist countries. According to Putnam it is the difficulties in *implementing sanctions* in the latter kind of networks which impede the building of mutual trust. 'Sanctions that support norms of reciprocity against the threat of opportunism are less likely to be imposed upwards and less likely to be acceded to, if imposed. Only a bold or foolhardy subordinate, lacking ties of solidarity with peers, would seek to punish a superior'.[52] Attractive and straightforward as this explanation is at first glance, it is nevertheless off the target.

Part of the problem is that there exist two theoretically different types of exchange relations in modern societies. Of these two types only one is really consistent with the notion of transfer of 'trust' from direct ties—or, rather, networks—between the actors to impersonal and collective bodies by force of the mechanism Putnam outlines. Although Putnam too is clear about this distinction, the real key to the problem concerning post-socialist societies is not the sanctioning of norms. Sanctions and mutual trust, we shall argue, are equally as much part of non-communitarian social capital as they are of communitarian social capital. Rather it is the *nature of transactions and the mode of reducing social transaction costs typical to non-communitarian social capital* that impede the building of trust in formal institutions. In the more elaborate (1993) version of the social capital theory Putnam's definition of social capital draws heavily on that of Coleman (1988, 1990).[53] In turn, the key concepts in both Putnam's and Coleman's understanding of exchange relations originally derive from game theory as introduced in American sociology in the 1950s as well as from Continental social anthropology, most notably represented by Mauss and Lévi-Strauss from the 1920s onwards.

Precisely as in the case of Putnam, the focus in the models of for example Homans and Blau was on the reduction of transaction costs,[54] the latter expression literally implying that, in an economist's way of thinking, social transaction 'costs' vary depending on the 'market' conditions. In contrast to what is the case in neoclassical market models, however, one of the most important tools for reducing transaction costs is for the market actors to enter reciprocal exchange relations based on trust.[55] That is, the relational properties of society intervene to reduce the uncertainties of the market. Two of the most important types of costs, according to Homans, can be summarised as 'attraction' and 'agreement'. This would equal Putnam's concept of 'reciprocity' as associated with 'networks of civic engagement'.[56]

In Homans's model high levels of 'attraction' and high levels of 'agreement' lead to increased 'trust', and therefore also lower transaction costs, something which indirectly results in more closely knit relations/networks among the actors. In Putnam's model 'reciprocity' works similarly to produce cohesion, trust and eventually 'civic networks'. Looked at the other way round, frequent interaction lowers the transaction costs and leads to ever-increasing levels of 'attraction' and 'agreement', or 'reciprocity'.[57] We should, however, be careful to note the nature of transaction costs implied by this model.

To be sure, at least during the initial phase of an exchange relationship, perceived qualities of 'attraction' and 'agreement' among the actors are to a considerable extent contingent on complicated psychological processes of a less than tangible nature. But this is far from the whole picture. If and when the frequency of exchange tends to accelerate, the mechanisms fostering attraction, agreement and trust become almost a *perpetuum mobile*. Trust and transaction costs are no longer, or at least not entirely contingent on the personal attributes and characteristics of the actors involved. 'Trust', according to Putnam—in turn following Coleman and indirectly Merton (1968)—becomes a 'social norm'.[58] This is also why 'trust' can be abstracted from social networks (or 'civic networks') to collective actors. In this kind of reciprocal exchange relations, then, the threat of sanctions on instances of breaking an agreement is definitely part of the problem, as breaking an agreement would automatically lead to loss of attraction, with consequently less to be gained for all parties involved. From this the hypothesis of 'virtuous' and 'vicious circles' may be deduced.

Obviously the mechanisms by which these processes are initiated were not exactly abundant in polities characterised by central planning, 'dictatorship of the revolution-ary vanguard' and top-down policy making. But if the reverse situation holds for countries such as Ukraine, how do the underpinnings of non-communitarian social capital match the logic behind Putnam's communitarian social capital? It is in this perspective that the type of exchange relations defined by the French social anthropol-ogists Mauss (1967 [1925]) and Lévi-Strauss (1969 [1949]) become of interest.[59] According to their line of thought exchange occurs to strict and often ritual principles of social behaviour tied to the social hierarchy of a particular society. Exchange is tied to mutual moral obligations of a kind that exceeds the limits of the actual exchange. Importantly, the social status of the individual actors serves as a regulator of which 'gifts' may be exchanged. For this reason one can also say that transaction costs in the sense of Homans, Blau, Coleman and Putnam do not really exist—or perhaps rather that the transaction costs for each type of exchange are always set at a fixed 'rate' as a result of social custom. The rules of transaction are regulated by force of social custom (or 'norms') but the actual cost is not contingent on the rate of exchange in the same manner as in Homan's or Putnam's examples.

Conventionally, exchange relations of this type have been regarded as typical of 'traditional' societies. Empirically, however, this distinction obviously does not stand up to scrutiny. Both modes of exchange occur conflated with each other in 'modern societies', although usually with a bias in favour for one type or the other. In exchange relations based more on status and social custom, though, trust is not as easy to transfer from the social networks in which the exchange occurs as in the case of game theory exchange, because of their being more tied up with the unique attributes of the individual actors. This, however, is far from implying lack of means to impose sanctions against the breaking of agreements or, as in this specific case, social custom.

To the contrary, although these kinds of networks are usually more vertical in nature, making clientelism part and parcel of non-communitarian social capital, the entire stability of the social structure depends on mutual honouring of agreements in accordance with social custom. Put simply, a patron's social standing and reputation in the community depend as heavily as those of his clients on the ability to perform in accordance with whatever rules, customs and expectations there are regulating social exchange. This necessarily involves trust and sanctions in both directions, despite the relations between patron and clients being vertical. This principle is, for example, illustrated by the nature and role of patron–client relations typical of society in early modern Europe, including the relations between magnates and their clients in pre-partition Poland.[60] Yet at the same time this mode of social transactions and the type of costs involved with exchange depend more on the personal attributes of the actors than in Putnam's game theory solution. Consequently, limits are also set precisely as to how far trust can be transferred to impersonal bodies and formal institutions. This is also the reason why we may label the exchange relations of Mauss and Lévi-Strauss 'non-communitarian' when cast in a post-socialist setting.

Social capital as typical of post-socialist societies constitutes a mix of the two above modes of exchange, but with some important differences. In some cases, to be sure, exchange and the formation of networks in the Ukrainian context depend on the social status of the actors. Attributes such as ethnicity, kin and other group-related criteria set the limits of social transactions. Yet, while such networks are particularistic along ethnic, linguistic and similar lines, they are not absolutely vertical in the same manner as patron–client relationships proper. Furthermore, there are presumably differences between different Ukrainian regions in this respect. Pirie, for instance, argued that high levels of inter-ethnic marriage—such as found to be the case in eastern Ukraine and in the Crimea—were important to the formation of mixed social identities.[61] This, in turn, would seem to indicate a lesser importance of particularistic exchange patterns in some dimensions. What is marriage, for instance, if not an integral part of those close affiliations from which a person's networks and social capital are built? The situation in eastern and southern Ukraine can thereafter be contrasted with the more clear-cut juxtaposition between 'Ukrainians' and 'Russians' found in western Ukraine, including in terms of marriage. Paradoxically this pattern speaks in favour of the hypothesis that the tendency to exchange at least across ethnic status group boundaries would actually be stronger in cities such as Donets'k compared with a more 'Western' and 'civic-minded' city such as L'viv.

Importantly, however, exchange—regardless of whether it took place within or across ethnic and similar lines of demarcation—was restricted for entirely different reasons as well during the Soviet period. While the costs and, indeed, also the 'currency' involved varied—vodka, cash, swapping of favours—exchange could often take place only within certain 'spatial' limits of social space. For one thing, the design and nature of state socialist institutions made compartmentalisation an intrinsic feature of society, thereby limiting the number of possible contacts and exchanges and thus favouring particularistic habits not only among the members of the *nomenklatura*. The fact that distrust and suspicion, more than trust, permeated the social fabric meant that exchange became limited within the boundaries of yet other types of closed networks such as those based on family ties, kin and close friendship. Secondly, as exchange in still other instances depended on the roles and positions of the actors in the hierarchy of Soviet institutions, exchange would also occur on the basis of vertical and informal patron–client-like relations, such as in the above case of 'Zenoviy's' bribed professors and their students. And the point is that even such instances of corruption depended heavily on certain 'social customs' and norms. This was simply because of the threat of sanctions imposed in both directions on subordinates and superiors alike by the state, if they were exposed.

Features such as these demonstrate why non-communitarian social capital is in principle incompatible with trust in formal institutions owing to the nature of exchange relations. This is the psychological legacy of state socialist institutions. Importantly, however, there is yet another aspect of importance, pointing more towards the problem of today's attempts at institutional reforms, namely efficiency. The very fact that state socialist institutions did not efficiently provide goods and services to the citizens, i.e. were not 'responsive' to the demands of the citizens, made personal contacts and networks—within reasonable limits—important as fairly efficient problem-solving devices for the man in the street. Not surprisingly, given the poor performance of reforms in Ukraine after independence, many tend to look back to the seeming stability of society during the Soviet period. This is reflected, for instance, by the results of the 1998 parliamentary elections. Although the Ukrainian Communist Party gained only 4.1% of the votes in L'viv *oblast'* in contrast to an average of 24.7%,[62] still many locals have a strong feeling of dissatisfaction with the present state of affairs. Well above 40.0% of those polled in L'viv thought that 'chaos and anarchy … [reigned] supreme in the country'.[63]

In fact, non-communitarian social capital rather than civic networks continues to permeate the daily life experience precisely because in certain respects it represents an efficient means of coping in the face of the difficulties connected with transition. Comparing the focus group discussions conducted in L'viv and Donets'k during 1996–97, this impression sticks regardless of other differences between the two cities. Commenting on the current situation of Ukrainians and Russians in L'viv, for example, 37-year-old 'Volodymyr', a former employee at the Institute for the Ukrainian Bus Industry, referred to family and rural connections as particularly important for local Ukrainians. 'It is easier for him from the point of view of food—those Ukrainians who have family in the countryside, they can go there and lay up potatoes or something else in store for themselves'.[64] The persistence of this and similar modes of practical problem solving often leaves people suspicious as regards the real use for Putnam-type civic networks.

Florist Olha Sadovska, born in 1957 and experiencing a 'typical Soviet kid' childhood in her own words, is another example. Sadovska could attend the 'right' schools with the help of family connections and she was later, after independence, able to open her business largely through the help of her husband and father. She did, during 1990, participate in the election demonstrations although such activities were, she admitted, not a regular part of her behaviour. On the contrary, even within her new line of work, she did not engage very actively in the new civic networks and organisations of the community.

> Even now, for example, there are lots of different clubs in L'viv. You know, women often get together in some business club, etc. I got into one of those clubs, paid my fees, but then I got bored going to those meetings. I don't know, probably this goes back in me to the days that I spent in the Komsomol. Ever since then I haven't liked such public activities. They seem to me to be a waste of time.[65]

Sadovska's comment serves as a pertinent illustration of the lack of trust placed in formal institutions: they are basically a 'waste of time' and they do not really constitute an efficient tool for practical problem solving. Now, personal networks constitute an intrinsic aspect of all societies. They are, to borrow Granovetter's expression, 'embedded' within the formal institutional and organisational structure of modern societies.[66] What we have in the case of post-socialist societies such as Ukraine, though, is a situation in which networks are not only embedded; in some cases they have even come to serve as a substitute for formal organisations and institutions. Neither do they, as might be the case in certain situations, serve the purpose of strengthening the legitimacy of such institutions.[67] To conclude from this, however, that societies characterised by non-communitarian social capital are therefore predestined to enter a 'vicious circle' as regards political culture, or that it would imply that the culture at large of such societies is incompatible with democratic ideas and institutions, would be erratic.

Summary and conclusions: social capital, institutional design and the state

We have argued for the persistence of non-communitarian social capital in post-socialist societies, illustrated by a case study of western Ukraine and L'viv during the first years following independence. Contrary to Putnam's argument, though, lack of trust in formal institutions is not due primarily to difficulties in implementing sanctions in the particularistic and often vertical networks from which non-communitarian social capital is built. Rather, we have put forward the hypothesis that the type of exchange relations that constitute the backbone of social capital, and in particular the mode of reducing social transaction costs which it represents, is the key to the problem. Contrary to indicating an unbreakable 'vicious circle' in Ukrainian political culture or making institutional design[68] and state policies redundant, though, the very nature of social capital indicates precisely the opposite. This in turn has to do with the function of social capital in post-socialist societies. By this we refer to their capacity of being so far and in some respects a more efficient device for practical problem solving compared with the relative failure of formal institutions and economic and political reforms introduced by the state.

Whether or not the new polity slowly evolving in Ukraine will eventually be 'efficient'—that is, will become truly 'responsive' to the demands and feed-back of the citizens according to Dahl's definition of democratic systems—is an open-ended question. Given the short time reforms have had to work, it is of course impossible to make any authoritative claims in this respect. To be sure the answer to the question depends on political culture and the success with which civic behaviour becomes an integral part of society. Yet as Putnam's 'virtuous' and 'vicious circles' are far from representing deterministic outcomes, it is important to note that institutional design and state polities are also very much part of the problem. In other words, as long as new institutions do not clearly prove themselves to be more efficient tools for collective problem solving, non-communitarian social capital and particularistic networks still fulfil a function in society. From this point of view, however, formal institutions and state agency would ultimately seem to be favoured. Complex, large-scale societies obviously cannot in the long run be efficiently managed only by mediation through personal contacts and networks.

In that perspective, though, it is equally important to acknowledge that democratic institutions differ in their design and that such differences are crucial to the compatibility of institutions with a particular set of social and cultural conditions. Under any circumstances it is clear that institutions cannot simply be imported just as they are lock, stock and barrel from Western polities without legislators and policy makers giving serious consideration to the social and cultural specifics of the country in question. To some extent this question lies at bottom of the issue of the 'clash of civilisations'. While these problems were not always stressed sufficiently among Western policy analysts at the beginning of the transition, some lessons have certainly been learned on the receiving side, something which in the case of Ukraine may be illustrated by the issue of individual rights vs. minority rights in society. Often these are referred to as incompatible alternatives from a 'Western' perspective stressing individual liberties. Extensive minority rights would simply favour the kind of particularism from which non-communitarian social capital breeds. But tentatively—at least in the short run—the situation is more as Resler has argued, i.e. that failing to make institutional amends for, in this specific case, the complex ethnic make-up of Ukrainian society would lead to more rather than fewer deficiencies in the polity.[69]

Social capital, structural factors and the nature of the state, we could therefore argue, simply constitute the 'environmental conditions' in which new institutions 'compete' with each other to become dominant political traits. Some institutional innovations and implants thus have a greater 'survival potential' than others to become dominant traits, or evolve into new path dependencies, given a particular social environment and a particular kind of social capital.[70] Consequently the crucial aspect in the future may well be our efforts to create a deeper and closer understanding of exactly how non-communitarian social capital and new institutions do or do not relate to each other in practical politics. After all, put somewhat drastically, it still holds that *lex bonae ex malis moribus procreantur* (Macrobius, *Saturnalia*, 3, 17, 10).

University College of South Stockholm

[1] This article was written in connection with the research project 'Institutionalising Democracy: A Study of City Regions in Poland and Ukraine', headed by the author. I am greatly indebted to my colleague Mikael Sandberg for valuable comments and critical remarks on previous versions of the manuscript.

[2] Robert D. Putnam, *Making Democracy Work. Civic Traditions in Modern Italy* (Princeton, 1993).

[3] See for instance Michael Harloe, 'Cities in Transition', in Gregory Andrusz, Michael Harloe & Ivan Szelenyi (eds), *Cities after Socialism. Urban and Regional Change and Conflict in Post-socialist Cities* (Oxford, 1996), pp. 1–29.

[4] See Thomas R. Cusack, 'Social Capital, Institutional Structures, and Democratic Performance: A Comparative Study of German Local Governments', Discussion paper FS III 97–201, Wissenschaftszentrum Berlin für Sozialforschung (WZB) 1997; Carol J. Hager, 'Building Democracy in Central Europe: Political Institutions and Political Culture in Two Border Towns', paper presented at the Annual Meeting of the American Political Science Association, Boston, 3–6 September 1998.

[5] Putnam, *Making Democracy Work*, p. 174.

[6] Arendt Lijphart, 'Comparative Politics and the Comparative Method', *American Political Science Review*, 65, 1971, p. 692.

[7] The survey in question was conducted in 1994, while the rest of the material was compiled in 1996–97. In both cases the projects were jointly carried out by the Centre for Russian and East European Studies, University of Michigan and the Institute for Historical Research, L'viv State University. The material is used by courtesy of the Institute for Historical Research, L'viv State University, for which the author is greatly indebted.

[8] See for instance Chris Pickvance, 'Comparative Analysis, Causality and Case Studies in Urban Studies', in Alasdair Rogers & Steven Vertovec (eds), *The Urban Context. Ethnicity, Social Networks and Situational Analysis* (Oxford and Washington DC, 1995), pp. 35–54.

[9] Samuel P. Huntington, 'The Clash of Civilization?', *Foreign Affairs*, 72, 3, 1993, pp. 22–49; Samuel P. Huntington, *The Third Wave. Democratization in the Late Twentieth Century* (Norman and London, 1991).

[10] Richard Pipes, *A Concise History of the Russian Revolution* (New York, 1995).

[11] See Sidney Tarrow, 'Making Social Science Work Across Time and Space: A Critical Reflection on Robert Putnam's *Making Democracy Work*', *American Political Science Review*, 90, 2, 1996, pp. 389–397.

[12] Robert A. Dahl, *Polyarchy. Participation and Opposition* (New Haven and London, 1971), pp. 2–9.

[13] Putnam, *Making Democracy Work*, p. 167.

[14] *Ibid.*, pp. 171–176.

[15] Robert D. Putnam, Robert Leonardi, Raffaella Y. Nanetti & Franco Pavoncello, 'Explaining Institutional Success: The Case of Italian Regional Government', *American Political Science Review*, 77, 1983, pp. 55–74. Importantly, Putnam does not actually use the concept 'social capital' or enter any real discussion of 'trust' in this early version of his model. Rather, what is referred to in this case is simply 'political culture', first and foremost by referring to Almond & Verba (1965).

[16] Putnam, *Making Democracy Work*, pp. 177–181.

[17] Huntington, *The Third Wave*, pp. 144–145.

[18] Lauri Karvonen, *Demokratisering* (Lund, 1997), p. 105.

[19] See John-Paul Himka, *Socialism in Galicia. The Emergence of Polish Social Democracy and Ukrainian Radicalism (1860–1890)* (Cambridge, MA, 1983), pp. 44–45; on Ukrainian socialism see pp. 138–140.

[20] Taras Kuzio, 'Restructuring from Below: Informal Groups in Ukraine Under Gorbachev, 1985–89', in Bohdan Krawchenko (ed.), *Ukrainian Past, Ukrainian Present* (New York, 1990), pp. 107–122. Also see the section on political behaviour, trust, and formal institutions in this article.

[21] Cusack, *Social Capital ...*, p. 40.

[22] *Ibid.*, pp. 46–47.

[23] Patrick. R. Ireland, *The Policy Challenge of Ethnic Diversity. Immigrant Politics in France and Switzerland* (Cambridge, MA, 1994).

[24] Roman Szporluk, 'The Strange Politics of L'viv: An Essay in Search for an Explanation', in Zvi Gitelman (ed.), *The Politics of Nationality and the Erosion of the USSR* (New York, 1992), pp. 215–223; Paul S. Pirie, 'National Identity and Politics in Southern and Eastern Ukraine', *Europe-Asia Studies*, 48, 7, 1996, pp. 1079–1104; Yaroslav Hrytsak & Victor Susak, 'Historical Legacies, Social Changes and Political Attitudes in L'viv, 1945–1998', paper presented at conference on 'Institutionalising Democracy: Poland and Ukraine in Comparative Perspective', Stockholm, 13–16 November 1998. See also for instance Michael Kennedy, 'Post-Soviet Identity and Environmental Problems in Transition: Estonia, Ukraine, and Uzbekistan Through Focus Groups', paper presented at conference on 'Identity Formation and Social Problems in Estonia, Ukraine and Uzbekistan', Kyiv, 4–8 August 1997.

[25] Pickvance, 'Comparative Studies, Causality and Case Studies ...'; J. Clyde Mitchell, *Cities, Societies and Social Perception: A Central African Perspective* (Oxford, 1987), pp. 7–17.

[26] Differences in mode of political mobilisation among Russians in the east and south, however, should of course be stressed. See for example David J. Meyer, 'Why have Donbass Russians not Ethnically Mobilized Like Crimean Russians have? An Institutional/Demographic Approach', in John S. Micgiel (ed.), *State and Nation Building in East Central Europe: Contemporary Perspectives* (New York, 1996), pp. 317–330.

[27] Precise data are, of course, lacking owing to problems of definition etc, but according to Polish estimates (1921 figures), Poles and Jews made up 63.8% and 25.9% respectively of the population; Germans and Ukrainians accounted for 1.4% and 8.9% respectively. See Fryderyk Papeé, *Historia miasta Lwowa w zarysie* (Lwów/Warszawa, 1924), footnote pp. 228–229.

[28] Szporluk, 'The Strange Politics of L'viv ...' pp. 215–231, quotation p. 230.

[29] Olga Malanchuk, 'Regional Influences in Ukrainian Politics', paper presented at conference on 'Identity Formation and Social Issues in Global Perspective', Ann Arbor, 11–15 May 1998, pp. 10–11.

[30] Kuzio, 'Restructuring from Below ...', pp. 109–113.

[31] This is, for example, indirectly illustrated by focus group discussions conducted among the local population in 1996–97. See Focus group discussion, men, L'viv, 6 October 1996, by courtesy of the Institute for Historical Research, L'viv State University.

[32] See *Hromads'ki ob'ednannia u L'vivs'kii oblasti* (L'viv, 1998).

[33] Paul Kubicek, 'Variations on a Corporatist Theme: Interest Associations in Post-Soviet Ukraine and Russia', *Europe-Asia Studies*, 48, 1, 1996, pp. 27–46.

[34] A. Levitas & P. Strzalkowski, 'What does "uwlaszczenie nomenklatury" ("Propertisation" of the Nomenklatura) Really Mean?', *Communist Economies*, 2, 3, 1990, pp. 413–416; Chris G. Pickvance, 'Environmental and Housing Movements in cities after Socialism: the cases of Budapest and Moscow', in Gregory Andrusz, Michael Harloe & Ivan Szelenyi (eds), *Cities after Socialism. Urban and Regional Change and Conflict in Post-socialist Societies* (Oxford, 1996), pp. 232–267.

[35] Pickvance, 'Environmental and Housing Movements in Cities after Socialism ...', p. 245.

[36] Natalie Chernysh, 'The Civil Society in Present-day Ukraine: Myth or Reality', paper presented at conference on 'Institutionalising Democracy: Poland and Ukraine in Comparative Perspective', Stockholm, 13–16 November 1998, p. 6.

[37] Table 2.

[38] Although it should also be noted that the revival of the Ukrainian Autocephalous Orthodox

Church in 1989 and the subsequent secession from the Russian Orthodox Church initially caused some tension between the former church and the Greek Catholics. See Kuzio, 'Restructuring from Below ...', pp. 111, 117.

[39] Pirie, 'National Identity and Politics ...', pp. 1079–1085.

[40] D. A. Yaremchuk (ed.), *Istoriya gorodov i sel ukrainskoi SSR. L'vovskaya oblast'* (Kiev, 1978), p. 118.

[41] Szporluk, 'The Strange Politics of L'viv ...', Table 9.13, p. 222.

[42] According to the 1994 survey ca. 80.0% of both parents of the respondents were of Ukrainian nationality. Pirie, 'National Identity and Politics ...', pp. 1086–1087.

[43] *Ukraine. The Social Sectors During Transition* (Washington DC, 1993), Table A 5, p. 130.

[44] David L. Hoffman, *Peasant Metropolis: Social Identities in Moscow, 1929–1941* (Ithaca and London, 1994); Stephen Kotkin, *Magnetic Mountain: Stalinism as a Civilization* (London, 1995).

[45] The original directive 755/213 has not been recovered. However, the document is cited and the initial problems highlighted in an evaluation report during the implementation process. Derzhavnyi arkhiv L'vivskoî oblasti, f. R-221, op. 1, spravka 263, pp. 162–172.

[46] That is, like Central European cities such as Kraków and Prague, L'viv should be regarded as a 'socialised' city rather than as a 'socialist city'. See Richard A. French & F. E. Ian Hamilton, 'Is there a Socialist City?', in Richard A. French & F. E. Ian Hamilton (eds), *The Socialist City. Spatial Structure and Urban Policy* (Chichester, 1979), pp. 1–21, p. 6.

[47] Antoni Z. Kaminski, *An Institutional Theory of Communist Regimes. Design, Function and Breakdown* (San Francisco, 1992), pp. 320–321.

[48] Focus group discussion, men, L'viv, 6 October 1996. On the topic of the elite, see also the case of Donets'k miner 'Alexander', Focus group discussion, men, Donets'k, 25 October 1996.

[49] Putnam, *Making Democracy Work*, pp. 163–176, quotation p. 169.

[50] Mark Granovetter, 'Economic Action and Social Structure: The Problem of Embeddedness' [1983], reprint in Mark Granovetter & Richard Swedberg (eds), *The Sociology of Economic Life* (Boulder and San Francisco, 1992) pp. 53–84; Putnam, *Making Democracy Work*, p. 172 *et passim*.

[51] In this case Putnam follows North's (1990) argument on the matter of 'third party enforcement'. Putnam, *Making Democracy Work*, p. 165.

[52] *Ibid.*, p. 174.

[53] *Ibid.*, p. 167; James S. Coleman, *Foundations of Social Theory* (Cambridge, MA, 1990), pp. 300–321, in particular pp. 302, 304; James S. Coleman, 'Social Capital in the Creation of Human Capital', *American Journal of Sociology*, 94, Supplement, 1988, pp. 95–120.

[54] See Peter M. Blau, *The Dynamics of Bureaucracy* (Chicago, 1955); George C. Homans, 'Social Behavior as Exchange', *American Journal of Sociology*, 63, 1957–58, pp. 597–606. In his (1988) conception of social capital Coleman criticised both Homans and Blau among other things for the limitation of theory to 'microsocial relations, which abandons the principal virtue of economic theory, its ability to make the micro-macro transition from pair relations to system'. See Coleman, 'Social capital ...' p. 98. In a sense this is the same problem facing Putnam regarding the transfer of trust based on networks of direct relations to impersonal interest organisations.

[55] One of the most influential albeit debated contributions to this strand of analysis became Oliver Williamson, *Markets and Hierarchies. Analysis and Antitrust Implications* (New York, 1975).

[56] Putnam, *Making Democracy Work*, pp. 171–174.

[57] Homans, 'Social Behavior as Exchange', pp. 601–603. According to Putnam, 'stocks of social capital, such as trust, norms, and networks, tend to be self-reinforcing and cumulative'. See Putnam, *Making Democracy Work*, p. 177.

[58] *Ibid.*, pp. 171–173; Coleman, *Foundations of Social Theory*, pp. 310–311; Robert K. Merton, *Social Theory and Social Structure* (New York, 1968), pp. 195–203. See also for instance Robert Axelrod, 'An Evolutionary Approach to Norms', *American Political Science Review*, 80, 4, 1986, pp. 1095–1111.

[59] Marcel Mauss, *The Gift* (New York, 1967 [1925]); Claude Lévi-Strauss, *The Elementary Structures of Kinship* (Boston, 1969 [1949]).

[60] Gunner Lind, 'Great Friends and Small Friends: Clientelism and the Power Elite', in Wolfgang Reinhard (ed.), *Power Elites and State Building* (London, 1996), pp. 123–147.

[61] Pirie, 'National Identity and Politics ...', pp. 1085–1092.

[62] *Ukraïns'kyi Shlyakh*, 2 April 1998; *Ekspres*, 4–12 April 1998.

[63] Chernysh, *The Civil Society in Present-day Ukraine ...*', pp. 8–10, quotation p. 10. Notwithstanding the differences between different countries in economic performance before and after the downfall of state socialism this has, of course, been a common phenomenon. In the case of Hungary, for instance, Chris Hann has argued that it was precisely parts of the state socialist institutional heritage and not the new ideas of a civil society that added stability and a sense of identity to local

communities following transition. Chris Hann, 'Civil Society at the Grass-roots: A Reactionary View', in Paul G. Lewis (ed.), *Democracy and Civil Society in Eastern Europe* (New York and London, 1992), pp. 152–165.

[64] Focus group discussion, men, L'viv, 6 October 1996.

[65] Interview with Olha Sadovska by Victor Susak, 13 and 15 May, 1997, by courtesy of the Institute for Historical Research, L'viv State University.

[66] Granovetter, 'Economic Action and Social Structure …'.

[67] See the analysis of the relation between social structure and formal organisation in Paul DiMaggio, 'Nadel's Paradox Revisited: Relational and Cultural Aspects of Organizational Structure', in Nithin Nohria & Robert G. Eccles (eds), *Networks and Organizations: Structure, Form, and Action* (Boston, 1992), pp. 118–142.

[68] Defined as design of electoral systems, executive-legislative relations and market economy institutions. See Arend Lijphart & Carlos H. Waisman, 'Institutional Design and Democratization', in Arend Lijphart & Carlos H. Waisman (eds), *Institutional Design in New Democracies. Eastern Europe and Latin America* (Boulder, 1996), p. 3.

[69] Tamara J. Resler, 'Dilemmas of Democratisation: Safeguarding Minorities in Russia, Ukraine and Lithuania', *Europe-Asia Studies*, 49, 1, 1997, pp. 89–106.

[70] Mikael Sandberg, 'Local Evolution of Democracy. Theory and Method for a Study of L'viv and Wroclaw', paper presented at conference on 'Institutionalising Democracy: Poland and Ukraine in Comparative Perspective', Stockholm, 13–16 November 1998.

Social Capital and Community Participation in Post-Soviet Armenia: Implications for Policy and Practice

BABKEN V. BABAJANIAN

Abstract

This article argues that the social capital framework used by development agencies in community-driven development projects in post-Soviet countries may not be adequate for analysing conditions affecting community participation. Research in Armenia shows that the availability of social capital in a community may not necessarily translate into participation. The governance environment plays a key role in affecting the nature and forms of community participation and in shaping local institutions in Armenia. The research argues against the 'cultural' view of institutional change, which presumes that the main barriers to participation are posed by cultural factors, such as interpersonal trust and the 'mentality' of post-Soviet citizens. Development interventions that focus on building social capital as a means to promote community participation may not be effective without addressing broader structural factors affecting participation.

COMMUNITY DRIVEN DEVELOPMENT PROJECTS AND PROGRAMMES have become popular in the former Soviet Union since the mid-1990s. Development agencies have been advocating and supporting a variety of decentralised and participatory programmes and projects as a means of improving service delivery, enhancing local self-reliance and empowering the poor. These initiatives are often referred to as Community Driven Development (CDD). Central to the thinking behind these projects is a concept of social capital that refers to norms and networks facilitating collective action (Woolcock & Narayan 2000, p. 226). It is believed that social networks based on shared norms, values, beliefs, knowledge and understanding can significantly enhance people's capacity to organise in their own collective interest, co-operate to perform collective tasks and achieve mutual benefits. In 2000, the World Bank developed a strategy to 'scale up' CDD in the region as part of its poverty

The author would like to thank Jane Falkingham for her invaluable support during this research. I am grateful to Jude Howell, David Lewis and Hakan Seckinelgin for their constructive comments and advice. This article has been produced as part of the Non-Governmental Public Action (NGPA) Programme funded by the UK Economic and Social Research Council (ESRC).

reduction and good governance agenda (World Bank 2000a, 2001a). Between 1995 and 2007, the World Bank, in partnerships with other donors, funded 30 social fund type projects in 13 countries in the ECA (Europe and Central Asia) region. The total financing of these projects up to 2007 exceeds $650 million (World Bank 2007).

The primary objective of CDD in the former Soviet Union has been seen in strengthening social capital and developing community institutions in order to enhance local self-reliance and self-organisation. Most development professionals and transitologists have attempted to explain the limits of citizen participation by the legacies of the Soviet regime that have arguably produced social distrust, apathy and dependence on the state. It is a commonplace assumption in development literature that ideological restrictions and domination by the Communist Party eroded the civic space and produced distrustful and atomised citizens (World Bank 2000a, 2000b, 2001a, 2001b). For example, a World Bank presentation on community development in the ECA region maintains that 'successful examples of autonomous local action are few' and that 'people still depend on the state for resources and guidance' (World Bank 2000b, p. 18). It goes on to argue that in most ECA countries 'people lack the trust in one another that is needed to foster community action groups' (World Bank 2000b, p. 18). It is assumed that in addition to the low levels of trust, the cultural and normative orientation of citizens, the so-called 'Soviet mentality' factor presents a serious obstacle to developing active, self-organising communities. For example, the World Bank's CDD Strategy Note for Armenia (World Bank 2001a, p. 3) maintains that the Soviet rule enforced 'citizen passivity' and an expectation that authorities or external donors should be responsible for community welfare. Thus the task set out by CDD in post-Soviet countries is to strengthen interpersonal trust, promote attitudinal changes and enhance capacity of communities to take part in local development.

This article examines the conceptual and operational utility of social capital for enhancing community participation within the social and institutional context of post-Soviet transition in Armenia. The conceptualisation and usage of social capital by development agencies has been criticised for de-politicising development by obscuring issues of politics and power relations (Fine 2001; Harriss 2002), the potential to reproduce existing social inequalities and poverty (Cleaver 2005), and the tendency to ignore gender dimensions of development (Molyneux 2002). However, there is still a pertinent need for detailed contextual studies that can help establish patterns of local social and institutional organisation within specific social, political and cultural settings and draw lessons for more general application in development policy and practice. This article discusses the usefulness and relevance of social capital by mapping out local social and institutional relations and establishing contextual factors affecting community participation in post-Soviet Armenia.[1] First, it discusses the

---

[1]The existing literature on local institutions and social capital in post-Soviet Armenia is limited (Kharatyan 2001; Shahnazaryan 2007; Tadevosyan & Shakhsuvaryan 2005). The locally existing ethnographic knowledge about Armenian communities has not been adequately systematised and framed so as to be useful for informing development projects and policies. In contrast, local institutions and communal practices in Central Asia have received greater international attention and have been explicitly recognised and utilised in development projects and policies. Perhaps one of the reasons for this is that traditional institutions in Central Asia, such as *mahallas* in Uzbekistan and Tajikistan, have historically been more visible and discernible than those in Armenia.

concept of social capital in the general literature on CDD projects; second it examines social capital in the forms and nature of interpersonal relations, networks of mutual support and solidarity and social participation in the sample communities in Armenia; third, it explores the forms and nature of citizen participation in service delivery and local governance and discusses the key constraints to participation in the sample communities. The article relates these findings to the wider literature and discusses their implications for the conceptualisation of social capital and community participation and for designing policies to promote institutional change in post-Soviet countries.

Promoting social capital in CDD projects

The CDD paradigm originated within the World Bank, and at the same time, similar 'community-driven', 'community-based' or 'community-linked' initiatives have also been actively supported by other development agencies and NGOs. Most CDD initiatives are based on a 'bottom-up development model' for service delivery and capacity building. On the one hand, the availability of social capital is thought to be a necessary precondition for successful project outcomes (Dongier *et al.* 2003, p. 6; Van Domelen 2003, pp. 10–11). Thus many initiatives, such as social investment funds (or social funds), group based micro-finance schemes or safety net targeting programmes draw on existing stocks of social capital in order to enhance their development effectiveness. On the other hand, CDD interventions seek to build and strengthen networks within and across communities as a means of empowering poor people and improving their access to resources and services (Dongier *et al.* 2003, pp. 7–8). The CDD bottom-up development model presumes that by strengthening social capital, promoting attitudinal changes and improving organisational capacity, bottom-up interventions can promote participation of people in local development (Jørgensen & Van Domelen 1999, p. 20; Kammersgaard 1999; Narayan 1995; Narayan & Ebbe 1997; OED 2002; Schmidt & Marc 1995; Serrano 2003; Van Domelen 2003).

The discussion of the CDD bottom-up model in this article draws on social funds literature, where it has been described in a more consolidated manner. Social funds and other CDD initiatives share a similar bottom-up, community-based institutional development model for promoting participation and institutional capacity building. This model presumes that participation and capacity building effects can be achieved in several ways.

First, it is thought that social fund micro-projects can enhance social capital by assisting communities in developing norms and networks. The CDD bottom-up model is primarily based on Putnam's (1993) conceptualisation of social capital. Putnam views social capital in terms of norms of trust and reciprocity and 'networks of civic engagement', measured as membership in and density of voluntary organisations, clubs, co-operatives and political parties. For Putnam, interpersonal trust is the key variable that facilitates societal co-operation. The definition of trust used by Putnam stems from game theoretical assumptions, in which trust is an assessment by an individual of whether or not the behaviour of other individuals is trustworthy. This view holds that overlapping positive expectations about other individuals' actions can lead to co-operation and collective action. In his review of 'causalities between social capital and social funds', Kammersgaard (1999, p. 2) follows Putnam to conceptualise social capital as 'trust influencing collective action'.

It is thought that social fund micro-projects can help establish institutional structures (for example, implementing agencies or community committees) that can continue functioning to solve other problems after micro-project completion and can become a focal point for community activity in the future (Narayan 1995; Narayan & Ebbe 1997; Schmidt & Marc 1995). By promoting the formation of community groups, bottom-up interventions can create spaces for community participation and interaction. Frequent interactions among community members and positive problem solving experiences can reinforce and cultivate norms of trust and relations of solidarity (Kammersgaard 1999; OED 2002; Serrano 2003). Successful co-operation and performance can help create expectations that future behaviour will be positively rewarded, make the probability of future collective action more likely and encourage future collaborative efforts in new areas.

Second, it is argued that participation in decision making and problem solving can have an empowering effect on individuals. It can lead to changes in attitudes, behaviour, and confidence and can enable people to become more actively engaged in local affairs, take initiative and exercise voice and leadership (Narayan 1995, p. 26). Finally, CDD projects are said to have a 'learning by doing' effect (Narayan & Ebbe 1997, p. 33). The positive experiences of interaction may enable community members to appreciate the benefits of collective action and community-based solutions to local problems. Participation in micro-project activities can enhance a community's access to information and experience and help develop organisational and technical skills. It is assumed that the strengthened social capital, attitudinal changes and improvements in people's skills and abilities will enhance a community's capacity to undertake mutually beneficial development initiatives and effectively solve collective action problems.

Social capital and community participation in rural Armenia

The following sections discuss the findings of the research that I conducted in seven rural communities in Armenia in July and August 2002. The objective of the research was to examine the existing forms and nature of social capital and community participation and identify social and institutional factors that affect participation in the sample communities. Armenia has a permanent population of 3.2 million and it is divided into 10 administrative regions (*marz*) comprising of 930 units of local government, or 'communities' (*hamaynk*). Rural communities (or villages) account for 872 of the 930 units of local government. More than half the population lives in communities of less than 1,000 inhabitants. All local governments have a directly elected community leader (*hamaynkapet*) or local mayor. I selected seven communities situated in different regions (*marz*) of Armenia, including Ararat, Vayots Dsor, Aragatsotn, Armavir and Shirak *marz*. The smallest community in the sample comprised 120 residents (90 households) and the largest 1,700 residents (760 households). I based my sampling design upon the assumption that the study of communities with different socio-economic, geographic and demographic character-istics in different regions of Armenia would enable me to capture a diverse range of contexts and impacts.

The research used in-depth qualitative methods, including semi-structured interviews and focus group discussions.[2] In total, 94 in-depth interviews and 14 focus group discussions (involving 51 respondents) were conducted. I identified two groups of respondents. The first group were selected from the community members who were most knowledgeable about local development issues (key informants), including local mayors, deputy mayors, school directors, heads and members of local associations as well as community members who were somehow involved in the initiation and implementation of local projects. Most key informants were men in the age range of 40–60. The key informant interviews lasted from one to two hours. The second group of respondents included community residents representing various social groups in the chosen communities. The sampling of community residents was stratified so as to reflect the social composition of the communities and represent a variety of views and circumstances. The names of the communities and respondents have been concealed in this article in order to ensure anonymity. In this article the seven sample communities have been coded as A, E, K, N, R, S and T and the individual respondents have been coded as 1–14. The respondents were purposefully selected to include men and women; the elderly; indigenous residents and ethnic Armenian refugees from Azerbaijan (only present in communities S, E and N); the disabled; the relatively better-off and marginally poor households; ethnic Armenians and Yezids[3] (only present in community R).

Social capital

The importance of 'human relations' has been traditionally cherished in Armenia. Kinship ties and a sense of communal affiliation performed an important regulatory function (Kilbourne Matossian 1962), and the patriarchal family (*azg*) was the primary unit of pre-Soviet social organisation in rural communities. The extended families formed a village commune and elected the village headman (*tanouter*), who was in charge of communal governance. There were no sharp class or social distinctions in these communities, although some traditionally better-off families (*ojakh*) retained privileged positions. Land, pastures and sometimes irrigation canals and mills were communal property. The Soviet state regarded the traditional Armenian family as a potential source of resistance to the regime and as a 'backward'

[2] I adopted a flexible, exploratory approach to semi-structured interviews and developed interview guides, which contained separate thematic sections with associated open-ended questions. Most questions in the interview guides served as topics. They provided indications of the issues to be explored, and the actual questions were formulated during the interview. Depending on the context of the interview, I modified the order of these topics. I retained open conversational interviewing style in order to allow the respondents to digress towards issues that they deemed to be important. I allowed greater probing beyond the answers and entered into a dialogue with the respondents. During my fieldwork, I also engaged in direct observation. I visited important communal infrastructure facilities, including community centres, schools, medical centres, irrigation and potable water facilities. I observed public meetings, social activities and interaction among community residents and between residents and their leaders.

[3] Yezids are the largest ethnic minority in Armenia. Currently, there are just over 42,000 Yezids in Armenia. They are related to ethnic Kurds and have been traditionally engaged in highland cattle breeding.

institution. Collectivisation and the new collective village organisation (*kolkhoz*) contributed to the fragmentation of the extended Armenian family. The large landholdings, which were necessary to maintain the extended family, were fragmented and distributed as household plots among the collective farmers. However, despite the attempts by the state to destroy the traditional family as a social institution, kinship based solidarity in Armenia has remained strong.

In all Soviet republics, informal social networks based on kinship and friendship as well as on diffused personalised relations (*blat* networks) provided an important social space through which individuals and groups could pursue their interests and identities in the absence of other legitimate avenues. These networks were crucial in providing Soviet citizens with access to scarce resources, the opening up of new economic and social opportunities, securing their rights and collective pooling against social risks (Ledeneva 1998; Lomnitz 1988; Shlapentokh 1989). Lomnitz (1988, p.43) argues that the informal networks in the Soviet Union were a result of the malfunctioning of the Soviet bureaucratic systems that failed to satisfy social requirements. She suggests that these networks were an 'adaptive mechanism' that attempted to compensate for the inefficiencies of the formal system. Informal social networks also played an important role in the emergence and sustenance of an informal or shadow economy in the Soviet Union (Grossman 1977; Katsenelinboigen 1977; Mars & Altman 1983; Simis 1982). In particular, relations of trust and reciprocity enabled Soviet citizens to successfully undertake informal entrepreneurial activities and establish illegal trade networks and remain unpunished. The shadow economy was especially well developed in the Caucasus. Most Soviet informal networks have continued their existence in the post-Soviet era, although in modified and reconfigured shapes and forms.

The findings of my fieldwork allow an examination of social capital in post-Soviet rural Armenia. In particular, my research examined the forms and nature of interpersonal relations, networks of mutual support and solidarity and social participation in the sample communities. There were strong endowments of social capital in all of the studied communities, which manifested in dense networks of mutual support and solidarity and high levels of social participation. The respondents often referred to the traditions of co-operation and solidarity in their villages by describing their communities as 'cohesive' or 'united'. Their interpretation of 'unity' referred to the extent to which people were willing to support each other and to participate in collective activities. According to a resident in community A, 'People help each other. It is important to support each other morally and we all do our best. We all participate in celebrations'.[4] Another resident in community A said, 'People trust each other, they help each other, this village is known in the whole country as very strong and united'.[5] A resident in community E reflected the opinion of other villagers, 'People help each other in difficult situations'.[6] A respondent in community S noted, 'We fully trust people here; the other day I accidentally gave an extra 5,000 *dram* to a villager, and he came back to me to return it'.[7] Another respondent in

---

[4]Author's interview, A-3, Shirak *marz*, 9 July 2002.
[5]Author's interview, A-1, Shirak *marz*, 9 July 2002.
[6]Author's interview, E-4, Ararat *marz*, 15 July 2002.
[7]Author's interview, S-13, Ararat *marz*, 6 July 2002.

community S said, 'The relations in our community are very good'.[8] According to a respondent in community K, 'People here are very united and they help each other. For example, when someone travels into town, he volunteers to deliver documents or sort out problems for other villagers'.[9] Another respondent in community K said, 'This village is very cohesive. You can trust people here, someone found my gold ring the other day and brought it back to me'.[10]

In the absence of effective state support, mutual assistance has become a crucial resource upon which many households can draw to survive the transition. Mutual support networks exist both within smaller groups, such as kinship and friendship networks, and between different groups in a community. Extreme poverty has made it difficult for people to co-operate and support each other. Due to extreme material and social deprivation, people are forced to concentrate on their own everyday survival needs, and have less time and resources to dedicate to their relatives, friends and fellow community members. Many respondents noted that despite their desire to help, it was often impossible or difficult to be helpful. As resources at the disposal of a household were limited, informal assistance prioritised kinship networks. Most of the respondents noted that their immediate priority was to help family members and relatives. In all studied communities, residents provided support to villagers, who were outside their kinship or friendship networks, where they had available resources. The respondents described many instances when they would help people to whom they were not connected with kinship ties. Relations with neighbours were no less important than relations with relatives and kin related villagers. A resident in community S said, 'It is the neighbours who come first to help you and not the relatives'.[11] Another resident in community S remarked, 'My husband fell ill and the whole village was in my house'.[12]

Three villages in the sample (communities S, E and N) hosted ethnic Armenian refugee families from Azerbaijan, who were well integrated into village life. A refugee woman in community S noted, 'There are three refugee families here from Azerbaijan and my family is one of them. They treat us very well here ... I would never leave this village'.[13] A respondent in community E said, 'I am a refugee from Baku, and there are lot of refugee families here. We live peacefully with each other and the locals treat us well'.[14] A refugee in community N noted, 'We like our village. For example, there were talks about joining the neighbouring village as one unit, but we refused it'.[15] Relations of reciprocity existed between Armenians and the Yezid residents in the ethnically mixed community of R. Armenians and the Yezid minority here co-operated and shared food and resources. A resident in community R noted for instance, 'Half of the households in this village are Yezid, but we have very good relations, the village is very

[8]Author's interview, S-9, Ararat *marz*, 6 July 2002.
[9]Author's interview, K-2, Vayots Dsor *marz*, 2 July 2002.
[10]Author's interview, K-8, Vayots Dsor *marz*, 2 July 2002.
[11]Author's interview, S-13, Ararat *marz*, 6 July 2002.
[12]Author's interview, S-14, Ararat *marz*, 6 July 2002.
[13]Author's interview, S-13, Ararat *marz*, 6 July 2002.
[14]Author's interview, E-7, Ararat *marz*, 15 July 2002.
[15]Author's interview, N-4, Aragatsotn *marz*, 17 July 2002.

peaceful. We are neighbours and neighbours should live in peace'.[16] Another resident in community R concurred: 'Armenian and Yezid children go to the same school and sit in the same classroom, and we have never had problems with each other'.[17]

Social networks and relations of solidarity developed in different ways in different communities in the sample. An important source of social cohesion is common kinship ties. The residents of community A, for example, originate from Sasoun region in Western Armenia (Eastern Turkey) and share common kinship, identity and a sense of belonging to the same place of origin. Descendants from Sasoun are known for their strong spirit and sense of solidarity. A resident in community A said, 'You cannot imagine what happens here during festivities and events like weddings, funerals, birthdays, graduations. The whole village celebrates together, not only just relatives. We are all from Sasoun!'[18] The community of K descends from three extended kin groups, who have lived in the same village for more than 100 years. The village is rather remote and difficult to access, and there has been little migration into the village, which has helped maintain the historical social composition of the village. Lack of kinship ties does not preclude the formation of social capital. A common positive history of interaction is crucial for establishing trusting relations. The village of S was founded in the early 1970s by young families, who came from different regions of Armenia. According to the residents, in the village they enjoyed 'peaceful' relations as they had all come there as very young families, without their parents-in-law. They believed that the presence of older community members would have compelled them to give greater significance to the kinship and origin of other villagers and hence reinforce traditional hierarchies. Finally, the degree of effectiveness and accountability of local mayors directly influences levels of economic development and social cohesion in the local communities (Babajanian 2008). Thus, the communities of N and E, composed of local Armenians and ethnic Armenian refugees from Azerbaijan, developed a sense of common identity mostly thanks to the positive experience of interaction facilitated by their local mayors.

In all the studied communities, people helped each other with 'what they could'. Mutual help included limited cash assistance (donation and lending), in-kind assistance (food donation and lending, donation of clothes, donation of agricultural inputs, such as fertilisers and pesticides, and lending machinery and spare parts), and labour assistance (agricultural works, for example, harvesting, or repairing houses and taking cattle to pastures). A resident in community N noted, 'People help each other; for example, one person fell ill and three of his villagers went to work in his field to help him out'.[19] Similarly, a resident in community K said, 'People help each other with physical labour, for example, they would help to harvest the crops or dig the orchard; they also lend money to each other'.[20] In the case of the death of a family member of a villager, the entire village raised money to help with the funeral expenses. People borrowed cash from other villagers, usually in small amounts, to cover the cost

---

[16]Author's interview, R-10, Armavir *marz*, 11 July 2002.
[17]Author's interview, R-7, Armavir *marz*, 11 July 2002.
[18]Author's interview, A-1, Shirak *marz*, 9 July 2002.
[19]Author's interview, N-4, Aragatsotn *marz*, 17 July 2002.
[20]Author's interview, K-2, Vayots Dsor *marz*, 3 July 2002.

of their essential needs (for example, for buying food and hygiene items and paying utility bills). In all studied communities, local shops sold goods on credit. People usually repaid their debt after they obtained cash from selling their crops or receiving remittances from abroad or social assistance benefits. Many respondents said they often lend small amounts of money without the expectation that the money would be returned. In most cases, people paid the loans back for the borrowed items, although sometimes repayment could take up to six months. As a participant of a focus group in community K said, 'Everybody in the village is indebted to each other'.[21] The shopkeeper in community K noted that requiring customers to pay cash at the time of purchase was not realistic, and the only way to continue their business was to sell goods for credit. He said,

> People do not have money, and the local café and the shop lend food to the villagers for an indefinite time. Often they may not receive their money back, or receive it in six months. It is the same situation in the other village shop. But how can we refuse lending? That means we will stop having business, as nobody can pay right away; but we trust people here; about 90% return the money eventually; especially in autumn, when people have the proceeds from their harvest. And we all help each other regardless of whether we are relatives or not.[22]

Social events, traditional celebrations and social interaction have historically played an important role in the life of Armenian communities. However, most respondents noted that there has been a decrease in the level of their social interaction as compared with that in Soviet times. For example, they complained that 'life these days is not the same as it used to be'.[23] They explained this by the lack of economic resources and time to entertain friends and relatives and pay the costs incurred in ceremonial events and festivities. At the same time, celebrations of birthdays, weddings, national and religious holidays, and visits to relatives, friends and neighbours are still important for uniting communities and strengthening social bonds. A respondent in community E said, 'We celebrate the anniversary of the establishment of this village in 1989; it is a big event; it brings together the entire village'.[24] A woman in community S noted, 'We get together with our friends and relatives for a birthday or a holiday celebration. We have not lost our humanity yet'.[25] Most respondents believed that participation in social life was crucial for keeping the community spirit and supporting people psychologically. A resident in community A expressed a common view: 'We all participate in communal events; it is important to support each other morally'.[26] A resident in community K described how social events are organised in his village:

> We do celebrate holidays and festivities, for example, return from army service, school graduation, New Year. It has become easier to do so recently than in the previous years. Life

---

[21]Author's interview, K, focus group 2, Vayots Dsor *marz*, 3 July 2002.
[22]Author's interview, K-4, Vayots Dsor *marz*, 3 July 2002.
[23]Author's interview, S, focus group 1, Ararat *marz*, 6 July 2002.
[24]Author's interview, E-5, Ararat *marz*, 15 July 2002.
[25]Author's interview, S-14, Ararat *marz*, 6 July 2002.
[26]Author's interview, A-11, Shirak *marz*, 9 July 2002.

has become better now compared with 10 years ago. We organise activities in the local Culture Club. For the village festivities we collect money, for example, from local shops, and the mayor himself contributes from his personal farm profits. For example, for the New Year's we collected 100,000 *dram*.[27]

Most conflicts and disagreements in the studied communities occurred over economic resources, mostly over sharing irrigation water. Scarcity of water was a major factor causing disagreement and negatively affecting interpersonal relations. Conflicts occurred when, for example, some villagers drew water above the amounts allocated to them. This often deprived other villagers, especially those whose fields were at the tail end of the irrigation system. The respondents reported that during the drought of 1999–2001, when water supply in Armenia was especially scarce, conflicts over water were very frequent. These conflicts were not violent and were usually resolved peacefully by the community members themselves or through the intermediation of the local mayor. A resident in community A said, 'We are all neighbours here and we have to spend our lives together. Sometimes we have conflicts, but they are always quickly resolved'.[28] According to a resident in community K, 'When there are conflicts people try to resolve them amongst each other. Everybody knows each other in this village'.[29] Another resident in community K noted, 'As we live with each other, we are compelled to resolve conflicts peacefully'.[30] A respondent in community S said, 'We all try to sort our problems amongst each other'.[31]

Community participation

The previous section demonstrated that strong networks of mutual support based on trust and reciprocity existed in the sample communities. But how are social capital and community participation related in the context of post-Soviet Armenia? Does the presence of social capital translate into active citizen participation? This section examines the forms and nature of people's participation in service delivery and local governance and discusses the key constraints to community participation in the sample communities. I use the term 'community participation' to refer to empowered participation, and use it as a normative benchmark in analysing and interpreting the research data. Participation is defined as a state of social and institutional organisation in which citizens are empowered to 'participate in, negotiate with, influence, control, and hold accountable institutions that affect their lives' (World Bank 2002, p. 11). Such a conceptualisation is different from the narrow definition of participation, in which participation of citizens in local development is limited to the provision of voluntary labour and resources. Thus, it implies that community members become active agents, not only in terms of their physical and material contribution. It refers to the ability of individuals to take part in important decision making, hold officials

[27]Author's interview, K-2, Vayots Dsor *marz*, 2 July 2002.
[28]Author's interview, A-3, Shirak *marz*, 9 July 2002.
[29]Author's interview, K-12, Vayots Dsor *marz*, 2 July 2002.
[30]Author's interview, K-13, Vayots Dsor *marz*, 2 July 2002.
[31]Author's interview, S-10, Ararat *marz*, 6 July 2002.

accountable and claim citizenship rights. This view implies that participation is broad-based and not dominated by local leaders and elites; it is bottom-up, driven by the community members themselves and not by top-down directives; and it is inclusive, allowing all members to have equal opportunities to take part in development processes. This conceptualisation of participation is based on the notions of citizen rights, inclusiveness and democratic accountability.

In all of the studied communities, residents took part in various local initiatives and communal projects, initiated by the local mayors and school directors. People were willing to contribute time and money towards the common community good and were dealing with their local problems as best they could. Most community residents took part in these initiatives even when they did not personally benefit from them, mostly as a sign of solidarity with other villagers. People seemed to be genuinely interested in the life of their community, their fellow community members and the future of their communities. Most respondents thought that the problems of their communities were their own problems. The most common form of participation in the sample communities was the contribution of voluntary labour in community infrastructure and environmental maintenance initiatives. In particular, residents participated in cleaning canals, rehabilitating roads and potable and irrigation water systems, collecting rubbish, planting trees and improving school areas. Residents also contributed money for the rehabilitation and maintenance of community infra-structure as well as for community events and celebrations. For example, residents in community K collected 3,000 *dram* per household and contributed free labour for the rehabilitation of the potable water system. As a result, the new system provided 120 villagers with access to clean water. They also worked as volunteers on the rehabilitation of the building for the new bakery. A local resident described how public works were organised in community K:

> People here contribute labour and time for local village wide initiatives. For example, we organise 'labour days'. We decide how many people we need and then make announcements in the village and ask villagers for their support. This is mainly organised by the local government. For example, we organised a clean-up of canals, rehabilitated some roads and planted trees. There were some 40 to 50 people joining in.[32]

A respondent in community S said, 'The other day we organised works to clean up the communal areas in the village. We collected money to buy fuel for the tractor to clean up the village yard. Everybody was present, probably one person from each household'.[33] The mayor in community R noted, 'When we need to conduct some maintenance works, we can always rely on the local residents, and I often personally contribute money to help them'.[34] Mobilisation of monetary contributions normally has a poverty targeting element—the poorest residents were exempt, and higher amounts were solicited from the relatively better-off residents. For example, the mayor

[32]Author's interview, K-5, Vayots Dsor *marz*, 2 July 2002.
[33]Author's interview, S-4, Ararat *marz*, 6 July 2002.
[34]Author's interview, R-1, Armavir *marz*, 11 July 2002.

in community A collected cash from the residents in order to dig a canal. The residents collected 400 *dram* from those who had owned a cow and 100 *dram* from those who only owned sheep.

Participation of residents in all of the communities, however, was restricted to the provision of 'physical' inputs, such as contributions of labour, cash and materials. Ordinary residents rarely assumed leadership roles to undertake independent initiatives and organise collective action to pursue their interests. The local mayors and school directors in the sample communities played the key role in organising communal initiatives and social events by mobilising cash, managing logistical arrangements and involving community residents. Participation in formal organisations and informal groups was not perceived by people as a viable means of pursuing their interests and achieving their goals. There were very few formal and informal groups or associations established by the residents in order to pursue their objectives. The existing formal associations such as community-based Water Users Associations (WUAs) were established by the central government, and most WUA members did not view the WUAs as vehicles through which they could advance their interests. Community associations established under CDD projects dissolved immediately after the completion of the projects. Ordinary residents were not active in claiming their rights and exacting accountability and transparency from local leaders. The rest of this section will explore some of the reasons for the limited community participation in the sample communities.

The lack of material resources significantly constrains the ability and willingness of community members to undertake local projects and initiatives. There are only limited activities that community members can successfully implement on their own. These are mostly clean-up works, minor repairs and other activities where limited technical skills and resource investment are needed. Otherwise, solutions to more significant problems require more labour and time and need a specialised workforce and monetary investment. Any local action requires significant resources and logistical effort, which local governments and community residents can rarely afford. Even relatively small-scale initiatives, such as cleaning up the communal areas, require cash for fuel and tractor hire. Thus local participation can often only provide limited solutions, and a lot of problems remain unsolved. A villager in community K said, 'We could have done a lot of things, but it all requires money'.[35] Another respondent in community K noted, 'People participate in common activities—they do not mind things like cleaning up the communal areas and other works, but it all requires money, which they don't have'.[36] A respondent in community A said, 'People participate, they contribute labour. But in many cases, some maintenance works are very demanding, and we simply cannot do them ourselves'.[37] According to a resident in community S, 'The major obstacle for solving common problems is financial. Everything requires money, for example, even to do some welding works or to buy electrical cords. Otherwise, people are willing to contribute labour to solve common problems'.[38] Community

---

[35]Author's interview, K-5, Vayots Dsor *marz*, 2 July 2002.

[36]Author's interview, K-7, Vayots Dsor *marz*, 2 July 2002.

[37]Author's interview, A-9, Shirak *marz*, 9 July 2002.

[38]Author's interview, S-4, Ararat *marz*, 6 July 2002.

residents struggle to sustain their livelihoods and have little time and energy to assume leadership roles, initiate collective action and solve problems of a community-wide nature. In all of the studied communities, men spent most of their time cultivating their fields, working on their land plots or taking care of animals. The workload of women is double that of men, as women have to combine their work responsibilities with their duties at home, including housework and care of children. People believed that in addition to material problems, psychological factors also discouraged their participation. A resident in community R said, 'People are breathless, the village is dying out, we don't have money, everybody is indebted, and there is no water—what can we undertake in this situation?'[39]

The poor governance environment in Armenia poses an especially significant constraint on citizen participation. The weakness of the rule of law and pervasive corruption affect all spheres of economic and social life in Armenia (Anderson & Gray 2006; Freedom House 2006; Greco 2006; Hansen 2002; ICG 2004; TI 2006; Stefes 2006; World Bank 2000c). Personalised relations, informal rules, cronyism, misuse of public positions, clientelism and rent seeking continue to be part of post-Soviet reality. In addition, the weak financial and administrative capacity of the state constrains its ability to reach out to the impoverished residents, engage with local communities and adequately respond to people's needs. The state institutions do not attempt to establish spaces where citizens can voice their needs and concerns, access information and enter into a constructive public dialogue. The inability and insufficient commitment of the state to adequately enforce the rule of law and social justice in Armenia encourages elitism and reinforces social polarisation. As income inequality widens, Armenian society is being divided into a small group of rich and powerful, the so called 'new Armenians' (*nor hayer*), and the poor who are powerless and marginalised. As Kharatyan (2001, p. 349) maintains,

> Today being poor in Armenia implies being deprived of any security and protection. A society is being formed in which human capabilities are determined by wealth and its various manifestations—cash, connections, authority, or all three of them together, as they become the societal capital that provides security. Various groups start reproducing themselves and become entrenched in their sub-cultures—the poor become poorer; they experience not only material deprivation, but also social and political apathy, fear, low self-esteem, and they perceive themselves as inferior and incapable of playing any role in their society. The rich continue to get richer, and in addition to their wealth, they acquire power and social status and engage in political activism, sometimes without any distinct political or civic agenda.

This situation has produced distrust and disillusionment among the Armenian population with the authorities and with the principles of democratic governance in general. Poor people do not believe that the government is committed to act on their needs and priorities and support them in difficult times. Instead, they feel that the government protects the rich and powerful. The analysis of people's perceptions demonstrates the enormous gap that exists between the state and its citizens in Armenia. As a resident in community A put it, 'It is very hard for people to get things

---

[39]Author's interview, R-6, Armavir *marz*, 12 July 2002.

done: wherever you turn, you encounter a reluctant attitude [of the authorities] or lack of finance'.[40] A resident in community R said, 'The situation is really bad. Nobody in the government cares about people, nobody wants to help and give support. They just don't care about what happens to us'.[41] Various accounts of the respondents indicate that when people directly appealed to regional or central authorities, they were, as a rule, neglected and encountered bureaucratic resistance. A resident in community R noted for instance, 'In order to deal with *marzpetaran* [the regional governor's office], you will need a written note from the mayor; and you also need a seal. How can we go and get things done with them? They will not give us anything there'.[42] A resident in community S said, 'If we go to the regional government, they will ask—who are you? You don't have a mayor? Who are we? They will never take us seriously'.[43] According to a resident in community T, 'The problem is we cannot defend our rights, they [the government] do whatever they wish. We feel that appealing and complaining is useless'.[44] The negative experiences of dealing with state institutions have produced distrust of people in the possibility of achieving beneficial outcomes through democratic forms of participation and collective action.

In a situation when access to important public services, information and opportunities is determined by connections, social status and informal payments, ordinary citizens have little power to attract external resources and advance the interests of the community by undertaking independent problem solving initiatives. They are often compelled to rely on local leaders, such as local mayors and school directors, who have a position of influence, access to important social networks and strong organisational skills. In all of the studied communities, most residents were almost entirely reliant on their local mayors for their survival. Most respondents of this study perceived that important things in local communities can be only done through influence, connections and cash. A resident in community A said, 'Connections are very important. In order to lay a single pipe, you need connections'.[45] Another resident in community A was convinced that the mayor used connections to rehabilitate the potable water network in their village, 'We rehabilitated the potable water network. We collected 2,000 *dram* and contributed labour. And we used some connections "from above" to make it happen'.[46] The mayor in community E was on friendly terms with the regional governor, who 'helps with what he can'.[47] According to the residents, thanks to his connections, the mayor organised the rehabilitation of the irrigation pipeline and renovation of the local club. There was a similar situation in community K: 'Without the mayor the [infrastructure rehabilitation] works would not have been successful. He managed a lot of things, provided vehicles, obtained material for construction'.[48] A resident in community S

[40]Author's interview, A-5, Shirak *marz*, 9 July 2002.
[41]Author's interview, R-13, Armavir *marz*, 12 July 2002.
[42]Author's interview, R-5, Armavir *marz*, 12 July 2002.
[43]Author's interview, S-7, Ararat *marz*, 7 July 2002.
[44]Author's interview, T-3, Aragatsotn *marz*, 18 July 2002.
[45]Author's interview, A-3, Shirak *marz*, 9 July 2002.
[46]Author's interview, A-5, Shirak *marz*, 9 July 2002.
[47]Author's interview, E-1, Ararat *marz*, 15 July 2002.
[48]Author's interview, K-6, Vayots Dsor *marz*, 2 July 2002.

said about their mayor, 'Without his intermediation it probably would not have worked'.[49] This is how the mayor in community S described the situation in his community:

> An ordinary farmer does not have the time and the motivation to be involved in community affairs. Such involvement requires lots of time and commitment, whilst most farmers are busy working on their fields. There must be someone like the mayor who has got the time and can set his mind on getting things done and mobilise efforts for achieving that goal. And, of course, the status of the mayor is crucial for success.[50]

Some residents believed that even development projects supported by international agencies could only be 'brought from above', through connections or cash. Thus, the respondents in community A were convinced that the personal connections of their local mayors were crucial in obtaining funding for local donor-funded projects. For example, the participants of a focus group in community A were convinced that the neighbouring village received donor funding because it offered a bribe to the project officer. One of the respondents said,

> God only knows how one can bring projects into the village. You don't want to get into their kitchen. Their project officer demanded interest from the grant money in order to bring it to the village. If you don't give them money, you will not get a project.[51]

A villager in community A noted, 'The former mayor brought the project. He and his deputy controlled everything in the village. He managed to obtain the funding through his contacts in the government'.[52] Another resident in community A said about the mayor, 'The mayor is trusted, and he has lots of really good connections; so it is good for the village. He used his contacts to bring projects for the village. It would have been very difficult without him'.[53]

The key formal and informal roles that local mayors play in managing local development and securing livelihoods for community residents provide them with significant discretionary power. The mayors themselves define the boundaries or 'spaces' (Cornwall 2002) for community participation in service delivery and local governance. Community members in the sample communities had access to their leaders and opportunities to exercise voice and express their demands and preferences. The local mayors, however, had full control over decision making with regard to the choice, design and implementation of local policies and projects and resource allocation. The extent to which the mayors were willing to involve local residents in decision making varied depending on the personality and leadership style of the mayor. The dependence on the local mayors weakened channels of accountability and restricted people's ability to hold their mayors responsible for their actions. People

[49]Author's interview, S-7, Ararat *marz*, 6 July 2002.
[50]Author's interview, S-1, Ararat *marz*, 6 July 2002.
[51]Author's interview, A-9, Shirak *marz*, 9 July 2002.
[52]Author's interview, A-4, Shirak *marz*, 9 July 2002.
[53]Author's interview, A-5, Shirak *marz*, 9 July 2002.

usually tolerated rent-seeking behaviour or mismanagement of local resources by those mayors who were effective in attracting development resources for their communities.[54]

Rethinking the social capital framework

The social capital framework used in the CDD bottom-up development model overlooks the importance of the broader structural and institutional constraints that predetermine how institutions at the local level develop and operate. This article shows that endowments of social capital may not necessarily translate into community participation. This research found strong networks of mutual support based on trust and reciprocity in all of the studied villages. They existed both within smaller groups, such as kinship and friendship networks, and between different groups within a community. Community members actively supported each other and participated in the economic and social life of their communities. Despite the availability of strong endowments of social capital, community participation in the sample villages remained restricted in its forms and nature. This article has demonstrated that the limited community participation in the sample communities was not conditioned by the weakness of social capital or attitudinal factors, but rather by the broader institutional, socio-economic and political context. A similar conclusion was reached by Rose (1998) in his study of social capital in Russia. According to Rose, the nature of governance in Russia affects the expectations and experience of citizens and determines the choice of social networks that individuals rely upon in 'getting things done'. People choose to join those networks that are most conducive to pursuing their interests and adopt strategies that are most likely to succeed under particular social, economic and political circumstances. Thus, the population largely relies on informal alternatives (for example, growing its own food and borrowing), personalised relationships and connections, or breaking or bending rules.

These findings have important implications for the understanding and conceptualisation of social capital and citizen participation in transition societies. Thus, post-Soviet informal networks have often been viewed as a 'problem' of individuals rather than of structures, without an attempt to understand the roots and sources of informal networks and behavioural patterns of individuals. For example, Howard (2003) argues that one of the factors prohibiting the development of a genuine civil society is the persistence of private friendship networks among ordinary citizens. Such views confuse cause and effect, as they fail to recognise that informal networks at the micro-level are produced and reinforced by the macro level institutions. Stepanenko (2004, p. 39) suggests that Putnam's (Western) concept of social capital mainly focuses on citizens and civil society, automatically assuming a certain degree of co-operation between the society and the institutions of the state. He argues that in its application to post-Soviet countries, where the state–society relations have been ruptured, this

---

[54]For a detailed discussion of governance, accountability and citizen participation in rural Armenia see Babajanian (2008).

concept does not adequately problematise the relationship between state policies and citizens' behaviour.

Based on this research, I would suggest that the theories of social capital in their current application in development practice are not adequate for analysing conditions affecting community participation, but mainly suggest a framework for analysing co-operation. Cognitive variables such as norms of trust and reciprocity governing interpersonal relationships represent mechanisms through which co-operation is built and optimised to produce mutually beneficial outcomes. However, they do not necessarily determine people's decisions to participate (or not to participate) and the specific forms that such participation may take. The explanatory power of social capital as a basis for co-operation has been best exemplified in collective action literature. Decisions to co-operate depend on a series of collective action problems determining who will share in the costs, how the benefits will be distributed and how the activities will be monitored and sanctioned (Ostrom 1990, 1992). A number of studies show that social capital can help resolve collective action problems by facilitating co-ordination of activities, information sharing and collective decision-making, diminishing opportunistic behaviour and free-riding, and reducing conflicts (Kähkönen 1999; Lam 1998; Ostrom 1990, 1992; Tang 1992). Thus, the social capital framework can be useful for the analysis and design of institutional arrangements and co-operation mechanisms within organisations and communities, rather than for the understanding of the forms and nature of people's participation within specific contextual settings.

These findings have implications for the operationalisation and measurement of social capital in development policies and projects. Promoting social capital is often defined in development projects as an end in itself (OED 2002, p. 41; Van Domelen 2003, p. 16). Meanwhile, it is not the availability of social capital, but rather how it is used that can make a difference. The availability of norms (for example, trust and reciprocity) and networks (formal and informal groups and partnerships) by themselves does not necessarily imply that they can facilitate collective action and serve developmentally beneficial outcomes. Norms and networks are important as far as they serve the objective of enhancing the ability of communities to organise and pursue their interests. In particular, high levels of trust may not necessarily translate into collective action outcomes, and the mere presence of networks and associations may not imply that they have a meaningful involvement in service delivery and local governance. It is important that development policies and projects explicitly address the specific factors that affect the willingness and ability of community members to participate.

Institutional change: culture or structure?

The social capital framework used in the CDD bottom-up development model reflects a 'cultural' view of institutional change. This view presumes that societal change can be achieved by altering social and interpersonal relations at the local level. This model places strong emphasis on the normative orientations that govern interaction between individuals. In particular, it implies that the absence of a 'trusting culture' and the attitudinal orientation of post-Soviet citizens are the main obstacles to community participation and that individual trust and active citizenship can be fostered through a process of social learning. As this article has shown, the main barriers to community participation in Armenia were posed not by a breakdown in interpersonal relations and the 'mentality' of citizens, but rather by the existing power structures that affect rules and arrangements for resource allocation, service delivery and decision making in local communities.

A more radical, 'structural' approach to institutional change suggests that effective societal transformation depends on poor people's political capabilities and their capacity to mobilise for political action and influence public policy (Gaventa 2004; Moore & Putzel 1999; Moore 2001; Mosse 2004). It holds that changing the existing power relations is an inherently political task, and hence building the political agency or 'political capital' of the poor is as important as strengthening their social capital. The main agents of change for these scholars are local citizens, who claim and negotiate their rights 'from below'. Thus, policies and projects that de-link social and political aspects of participation may not be effective in addressing the existing structural constraints and promoting institutional change.

The issues of governance and politics are increasingly becoming part of the formal discourse on participation by development agencies. The latest World Bank view of social capital emphasises the importance of institutions and political participation. Thus, the World Bank's social capital framework has been further developed with the introduction of the notion of 'linking' social capital, which refers to building ties between citizens and people in positions of authority, such as government representatives and private institutions (Grootaert *et al.* 2004). The CDD approach to governance is based on the idea of a 'state–society partnership' (Dongier *et al.* 2003; Helling *et al.* 2005; World Bank 2004). This view assumes that local development can be promoted through institutional arrangements encouraging collaboration and partnerships between the state, local governments, service providers and local community groups, and through improvements in the legal and regulatory framework and sectoral policies. In practice, this view is manifested in a new generation of CDD projects that aim at addressing the issues of local governance and social inclusion (World Bank 2007). These projects are based on the bottom-up development model described earlier, but place a greater emphasis on the involvement of authorities in participatory processes and provide capacity building support to local governments (as, for example, the World Bank supported Village Investment Project in Kyrgyzstan).

One has to doubt, however, whether policy reforms and partnerships can bring about institutional change. Thus, it is questionable whether changes in formal laws and public sector rules in post-Soviet countries can transform historically established informal norms and practices within public institutions. This conceptualisation of participation still ignores the importance of power structures in affecting participation outcomes. It is still based on the cultural view of institutional change as it assumes that poor governance is a result of 'ignorance' (Fritz 2006, p. 2) and that collaboration between citizens and authorities can be encouraged through the 'learning by doing' effect of CDD projects. The partnerships' framework does not offer effective operational links with the issues of political and social rights, representation, transparency and accountability. For example, it is not clear why central or local governments should be more accountable to local communities once they enter into 'partnerships' with them. The experience of the Armenia Social Investment Fund project demonstrates that state–society partnerships can be formed on unequal terms and that collaboration does not necessarily imply better accountability or responsiveness. This finding is likely to be true in most settings where the elites derive economic and political benefits from patronage and rent-seeking and have little desire to share power with citizens.

There is an inherent difficulty in identifying and designing effective mechanisms for establishing democratic governance. Institutionalising participation requires concerted action, which would go beyond the scope of individual projects, sectoral interventions and policy reforms. It requires a change in political systems that reproduce unequal power relations. Building political capabilities is crucial for empowering ordinary citizens. At the same time, any external involvement in politicising local development is prone to risks and conflicts (Cleaver 2004, p. 275; White 1996, p.15). In contexts where patron–client relationships provide important welfare and political functions, a more radical political approach may antagonise and fragment local communities and jeopardise people's livelihoods.

Citizen participation cannot be fostered in the absence of an enabling governance environment. Bottom-up community-driven initiatives, even if they are 'politicised', need to be combined with top-down efforts to democratise both formal and informal institutions of the state. Bottom-up development in post-Soviet countries represents an attempt to establish 'islands of democracy' within largely undemocratic environments and it is questionable whether these 'islands' can survive. It is crucial that state institutions support and actively enforce the rule of law and democratic freedoms. This cannot be achieved in the absence of political will on the part of a country's ruling elite. State leaders must be genuinely convinced of the importance of citizenship rights and must actively create spaces for public participation. In my view, institutional change and democratisation in post-Soviet countries can only be possible when there are 'altruistic' leaders (Brett 1995, p. 213), who genuinely believe in the principles of justice and democracy and who are able to mobilise public support for political and economic reforms.

London School of Economics and Political Science

References

Anderson, J. H. & Gray, C. W. (2006) *Anticorruption in Transition 3: Who is Succeeding . . . and Why?* (Washington, DC, World Bank).
Babajanian, B. (2008) 'Local Governance in Post-Soviet Armenia: Leadership, Local Development and Accountability', *Communist and Post-Communist Studies*, 41, 3.
Brett, E. A. (1995) 'Institutional Theory and Social Change in Uganda', in Harriss, J., Hunter, J. & Lewis, C. M. (eds) (1995) *The New Institutional Economics and Third World Development* (London and New York, Routledge), pp. 200–14.
Cleaver, F. (2004) 'The Social Embeddedness of Agency and Decision-Making', in Hickey, S. & Mohan, G. (eds) (2004), pp. 271–77.
Cleaver, F. (2005) 'The Inequality of Social Capital and the Reproduction of Chronic Poverty', *World Development*, 33, 6, pp. 893–906.
Cornwall, A. (2002) *Making Spaces, Changing Places: Situating Participation in Development*, IDS Working Paper No. 170 (Brighton, Institute of Development Studies).

Dongier, P., Van Domelen, J., Ostrom, E., Ryan, A., Wakeman, W., Bebbington, A., Alkire, S., Esmail, T. & Polski, M. (2003) *The PRSP Sourcebook* (Washington, DC, World Bank).

Fine, B. (2001) 'The Social Capital of the World Bank', in Fine, B., Lapavitsas, C. & Pincus, J. (eds) (2001) *Development Policy in 21st Century: Beyond the Post-Washington Consensus* (London, Routledge), pp. 136–53.

Freedom House (2006) *Countries at the Crossroads 2006. Country Report—Armenia* (New York, Freedom House).

Fritz, V. (2006) *How to Move Forward on Governance and Corruption*, ODI Opinion Paper No. 72 (London, ODI).

Gaventa, J. (2004) 'Towards Participatory Governance: Assessing the Transformative Possibilities', in Hickey, S. & Mohan, G. (eds) (2004), pp. 25–42.

Greco (2006) *Evaluation Report on Armenia. Joint First and Second Evaluation Round* (Strasbourg, Groupe d'Etats contre la Corruption).

Grootaert, C., Narayan, D., Nyhan Jones, V. & Woolcock, M. (2004) *Measuring Social Capital: an Integrated Questionnaire*, World Bank Working Paper No. 18 (Washington, DC, World Bank).

Grossman, G. (1977) 'The Second Economy of the USSR', *Problems of Communism*, September–October, pp. 25–40.

Hansen, G. (2002) *The Programming Environment and Donor Co-ordination on Anti-Corruption Assistance in Armenia. A Case Study Prepared for the Donor Standards in Anti-Corruption Project (DSACP)* (Cambridge, MA, The Collaborative for Development Action (CDA) Inc.).

Harriss, J. (2002) *Depoliticizing Development. The World Bank and Social Capital* (London, Anthem Press).

Helling, L., Serrano, R. & Warren, D. (2005) *Linking Community Empowerment, Decentralized Governance, and Public Service Provision Through a Local Development Framework*, Social Protection Discussion Paper No. 0535 (Washington, DC, World Bank).

Hickey, S. & Mohan, G. (eds) (2004), *Participation: From Tyranny to Transformation? Exploring New Approaches to Participation in Development* (London and New York, Zed Books).

Howard, M. (2003) *The Weakness of Civil Society in Post-Communist Europe* (Cambridge, Cambridge University Press).

ICG (2004) *Armenia: Internal Instability Ahead*, Europe Report No. 158 (Yerevan/Brussels, International Crisis Group).

Jørgensen, S. L. & Van Domelen, J. (1999) *Helping the Poor Manage Risk Better: the Role of Social Funds*, Social Protection Discussion Paper No. 9934 (Washington, DC, World Bank).

Kähkönen, S. (1999) *Does Social Capital Matter in Water and Sanitation Delivery? A Review of Literature*, Social Capital Initiative Working Paper No. 9 (Washington, DC, World Bank).

Kammersgaard, J. (1999) *Causalities between Social Capital and Social Funds*, Social Protection Discussion Paper Series (Washington, DC, World Bank).

Katsenelinboigen, A. (1977) 'Coloured Markets in the Soviet Union', *Soviet Studies*, 29, 1, pp. 62–85.

Kharatyan, H. (2001) *Patmutyunner Aghkatutyan Masin* (Yerevan, Lusakn).

Kilbourne Matossian, M. (1962) *The Impact of Soviet Policies in Armenia* (Leiden, E.J. Brill).

Lam, W. F. (1998) *Governing Irrigation Systems in Nepal: Institutions, Infrastructure, and Collective Action* (Oakland, CA, ICS Press).

Ledeneva, A. (1998) *Russia's Economy of Favours* (Cambridge, Cambridge University Press).

Lomnitz, L. A. (1988) 'Informal Exchange Networks in Formal Systems: a Theoretical Model', *American Anthropologist*, 90, 1, pp. 42–55.

Mars, G. & Altman, Y. (1983) 'The Cultural Bases of Soviet Georgia's Second Economy', *Soviet Studies*, 35, 4, pp. 546–60.

Molyneux, M. (2002) 'Gender and the Silences of Social Capital: Lessons from Latin America', *Development and Change*, 33, 2, pp. 167–88.

Moore, M. (2001) 'Empowerment at Last?', *Journal of International Development*, 13, 3, pp. 321–29.

Moore, M. & Putzel, J. (1999) *Thinking Strategically about Politics and Poverty*, IDS Working Paper No. 101 (Brighton, Institute of Development Studies).

Mosse, D. (2004) 'Power Relations and Poverty Reduction', in Alsop, R. (ed.) (2004) *Power, Rights, and Poverty: Concepts and Connections* (Washington, DC, World Bank), pp. 52–66.

Narayan, D. (1995) *Designing Community Based Development*, Social Development Paper No. 7 (Washington, DC, World Bank).

Narayan, D. & Ebbe, K. (1997) *Design of Social Funds: Participation, Demand Orientation and Local Organisational Capacity*, World Bank Discussion Paper No. 375 (Washington, DC, World Bank).

OED (2002) *Social Funds: Assessing Effectiveness*, Operations Evaluation Department Report (Washington, DC, World Bank).

Ostrom, E. (1990) *Governing the Commons: The Evolution of Institutions for Collective Action* (Cambridge, Cambridge University Press).

Ostrom, E. (1992) *Crafting Institutions for Self-governing Irrigation System* (San Francisco, ICS Press).

Putnam, R. (1993) *Making Democracy Work: Civic Traditions in Modern Italy* (Princeton, NJ, Princeton University Press).

Rose, R. (1998) *Getting Things Done in an Anti-Modern Society: Social Capital Networks in Russia*, Social Capital Initiative Working Paper No. 6 (Washington, DC, World Bank).

Schmidt, M. B. & Marc, A. (1995) *Participation in Social Funds*, Social Development Publication No. 18180 (Washington, DC, World Bank).

Serrano, R. (2003) 'Social Funds and Social Capital', conference presentation, *Social Funds ECANET Conference*, Antalya, Turkey, 21–23 October, available at: http://www.worldbank.org/social funds, accessed 15 January 2005.

Shahnazaryan, G. (2007) 'Socialakan Kapital: Sociologiakan Tesutjan Meknabanman Himnaxndiry', *Sociologiaji Fakulteti Taregirq* 2006–2007 (Yerevan, EPH Hratarakchutjun).

Shlapentokh, V. (1989) *Public and Private Life of the Soviet People* (New York, Oxford University Press).

Simis, K. M. (1982) *USSR: The Corrupt Society. The Secret World of Soviet Capitalism* (New York, Simon and Schuster).

Stefes, C. (2006) *Understanding Post-Soviet Transitions: Corruption, Collusion and Clientelism* (Basingstoke, Palgrave Macmillan).

Stepanenko, V. (2004) 'Sotsial'nyi kapital v sotsiologicheskoi perspektive: teoretiko-metodologicheskie aspekty issledovaniya', *Sotsiologiya: teoriya, metody, marketing*, 2, pp. 24–41.

Tadevosyan, G. & Shakhsuvaryan, A. (2005) 'Socialakan Kapitali Dery Zhamanakakic Hay Hasarakutjan Genderajin Mobiliutjan Gorcyntacum', *Banber*, 3, pp. 117–25.

Tang, S. Y. (1992) *Institutions and Collective Action: Self-governance in Irrigation* (San Francisco, ICS Press).

TI (2006) *Transparency International Corruption Perceptions Index 2006* (Berlin, Transparency International).

Van Domelen, J. (2003) *Social Capital in the Operations and Impacts of Social Investment Funds* (Washington, DC, World Bank).

White, S. C. (1996) 'Depoliticising Development: the Uses and Abuses of Participation', *Development in Practice*, 6, 1, pp. 6–15.

Woolcock, M. & Narayan, D. (2000) 'Social Capital: Implications for Development Theory, Research, and Policy', *The World Bank Research Observer*, 15, 2, pp. 225–49.

World Bank (2000a) *The Europe and Central Asia CDD Strategy: Scaling Up Community-Driven Development in Europe and Central Asia* (Washington, DC, World Bank).

World Bank (2000b) 'Community Development in ECA: Accomplishments, Challenge and Strategy', seminar presentation, Washington, DC, World Bank, 27 January, available at: http://www.worldbank.org/ECA/ECSSD, accessed 7 December 2006.

World Bank (2000c) *Armenia Institutional and Governance Review. Executive Summary* (Washington, DC, World Bank).

World Bank (2001a) *Scaling Up Community Driven Development in Armenia: a Strategy Note* (Washington, DC, World Bank).

World Bank (2001b) *Making Transition Work for Everyone: Poverty and Inequality in Europe and Central Asia* (Washington, DC, World Bank).

World Bank (2002) *Empowerment and Poverty Reduction: A Sourcebook*, Draft, PREM (Washington, DC, World Bank).

World Bank (2003) *Measuring Empowerment—An Analytical Framework*, Poverty Reduction Group (Washington, DC, World Bank).

World Bank (2004) 'Local Development Discussion Paper', paper prepared for the *International Conference on Local Development* 16–18 June (Washington, DC, World Bank).

World Bank (2007) *From Social Funds to Local Governance and Social Inclusion Programs*, A Prospective Review from the ECA Region, in Two Volumes, Report No. 39953-ECA (Washington, DC, World Bank).

Social Capital, Ethnicity and Support for Democracy in the Post-Communist States

KATHLEEN M. DOWLEY & BRIAN D. SILVER

FEW THEORETICAL CONCEPTS have received more attention among social scientists in the past half dozen years than that of 'social capital', particularly among students of countries undergoing democratisation (or, in some cases, redemocratisation). Putnam notes that social capital 'refers to features of social organisation such as trust, norms and networks, that can improve the efficiency of society by facilitating coordinated action' (Putnam, 1993, p. 167). Thus communities with higher levels of social capital are thought to be able to cooperate more often to overcome social problems, keep their governments more responsive and more honest, and improve democratic institutional performance. Communities with low levels, in contrast, seem unable to break the vicious circle and remain with governments that are less responsive, less efficient and less honest.

Much of this argument echoes an earlier literature on the role of intermediate groups in moderating political views and mediating between political elites and masses. Voluntary organisations, and especially multiple and cross-cutting group affiliations, were said to be vital to the development of democracy (Kornhauser, 1959; Lipset, 1960). This idea also underlies earlier discussions of political cleavage and political culture (Almond & Verba, 1963).

Putnam's social capital thesis has been subjected to any number of scholarly responses, retorts and replications. The concept is attractive theoretically, as it places so much emphasis on the activities of ordinary citizens, after a decade of bringing the state back into the centre of comparative political analysis. Promoting civic engagement and an active civil society, with individuals assuming responsibility for their own government and getting the government they therefore deserve, are messages that resonate with scholars and policy makers alike. If democracy needs civil society, we will support civil society, we will fund voluntary organisations, we will make social capital wherever it is lacking.

Yet the criticisms have been pointed as well. Are all networks or voluntary organisations democratic? Does participation in narrowly defined organisations promote the kind of social trust that Putnam sees as so critical to a functioning democracy, or do they more often, particularly in already divided societies, serve only to reinforce existing cleavages rather than help to cut across them? Might not, as Hardin (1995) notes, differential mobilisation of small groups of the population, particularly along ethnic, racial or religious lines, often undermine democratic institutions as they make particularistic demands, not those that necessarily promote the public good?

In her critique of the theory Levi (1996) notes that the emergence of social trust depends on experiences with institutions outside the small groups normally identified in the scholarly literature on social capital. The expectations about the behaviour of others that would allow individuals to agree to cooperate in the first place form as a 'result of interactions among groups defined by ethnicity, religion or some other shared value, confidence in a backdrop of third party sanctions, or sufficient costs to discourage the betrayal of trust' (Levi, 1996, p. 48). Thus, for Levi, Francophones in Canada have come to distrust the Canadian federal government not because of a lack of civic engagement but because that engagement has often been met with broken promises from that government. Our previous research has shown large differences between groups in divided states such as Canada in evaluations of democratic institutions, subjective political competence and patriotism, and interpersonal trust (Silver & Dowley, 2000).

These conflicting views of the value of social (and unsocial) capital for democratic performance and overall support for democratic institutions in plural societies are particularly relevant to the study of politics in East-Central and post-Soviet Europe. With the history of the region replete with examples of ethnic mobilisation and its devastating consequences present even today in the former Yugoslavia and Chechnya, a thorough examination of the propositions suggested above seems warranted. The usual measures of social capital seem problematic in plural societies, especially ones undergoing rapid political transitions.

For example, scholars studying civic communities have generally gauged the degree of 'civicness' by examining mean levels of participation in voluntary organisations (excluding religious organisations and those that are said to be hierarchical), mean levels of interest in politics, and mean levels of interpersonal trust. But in plural societies undergoing transition, interest in politics and high levels of participation in voluntary associations may in fact signal the ethnic polarisation of society. With the breakdown of old institutions and the expectations that they had for so long generated, a condition of domestic anarchy may have emerged that forces *ethnies* to mobilise to protect themselves in an uncertain environment (Posen, 1993; Snyder, 1993). In these cases, higher levels of participation along ethnic lines and high interest in politics will not signal democratic social capital in the making but instead an ethnic mobilisation and countermobilisation that threaten new democratic states. Communal organisations are not necessarily community organisations.

The release of data from the 1995–98 World Values Survey, which includes a large number of countries from the post-communist space, provides an opportunity to explore the nature and consequences of social capital in this region. The countries vary enough in the quality and completeness of their democratic transitions to allow us to make some preliminary observations. First, do the usual markers of social capital (interpersonal trust, political interest and voluntary group participation) correlate with the most and least successful cases of democratisation in East-Central Europe and the post-Soviet states? Are the countries with the highest overall levels of apparent social capital the most democratic? Are they the countries in which individuals report the highest levels of satisfaction with democratic institutions (one of Putnam's measures of institutional performance)? Are they the same countries as those in which respondents are most confident in democracy?

Second, are the effects the same when one takes into account the ethnic diversity of the country? Does social capital function in the same manner in plural countries, or are the usual markers instead more likely to indicate dangerous polarisation in that society instead of social engagement that keeps democracy healthy and strong? These are the questions this article seeks to answer by analysing the latest round of surveys from the World Values Survey project.

Democratisation and social capital in the post-communist world

A survey of the vast literature on democratisation in both Central-Eastern Europe and the former Soviet Union yields mixed assessments of its relative success, completeness and durability. In a symposium commemorating the 10th anniversary of the fall of communism, Roeder characterised the transitions in the region as fraught with ethnic conflict and ethnoconstitutional crises. Indeed, 54 of the 69 ethnic groups comprising at least 1% of any state's population have been engaged in some kind of constitutional struggle with the state since 1989 (Roeder, 1999, p. 867).

In the same symposium, however, Fish noted that 'the region has scarcely been the seething cauldron of interethnic violence that it is often assumed to be ...' (Fish, 1999, p. 811). In Fish's view, democratisation has been associated with a decrease in ethnic tensions in places such as Georgia, Bulgaria, Romania and Hungary. Where tensions have flared, such as in Chechnya or Serbia, the problem is the absence of real democratisation, not mass participation itself.

Freedom House indicators of democratisation, measured in terms of both political and civil liberties, yield the ranking of countries identified in Table 1. Scores of 1 on each indicate that the highest levels of political and civil liberties are being protected, while scores of 7 indicate that virtually none is.[1] In 1991 the regional mean for political rights was 3.4 and for civil liberties 3.6; in 1996 (the time of the latest World Values Surveys) the means were 3.0 for political rights and 3.4 for civil liberties, marking a small improvement during the five years.[2] And in 1999 the mean scores on the two indicators further improved to 2.7 and 3.2. The general trend is towards a steady improvement in the democratic quality of life in most East European states, except the former Yugoslavia, and towards a decline in the democratic quality of life in the former Soviet republics, except the Baltic countries.

The indicators for social capital in the World Values Survey stem from responses to three questions, consistent with how most of the scholars in this literature have used the survey (e.g., Newton & Norris, 2000). The first is a question about the respondent's level of interest in politics: 'How interested would you say you are in politics?'. The respondents could answer 'Very interested, somewhat interested, not very interested or not at all interested.' We coded the responses to allow 4 to represent those 'very interested' and 1 'not at all interested'.

Second, we constructed a variable to measure participation in voluntary organisations that counts whether individuals claimed to be ordinary members or active in any of these groups:

TABLE 1

Freedom House Rating of Post-Communist Countries in the Study, 1991–1992, 1996–1997 and 1999–2000 (Most freedom = 1, Least freedom = 7)

	Political rights scale			Civil liberties scale		
	1991	1996	1999	1991	1996	1999
Czech Republic[a]	2	1	1	2	2	2
Hungary	2	1	1	2	2	2
Poland	2	1	1	2	2	2
Estonia	2	1	1	3	2	2
Slovenia	2	1	1	3	2	2
Lithuania	2	1	2	3	1	2
Slovak Republic[a]	2	2	1	2	4	2
Latvia	2	2	1	3	2	2
Bulgaria	2	2	2	3	3	3
Macedonia	3	4	3	4	3	3
Ukraine	3	3	3	3	4	4
Russia	3	3	4	3	4	5
Romania	5	2	2	5	3	2
Moldova	5	3	2	4	4	4
Georgia	6	4	3	5	4	4
Armenia	5	5	4	5	4	4
Azerbaijan	5	6	6	5	5	4
Bosnia-Herzegovina	6	5	5	6	5	5
Yugoslavia	6	6	5	5	6	5
Belarus	4	6	6	4	6	6
Mean	**3.4**	**3.0**	**2.7**	**3.6**	**3.4**	**3.2**

Note: [a] 1991–92 scores for Czech Republic and Slovak Republic are based on Czechoslovakia.
Source: Freedom House Annual Survey of Freedom Country Ratings, 1972–73 to 1999–2000. Includes countries that participated in World Values Survey 1990–93 or 1995–97 waves only. For Bosnia-Herzegovina and Macedonia the first year's scores are from 1992 to 1993.

- Church or religious organisations
- Sport or recreation organisations
- Art, music or educational organisations
- Trade unions
- Political parties
- Environmental organisations
- Professional associations
- Charitable organisations
- Any other voluntary organisations

On the basis of Putnam's (1993) discussion of social capital in Italy, we eliminated membership in religious organisations because of their hierarchical character. This is somewhat at odds with the work of Mishler & Rose (1999, p. 95), who use church attendance as a measure of the civic community in East-Central Europe, though they acknowledge this is a crude indicator. Using church attendance and membership in a political party, though, they too found a positive relationship between these measures and individual responses on their political support thermometer (Mishler & Rose, 1999).

For a third indicator of social trust we used the dichotomous question (V27)

TABLE 2

CORRELATIONS BETWEEN SOCIAL CAPITAL INDICATORS AND FREEDOM HOUSE INDICATORS OF DEMOCRATISATION FOR 20 POST-COMMUNIST STATES IN 1995–1997 WORLD VALUES SURVEY[a] BASED ON DATA AGGREGATED BY COUNTRY

Social capital indicator	Freedom House political rights 1996	Freedom House civil liberties 1996	Freedom House political rights 1999	Freedom House civil liberties 1999
Mean political interest	0.152	0.080	− 0.152	0.111
	($p = 0.522$)	($p = 0.737$)	($p = 0.522$)	($p = 0.641$)
Mean interpersonal trust	− 0.161	− 0.354	0.203	− 0.357
	($p = 0.498$)	($p = 0.125$)	($p = 0.391$)	($p = 0.122$)
Mean number of organisation memberships	− 0.355	− 0.321	0.355	− 0.340
	($p = 0.136$)	($p = 0.180$)	($p = 0.138$)	($p = 0.154$)

Note: [a] We have reversed the standard polarity of the Freedom House indicators so that a higher score indicates greater democracy or freedom.

'Generally speaking, would you say most people can be trusted or that you can't be too careful in dealing with people?'. Individuals who responded 'most people can be trusted' were recoded as 1 and those who said 'you can't be too careful' as O. Thus, for all three sets of indicators, higher scores indicated someone with higher levels of civic engagement/capital.

Table 2 presents the product-moment correlations between the aggregate measures of social capital and the Freedom House scores for those countries in both 1996 and 1999.[3] One might expect social capital at a given time to predict democratic outcomes at some later time, so we ran the 1996 social capital scores from the World Values Survey against the 1999 democracy scores for this reason.

Social capital is not correlated with democratisation in these post-communist countries. None of the bivariate correlations is statistically significant (at $p \leqslant 0.05$). Indeed, the mean levels of social trust and organisational membership are consistently *negatively* related to levels of overall democratisation across the 20 post-communist countries included in this analysis.

No one would contend that social capital is the only or a sufficient explanation of the level of democracy. But one might expect to find a positive correlation. Another possible source of the negligible (and negative) correlations may be the Freedom House measures. More recent scholarship on political support in both established and emerging democracies has attempted to distinguish between support for the political community, support for regime principles, support for the regime's performance and support for individual democratic institutions, all seen as independent of evaluations of a particular political leader (Norris, 1999, pp. 17–20). The social capital literature, beginning with Putnam's work in Italy, has typically emphasised support for or confidence in democratic institutions as an indicator of regime capacity or effectiveness. Consistent with recent research, we used the World Values Survey questions that asked respondents about their confidence in democratic institutions. The questions were worded as follows:

I am going to name a number of organisations. For each one, could you tell me how much

TABLE 3

CORRELATIONS BETWEEN SOCIAL CAPITAL INDICATORS AND SUPPORT FOR DEMOCRATIC INSTITUTIONS FOR 20 POST-COMMUNIST STATES IN 1995–1997 WORLD VALUES SURVEY[a] BASED ON DATA AGGREGATED BY COUNTRY

Social capital indicator	Confidence in legal system	Confidence in parliament	Satisfaction with the government	Support for democracy
Mean political interest	− 0.022	0.195	− 0.209	− 0.009
	($p = 0.928$)	($p = 0.411$)	($p = 0.421$)	($p = 0.972$)
Mean interpersonal trust	0.239	− 0.388	− 0.042	0.265
	($p = 0.310$)	($p = 0.093$)	($p = 0.872$)	($p = 0.303$)
Mean number of organisation memberships	0.364	0.175	0.410	0.145
	($p = 0.125$)	($p = 0.473$)	($p = 0.102$)	($p = 0.577$)

Note: [a] World Values Survey Data on Satisfaction with the Government and Support for Democratic Principles are available for only 17 of the countries. All variables are scored so that if social capital is a cause of democratisation, there should be a positive correlation between social capital and support for democratic institutions and principles.

confidence you have in them: is it a great deal of confidence, quite a lot of confidence, not very much confidence or none at all?

We looked at evaluations of the legal system (V137) and the parliament (V144) as indicators for the efficacy of new democratic institutions.[4] We recorded the confidence indicators to range from a high of 4 (a great deal) to a low of 1 (no confidence at all). Table 3 reports the product-moment correlations between the mean confidence in democracy score and the mean scores on the three social capital indicators.

To tap into what Norris (1999) refers to as support for 'regime performance' we also examined an indicator of 'satisfaction with the government' (V165):

How satisfied are you with the way the people now in national office are handling the country's affairs? Would you say very satisfied, fairly satisfied, fairly dissatisfied or very dissatisfied?

We coded the responses on a scale ranging from 4 (very satisfied) to 1 (very dissatisfied).

Finally, to assess the level of support for the 'democratic principle', as opposed to support for particular institutions or regime performance in a particular country, we constructed a 'pro-democracy' scale based on answers to four questions, each with 4-point strongly agree, agree, disagree, strongly disagree response categories:

In democracy, the economic system runs badly (V160).

Democracies are indecisive and have too much squabbling (V161).

Democracies aren't good at maintaining order (V162).

Democracy may have problems but it's better than any other form of government (V163).

We treat 'disagree' responses to the first three questions, and 'agree' responses to the last question as 'pro-democracy' responses. The mean score of the responses to the four questions ranges from 4 (most in favour of democracy) to 1 (least in favour of democracy). We assume that responses mainly reflect the respondents' commitment to the abstract principles of democracy, not just to the performance of the government in their country.

We expected to find that countries with higher levels of social capital would have a higher percentage of people expressing support for the performance of the regime, higher confidence in its political institutions and, more broadly, a higher percentage committed to the principles of democracy. However, when we examine the relationship between the levels of confidence in new institutions and the indicators of social capital, we find no statistically significant relationships between social capital and aggregate confidence in or satisfaction with democratic institutions. We find no positive relationships even if we eliminate the non-democracies from our pool of countries.

Thus, within the first 10-year post-communist transition period, we find scant evidence of a link between social capital and aggregate levels of democratisation. It is not just that other factors (such as internal war) have shaped the outcome of the transition, but that social capital does not seem to contribute to democratic development, since without a correlation the former cannot be even a partial cause of the latter.

Why do the measures of social capital that have commonly been employed to predict democracy and democratic performance not work in these societies undergoing transition? Are the measures flawed in this context? Is the theory wrong or underspecified in this setting?

In the extant criticisms of the theory we note a repeated concern that the survey-based indicators of social capital might have different meanings in different social contexts. In particular, high levels of interest in politics and high rates of participation in voluntary organisations in ethnically plural societies, especially but perhaps not uniquely in countries undergoing significant political transformations, might signal the ethnic polarisation of society and a consequent threat to democratic institutions, democratic values and liberal notions of civil and political rights.

Social capital and support for democracy

According to Rustow (1970), the only prior condition for successful democratisation is national unity. This does not mean that everyone has to trace his ancestry back to the same clan, nor does it mean that everyone has to speak the same language, or even practice the same religion. Instead it means that nearly everyone must believe they belong together in a single political community. Later scholars doing cross-national work on support for regime performance, institutions and principles suggest that support for the *political community* is the first level of identification in a multidimensional scheme of political support (Norris, 1999). It may well be that social capital operates in the expected manner at some of these levels but not others, i.e. at the level of support for regime performance but not at that of the political community. Or it may be that national unity as measured by general support for the political community by all relevant sub-national groups is a necessary precondition for social capital to predict democratisation.

Support for the political community has often been measured by means of the 'patriotism' question employed by the World Values Survey and countless other surveys. With this in mind, and to demonstrate the validity of our concern about the potential impact of pluralism on social capital markers, we turn to a survey question on national pride (V205) to explore differences in mean responses of significant groups within states in transition. The existence of substantially different evaluations of the country as a whole by large sub-national groups would be evidence of a lack of national unity and, as such, would potentially challenge the way in which social capital affects the democratisation process. The national pride question reads as follows:

How proud are you to be an [American]? Very proud, somewhat proud, not very proud, not proud at all?

To evaluate support for the political community within significant sub-national ethnic groups we needed first to adapt the World Values Survey data to determine to which ethnic groups the respondents may have belonged. The World Values Surveys were not designed, for the most part, to study ethnic variation (Silver & Dowley, 2000). Although we did our best to classify respondents using one or more indicators that are typically linked to ethnic self-identification or consciousness, we had to rely on different variables in different countries. In some cases ethnicity was derived from an ethnic self-identification question; in others it is based on the survey organisation's or the interviewer's identification of the respondents by ethnicity; and in still others it is based on religious identification, language used at home or the region in which the respondent resided.[5] However, we were able to derive ethnic variables for all countries in which the population had at least a 10% minority except Croatia and Slovenia.

Using the responses to the national pride question, we calculated the mean for each ethnic group as well as the difference between the mean scores for each ethnic group and the grand mean (2.3) for all World Values Survey respondents in the region. By using the grand mean (a common metric), we can compare groups within countries as well as across countries. In Figure 1, in addition to reporting the mean scores by ethnic group relative to the grand mean, for cases in which the mean score of an ethnic minority population is significantly different from the mean score of the majority or titular ethnic group in the same country the bars are marked by a white bar.[6] Those for which the difference from the titular ethnic group is not statistically significant are marked by a black bar. Almost universally, the minority populations report lower levels of pride in the country. If we accept the common interpretation that the question captures support for the political community, then ethnic pluralism matters, and it matters in a meaningful and predictable manner.

Now that we have found evidence that people view the political community through an ethnic lens, we address again the bivariate relationships between social capital and support for regime performance, regime institutions and regime principles. This time, however, we add the ethnic component to the mix. Figures 2 to 5 report the mean scores of majority groups and minority groups in each of these societies, by expressing the means relative to the regional grand mean scores for confidence in the

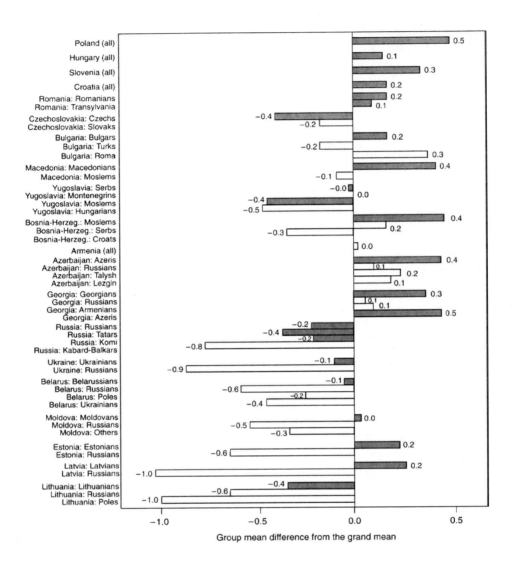

FIGURE 1. DIFFERENCES IN PRIDE IN COUNTRY AMONG 49 ETHNIC GROUPS IN 20 POST-COMMUNIST COUNTRIES. ORIGINAL RANGE 1 (NOT AT ALL PROUD) TO 4 (VERY PROUD) MEAN 3.20 ± 0.85, $n = 27 363$.

Source: Calculated from World Values Survey: 'How proud are you to be [Czechoslovak]? Very proud, quite proud, not very proud, not at all proud' (V205). Answers are recorded so that they range from 4 (very proud) to 1 (not at all). White bars lines represent minority groups whose mean level of national pride is statistically significantly different from the mean level for the majority or titular ethnic group in the same country (at $p = 0.05$, two-tailed test).

legal system, the parliament, the current national government and the pro-democracy scale.

We find no easily apparent pattern across the political support measures. About 55%

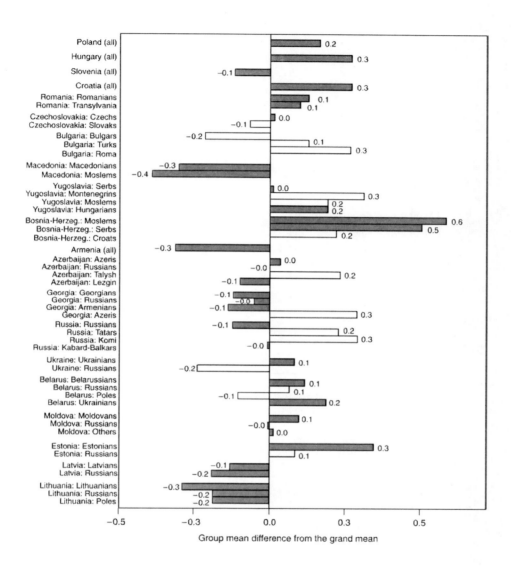

FIGURE 2. DIFFERENCES IN CONFIDENCE IN THE LEGAL SYSTEM AMONG 49 ETHNIC GROUPS IN 20 POST-COMMUNIST COUNTRIES.

ORIGINAL RANGE 1 TO 4, MEAN 2.38 ± 0.86, $n = 27\ 849$.

Source: Calculated from World Values Survey: '... How much confidence do you have in the legal system? A great deal, quite a lot, not very much or none at all. (V137). Answers are recoded so that they range from 4 (great confidence) to 1 (none at all). White bars represent minority groups whose mean level of confidence is statistically significantly different from the mean level for the majority or titular ethnic group in the same country (at $p = 0.05$, two- tailed test).

of the minority ethnic groups in our sample (16 out of 29 minority groups) are less confident than the majority population in the legal systems in their country. Only 45% of the minority groups are less confident than their majority populations in the

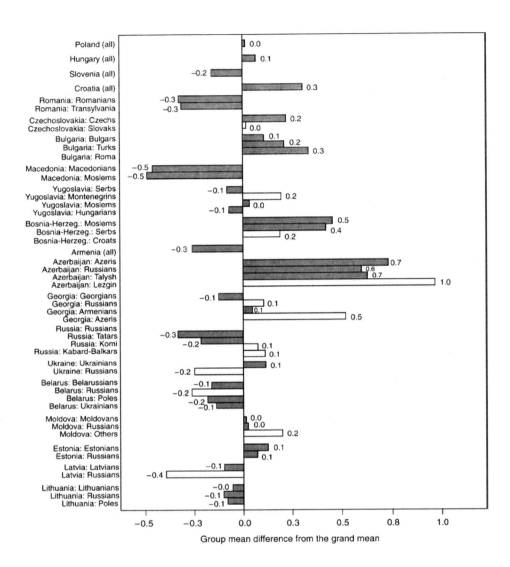

FIGURE 3. DIFFERENCES IN CONFIDENCE IN THE PARLIAMENT AMONG 49 ETHNIC GROUPS IN 20 POST-COMMUNIST COUNTRIES.

ORIGINAL RANGE 1 TO 4, MEAN 2.20 ± 0.87, $n = 27\,190$.

Source: Calculated from World Values Survey: '… How much confidence do you have in the parliament? A great deal, quite a lot, not very much or none at all' (V144). Answers are recoded so that they range from 4 (great confidence) to 1 (none at all). White bars represent minority groups whose mean level of confidence is statistically significantly different from the mean level for the majority or titular ethnic group in the same country (at $p = 0.05$, two-tailed test).

national parliament. But 63% of the minority groups are less satisfied than the majority groups with the performance of the regime, and 60% express less support than the majority groups do for democratic principles.

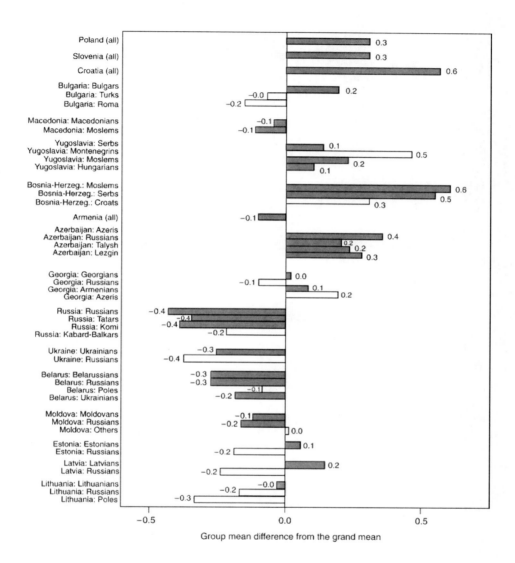

FIGURE 4. Differences in Satisfaction with Government Performance Among 44 Ethnic Groups in 17 Post-Communist Countries.

Original range 1 (very dissatisfied) to 4 (very satisfied) mean 1.92 ± 0.75, $n = 23\,895$.

Source: Calculated from World Values Survey: 'How satisfied are you with the way the people now in national office are handling the country's affairs? Very satisfied, fairly satisfied, fairly dissatisfied or very dissatisfied?' (V165). Answers are recoded so that they range from 4 (very satisfied) to 1 (very dissatisfied). White bars represent minority groups whose mean level of satisfaction is statistically significantly different from the mean level for the majority or titular ethnic group in the same country (at $p = 0.05$, two-tailed test).

The clearest cross-national tendency is that the Russian minority populations in the post-Soviet states are consistently less confident in the new institutions, less satisfied with the new national government, and less supportive of democracy as a system of governing

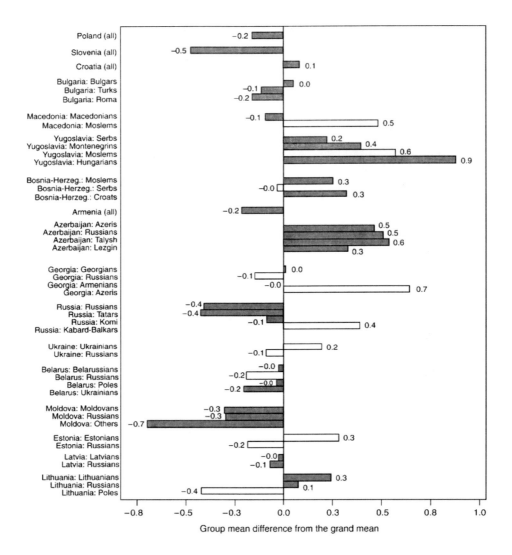

FIGURE 5. Differences in Support for Democracy Among 44 Ethnic Groups in 17 Post-Communist Countries.

Original range 1 to 4, mean 3.02 ± 1.16, $n = 23\ 638$.

Source: Calculated from World Values Survey. Mean score in the 'democratic' direction on four 4-point agree–disagaree questions: 'In democracy the economic system runs badly' (V160), 'Democracies are indecisive and have too much squabbling' (V161), 'Democracies aren't good at maintaining order' (V162) and 'Democracy may have problems but it's better than any other form of government' (V163).

ideals than their new majority populations. Of course, this may not be due entirely to their status as ethnic minorities in new countries, as the Russian majority in Russia itself is also the least supportive of democratic principles, the least satisfied with their current government, and among the least confident in new governing institutions of the majority populations in our sample.[7]

Although the differences between majority and minority groups are generally small and run in both directions, in 55 of 116 possible differences the gaps between the majority and minority populations were statistically significant. This is 49 more statistically significant differences than one would expect due to chance alone. By chance alone one would expect to find six statistically 'significant' differences out of 116 (at $p \leqslant 0.05$). As noted previously, however, the sample designs in most of the World Values Survey countries either undersampled the minority populations or else failed to sample enough members of the minority groups to permit reliable estimates of inter-group differences. That despite this 55 of 116 of the relationships are statistically significant makes our finding of so many statistically significant differences even more notable.

How does social capital fit into this complex relationship? If we first examine differences in the level of interest in politics among the ethnic groups in the countries under consideration we find that Czechs and Slovaks in the early 1990s were far more interested in politics than the rest of the ethnic groups in the region. This high level of interest did not signal health of the polity, but instead polarisation and subsequent dissolution of the state. In fact, the most successful cases of democratisation are those in which levels of interest, participation and trust were at or below the regional mean.[8] Indeed, Czechs and Slovaks notwithstanding, the only other groups with expressed levels of political interest higher than the regional mean are the Montenegrins in Yugoslavia, Serbs in Bosnia, Russians and Ukrainians in Belarus, Russians and Talysh in Azerbaijan, Latvians and Estonians. Interestingly, in the two former Soviet republics with the highest level of democratisation, Estonia and Latvia, the Russian populations express mean levels of interest in politics lower than the regional mean, and significantly lower than the majority populations in the successor states.

Using interpersonal trust variables to indicate democratic social capital in this part of the world is also problematic. The most trusting groups (judging by the World Values Survey data) are the Roma in Bulgaria, Hungarians in Yugoslavia and Kabards and Balkars (small Moslem ethnic groups residing in the North Caucasus) in Russia. Above the mean are also Serbs in all settings, Moslems in Bosnia and Yugoslavia, Croats in Bosnia and Azeris in Georgia. In Russia the Tatars and Kabards and Balkars are significantly more trusting than titular Russians, just as Roma and Turks are more trusting than Bulgars in Bulgaria.

Because voluntary group membership is so central to the social capital thesis, we report in Figure 6 the percentage of individuals within each group that belong to at least one voluntary association. Once again we find evidence against the applicability of standard social capital indicators. The ethnic groups with the highest percentages belonging to at least one voluntary organisation are located in the states of the former Yugoslavia. A phenomenal 79% of Bosnian Serbs belong to at least one voluntary organisation—compared with only 42% of Hungarians (in Hungary) and 11% of Poles (in Poland). The latter two countries are sometimes taken as paragons of the democratic transition in the post-communist world. Although conceivably this evidence signals an emerging civic involvement among the Bosnian Serbs, it is more likely that it reveals high engagement in communal organisations that are far from helping to reconcile relations with non-Serbs. When we examine the individual forms of membership, we note that 164 of the 369 Bosnian Serbs who are members of voluntary associations identify these organisations as political parties, more than any other category of voluntary organisation except sports clubs, to which 176 of the 369 reported belonging.

We turn now to a multivariate statistical analysis of the relationships between social capital, ethnicity and support for democracy, using the same indicators of support for regime institutions, government performance and democratic principles. For this purpose we rely on individual-level rather than aggregated data. In addition, we pool the approximately 29 000 cases from the post-communist countries in the 1995–97 World Values Survey.[9]

Table 4 reports the Pearson's r coefficients and significance levels for all respondents in the 20 countries under investigation, as well as separately for just the titular majorities, the new Russian minorities in the 'near abroad' (former non-Russian republics of the USSR) and all other minority groups in the post-communist space. Because Russians themselves were so consistently more negative in their evaluations of state institutions and democratisation, we needed to determine whether they alone were driving some of the negative correlations between social capital and democratisation that we reported earlier in the aggregate analysis. Is minority status in states undergoing transition responsible for the negative signs, is it simply Russians who are more negative in this context, or are small or negative correlations between social capital and evaluations of regime institutions found also among the titular nationalities?

For all respondents combined, of the three social capital indicators interpersonal trust is most consistently positively correlated with support for regime institutions, regime performance and democratic principles. The coefficients are statistically significant at the $p \leqslant 0.05$ level for titular majorities as well on all four measures of support for the regime, government and democracy.

However, for Russians in the near abroad, although higher levels of interpersonal trust are associated with greater confidence in new institutions, trust is not correlated with the evaluation of regime performance or support for the principles of democracy. This is similar to the attitudes of all other minority populations, where higher levels of interpersonal trust are negatively associated with support for democratic ideals, though the negative correlation is not statistically significant.

Interest in politics and organisational membership are the two social capital indicators that we anticipated might predict differently in plural settings. Specifically, political mobilisation might be expected to occur among those who are less satisfied with the newly established political order. Our expectations are borne out by Table 4. While for the titular nationalities interest in politics is positively correlated with support for institutions and democracy, for the Russian and other minority populations greater interest in politics is negatively correlated with support for democratic principles. Hence, high levels of explicitly political interest among ethnic minorities do not represent social capital in the making, but perhaps political mobilisation against democratic development.

We find a less consistent pattern for organisational membership. For the titular

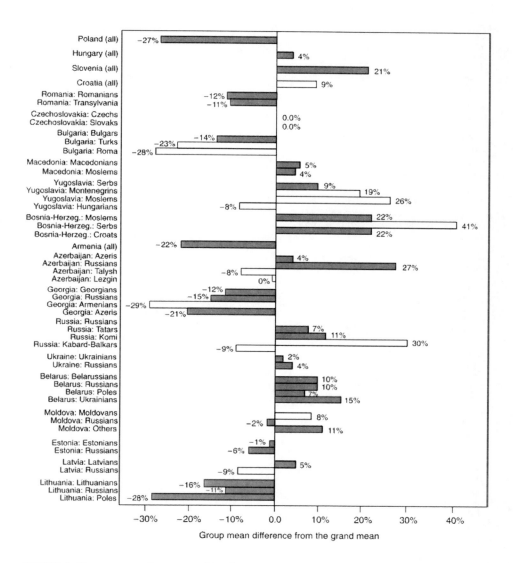

FIGURE 6. DIFFERENCES IN PERCENTAGE WHO BELONG TO ANY NONRELIGIOUS VOLUNTARY ORGANISATION AMONG 49 ETHNIC GROUPS IN 20 POST-COMMUNIST COUNTRIES.

MEAN PERCENTAGE WHO BELONG TO ANY NONRELIGIOUS ORGANISATION: 38 ± 48, $n = 27\ 641$.

Source: Calculated from World Values Survey: 'Now I am going to read off a list of voluntary organisations: for each one, could you tell me whether you are an active member, an inactive member or not a member of that type of organisation?' (V28 through 36). This chart counts as a 'member' whether the person was either an active member or an inactive member. The organisational types are: church/religious, sports/recreation, art/music/educational, trade union, political party, environmental, professional, charitable, any other voluntary organisation. This chart excludes churches and religious organisations from the count.

ethnic groups, organisational membership seems to act as social capital theory predicts: involvement in voluntary organisations is associated with higher levels of confidence in new institutions, and higher levels of support for the current regime. It

TABLE 4

PRODUCT-MOMENT CORRELATIONS BETWEEN SOCIAL CAPITAL INDICATORS AND SUPPORT FOR INSTITUTIONS AND DEMOCRACY IN POST-COMMUNIST STATES, 1995–1997 WORLD VALUES SURVEY (POOLED INDIVIDUAL-LEVEL DATA)

	Inter-personal trust	Interest in politics	Organisational memberships (non-church)
All respondents (max. *n* = 27 942)			
Confidence in legal institutions	0.043**	0.017**	0.016**
Confidence in parliament	0.061**	0.079**	0.024**
Satisfaction with the government	0.038**	0.043**	0.030**
Support for democracy	0.041**	−0.032**	0.002
Titular nationalities (max. *n* = 22 234)			
Confidence in legal institutions	0.039**	0.013*	0.011
Confidence in parliament	0.060**	0.083*	0.025**
Satisfaction with the government	0.034**	0.043**	0.017*
Support for democracy	0.052**	−0.023	0.005
Russians in 'near abroad' (max. *n* = 2773)			
Confidence in legal institutions	0.050*	0.032	−0.015
Confidence in parliament	0.063*	0.048*	0.000
Satisfaction with the government	0.032	0.021	0.011
Support for democracy	0.024	−0.053**	0.021
Other minorities (max. *n* = 2661)			
Confidence in legal institutions	0.075**	0.012	0.063**
Confidence in parliament	0.076**	0.051**	0.014
Satisfaction with the government	0.085*	0.070**	0.129**
Support for democracy	−0.035	−0.079**	−0.076**

* $p \leqslant 0.05$ (two-tailed), ** $p \leqslant 0.01$ (two-tailed).
Interpersonal trust: Can 'most people be trusted?' (1/0)
Interest in politics: How interested in political affairs? (4-point scale)
Organisation membership: Belong to (or activist in) any nonreligious voluntary organisation? (1/0)
Confidence in legal institutions: How much confidence in the legal system? (4-point scale)
Confidence in parliament: How much confidence in the parliament? (4-point scale)
Satisfaction with Government: How satisfied with how the government is handling nation's affairs? (4-point scale)
Support for democracy: How strongly support democracy? (4-point scale based on four questions)

is also positively correlated with support for democratic ideals (though not at a statistically significant level).

For Russians in the near abroad, however, none of the coefficients with organisational membership was statistically significant, suggesting that among those Russian minorities involved in voluntary organisations such participation is not correlated with their levels of support for democratic institutions. Among other minorities in the region, while involvement is positively and significantly related to greater confidence in the legal system and satisfaction with the government's policies, those who are involved in voluntary organisations are less likely to support democracy as an ideal form of government than those who are not involved in organisations.

We fit a multivariate OLS regression model to summarise the typical effect of the social capital measures on each of the four dependent political support indicators. As predictors we include the three social capital indicators as well as dummy variables for the two minority ethnic categories.[10] Furthermore, we specify interaction terms to capture the joint effects of being a member of a minority group and having an interest in politics as well as being a member of a minority group and being a member of at least one voluntary organisation. In addition, we control for the economic situation of the respondent by including responses to the following question (V64):

> How satisfied would you say you are with the financial situation of your household? If 'I' means you are completely dissatisfied and '10' means you are completely satisfied, where would you put your satisfaction with your household's financial situation?

Our goal is not to account fully for the variance in support for democracy but to test for the effects of social capital and ethnicity. Because economic well-being is likely to be an important factor that differentiates the situations of ethnic groups in society, it is necessary to control for this factor in the analysis.[11]

The results in Table 5 provide support for our hypothesis that the impact of social capital differs according to whether the individuals belong to the titular or a minority ethnic group in a state in transition. First, interpersonal trust has a consistently positive association with support for democracy, regime institutions and regime performance. The greater the interpersonal trust, the greater is the support for democracy as an ideal, the greater the confidence in the legal system and the parliament, and the greater the satisfaction with governmental performance.

Second, interest in politics has a consistently positive relationship with three of the four dependent variables, but not with support for democratic principles. Indeed, interest in politics is negatively and significantly predictive of support for democracy, which implies that those who are more psychologically engaged in politics are less supportive of democratic ideals in the post-Soviet, post-communist context.

Third, membership in voluntary organisations is not consistently correlated with any of the political support indicators. Bear in mind that, given the specification of variables in the equations, the effect of organisational memberships on the dependent variables (row 3) mainly reflects the relationship for the titular nationalities. Nonetheless, we find again that being a member of a voluntary organisation is not correlated with support for democratic principles. In fact, among minority populations voluntary group membership is more often associated with lower support for democratic institutions and principles.

That the mobilisation of political interest and associational life among the ethnic minority populations in the post-communist countries is correlated with weaker support for democracy should be placed in context. On the whole, the minority nationalities (excluding the Russians) are likely to be substantially more positively disposed toward democratic principles than even the titular nationalities (see the positive coefficients in the fifth row of numbers in Table 5). But the more socially engaged of those minorities are likely to be somewhat less favourably disposed toward regime institutions and democracy than the socially passive.

Furthermore, on all four indicators of support for political institutions and democracy Russians are less supportive than the titular nationalities in the countries of the near abroad, though the negative coefficients are statistically significant only for satisfaction with governmental policies and confidence in the legal system. If we

TABLE 5

Effects of Social Capital and Ethnicity on Support for the Democratic System in Post-Communist Countries (Pooled Individual-Level Data)

Dependent variable	Confidence legal system		Confidence parliament		Satisfaction with government performance		Support for democracy	
Social capital								
Interpersonal trust	0.086**	(6.748)	0.106**	(8.187)	0.062**	(5.634)	0.100**	(5.597)
Interest in politics	0.019**	(2.760)	0.075**	(10.778)	0.043**	(7.121)	−0.026**	(−2.707)
Voluntary organisation membership[a]	−0.011	(−0.857)	−0.049	(−0.038)	−0.025	(−2.243)	−0.006	(−0.325)
Ethnic group[b]								
Russian in near abroad	−0.112*	(−2.103)	−0.047	(−0.864)	−0.113*	(−2.547)	−0.073	(−0.991)
Other minority	0.035	(0.629)	0.073	(1.299)	0.138**	(2.743)	0.316**	(3.906)
Social capital and ethnic group jointly								
Russian* interest	0.009	(0.413)	−0.025	(−1.161)	−0.035*	(−1.987)	−0.040	(−1.371)
Other minority *interest	0.061	(1.523)	0.019	(0.841)	−0.026	(−1.287)	−0.054	(−1.678)
Russian* organisation membership	−0.042	(−1.135)	−0.041	(−1.059)	0.004	(−0.124)	0.066	(1.297)
Other minority* organisation membership	−0.061	(1.523)	−0.012	(−0.304)	0.197**	(5.492)	−0.168**	(−2.937)
Household finances								
Satisfaction with finances	0.030**	(13.165)	0.036**	(15.448)	0.065**	(31.868)	0.021**	(6.377)
Constant[c]	2.206	(114.453)	1.862	(94.003)	1.539	(89.890)	3.022	(108.068)
Adjusted R²	0.032		0.035		0.104		0.020	
SEE	0.85		0.86		0.70		1.132	
n	24 995		24 403		22 536		22 319	

* Indicates coefficient significant at $p \leq 0.05$ (two-tailed); ** Indicates significant at $p \leq 0.01$ (two-tailed). The coefficients are unstandardised regression coefficients (b's); t-ratios are given in parentheses.

Notes:

[a] Excludes membership in church or religious organisations.

[b] Dummy variables: Russian in near abroad: 1 if a Russian living in non-Russian successor state of Soviet Union, 0 if not; Other minority: 1 if a non-Russian minority, 0 if not. The 'omitted' category is the titular nationality of the country, e.g., Estonians in Estonia, Bulgarians in Bulgaria.

[c] In addition to the constant shown, the equations also included a set of dummy variables to capture the fixed effects of the countries in which no minority ethnic group members were identified.

examine the joint effects of minority status and civic engagement, we find that, for Russians, those who express greater interest in politics are less likely to support the regime and democracy than those who have little or no interest in politics.

If we focus on just these statistically significant relationships, however, we obtain results that somewhat contradict those presented in Table 4. In the equations in Table 5 interest in politics among Russians predicts less support for the regime, while in Table 4 it predicted in the opposite direction (though not significantly). While we cannot readily reconcile this difference, we do not find any support for the idea that Russians who are more engaged in civic or political life are more likely to support either the new regime under which they live or the ideals of democratic governance.

In contrast, being a *non*-Russian minority is associated with having a more *positive* attitude toward governmental performance and democracy. Why this difference between Russians and the other minorities? We propose that for Russians in the near abroad, political development and the process of democratisation over the past 10 years has meant a loss of status as a corporate group. But for many other minorities, although there are certainly several major exceptions (including major cases of civil strife and civil war), post-communist development has opened up new opportunities for a flourishing of cultural life or even an independent political life and has provided a stake for them in achieving a further democratisation of the system to protect their civil rights.

Conclusions

Our first significant finding is the weak overall relation between indicators of social capital and democratisation in the post-communist countries. An analysis of aggregate measures of social capital and democratisation failed to find a positive correlation between the aggregate amount of social capital and the level of democratisation. This remained true whether we used external evaluations of the level of democratisation or survey-based responses about the degree of confidence in and satisfaction with democracy.

The analysis of individual-level data did, however, find some evidence of a positive correlation between social capital and *attitudes supportive of democracy*. This was especially so for social trust, though we urge caution about assuming that interpersonal trust only works in a pro-democratic direction. Viewed as a political resource, being able to rely on others can help the democrat and the anti-democrat, the individual engaged in regime-supportive participation or the one who adopts unconventional political methods or espouses unconventional goals (Bahry & Silver, 1990).

When we examined the impact of political interest and membership in voluntary associations, we found a more mixed result. By and large, for members of the titular majority, greater political involvement and social engagement were associated with greater support for democracy, the government and regime institutions. But among ethnic minorities we found that the more mobilised members of those groups were less supportive of democracy than the more passive members.

Thus, social capital theory cannot be easily transported from the established democracies to ethnically plural societies in transition. In the post-communist countries the transition unleashed the potential not only for a liberation of minorities but also for their suppression, not only for minority groups to proclaim and seek to protect their interests by endorsing a strong civil rights regime or cultural and political autonomy, but also for majority groups to want to deny or limit those claims and aspirations in the interest of preserving the physical boundaries of the state or their own newly dominant position in the system.

Researchers also need to be cautious about assuming that indicators that apply to the more homogeneous societies work just as well in ethnically plural societies. Social scientists do not yet understand well the conditions under which people's sub-national loyalties are mutually exclusive with national and state identities (Dowley & Silver, 2000). Our message is not that ethnically plural societies cannot democratise but that it is more difficult for them to do so if the majority ethnic groups are exclusive in their post-communist nation-building project, or if a past history of injustice against minority populations mobilises them during periods of uncertainty in a way that makes the national unity condition impossible to satisfy.

Our findings regarding the Russian minority lead us to wonder about similar tendencies among other former dominant or imperial nationals who suddenly find themselves in an inferior position. Does their undemocratic national 'mean' imply that some cultures never adopt democratic principles, no matter how interested or involved in organisations their peoples become? Or does their attitude stem more from their newly diminished position in these societies, which suggests parallels to other former dominant or colonial elites in parts of Africa and Asia? These are some of the questions suggested by our findings, and to which we shall direct our attention as we search for the conditions under which diverse peoples can make the transition from authoritarian rule to national unity under freer and fairer governing institutions.

State University of New York, New Paltz
Michigan State University

A previous version of this article was presented at the annual meeting of the Midwest Political Science Association, 18–22 April 2001. Dowley's work on the article was supported by a Research and Creative Projects Grant from SUNY, New Paltz. The World Values Survey data were obtained from the Inter-University Consortium for Political and Social Research (ICPSR Study No. 2790). Neither SUNY, New Paltz nor the ICPSR nor the creators and sponsors of the WVS data are responsible for our use or interpretation of the data.

[1] Freedom House uses the following checklist to evaluate *political rights*: Is head of state/ government elected through free and fair elections? Are legislative representatives elected in free and fair elections? Are there fair electoral laws, equal campaigning opportunities, fair polling and honest tabulating of results? Do people have the right to organise into political parties? Is there a significant opposition vote or de facto opposition power? Are the people free from domination by the military, foreign powers or economic oligarchies? Do ethnic, cultural and minority groups have reasonable self-determination? For *civil liberties*, the emphasis is on free and independent media, free religious institutions, freedom of assembly, speech and organisation, the availability and legality of trade unions, an independent judiciary and secure property rights. For details, see the methodology report at www.freedomhouse.org.

[2] These figures are based only on the 20 countries included in Table 1—countries that participated in the World Values Survey in either the 1990–93 or 1995–97 rounds.

[3] The World Values Survey indicators are based on weighted data, which make the scores from the sample more representative of the population of each country. Except as noted, we rely on V236 from the World Values Survey as the weight variable.

[4] Initially we included confidence in the government (V142). The question was worded: '... confidence in the government in [capital city]', presumably so that respondents would think not of

their regional or local leaders but instead of the national leaders. However, it appears that many respondents took the reference to the capital city literally, so that, for example, respondents in Russia might think the question referred to the leaders of Moscow city, not of the Russian Federation.

[5] Detailed recoding information is available from the authors in the form of an SPSS syntax file.

[6] Whether the scores for a given ethnic group are significantly different from average depends not only on the magnitude of the mean difference but also on the variance and on the number of cases. That the World Values Survey did not intentionally over-sample minority populations makes it more difficult to find statistically significant differences among ethnic groups.

[7] For example, the mean evaluation by Russians of the Duma of the Russian Federation is 1.88. Only the Macedonians in Macedonia have a lower mean evaluation (1.75) of parliament among titular nationalities in the third wave of the World Values Survey, although the overall samples in a few other World Values Survey countries give lower marks than the Russians to their legislature: Colombia 1.77, Argentina 1.78, Dominican Republic 1.82 and Peru 1.85.

[8] These conclusions are based on World Values Survey data that are not shown in a table or figure here.

[9] We again use V236 from the World Values Survey data to weight the cases. However, in the pooled data analysis we adjust the weights so that the total Ns from each country equal the actual N of respondents. Further information about the weighting procedures is available from the authors.

[10] The titular nationalities become the 'omitted' or reference category needed for specifying the equations.

[11] We assume that 'satisfaction with household financial situation' encapsulates a combination of factors (e.g. the respondent's objective economic situation and frustration in meeting aspirations for economic success). Norris (1999) includes a measure of 'satisfaction with life as a whole' to predict support for political institutions in a regression analysis based on advanced Western democracies. Although this variable also correlates with the same dependent variables in the post-communist states, we are concerned that the answers to a question on 'satisfaction with life as a whole' are likely to be more contaminated by the respondent's views of the overall political situation and thus impart a simultaneity bias to the analysis.

References

Almond, Gabriel A. & Verba, Sidney, *The Civic Culture: Political Attitudes and Democracy in Five Nations* (Princeton, Princeton University Press, 1963).

Bahry, Donna & Silver, Brian D., 'Soviet Citizen Participation on the Eve of Democratization', *American Political Science Review*, 83, September 1990, pp. 821–848.

Dowley, Kathleen M. & Silver, Brian D. 'Subnational and National Loyalty: Cross-National Comparisons', *International Journal of Public Opinion Research*, 12, November 2000, pp. 357–371.

Fish, M. Stephen, 'Postcommunist Subversion: Social Science and Democratization in East Europe and Eurasia', *Slavic Review*, 58, Winter 1999, pp. 794–823.

Hardin, Russell, *One For All* (Princeton, Princeton University Press, 1995).

Kornhauser, William, *The Politics of Mass Society* (Glencoe, IL, The Free Press, 1959).

Levi, Margaret, 'Social and Unsocial Capital: A Review Essay of Robert Putnam's *Making Democracy Work*', *Politics and Society*, 24, March 1996, pp. 45–55.

Lipset, Seymour M., *Political Man: The Social Bases of Politics* (Garden City, NY, Doubleday, 1960).

Mishler, William & Rose, Richard, 'Five Years After the Fall: Trajectories of Support for Democracy in Post-Communist Europe', in Pippa Norris (ed.), *Critical Citizens: Global Support for Democratic Governance* (Oxford, Oxford University Press, 1999), pp. 78–102.

Newton, Kenneth & Norris, Pippa, 'Confidence in Public Institutions: Faith, Culture or Performance?' in Susan Pharr & Robert Putnam (eds), *Disaffected Democracies: What's Troubling the Trilateral Countries?* (Princeton, Princeton University Press, 2000), pp. 52–73.

Norris, Pippa (ed.), *Critical Citizens: Global Support for Democratic Governance* (Oxford, Oxford University Press, 1999).

Posen, Barry, 'The Security Dilemma and Ethnic Conflict', in Michael Brown (ed.), *Ethnic Conflict and International Security* (Princeton, Princeton University Press, 1993).

Putnam, Robert, *Making Democracy Work: Civic Traditions in Modern Italy* (Princeton, Princeton University Press, 1993).

Roeder, Philip, 'Peoples and States After 1989: The Political Costs of Incomplete National Revolutions', *Slavic Review*, 58, Winter 1999, pp. 854–882.

Rustow, Dankwart, 'Transitions to Democracy', *Comparative Politics*, 1, April 1970, pp. 337–363.

Silver, Brian D. & Dowley, Kathleen M., 'Measuring Political Culture in Multiethnic Societies: Reaggregating the World Values Survey', *Comparative Political Studies*, 33, May 2000, pp. 517–550.

Snyder, Jack, 'Nationalism and the Crisis of the Post-Soviet State', in Michael Brown (ed.), *Ethnic Conflict and International Security* (Princeton, Princeton University Press, 1993).

Citizen Participation in Local Governance in Eastern Europe: Rediscovering a Strength of Civil Society in the Post-Socialist World?

TSVETA PETROVA

Abstract

This article studies the impact of citizen participation on local government performance in Bulgaria. Both survey and interview data are used to suggest that, all else being equal, municipal efficacy grows with the increasing involvement of social and economic actors in the policy-making process. This improved government efficacy is most likely a result of the professionalisation and organisational strength of the third sector. Although the politicisation of the local state has undermined its capacity, municipalities have been able not only to reconstitute some of their authority but also to improve the output and the quality of their policy making by employing the expertise and support of major local civic organisations.

THE DESIRE TO DENY THE SOCIALIST ELITE THE ability to set goals with only marginal input from or control by domestic groups was a focal point for the mobilisation of opposition to state socialism and the impetus for the democratisation project in many Central and Eastern European countries. Since the collapse of state socialism, issues such as accountability, legitimacy, popular representation and responsiveness of governments to citizen demands have become central to discussions about democratisation among scholars, politicians and activists. However, studies of Central and Eastern European civil society have largely neglected to examine the contributions of non-state actors to governance in the region. This article seeks to begin addressing this gap in the literature by examining the impact of citizen participation in local government in Bulgaria on the efficacy of municipal policy making. The article shows that despite the passivity of local government in many municipalities, and their preference for working primarily with political actors, there has been widespread and diverse, if weakly institutionalised, cooperation between local authorities and societal actors. Moreover, it seems that in the Bulgarian

The author acknowledges the support of the Institute of European Studies, the Institute for Public Affairs, and the Johnson Business School at Cornell University. The author also wishes to express her gratitude to the Foundation for Local Government Reform in Bulgaria for providing the survey data for this study and to Sidney Tarrow, Valerie Bunce, Devra Moehler, Nicolas van de Walle, Mitchell Orenstein, Susan Rose-Ackerman, Milada Vachudova, Daniel Epstein, and Jerome Ziegler for their comments on earlier drafts of this paper.

case, but perhaps throughout the region as well, the problem-solving capacity of municipalities grows with the increasing involvement of social and economic actors in the policy-making process. This improved government efficacy is most likely a result of the professionalisation and organisational strength of the third sector. Although the politicisation of the local state has undermined its capacity, many municipalities have been able not only to reconstitute some of their authority but also to improve the output and the quality of their policy making by employing the expertise and support of major local civic organisations.

The article begins by reviewing the literature on civil society in Eastern Europe in order to motivate the research question and to provide some context for examining civic participation in policy making. After describing local government performance and civic–municipal interaction trends in Bulgaria, it examines the relationship between civic inclusion and municipal efficacy. Both variables are gradually aggregated from their various components into factors corresponding to stages or aspects of policy making, then into composite indices of overall participation and performance, and finally into latent variables in a structural equation model of the participation–performance relationship. The article concludes by offering an interpretation of the results and their implication for democratisation in the country and the region.

Research agenda: civil society and democracy in Eastern Europe

Most scholars and practitioners assessing the contribution of Central and Eastern European civil society to democracy in the region focus on the overall quality of citizens produced in the process of civic participation. Many have warned that despite wide interest in politics and a general regard for the common good in Eastern Europe (Raiser et al. 2001), the post-socialist region is characterised by low mass participation in civic groups (Howard 2003), low levels of general interpersonal trust and social capital (Crawford & Lijphart 1995; Rose 2000; Theesfeld 2004), and low levels of trust in and approval of civic and political institutions (Carnaghan 2001; Mishler & Rose 1997; Rose 2001). However, some have also pointed to the existence of broad, porous and politically relevant interpersonal networks to argue that such higher-trust connections might be bridging the gap between the private and public spheres (Gibson 2001; Ledeneva 1998; Marsh 2000).

In addition to such individual-level studies of civic participation and the norms associated with it, there has been much organisation-level work on the predominance of 'third sector' groups within East European civil societies—the formal and functionally differentiated and frequently professional, hierarchical, centralised, and even 'corporate', non-profit and non-governmental organisations (NGOs) (Toepler & Salamon 2003). Many have expressed concerns that such groups tend to be sustained primarily by foreign funding and interact mostly with state and market actors and therefore frequently value their own survival over their social mission (Glenn & Mendelson 2002). Thus, the debate in this group of studies has been about the strength of the cooperation within the civic sector as well as about the thickness of the links between third-sector organisations and the constituents they claim to represent. Some have uncovered civic fragmentation (mistrust, bitterness and secrecy, as well as accentuation of new–old hierarchies, networks and privileges), especially where foreign assistance is at stake (Evans 2002; Henderson 2002; Sperling 1999), whereas others point to both horizontal and vertical communication networks, which raise public awareness and help make civil society groups more professional, organised and strategic in their planning and activism (Petrova & Tarrow 2007; Powell 2002). In addition, in studying the responsiveness, legitimacy and capacity of NGOs, some have suggested that chronically underfunded advocacy groups have frequently been more sensitive to demands by outside donors than to those by their internal constituencies (Krastev 2001; Glenn & Mendelson 2002; Henderson 2002; Narozhna 2004), while others demonstrate a systematic relationship between the patterns of foreign ties and those of domestic integration (Stark *et al.* 2006).

Much less researched, however, has been the contribution of Central and Eastern European civil society in providing citizens with institutional leverage for relating to the state—aggregating interests and articulating demands in the process of counselling the government, ensuring its accountability to the citizens, and protecting them against the state's unwanted intrusion (Kubik 2005). This is an unfortunate oversight, especially given the third-sector nature of civil society in the post-socialist region and particularly since some have already documented that third-sector organisations have earned certain official and societal acceptance as legitimate social actors, have begun interacting with state and market actors on behalf of certain constituents, and have become incorporated into transnational civil-society networks that pressure the state (Glenn & Mendelson 2002). Finally, this is also an important policy question given the efforts of many donors to strengthen the role of civil society in the policy process as a way to improve governance (World Bank 2001).

The few studies that touch upon the role of civil society in policy making in Central and Eastern Europe present mostly anecdotal evidence, primarily about the merits and limitations of NGOs, and rarely focus on their interaction with the state.[1] Such works also study predominantly the national level, where the 'success' of influencing the government is difficult to achieve and to evaluate. This article seeks to begin filling this gap in the literature by studying the consequences of political inclusion on local government efficacy. It asks the question: how has civic participation in local policy-making affected municipal performance?

Research design

Studying the effects of participation on government performance at the local level seems particularly appropriate. Because of the smaller scale of local politics, citizens perceive a more immediate and tangible interest in the outcome of political decisions. In addition, a greater sense of responsibility for one's actions and a heightened sense of personal efficacy are easier to develop at the subnational level. Last, it is within their own communities that citizens have the greatest number of opportunities to take part in and actually influence policy making (Illner 1998).

---

[1]With the exception of Cook and Vinogradova (2006), such discussions usually present observations about the existence of representation and accountability channels, governmental receptivity and third-sector motivations, and legitimacy and capacity of NGOs.

The 'Indicators of Local Democratic Governance in Central and Eastern Europe Project' (EE LG Indicators Project), conducted by the Local Government and Public Service Reform Initiative and the Tocqueville Research Center in Budapest, Hungary, is one of the few studies of civic participation and local governance in Eastern Europe.[2] The series of administrative leader surveys conducted in Latvia, Poland, Hungary and Romania in 2001 and 2002 and in Estonia, Bulgaria and Slovakia in 2003 and 2004 (Soós & Zentai 2005) reveal weak unmediated citizen participation in local government decisions but 'a positive role of civic groups' in the context of 'mutual [NGO-municipal] financial and non-financial support' (Wright 2002, p. 400). However, the EE LG Indicators Project mostly surveys the levels of civic participation and local governance efficacy in the region without exploring the relationship between the two. This article seeks to build on and extend the EE LG Indicators Project analysis by examining the relationship between participation and government performance.

The case study here focuses on research in Bulgaria. According to the NGO Sustainability Index for Central and Eastern Europe and Eurasia, prepared by USAID from 1998 to the present, Bulgaria is the closest to an 'average performer' of the countries in the post-communist region in terms of the development of the strength and viability of its NGO sector.[3] Moreover, Bulgaria is also near to the mean in terms of the average of citizens' network political capacity (Gibson 2001). Similarly, according to the EE LG Indicators Project, the overall government performance and civil society development at the local level in Bulgaria, as well as the relationship between the two, are typical for Eastern Europe (Swianiewicz 2006). Therefore, the Bulgarian case seems to be well suited to generate conclusions that are representative of developments in the post-communist region in general.[4] It may be reasonable to suggest therefore that processes similar to the positive civil society–government interactions found by the EE LG Indicators Project in the Bulgarian case are unfolding in other East European countries as well.[5]

This article incorporates some of the descriptive data from the Bulgarian EE LG Indicators Project. However, the analysis is based on the more reliable and to-the-point 2004 Ministry of Regional Development survey of all Bulgarian municipalities. The survey was administered by UNDP officials or their assistants from the National Association of Municipalities in the Republic of Bulgaria and from the Foundation

[2]For more information, see www.t-rc.org/ProjectActivities/Indicators/IndicatorsDescription.html, last accessed 1 February 2009.

[3]The Index is based largely on the understandings of both local and international donor experts and is collected, in part, through field-based focus groups. The Index is available at http://www.usaid.gov/locations/europe_eurasia/dem_gov/ngoindex/, accessed 1 February 2009.

[4]However, it should be noted that even though the Bulgarian case is a typical one for the region, there still might be a unique mechanism at work in the country. On typical case study research, see Gerring (2007).

[5]In addition to the EE LG Indicators Project, Gotchev (1998) and Dainov (2004) also find a 'positive' impact of civic inclusion in local governance on municipal performance in the Bulgarian case. This article thus builds on these arguments by testing them more rigorously and systematically on the population of all municipalities in the country. Moreover, this article links the contributions of civil society to local development to the professionalisation and organisational strength of Bulgarian NGOs and thus to the broader debate about the merits and drawbacks of the third sector nature of civil society in Eastern Europe.

for Local Government Reform. The majority of respondents were high-ranking municipal officials (a deputy mayor or a senior expert). Their answers were validated by district focus groups of local government employees and local and regional civil society representatives. The set of local authorities who responded ($N = 209$ or 80% of all municipalities) is highly representative of all municipalities in the country in terms of geography, size, development, performance and political inclusion (UNDP 2004).[6]

The survey was conducted to establish the training needs of local governments in Bulgaria, so there was no incentive for municipal officials to exaggerate their performance. Moreover, the answers to the survey were vetted and validated by regional focus groups in which local civil society participated. These groups were organised by officials from UNDP and from one of the two national civic organisations working with local governments in Bulgaria—the National Association of Municipalities in the Republic of Bulgaria, and the Foundation for Local Government Reform. The focus groups thus not only served to add details to the survey answers but also to correct any reports, which might have (intentionally or not) inflated the indicators of good municipal performance or deflated the indicators of poor municipal performance. Finally, the questions used in the analysis for this article do not rely on the self-assessment of local officials; rather, the questions ask those officials to report factual information about the work of their municipality, such as the date the local development strategy was developed, whether the citizenry was consulted in drafting the strategy, and the number of municipal projects which were funded by the EU.[7]

Furthermore, the survey analysis in this article is interpreted and supplemented with 60 interviews conducted by the author in six municipalities in two of the six Bulgarian regions. The municipalities were chosen to ensure variation on the independent variable (municipalities with high inclusion compared to municipalities with low inclusion rates) and (clusters of low, medium, and high values of) the control variables. The interviewees included some local government employees but mostly they were civil society and business representatives as well as some knowledgeable observers of local governance in Bulgaria such as donors, journalists and academics. The interviews independently verified the municipal survey answers for those regions and investigated the mechanisms underlying the impact of local civic participation on municipal performance.[8]

In examining the relationship between civic participation and local government performance, the latter is studied here as a measure of government efficacy, that is, the extent to which municipalities make and carry out prompt and relevant decisions in response to developments in their communities.[9] The scope of the participatory activities examined includes having a voice, taking part, and sharing in the policy-making process at the local level. Excluded are ceremonial support and protest, and

---

[6]Moreover, less than 0.05% of the answers to all questions were returned blank.

[7]For a full list of the questions used, see Appendix 1.

[8]All interviews were conducted in confidentiality and the names of the interviewees and their municipalities are withheld by mutual agreement. Again, for reasons of confidentiality, the names of the case study municipalities in this article are also omitted; these are referred to in the text by their initials.

[9]On government performance as operational efficacy, see Eckstein (1971).

influencing the selection of government officials through voting and voluntary associational activity not directed at the state.

The operationalisation of government performance and of civic participation are derived from municipal and civic practices in the process of crafting and implementing local development strategies.[10] In Bulgaria, these strategies detail government commitments in the realms of economic, social, infrastructural, environmental and other policies on the basis of which annual municipal budgets are drafted. Their preparation requires that local authorities assess the opportunities and challenges in their community, devise concrete proposals to address them, and then integrate those policies into a coherent vision, whether short-term, medium-term, and sometimes even long-term, for the development of the municipality. Local development strategies are a 'successor' practice of the socialist-era five-year plans, but have acquired new importance, as they are currently used by regional and national governments in the crafting of regional and national development strategies, as well as in the distribution of national investments and in applications for EU structural funds.

In addition, several variables are used to facilitate comparisons between different types of local governments and to control for competing explanations of government performance in analyses of the participation–performance relationship. Financial outlook combines mean wage, GDP *per capita*, income from taxes collected *per capita*, and other generated income *per capita* to measure the wealth of a municipality. Urbanisation levels are based on population density, population education levels, housing, water and waste-water treatment coverage, and income generated; they capture the municipal social development level. The minority unemployment rate is a proxy for the extent to which there is social conflict in the municipality. Population size stands in for the general socio-economic and human resources available to a local government. The extent to which a municipality consulted with and involved the central authorities in the preparation of its local development strategy and the projects under it is used to assess municipal relations with (and importance to) the centre. Finally, NGO capacity, or the number of civic groups per 10,000 people, equalises differences in civicness.

Municipal performance

In assessing government performance, this article is modelled after works on institutional performance that emphasise policy output (Putnam 1993; Stoner-Weiss 1997). It should be noted that even non-democratic governments might perform well according to these output-based performance indices. Thus, such measures have been criticised by those who believe that democratic governments should satisfy local needs with openness, transparency, fairness and inclusion of local citizens in the decision-making process (Laitin 1995). It seems, however, that this limitation of output-based policy measures is in fact a positive factor given the research question of this article: it helps distance performance from participation, and moreover, it also helps distinguish

---

[10]Municipal policy making is also frequently evaluated through the budget cycle practices of local governments; however, public involvement in the budget would not be a good measure in the Bulgarian context because public budget hearings have been mandatory in the country since 2004.

policy output from policy outcomes, as outcomes are the result of more than just government policy making.

In this article, government efficacy is evaluated on four institutional performance scales (for a summary of the dependent variable components, please refer to Appendix 1). First, the responsiveness scale aims to capture the ability of municipalities to respond quickly to developments in their communities. Given the dynamic nature of the country's transition to capitalist democracy, a responsive administration probably updates the local development strategy every year (most likely in the context of preparing the budget). Therefore, municipalities that updated their local development strategies every year received the highest score. It should be noted that the responsiveness scale does not assess the congruence between government policy and constituent demands. However, an attempt to capture the quality and relevance of municipal responsiveness is made through the policy process scales.

Secondly, the local development strategy implementation scale focuses on the degree to which municipalities have achieved their declared policy objectives. It measures the percentage of the local development strategy that has been actually implemented. Should there be a huge difference between municipalities in the number of political, socio-economic, or environmental problems to be resolved or in the aspirations (number of declared policy objectives) of local government, this index would obviously under-reward performing administrations. However, the introduction of a policy process scale in the performance measure and of control variables in the analysis is an effort to address this limitation of the implementation scale.

Thirdly, the two policy process scales link the two previous measures and improve their precision. Their purpose is to capture the quality of the local development policy. The municipal capacity to attract EU structural funds is taken into account to ensure that in their strategies and the programmes under them municipalities have identified real social needs and proposed sound solutions. According to two of our respondents, foreign donors reward municipalities that react comprehensively, coherently, and creatively to issues arising in their community, including difficult and often neglected problems (such as integration of vulnerable social groups).[11] External funding is important for another reason as well: the bulk of municipal budgets is spent either on remuneration of the municipal administration and public service (education and health care) personnel or on the maintenance of schools and hospitals;[12] therefore, any additional programmes usually require external funding, the securing of which thus becomes related to implementation. Therefore, the higher the ratio of ideas to proposals to approved EU structural funds projects, the higher the local government's ranking. Looking at EU funding seems particularly appropriate given Bulgaria's preparation for EU membership at the time of the survey and given the Union's attention to subsidiarity. In addition to external funding, another proxy for the quality

[11]Interviews with the author with: anonymous USAID Official, individual interview, 17 July 2004, Sofia, Bulgaria; anonymous individual from Foundation for Local Government Reform, individual interview, 14 July 2004, Sofia, Bulgaria.

[12]Other services, such as refuse collection and disposal, public transport, water supply, central heating, construction, reconstruction, and maintenance of roads and infrastructure, are provided by a variety of public and private agencies.

of local programmes is the competence of local officials in preparing and managing them. Because strategic planning and EU structural-funds' applications represent crucial but new and challenging municipal tasks, local officials who received recent training on both received the highest scores.

Patterns of municipal performance

A majority of Bulgarian local governments tried to respond to challenges and opportunities in their communities. A total of 65% of the municipalities created their current local development strategy within a year of the 1999 local elections, after which new decentralisation legislation was passed. Most (72%) of the municipalities had updated their strategies within the two years before the survey; small, poor, and underdeveloped governments were as responsive as large, rich, and/or modernised ones. However, 17% of local governments continued using their pre-2000 strategies and a half of this 17% did so without updating them.

The municipal record in implementing these strategies however, is less commendable: 48% of local authorities realised less than half of the goals listed in their development strategies. Surprisingly, it is not just poor, small or underdeveloped municipalities that have difficulties honouring their commitments. However, large urban and wealthy municipalities accumulated stronger experience in turning ideas into proposals and then receiving EU funding for the projects they propose. On average local governments proposed 5.7 ideas for programmes in their communities that could qualify for EU structural funding; they then prepared projects for 2.6 of them and obtained funding for 0.7 projects. Of all municipalities, 72% had no approved EU projects, 33% prepared no proposals and 20% had no ideas. Moreover, 31% of local governments reported that they would like help with or had experienced some difficulties in all aspects of project and programme preparation, 30% in formulating programme goals, 38% in properly aligning the programme with municipal strategic priorities, 25% in programme budget preparation, 31% in preparing project proposals, 48% in project management, 45% in project monitoring and 36% in project evaluation. Municipal reports are similar when it comes to strategic planning: 59% of local authorities mentioned difficulties with conducting assessment studies, 42% with formulating strategic priorities, 54% with the programmes for achieving them, and 39% with their monitoring and evaluation. Perhaps seeking to improve their implementation record, 39% of all municipal authorities trained their employees in both strategic planning and structural-funds applications; however, 28% of local governments (usually small municipalities but not necessarily poor or underdeveloped ones) trained employees in neither.

The EE LG Indicators Project adds some more detail (see Table 1) and helps explain these implementation rates by revealing an overall poor administrative competence in the country. Municipal councillors assessed the competence of their local administrations as an average of 3.88 on a 1–7 scale, and they considered their administrations to be politically biased to a similar extent: 3.49 on a 1–7 scale. It is usual practice in the country that each newly elected mayor dismisses all chief administrative officers (the secretary of the municipal administration and the heads of departments) (Minkova *et al.* 2006). Quite a few local governments continued to be exploited by political

TABLE 1
LOCAL STATE ADMINISTRATIVE CAPACITY IN BULGARIA

	High capacity	Medium capacity	Low capacity
Quorum	Always (55.5%)	—	None (44.5%)
Extraordinary sessions	< 10% (82%)	10–20% (5.8%)	> 20% (12%)
Postponement of decisions	Rarely (56%)	Occasionally (37%)	Every session (7%)
Budget promptness	Yes (90%)	—	No (10%)
Difference between real and projected budget costs	Most (32%)	Half (15%)	Some (38%)
Projects completed on time	Most (33%)	Half (24%)	Some (38%)

Source: EE LG Indicators Project, available at: www.t-rc.org/ProjectActivities/Indicators/Indicators Description.html, last accessed 1 February 2009.

parties seeking to draw reputational as well as material resources and to favour allies in state appointments and contracts (Bluebird Group 2003; Ganev 2007; Grzymala-Busse 2007). When asked about the most frequent reason for delay in council decisions, 39% of municipalities pointed to ineffective communication between inexperienced municipal administrations and municipal councils and 40% of municipalities pointed to frequent interparty conflicts and time-consuming, unproductive partisan debates, which repeatedly provoked a 'failing quorum' or postponed decisions (Minkova *et al.* 2006). Given the rapid pace of the transition, the politicisation of local governments and the subsequent high official turnover within them made learning difficult and compromised the ability of Bulgarian municipalities to develop and implement policies. Therefore, even though local officials were familiar with municipal problems (UNDP 2004) and were deeply integrated into the life of their local community (Minkova *et al.* 2006), many local governments had not become effective as an administrative and executive force.[13]

In sum, local officials were well integrated into their communities and generally sought to respond to local developments; however, their ability to do so was somewhat compromised in quite a few cases by their relatively low administrative capacity.

Participation in municipal governance

Participation is measured here on five scales, which together are designed to capture the extent and the nature of the involvement in the local development policy-making of private citizens and organised social and economic interests directly or through intermediary organisations or persons.[14]

At the planning stage, some municipalities conduct polls and hold public discussions, advisory council meetings, stakeholders' focus groups, and public forums as a way to solicit feedback on municipal performance, to learn about the needs of their constituents, and to gather their input on the programmes they would like to see in the future. Different agenda-setting opportunities, however, produce different

---

[13]On similar challenges in the other Central and Eastern European countries, see UNDP (2001) and von Breska and Brusis (1999).

[14]For a summary of the independent variable components, see Appendix 1.

qualities of interaction among civic groups and between civic groups and local authorities. For example, a forum is conducted to facilitate an agreement that is as acceptable to as many societal actors as possible and that is binding to the government; a poll, on the other hand, can be rather limited in terms of the amount, quality, and impact of the information that citizens submit in their answers. Interviewed municipal officials identified forums, meetings with stakeholders, and advisory councils as the most useful, followed by general public meetings, and then by polls. Therefore, the more transformative the participation channels frequently used, the higher the score the municipality received. In addition, some municipalities solicited feedback on their local development strategy as well as on the project drafts that were parts of it. The more diverse the set of actors that were consulted, the higher the municipality was ranked.

At the implementation stage, local governments were ranked according to the frequency and extent to which they involved private citizens and major social and economic actors in implementing projects and programmes that realised the policy objectives detailed in the municipality's local development strategy. Municipalities invited civic participation in the provision of local services and in the achievement of other local development goals by sharing with relevant societal actors a project's management, funds and technical equipment. The types of civic–municipal coopera-tion considered here include delegating through material or non-material support for projects by private citizens, NGOs and local businesses and partnering with any of these actors in running externally funded joint projects. The more such initiatives a municipality took on, the higher was its ranking. Also, local authorities that participated with both financial and non-financial resources (relative to the wealth of the municipality) received the highest scores because the pledging of material resources usually increased the commitment of both societal actors and their government to work together towards shared development goals.

Tendencies of citizen–municipal interaction

Cooperation between local governments and societal actors seems widespread and takes various forms. There are three agenda-setting opportunities on average each year in larger municipalities and 2.5 in smaller municipalities (Minkova *et al.* 2006). Eighteen percent of local authorities frequently set up public forums, 34% consulted stakeholders' focus groups, 53% organised public discussions, 35% held advisory council meetings and 31% conducted polls. Only 12% of all the municipalities attempted none of these. Generally, poorer municipalities relied relatively more on public discussions (perhaps because they are inexpensive and easy to organise), whereas bigger municipalities consulted with stakeholder focus groups (rather than with their large general population) and held more public forums more frequently.

Moreover, 51% of local governments invited societal actors to participate in the drafting of the local development strategy, with small, rural and poor authorities equally represented. Of all the municipalities, 56% invited NGOs to help them improve the projects planned under the strategy, 48% consulted businesses, and 25% the local citizenry; 9% solicited feedback from all three groups of actors, whereas 22% involved none. Consultations with the citizenry occurred in all types of municipalities, but the more developed and bigger municipalities tended to also invite more NGOs and businesses.

At the same time, the EE LG Indicators Project reported that even though one fifth of all municipal councillors and one third of all mayors held a position in a civic organisation, the influence of societal actors on decision making on local policy was perceived to be lower than the influence of political actors. On a scale of 0–7, municipal councillors ranked the influence of NGOs at 2.8, of affected citizens at 3.5, and of businesses at 3.8, compared with the influence of the mayor at 5.3, of municipal council committees at 4.6, of civil servants at 3.5, of local political parties at 4.4, and of the central government at 4.3. Local chief administrative officers ranked civic influence even lower: NGOs at 2.2, affected citizens at 2.8, and businesses at 3.0, compared with the mayor at 6.4, municipal council committees at 5.3, civil servants at 3.7, local political parties at 3.4 and the central government at 4.4.

At the implementation stage, 36% of the municipalities had extensive experience in implementation cooperation, and urban, rich and large municipalities were disproportionately represented in the latter group. Only 17% of local governments reported that they have not cooperated with civil society in implementing any projects. Societal actors seem to be the leading partners in those. A total of 39% of municipalities committed mainly non-material resources, while 51% committed both non-material and financial resources. The committed material resources seem to be primarily concentrated in a few projects: 33% of local governments reported financial commitment to a few joint projects, whereas only 16% reported financial commitment to many such projects. Compared with other municipalities of the same financial status, while 42% of local government under-committed financial support, only 18% over-committed material resources. At the implementation stage, as at the planning stage, municipalities seemed to prefer working with NGOs to cooperating with businesses or individual citizens: 19% of local authorities had not supported an NGO, compared with 38% who had not supported initiatives by individual citizens.

Overall, 21% of local governments noted difficulties in developing partnerships with societal actors at the implementation stage; in addition, 33% of Bulgarian municipalities assessed their overall cooperation with local NGOs as poor, and 42% saw their cooperation with local businesses as unsatisfactory. This might have been partially due to the preference for and ease of involving formal civic actors and their uneven distribution across the country—there were no formal civil-society organisations in 24% of all municipalities, and smaller, less urbanised, and less wealthy municipalities were disproportionately represented in this group. There was an average of 8.5 NGOs in municipalities with over 50,000 residents compared with an average of 0.98 in municipalities with fewer than 10,000 people; the average number of NGOs per municipality was three.

In sum, municipalities tended to rely more on municipal councils for public representation than on social and economic actors. This is probably not surprising given that allowing for broader participation requires the institutionalisation of special mechanisms for consultation. Furthermore, still quite a few local governments remained somewhat passive when it comes to encouraging participation at the implementation stage. However, because of the strong initiative of citizens, businesses, and especially NGOs, societal actors were increasingly involved in the development of their communities. Finally, bigger and more urban municipalities appeared to be more inclusive, and NGOs were the preferred but not exclusive partners of local authorities.

The impact of participation on municipal performance

Scholarly and policy debates point to several implications of citizen involvement in public affairs. The greater inclusion of citizens in the policy-making process is believed to sometimes slow down or even paralyse decision making and policy implementation or to compromise the coherence and consistency of government policy, in part because of the mere cacophony of demands it introduces, and in part because some of the potential participants might lack the democratic loyalty or the technical knowledge necessary to take part in governance. Moreover, practitioners also point out that in some cases participation can create animosities between participating groups and in the community at large, further complicating policy making (Huntington 1975; Schumpeter 1962; Strange 1972; Verba 2003).

At the same time, it has been argued also that greater citizen involvement can increase information on which policy makers draw in developing and implementing policies and evaluating their effects. In addition, participation in the making of political decisions increases the likelihood that decisions will be effectively carried out, because such policies would respond to social needs and because those who take part in the decisions are more likely to support those decisions. Finally, it is argued that public involvement can mitigate social conflict because of the transformative effects of political empowerment through participation: individuals become more public-spirited, tolerant, knowledgeable and attentive to the interests of others (Barber 1984; Lane & Wolf 1990; Pateman 1970; Stiglitz 2002; Verba 2003).

Thus, the literature suggests two sets of competing mechanisms—first, information and noise, and second, cooptation and conflict—that may be at work at the same time. To examine such a possibly uneven impact, this article first looks at the correlations between the various inclusion and efficacy components, and then aggregates them and studies the relationship of the aggregated participation and performance measures.

A differential impact of inclusion?

The only component of participation that affects local development strategy currency is feedback on the strategy draft. The implementation rate of the local development strategy, on the other hand, is significantly and positively influenced by all participation components. However, transformative agenda-setting and strategy-draft feedback are the most influential factors shaping implementation rates. Inclusion at the implementation level is the kind of participation that is most important in obtaining external assistance (see Table 2).

All planning components influence strategy implementation positively. Moreover, broad (strategy and project) draft feedback probably makes plans more realistic and socially grounded, and therefore more implementable, but also improves the quality of the strategy and the programmes under it, as demonstrated by the increased EU validation for their coherence and innovation. In addition to inclusion in planning, cooperation over implementation is also significant to policy quality and output.

TABLE 2

PARTICIPATION AND PERFORMANCE COMPONENTS CORRELATIONS

Kendall's tau-b sig (2-tailed)	Strategy currency	Strategy implementation	EU funding	Training
Agenda setting	0.104	0.258	0.106	0.154
	(0.123)	(0.002)	(0.086)	(0.018)
Strategy feedback	0.227	0.246	0.147	0.308
	(0.000)	(0.001)	(0.033)	(0.000)
Project feedback	0.061	0.142	0.155	0.239
	(0.357)	(0.023)	(0.011)	(0.000)
Common projects	−0.020	0.145	0.411	0.458
	(0.790)	(0.043)	(0.000)	(0.000)
Resource commitment	0.018	0.100	0.336	0.329
	(0.806)	(0.149)	(0.000)	(0.000)

Not only does civic involvement appear to increase the range of provided services by bringing in expertise, equipment, volunteers and funding, but it also seems to be useful in helping local authorities introduce ideas, turn them into proposals and then secure funding for them. Finally, it seems that participation does not slow down policy making (or at least, it does not interfere with regular updates of the local development strategy). In fact, consulting with societal actors on the development strategy draft itself appears to encourage local governments to update it regularly; perhaps, instead of existing just on paper, the strategy acquires real meaning, stemming from real social needs, so local authorities find it useful in guiding local development.

This article proceeds by analysing the relationship of the integrated participation and performance variables. The five components of participation aggregate into a moderately reliable (Cronbach's Alpha = 0.689) one-dimensional inclusion factor (one Varimax principal component according to the Kaiser criterion). However, it captures only about half of the variation of the original components. To preserve some more of this variation, the five components of participation were also split into two factors, which seem to be not just empirically but also theoretically meaningful since they have significant (above 0.6) positive component loadings and correspond to the combined participation measures at the two stages in the policy-making process: planning and implementation. The performance measures also aggregate into a moderately reliable (Cronbach's Alpha = 0.547) one-dimensional inclusion factor (one Varimax principal component according to the Kaiser criterion), which was also split into two factors. These principal components are both empirically and theoretically meaningful as well: they, too, have significant positive component loadings and gravitate around the two theoretical dimensions of municipal efficacy—responsiveness and implementation (with the policy process scales being a part of the implementation factor).

Even when controlling for municipal size, development, wealth, social conflict and relations with the centre, the planning inclusion factor is weakly positive but still significantly correlated with responsiveness, and both planning participation and implementation participation factors are moderately positively correlated with implementation. Moreover, there is positive and moderate correlation between the overall inclusion factor and the implementation factor, and a positive and weak but still significant correlation between the overall inclusion factor and the responsiveness factor (see Table 3).

Another way to study the relationship between inclusion and performance is to aggregate their components into composite indices. Because there is no theoretical reason why some components of participation or performance would matter more than others, and because the original participation and performance components are constructed on the same scales, they can be aggregated by simple summation. While this reduces both participation and performance to one-dimensional constructs (which is somewhat problematic for performance), it recaptures the variation lost in the factor analysis and allows for some result triangulation. It also allows for aggregating performance into a single variable and evaluating the impact of the different types of participation on overall performance. Participation again is significantly and positively correlated with performance. Even when controlling for municipal size, development, wealth, and social conflict, implementation participation and overall inclusion are moderately associated with overall performance, whereas planning participation is weakly but still significantly associated with overall participation (see Table 4).

In conclusion, participation appears to be a factor in improving local government efficacy: first, planning participation is correlated with responsiveness, implementation and overall performance, but weakly; secondly, implementation cooperation is associated with both implementation and overall performance improvements; and thirdly, overall inclusion affects both implementation and overall performance more than does responsiveness.

TABLE 3
PARTICIPATION AND PERFORMANCE FACTORS CORRELATIONS

Partial correlation coefficient sig (2-tailed)	Responsiveness factor	Implementation factor
Planning participation factor	0.321 (0.001)	0.287 (0.003)
Implementation participation factor	0.113 (0.246)	0.334 (0.000)
Overall participation factor	0.316 (0.002)	0.523 (0.000)

Note: control variables: municipal size, municipal wealth, urbanisation level, social conflict and relations with the centre.

TABLE 4
PARTICIPATION AND OVERALL PERFORMANCE COMPOSITE INDICES CORRELATIONS

Partial correlation coefficient sig (2-tailed)	Overall performance composite index
Planning participation composite index	0.255 (0.011)
Implementation participation composite index	0.528 (0.000)
Overall participation composite index	0.569 (0.000)

Note: control variables: municipal size, municipal wealth, urbanisation level, social conflict and relations with the centre.

A virtuous cycle?

What underlies this positive association between inclusion and performance; and what is the direction of causality? It is important to note that when asked how local development could be strengthened, 62% of local governments suggested improving municipal cooperation with the public, NGOs and businesses. Moreover, this recognition that better cooperation with societal actors would improve local development is also positively correlated with the implementation factor and both inclusion factors. In other words, 'the longer the experience of working with NGOs, the greater the number of problems that have been solved and the greater the [local] administration's inclination to cooperate with NGOs' (Dainov 2001, p. 12).

The interviews conducted for this project reveal that early attempts at cooperation are often initiated by proactive mayors or by representatives of civil society itself, sometimes on the suggestion of (foreign or domestic) donors or of one of the two associations of municipalities in the country, and frequently in relation to some external funding opportunity.[15] Such proactive mayors welcomed NGOs because of their expertise in developing and implementing projects, the fresh resources secured through them, and the (resultant) influence of NGOs over sections of the public that were most likely to be unserved and therefore discontented (Dainov 2004). To improve their service provision and win votes in the future, many local governments also adopted some NGOs' suggestions for more efficient and friendly administration such as providing information services about the municipality, setting up front offices in the municipality, and moving to a 'single-point' service culture (Dainov 2004). Having demonstrated that participation can be beneficial to local authorities in working towards local development, such early cooperation helped create something of a 'virtuous cycle' of further (broader and more involved) participation and improved municipal performance. Subsequently, mayors began introducing new channels for civic participation from regular town hall meetings to local media broadcasts of municipal council meetings, thus inviting NGOs to monitor policies and participate in the making of local decisions. With such practices came the appreciation that NGOs have the capacity and expertise to 'be part of the entire process of policy—from strategy and policy design, to policy implementation and evaluation' (Dainov 2004, p. 5).

An example of this is the cooperation of municipality V with local civic groups working with people with disabilities. Cooperation began in the mid-1990s with a few projects aimed at providing social assistance (such as transport and specialised healthcare) to members of the minority group. Recognising that such local state–civic cooperation improved the level and quality of the municipal social services as well as the ability of the local authorities to provide them, in 1998 municipality V and its civic

---

[15]Dainov (2004, p. 6) reports similar findings: 'What usually happens is that NGOs (or independent experts) become aware that funding (increasingly EU funding) is available for a big initiative. They take it to a municipality with a good track record in the problematic or in dialogue with NGOs. Then other stakeholders come in (local businesses, central authorities etc.) and become partners in the design and then the implementation of the project. Or a municipality seeks out NGO expertise to structure a big project, gets the funding and then implements it in partnership with the NGO and other stakeholders'.

partners created an advisory council for the 'Social Integration of People with Disabilities'.[16] The council, which included representatives of seven NGOs working with this minority and municipal officials responsible for local education, employment, city planning, social services and cultural policies, discussed the special needs of this minority and developed policies to meet them. An example of a council recommendation implemented by municipality V was a set of local taxes and fees relief measures for people with disabilities. The work of the council was such a success that the number of NGOs involved grew twofold in the first five years. Moreover, the integration of people with disabilities was included as one of the four priority areas in municipality V's Social Policy Initiative which was launched in 2003. The initiative committed municipality V to a set of social measures prepared in consultation with municipality V's civil society and implemented in part through joint projects financed at least partially through the local budget. An example of civic input for improving municipal programmes was a suggestion by the local NGOs working with people with disabilities that a representative of theirs be included in the city planning committee to advise and monitor the implementation of the Access for Disabled People Act, and that a municipal ombudsman dealing with complaints by people with disabilities be set up; municipality V put both suggestions into practice within a year. At the implementation stage, an example of the joint municipal–civic efforts was the local shuttle service for people with disabilities; Foundation E secured the capital investment for the service and trained the service staff, while municipality V covered the operating expenses for the service, which is now provided to more than 250 people a month.

The focus groups conducted with the 2004 Ministry of Regional Development survey also revealed another related trend. With the strengthening of participation in local policy-making, the subsequently enhanced government efficacy changed the nature of public involvement. Local governments in Bulgaria can be grouped into three broad categories depending on the extent and type of citizen participation in policy making (UNDP 2004). First, there is a group of usually small municipalities with weak civil societies in which public involvement is limited to representation through municipal councillors and sometimes direct engagement with the citizenry. Second, there is a group of local governments with limited experience in involving NGOs and local businesses on an *ad hoc* basis and in addressing specific local problems. These local governments tend to depend on non-governmental organisations for project or programme preparation and management, but as they accumulate experience with common projects with civil society, they are also more likely to invite NGOs to give feedback on the local development strategy and/or the programmes under it. Last, there is a group of local governments that already have an extensive record in engaging the citizenry in local development. In those cases, civil society participates in both the planning and the implementation of both local development in general and individual programmes under it in particular. Moreover, in these instances, municipal officials seek partners for joint projects rather than for project management and further ask for counsel on specific issues or tasks (such as

---

[16]Interview no. 7: anonymous civic activist working with people with disabilities, individual interview, 7 June 2004, municipality V, Bulgaria.

assessments or monitoring schemes) rather than on programme preparation or implementation.

In other words, it seems that local governments grow in the evolution of their partnership with civil society, from requiring fairly comprehensive assistance to being able to utilise the strengths of their civic partners in different policy settings as their experience grows. This dynamic is well documented in the case of municipality V, in which cooperation began with the implementation of several *ad hoc* projects, then moved to the inclusion of NGOs working with people with disabilities in the development of the local social policy through the advisory council, and eventually to implementation (and planning) of the individual social programmes through the Social Policy Initiative. In addition, over time municipality V began inviting more and more cooperation on specific tasks such as monitoring of specific municipal commitments (for instance, accessibility of public buildings) rather than wholesale management of programmes.

To confirm this 'virtuous cycle' relationship between inclusion and performance, a non-recursive structural equation model was constructed (see Figure 1).[17] Socio-economic factors (Dahl 1971; Lipset 1960) and socio-cultural factors (Almond & Verba 1963) have long been offered to explain government performance and are used here to define the model.[18] Since it is theorised that social development and economic wellbeing underlie effective government, whereas social conflict undermines it, the model includes municipal urbanisation, wealth and size (capturing the general human resource endowment) and minority unemployment (as a proxy for social conflict in the municipality) as exogenous factors affecting the performance of local authorities. In addition, since relations with the national authorities have also been seen to be important to local government performance, to the extent that the centre can facilitate local policy formulation and implementation in a financial and non-material manner (Stoner-Weiss 1997), a 'relations with the centre' indicator was also included as an exogenous influence on municipal efficacy.

Finally, NGO capacity and inclusion are the variables included in the model to represent the socio-cultural factors theorised as influencing government performance. NGO capacity captures the social structure that allows for and in part mediates political inclusion, which is in turn hypothesised to affect municipal efficacy but to also be influenced by it. Both inclusion and performance are modelled as latent variables, which are indirectly measured by the respective civic participation and municipal efficacy components described earlier. Urbanisation, wealth and size—but not necessarily social conflict—are theorised as both accompanying and also creating an environment for the development of civil society (Putnam 1993, 2000). These relationships are captured by the covariances between these variables in

[17]Researchers have found that 'normally distributed' variables containing four or more ordered categories treated as continuous produce robust and only slightly underestimated fit indices (Green *et al.* 1997), parameter estimates, and standard errors and factor correlations (Babakus *et al.* 1987); therefore, since the ordinal variables in the model contain four categories and appear approximately normally distributed, maximum likelihood estimation is used (on categorical data in structural equation modelling; see also Finey and diStefano (2006).

[18]Institutional design, which has also been deemed to have an impact on government efficacy (Eckstein & Apter 1963), is held constant in this study.

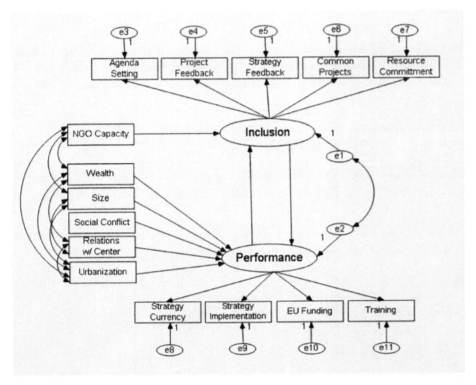

FIGURE 1. INCLUSION–PERFORMANCE CYCLE STRUCTURAL EQUATION MODEL

the model. The second set of covariances represents the understanding that big urban municipalities are more important to the centre and (as a result) are wealthier too.

The model is significant and stable overall. It confirms the understanding that a virtuous cycle relationship between inclusion and performance is appropriate given the data (see Table 5). Both inclusion and performance are significant and positively associated with each other.[19] Performance has a slightly stronger effect on inclusion than the other way around, which may be in part due to the fact that there are fewer factors that are important to inclusion than there are determinants of performance. It should also be noted that the NGO capacity of a municipality is not a good predictor of inclusion—a finding that perhaps reflects a trend of civic–municipal cooperation even where the formal civic mediating structures are weak as well as a trend of their possible under-utilisation where they are developed.

[19]It is noteworthy that neither of the social-economic variables significantly contributes to explaining the differences in overall local government performance. However, since the goal of the article is to study the relationship between performance and inclusion (rather than to account for municipal efficacy), the social-economic variables are kept in the model because of their importance as controls.

TABLE 5

INCLUSION–PERFORMANCE STRUCTURAL EQUATION MODEL MAXIMUM LIKELIHOOD ESTIMATION RESULTS

Relationship	Standardised estimate	P-level
Inclusion ← Agenda Setting	0.473	0.000
Inclusion ← Strategy Feedback	0.581	0.000
Inclusion ← Project Feedback	0.542	0.000
Inclusion ← Common Projects	0.598	0.000
Inclusion ← Resource Commitment	0.629	0.000
Performance ← Strategy Currency	0.126	0.106
Performance ← Strategy Implementation	0.330	0.000
Performance ← EU Funding	0.344	0.002
Performance ← Training	0.481	0.000
Inclusion ← NGO Capacity	0.106	0.287
Performance ← Municipal size	0.152	0.294
Performance ← Municipal Wealth	−0.014	0.666
Performance ← Urbanisation Level	0.060	0.355
Performance ← Social Conflict	−0.062	0.337
Performance ← Relations with the Centre	0.034	0.454
Performance ← Inclusion	0.723	0.037
Inclusion ← Performance	0.896	0.001

Notes: CMIN (3.88), P (0.144), CMIN/DF (1.940); RMSEA (0.067). Model probability (0.000); model stability (0.648).

Civil society and the state: different configurations and different relationships?

Before concluding that civic inclusion has served to improve local government efficacy in Bulgaria, a final word of caution is in order. Scholarly debates on the implications of citizen involvement in public affairs emphasise that the impact of inclusion can also differ according to the strength and thickness of state–society connections in a polity (Bermeo & Nord 2000). A strong state and a strong civil society is believed to be the optimal (and the only) power configuration that is good for democracy. In this scenario, the state has the capacity to be effective, while society has the capacity to prevent the state from becoming so autonomous as to be unresponsive. The worst constellation for democracy is a weak state and a strong society in which the state's capacity for policy implementation is likely to be overwhelmed by society's demands, leading to overburdening, ineffectiveness and a potential breakdown or overthrowing of the state by powerful interests within civil society. If a weak civil society faces a strong state, actors linked to the state rule in their own interests autonomously from civil society. Where both the state and society are weak, there is likely to be a power vacuum and thus a regime vulnerable to overthrow (Bernhard 1996). These hypotheses are useful for and can be adapted to understanding the quality of local democracy.

To examine the differential impact of participation on municipal performance in relation to the local state–society balance, the article proceeds by splitting the data into four clusters, according to the combined strength of the local authorities and local civil society. The first is evaluated on the basis of municipal capacity self-assessments (reports of low capacity), and the second is based on the number of civic groups per 10,000 people. Unfortunately, because two of the clusters have too few municipalities in them, they returned unstable (not well-defined) relationships when run with the non-recursive structural equation model described above. However, although it is not possible to separate accurately the impact of participation on performance from the influence of performance on participation for each cluster, the correlations between inclusion and efficacy in the four scenarios still tell an interesting story. The association between participation and performance is positive in all four state–society configurations and is significant in all but the strong state and weak society case. The correlation is the strongest in the weak state and strong society scenario and weakest in the strong state and weak society case. Furthermore, within the strong society category, the performance–participation association grows when moving from the strong-state group to the weak-state group and, within the weak society category, the association becomes significant (see Table 6). In other words, at least in Bulgaria, at the local level, it seems that if societal strength is held constant, participation improves municipal efficacy (more) where state capacity is lower.

Interpreting the results: reconstituting state capacity through civic participation

How can the findings in this article be interpreted? What is the civic contribution to local government performance in Bulgaria and possibly elsewhere in the region? Previous works on local democracy suggest that civil society 'has found a way to compensate for the deficits of government' (Dainov 2004) by bringing in additional expertise, representing different community interest and mobilising citizen support for local development initiatives (Gotchev 1998; Dainov 2004). The survey data and the focus groups conducted with it, as well as the interviews for this study, also indicate that local governments seek to enhance local state capacity and consequently improve government efficacy by devolving parts of their authority to societal actors through civic participation in the different stages and aspects of policy making. Many local governments lack personnel with extensive experience in policy formulation, implementation and evaluation, and moreover, do not retain highly competent personnel. Faced with the challenges of decentralised governance, many subnational authorities have discovered valuable problem-solving expertise, experience in representing particular constituents, and new resources in the third sector, precisely because of its professionalism and organisational strength.

As the state–society cluster analysis presented above suggests, NGO professionalism seems to make up for municipal expertise where it is underdeveloped. Many

TABLE 6

PARTICIPATION–PERFORMANCE COMPOSITE INDICES CORRELATIONS BY STATE–SOCIETY CONFIGURATION

Partial correlation coefficient *sig (2-tailed) (% municipalities)*	*Weak society*	*Strong society*
Strong state	0.264 (0.213) [32%]	0.641 (0.000) [21%]
Weak state	0.628 (0.000) [35%]	0.679 (0.031) [11%]

Note: control variables: municipal size, municipal wealth, urbanisation level, social conflict and relations with the centre.

interviewees mentioned that the most immediate and tangible benefit of cooperating with civil society comes when NGOs bring funding from external or private donors and run all or part of a project. Not only do donors like to see some civic involvement in a government project, but NGOs usually have much experience in identifying priorities and ways to achieve them, developing proposals, and then managing their implementation, since NGO survival frequently depends on obtaining support with exactly those skills.

An example of how such NGO expertise is utilised in local governance can be seen in the following case. Most of the large Roma population in municipality M lives in the outskirts of the municipal city and thus has poor access to a variety of social services. In the early 2000s, a local NGO, Foundation S, which had been working with Roma youth, began putting together a programme for reducing drop-out rates among local Roma students. Foundation S's assessment determined that the low quality of the education at the Roma school doomed the children to almost no career opportunities and to a future of high unemployment and low social status. The municipality, which also wanted to improve the social integration of the Roma minority, invited Foundation S to several informal meetings to discuss the challenges the minority faced. Foundation S proposed a two-pronged strategy: Roma school desegregation and involving the Roma community in keeping Roma youth in school. Foundation S and municipality M decided to cooperate to implement Foundation S's proposal. The Foundation prepared a project proposal and secured $43,000 of funding for it from a foreign donor. Foundation S and municipality M (in cooperation with the Regional Inspectorate of Education of the Ministry of Education and Science) worked together to place more than 200 Roma children living in the municipal outskirts in five Bulgarian-dominated schools and two Bulgarian-dominated kindergartens in the city. The Foundation also provided free textbooks, transport to school and after-school tutoring to the Roma students participating in this programme. Moreover, the Foundation encouraged informal leaders of the Roma community to liaise between the Roma parents and the Bulgarian teachers to improve the educational experience of the Roma students in order to keep them in school. Some of the results of this initiative included full participation in school by the relocated students, improved educational achievements of these Roma children, and the increased involvement of Roma students in extracurricular activities, which not only helped to keep them in school but also contributed to their social integration.

In sum, 'NGO initiatives [... have] gradually substituted for government programs which have limited impact due to budget constraints, scarce resources, and also because they are not participatory' (Gotchev 1998, p. 40). Such civic inclusion is most developed in 'the provision of social and health services, vocational training and retraining of the unemployed, introduction of alternative employment, development of anti-poverty strategies and strategies for socializing of individuals and groups marginalized for economic, ethnic, religious and other reasons, taking care of people with disabilities, drug addicts and homeless children' (Gotchev 1998, p. 40).

Moreover, many interviewees mentioned that having observed the work of local, regional or national NGOs, many Bulgarian municipalities also quickly recognised that the expertise of these non-state actors could be useful in a variety of aspects of strategic planning as well, including 'collecting or donating and analysing data to come up with a precise and realistic picture of the opportunities and challenges for development in the municipality' as well as finding 'innovative solutions to some serious problems in the community' (NAMRB 2001b, p. 4). Returning to the example of municipality M, the local authorities built on the success of their cooperation with Foundation S by inviting it and other local NGOs to work with several Roma municipal councillors and municipal experts on ethnic and demographic issues in order to develop a long-term Plan for Educational Integration of Children and Students of Roma Origin, to be implemented with municipal funding and in part in cooperation with local youth and minority NGOs. Additionally, the municipality set up an Advisory Board on the Education of Children from Ethnic Minorities to the M Municipal Council. The Board invited Roma NGOs, representatives of the Regional Inspectorate of Education and school and kindergarten principals and teachers to participate in the development of local education policies.

In another example, in the late 1990s, civil society representatives in municipality L began discussing ways of working with the local authorities in order to cooperate in seeking solutions to current municipal problems. In 1999, under the leadership of a local NGO, Association K, 12 NGOs and the local government developed and secured funding from the EU Phare Program for Bulgaria for a project called 'Building Sustainable Mechanisms for Cooperation Between NGOs and Local Authority in the Municipality of L'. NGO–state cooperation under the project focused on three municipal policy priorities: women's health, the integration of mentally and physically disabled children, and the effective use of municipal property. Participating civic elite members, government officials, and media representatives took part in three focus groups, which were tasked with analysing the local challenges and opportunities in their issue area and with coming up with concrete proposals for addressing the needs of the local population. The municipality and the NGOs then worked individually and collectively on attracting local and foreign business sponsors and donors to supplement the project funds and implement several projects that came out of the focus group proposals. By the end of the year, programmes had been implemented for: a women's health free clinic at the local hospital; some local affordable housing improvements; a service centre for children with special needs; and an information bureau to catalogue the services that the municipality offers to citizens (NAMRB 2001a). Moreover, municipality L began including in its budget funds for continuing the cooperation between state and non-state actors related to problems in the municipality, including cooperative research on important social problems, participation of NGO representatives in the established permanent committees and temporary bodies of the municipal council, participation of NGOs in the initiatives of the local government, future joint activities, and active partnership for educating citizens on the problems of local self-government and stimulating their motivation for finding solutions of municipal problems. (See Appendix 2 for further examples of common civic inclusion practices from municipalities throughout Bulgaria.)

Lastly, many NGOs have contributed to local development not just by effectively representing and advocating for the interests of their constituents but also by encouraging further broader inclusion (even if their motivation for cooperating with a municipality might also include gaining legitimacy and ensuring their own survival). Civic actors have worked to stimulate indigenous civic initiatives and to mobilise citizens' support for local development projects and programmes by encouraging local philanthropy and volunteerism (Gotchev 1998). As a mayor who invited local NGOs to participate in a municipal advisory council explained his decision, 'local non-governmental organizations have a lot of experience in involving the citizenry in public life, in polling public opinions and preferences, and aggregating local interests and solving conflicts' (NAMRB 2001a, p. 4). Indeed, the UNDP survey, too, indicates that the local authorities in municipalities with high NGO capacity are more inclusive in planning and have a higher rate of supporting common citizen and business initiatives. Such broader inclusion not only improves the quality of municipal plans but also adds to the implementation roles of NGOs.

For instance, in 2000, municipality S signalled its readiness to work with the local civic society by inviting two national NGOs working with Bulgarian municipalities to help the mayor's office organise a local development forum. The same year, five NGOs from the municipality formed a coalition of civic groups interested in cooperating with the local authorities on local development issues. In 2001, the municipality began looking for foreign technical and financial assistance to develop and adopt methodologies and tools for long-term investment planning while promoting state–civic partnerships in the investment planning process. At the same time, the NGO coalition approached the local government with a proposal for two joint initiatives: since the municipality had identified environmental sustainability as one of its priorities, and given the strength of local ecological groups, the NGO coalition suggested organising an Ecological Awareness week and preparing a public discussion on illegal deforestation. Both initiatives invited local journalists and citizens to volunteer in and organise programmes for local environmental preservation as well as to participate in educating the local residents about the issue. The state–civic cooperation was further strengthened through the local development forum implemented in municipality S in 2002.

Building on the achievements of the forum, in 2002 the civic local development coalition, which had grown to 14 local NGOs, called on the local government to implement a municipal Programme for Civic Initiatives, which would support projects prepared not only by NGOs but also by school boards, community centres and even informal citizen groups. The coalition saw the programme as an opportunity for citizens and non-state actors to identify and address local communal concerns. In 2003, the local authorities, which had secured the support of a US donor, began putting in place a community-driven municipal investment process that provides a framework and a process for participatory local governance. As a result, local NGOs, school boards, community centres and informal citizen groups are now invited annually to present proposals for improving the quality of life in the municipality. A steering committee (staffed by local political and civic elite members) decided which projects the local government would support by providing up to 70% of the necessary resources and 90% of the funding for each of them. In the first year alone, NGOs, community centres, school and church boards, businesses and informal citizen groups submitted 60 proposals, which clearly signalled the local development priorities of residents in municipality S. Moreover, the civic partners for each of the approved seven projects additionally mobilised the local population to volunteer labour, and local businesses to donate money, for the implementation of the proposed improvements of the local infrastructure, education, sports and culture, and tourism. (See Appendix 3 for additional examples of how civic actors mobilised the public to participate in local development.)

In sum, although the politicisation of the local state undermined its capacity, many local governments were able not only to reconstitute some of their authority but also to improve the quality of their policy making by employing the capacity and authority of key local civic actors. Many municipalities have been cooperating with local NGOs and thus borrowing their expertise in identifying local development priorities, developing projects and programmes to pursue them, securing external funding for such community needs and managing their implementation. Such civic inclusion has not only created support for the implementation of policies in which the citizenry had input but has also made such programmes more realistic and socially grounded, and therefore more fundable and more implementable. At the same time, local governments have not only provided financial, material, and political support to NGOs but have also enhanced their ability to serve their constituents as well as their community. Moreover, an increasing number of municipalities have reached out to a variety of civic organisations and sometimes even some informal non-state actors to invite them to represent various local agendas and groups. Lastly, local governments have also benefited from the experience of NGOs and business groups in mobilising public interest in the preparation of and support for the implementation of local policies.

Conclusion: rebuilding state and strengthening democracy from below?

Despite the weak institutionalisation of state–society cooperation, the passivity of many municipalities and their preference for working primarily with political actors, there is evidence of widespread and diverse cooperation between local authorities and societal actors in Bulgaria (which, as mentioned above, is typical in the Eastern European region in terms of overall government performance and civil society development at the local level).

Moreover, local officials appear well integrated into their local communities and generally seek to respond to local developments, even if their ability to do so is somewhat compromised in quite a few cases by their relatively low administrative capacity. However, municipalities also seem to compensate for such underdeveloped local state capacity and consequently to improve government efficacy by devolving parts of their authority to societal actors through civic participation in the different stages and aspects of policy making.

This article suggests that (with all else being equal) extending citizen participation in local policy making in Bulgaria has been associated with enhanced government efficacy, which in turn further improves inclusion. This virtuous participation–performance cycle appears to be primarily a consequence of the professionalism and organisational strength of the third sector. However, the participation of the third sector in local development in Bulgaria does not seem to be at the expense and to the exclusion of the general public since further broader inclusion and public empowerment is also part of the expertise the third sector brings to improve municipal performance. The implications of these findings for democratisation in Bulgaria and possibly the region as well seem significant. Rebuilding the state from below through extended participation would not only boost the legitimacy and thus the quality of the country's democratic order but would also improve its performance and therefore its stability as well.

Harvard University

References

Almond, G. & Verba, S. (1963) *The Civic Culture: Political Attitudes and Democracy in Five Nations* (Princeton, NJ, Princeton University Press).

Babakus, E., Ferguson, C. E. & Joreskog, K. G. (1987) 'The Sensitivity of Confirmatory Maximum Likelihood Factor Analysis to Violations of Measurement Scale and Distribution Assumptions', *Journal of Marketing Research*, 24, 2.

Barber, B. (1984) *Strong Democracy: Participatory Politics for a New Age* (Berkeley, CA, University of California Press).

Bermeo, N. & Nord, P. (eds) (2000) *Civil Society before Democracy: Lessons from Nineteenth-Century Europe* (Lanham, MD, Rowman & Littlefield).

Bernhard, M. (1996) 'Civil Society After the First Transition: Dilemmas of Post-Communist Democratization in Poland and Beyond', *Communist and Post-Communist Studies*, 29, 3.

Bluebird Group (2003) *In Search of Responsive Government: State Building and Economic Growth in the Balkans*, Policy Studies Series, Center for Policy Studies, Central European University, available at: http://pdc.ceu.hu/archive/00002071/, accessed 1 February 2009.

Carnaghan, E. (2001) 'Thinking about Democracy: Interviews with Russian Citizens', *Slavic Review*, 60, 2.

Cook, L. J. & Vinogradova, E. (2006) 'NGOs and Social Policy-Making in Russia's Regions', *Problems of Post-Communism*, 53, 5.

Crawford, B. & Lijphart, A. (1995) 'Explaining Political and Economic Change in Post-Communist Eastern Europe: Old Legacies, New Institutions, Hegemonic Norms, and International Pressures', *Comparative Political Studies*, 28, 2.

Dahl, R. A. (1971) *Polyarchy: Participation and Opposition* (New Haven, CT & London, Yale University Press).

Dainov, E. (ed.) (2001) *Civil Society and Sustainable Development: Non-Governmental Organizations and Development in the New Century* (Sofia, Center for Social Practices).

Dainov, E. (2004) 'Civil Society as Partner in Local Development: a Bulgarian Experience', Paper prepared for the IC Regional Workshop *Partnerships for a Successful Transition in Eastern Europe*.

Eckstein, H. (1971) *The Evaluation of Political Performance: Problems and Dimensions* (Beverly Hills, CA, Sage).

Eckstein, H. & Apter, D. (1963) *Comparative Politics: A Reader* (New York, McMillan).

Evans, A. (2002) 'Recent Assessments of Social Organizations in Russia', *Demokratizatsiya*, 10, 2.

Finey, S. J. & DiStefano, C. (2006) 'Non-normal and Categorical Data in Structural Equation Modelling', in Hancock, G. & Mueller, R. (eds) (2006) *Structural Equation Modelling: A Second Course* (Charlotte, NC, Information Age Publishing).

Ganev, V. (2007) *Preying on the State: The Transformation of Bulgaria after 1989* (Ithaca, NY, Cornell University Press).

Gerring, John. 2007. *Case study research: principles and practices* (New York: Cambridge University Press).

Gibson, J. (2001) 'Social Networks, Civil Society, and the Prospects for Consolidating for Russia's Democratic Transition', *American Journal of Political Science*, 45, 1.

Glenn, J. & Mendelson, S. (eds) (2002) *The Power and Limits of NGOs: A Critical Look at Building Democracy in Eastern Europe and Eurasia* (New York, Columbia University Press).

Gotchev, A. (1998) *NGOs and Promotion of Democracy and Civil Society in East-Central Europe*, Report, NATO Research Fellowships Programme 1996/1998, available at: www.nato.int/acad/fellow/96-98/gotchev.pdf, accessed 1 February 2009.

Green, S. B., Akey, T. M., Flemming, K. K., Hershberger, S. L. & Marquis, J. G. (1997) 'Effect of the Number of Scale Points on Chi Square Fit Indices in Confirmatory Factor Analysis', *Structural Equation Modeling*, 4, 2.

Grzymala-Busse, A. (2007) *Rebuilding Leviathan: Party Competition and State Exploitation in Post-Communist Democracies* (New York, Cambridge University Press).

Henderson, S. (2002) 'Selling Civil Society: Western Aid and the Nongovernmental Organization Sector in Russia', *Comparative Political Studies*, 35, 2.

Howard, M. M. (2003) *The Weakness of Civil Society in Post-Communist Europe* (New York, Cambridge University Press).

Huntington, S. (1975) 'The Democratic Distemper', *Public Interest*, 41, 4.

Illner, M. (1998) 'Local Democratization in the Czech Republic', in Rueschemeyer, D., Rueschemeyer, M. & Wittrock, B. (eds) (1998) *Participation and Democracy, East and West: Comparisons and Interpretations* (Armonk, NY, M.E. Sharpe).

Krastev, I. (2001) 'Think Tanks: Making and Faking Influence', *Southeast European and Black Sea Studies*, 1, 2, May, pp. 17–38.

Kubik, J. (2005) 'How to Study Civil Society: The State of the Art and What to Do Next', *East European Politics and Societies*, 19, 1.

Laitin, D. (1995) 'The Civic Culture at 30', *American Political Science Review*, 89, 1.

Lane, L. & Wolf, J. (1990) *The Human Resource Crisis in the Public Sector: Rebuilding the Capacity to Govern* (New York, NY, Quorum Books).

Ledeneva, A. (1998) *Russia's Economy of Favours: Blat, Networking, and Informal Exchange* (Cambridge, Cambridge University Press).

Lipset, S. M. (1960) *Political Man: The Social Bases of Politics* (Baltimore, MD, Johns Hopkins University Press).

Marsh, C. (2000) 'Social Capital and Democracy in Russia', *Communist and Post-Communist Studies*, 33, 2.

Minkova, M., Stefanova, M., Kolarova, R. & Dimitrov, D. (2006) 'Report on the State of Local Democracy in Bulgaria', in Soós, G., Toka, G. & Wright, G. (eds) (2006).

Mishler, W. & Rose, R. (1997) 'Trust, Distrust, and Skepticism: Popular Evaluation of Civil and Political Institutions in Post-Communist Societies', *Journal of Politics*, 59, 2.

Narozhna, T. (2004) 'Foreign Aid for a Post-Euphoric Eastern Europe: the Limitations of Western Assistance in Developing Civil Society', *Journal of International Relations and Development*, 7, 3.

National Association of Municipalities in the Republic of Bulgaria (NAMRB) (2001a) *Bulletin of the National Association of Municipalities in the Republic of Bulgaria*, 6, March.

National Association of Municipalities in the Republic of Bulgaria (NAMRB) (2001b) *Bulletin of the National Association of Municipalities in the Republic of Bulgaria*, 9, May.

Nichols, T. (1996) 'Russian Democracy and Social Capital', *Social Science Information*, 35, 4.

Pateman, C. (1970) *Participation and Democratic Theory* (New York, Cambridge University Press).

Petrova, T. & Tarrow, S. (2007) 'Transactional and Participatory Activism in the Emerging European Polity', *Comparative Political Studies*, 40, 1.

Powell, L. (2002) 'Western and Russian Environmental NGOs: A Greener Russia?', in Glenn, J. & Mendelson, S. (eds) (2002).

Putnam, R. (1993) *Making Democracy Work* (Princeton, NJ, Princeton University Press).

Putnam, R. (2000) *Bowling Alone: The Collapse and Revival of American Community* (New York, Simon and Schuster).

Raiser, M., Haerpfer, C., Nowotny, T. & Wallace, C. (2001) *Social Capital in Transition: A First Look at the Evidence*, Working Paper 61 (London, EBRD).

Richter, J. (2002) 'Promoting Civil Society? Democracy Assistance and Russian Women's Organizations', *Problems of Post Communism*, 49, 1.

Rose, R. (2000) 'Uses of Social Capital in Russia: Modern, Pre-Modern and Anti-Modern', *Post-Soviet Affairs*, 16, 1.

Rose, R. (2001) 'How People View Democracy: A Diverging Europe', *Journal of Democracy*, 12, 1.

Schumpeter, J. (1962) *Capitalism, Socialism, and Democracy* (New York, Harper).

Soós, G., Toka, G. & Wright, G. (eds) (2006) *The State of Local Democracy in Central Europe, Local Government and Public Service Reform Initiative* (Budapest, Open Society Institute).

Soós, G. & Zentai, V. (eds) (2005) *Faces of Local Democracy: Comparative Papers from Central and Eastern Europe* (Budapest, OSI).

Sperling, V. (1999) *Organizing Women in Contemporary Russia* (Cambridge, MA, Cambridge University Press).

Stark, D., Vedres, B. & Bruszt, L. (2006) 'Rooted Transnational Publics: Integrating Foreign Ties and Civic Activism', *Theory and Society*, 35, 3.

Stiglitz, J. (2002) 'Participation and Development: Perspectives from the Comprehensive Development Paradigm', *Review of Development Economics*, 6, 2.

Stoner-Weiss, K. (1997) *Local Heroes: The Political Economy of Russian Regional Governance* (Princeton, NJ, Princeton University Press).

Strange, J. (1972) 'The Impact of Citizen Participation on Public Administration', *Public Administration Review*, 32, 5.

Swianiewicz, P. (2006) 'Comparing Local Democracy in Central and Eastern Europe', in Soós, G., Toka, G. & Wright, G. (eds) (2006).

Theesfeld, I. (2004) 'Constraints on Collective Action in a Transitional Economy: The Case of Bulgaria's Irrigation Sector', *World Development*, 32, 2, pp. 251–71.

Toepler, S. & Salamon, L. M. (2003) 'NGO Development in Central and Eastern Europe: An Empirical Overview', *East European Quarterly*, 37, 3.

United Nations Development Project (UNDP) (2001) *Rebuilding State Structures: Methods and Approaches—The Trials and Tribulations of Post Communist Countries* (New York, NY, UNDP).

United Nations Development Project (UNDP) (2004) *Otsenka na Obshchinskya i Oblastnya Kapatsitet za Usvoyavane na Sredstvata ot Strukturnite Fondove i Fonda za Socialno Sblizhavane na Evropeiskia S''yuz* (Sofia, UNDP Bulgaria).

Verba, S. (2003) 'Would the Dream of Political Equality Turn Out to Be a Nightmare?', *Perspectives on Politics*, 1, 4.

von Breska, E. & Brusis, M. (eds) (1999) *Central and Eastern Europe on the Way into the European Union: Reforms of Regional Administration in Bulgaria, the Czech Republic, Estonia, Hungary, Poland and Slovakia* (Brussels, Bertelsmann Foundation).

World Bank (2001) 'Participation in Development Assistance', *Precis: World Bank Operations Evaluation Department*, 209, Fall.

Wright, G. (2002) 'Assessment of Progress Toward Local Democratic Systems', in Soós, G., Toka, G. & Wright, G. (eds) (2002) *The State of Local Democracy in Central Europe* (Budapest, OSI).

Appendix 1. Participation and performance components

TABLE A1
LOCAL GOVERNMENT PERFORMANCE COMPONENTS

Policy aspect	Components	Description	Scale
Responsiveness	Currency of policy	Date last local development strategy was updated	0–3
Policy output	Implementation capacity	Percent of local development strategy implemented	0–3
Policy process 1	Policy quality	Ratio of ideas to proposals to EU-funded projects	0–3
Policy process 2	Municipal competence	Training received on strategic development and EU structural funds	0–3

TABLE A2
LOCAL CIVIC PARTICIPATION COMPONENTS

Policy stage	Components	Description	Scale
Planning	Evaluation & agenda setting	Input through polls, focus groups, public discussions, advisory council meetings and/or public forums	0–3
Planning	Strategy draft feedback	Consultations with citizens, civic groups, and/or local businesses on drafts of the local development strategy	0–3
Planning	Projects drafts feedback	Consultations with citizens, civic groups, and/or local businesses on drafts of the projects planned under the local development strategy	0–3
Implementation	Joint programmes/projects	Programmes/projects implemented with citizens, civic groups and/or local businesses	0–3
Implementation	Resource commitment	Non-material and/or non-material participation in initiatives by citizens, civic groups and/or local businesses	0–3

Appendix 2. Common civic inclusion practices at the local level in Bulgaria: nine case studies

Contribution	Inclusion practice	Description
Planning	*Public forums* • on local or regional development • funding is secured sometimes before and sometimes after the forum	In 2004, municipality G secured foreign funding to organise a local development forum and implement the best projects formulated in the process. The municipality reached out to all constituent communities and invited them to a series of public meetings to discuss citizen proposals for improving the quality of life in G. Each participant joined a policy 'table' (such as small business, education, etc.), which developed project proposals to be presented to the forum. Then all participants decided together which projects would be implemented with the money from the fund set up by the foreign donor. Some participants also volunteered labour and donated resources so that two additional projects could be realised.
	Advisory councils • around local development in general or specific policy areas such as social, economic, or environmental policy • around the citizenry or specific constituent communities such as young people, ethnic minorities, etc.	In the mid-2000s, several local NGOs began looking for ways to be more actively involved in the development of municipality R's economy. The local government invited them and other civic groups to participate in an advisory council on tourism in R. The NGOs have participated in the drafting and updating of the local development strategy and various tourism programmes and projects under it as well as in the preparation of campaigns marketing their municipality. The NGOs have prepared their own analyses of and collected input from the citizenry about the local resources for the development of tourism in R. As a result, the NGOs have actively contributed to the municipal discussions of the local development priorities, goals and their implementation.
	Public discussions and polls • usually at the programme or project level	In 2005, municipality K and the local community centre organised a public hearing to discuss improving the quality of life of young people in the community. A majority of the participants threw their support behind the idea that a modern media centre be created in the municipality to provide local youth with free educational as well as leisure opportunities. The municipality purchased the equipment, the community centre offered space, and the citizenry donated labour and money for additional equipment. In the late 1990s, municipality Vl began working on a strategy for local sustainable development. First, the local government conducted a survey of 1,000 local residents about their perception of the environmental problems and habits in the municipality. The results were then publicly discussed with the local population. As a result, the municipality

(continued)

Appendix 2. (Continued)

Contribution	Inclusion practice	Description
		identified its sustainable development priorities and prepared a programme for achieving them. The local government also partnered with local school boards, NGOs, and media to launch a municipal ecological awareness campaign. Lastly, the municipality invited local NGOs and neighbourhood groups to start a municipal environmental watch.
	Ad hoc consultations • usually at the programme or project level	Seeking to stimulate the local economy, the government elected in municipality Pv in 1999 pledged to work to attract foreign investors. The mayor invited the three local business groups to participate in the organisation of an international business expo in Pv. The NGOs worked with local businesses and municipal officials responsible for the local economy to prepare a set of 'Invest in Pv' promotional materials, which highlight Pv's resources and comparative advantages. The expo resulted in the signing of three new foreign investment agreements.
Implementation	*Joint programmes* • mostly for socio-economic and national minorities but also for economic development and sustainable development	In 1997, a local NGO from municipality B, PFA, began developing a programme 'From Social Care to Employment' to address the high unemployment among local women. The NGO approached the local government to be a partner in the project. The participating women had individual meetings with a social worker and a labour market broker from the municipality. Additionally, the women attended a roundtable with employers and a series of trainings on searching for jobs or starting their own business or civic group.
	• sometimes building up on partnerships at the planning stage	In 2005 municipality Pz set up a Local Development advisory council, which included representatives of 17 local NGOs as well as some local officials. The council began meeting several times a year to discuss ways to improve the local quality of life. In cooperation with three of the participating NGOs, the municipality financed the provision of a variety of social services to five groups of underprivileged citizens: people with disabilities, people living in poverty, homeless people, orphans and the elderly. A board of directors, which included representatives from other local NGOs and businesses, managed these programmes financially. Moreover, several plans for joint municipal–civic projects were developed in the first year alone and submitted to various funding competitions organised by foreign donors.

(continued)

Appendix 2. (Continued)

Contribution	Inclusion practice	Description
	Public–private funds and ad hoc resource commitments • budget resources • free use of municipal property by non-state actors	In 2005, a regional NGO, BCK, developed and secured external funding for a project called 'Care for the Elderly', which was to provide a range of services to senior citizens living alone and in poverty. Municipality Pk agreed to support the project by contributing financially to the home-delivered meals service by paying the wages of the staff as well as by paying for the locally-grown produce used. In 2003, the municipal council in K voted to allow a local NGO, AMK, to use for free one of the local government's properties in a picturesque part of the municipality. AMK wanted to turn the property into an international cultural venue, which was to revive the cultural life and thus develop the tourist industry in the area. AMK's 'art house' opened its doors in 2005 and hosted more than 200 artists from the US, the EU, Asia and the Middle East. Since some of them donated their work to the NGO, the municipal council in K voted to allow AMK to use for free another building in the city as an art gallery, which was to further establish K as a cultural centre in the region.

Note: the case studies in this Appendix are based on the archival materials of the Foundation for Local Government Reform.

Appendix 3. Common practices of popular mobilisation in local governance in Bulgaria: four case studies

Contribution	Description
Planning	In municipality P, there is a large minority of ethnic Turks (10% of the local population) and an even larger Roma community (35% of the local population), neither of which was civically mobilised. In 2006, the local community centre began working with informal leaders from these minorities to help them organise and become more actively engaged in the governance of the municipality. The centre invited a national NGO to train these elites in various participatory techniques and took them to a neighbouring town to learn from the experience of local NGOs that had been actively involved in their local governance. The minority elites in P set up their own NGO shortly thereafter and continued to cooperate with the community centre and organised four discussions about the current problems of P's minorities within the first year alone. As a result, the municipality invited the NGO to consult for several municipal committees and to broadcast and print for free in the municipal media. By the end of the year, the local government had approved a Plan for Social Integration of P's minorities.
	In the mid-1990s, municipality Z allowed a newly set up local community foundation to use one of the local government's properties for free while local businesses donated labour and money to renovate the office. The foundation has been working closely with the local authorities to sponsor neighbourhood action groups and to set up an economic development commission to draft a local development strategy for the municipality.
Implementation	In 2006, a group of civic activists from municipality S launched a campaign for ecological restoration of a nearby park. Three local ecological groups approached the local government with an initiative to repair and manage the nearby park in order to not only preserve its biological diversity but also to encourage local ecotourism. The NGOs also worked to mobilise popular support for the implementation of the project as well as for long-term ecological preservation in the municipality by working with school boards and media in the municipality. The campaign relied on volunteer labour for clean-up and reforestation, and for the installation of park benches, water fountains and refuse cans.
	The mayor of L invited local business groups to advise on economic development in the municipality. The NGOs subsequently mobilised local businesses to support several other municipal initiatives that benefited the public at large: within the first year of inclusion, businesses donated resources for a 'spring clean-up' of the town and for an anti-littering programme, helped secure funds for several town renovations under 'Beautiful Bulgaria' (a UNDP countrywide project), and helped devise a plan for improvement of the local infrastructure (sewage system).

Note: the case studies in this Appendix are based on the archival materials of the Foundation for Local Government Reform.

The Structure and Culture of Post-Communist Civil Society in Latvia

ANDERS UHLIN

Abstract

This article provides an account of post-communist civil society in Latvia. Based on original survey data, the structure of civil society is analysed on both individual and organisational levels and cultural aspects are examined. The weakness of post-communist civil society found in much previous research is confirmed when measured on the individual level and in relation to some organisational aspects. The political culture of civil society in Latvia is relatively trusting, tolerant and pro-democratic, but elitist. The specific weaknesses of post-communist civil society can be attributed to the historical heritage of the communist regime as well as the context in which new foreign-funded civil society organisations emerged.

DURING THE LAST TWO DECADES THERE HAS BEEN A growing interest in studying the development of civil society in different countries. Donor agencies as well as academics have tried to 'measure' civil society in Africa, Asia, Latin America, and not least in post-communist Europe. However, there is no agreement on what indicators should be used when trying to make sense of what is labelled civil society in very different contexts. Despite a number of efforts at large comparative studies of civil society developments (CIVICUS 1997; Anheier 2004; Salamon & Sokolowski & Associates 2004; Heinrich & Fioramonti 2008), and more specifically on civil society in post-communist and post-Soviet societies (Howard 2003; Uhlin 2006), there are still many countries in post-communist Europe on which we lack systematic research of the development of civil society. One such country is Latvia.

Most researchers focusing on post-communist civil society tend to agree on one thing: the weakness of civil society in this particular context. For example, the civil society index constructed by CIVICUS (World Alliance for Citizen Participation) drawing on expert evaluations of civil societies in different countries, gives Eastern European countries consistently lower scores than Western European countries (Celichowski 2008, p. 14). Also in a broader international comparison, citizen participation in civil society organisations (CSOs)[1] is very limited in post-communist

---

[1] I use the concept 'civil society organisations' (CSOs) as it is somewhat more inclusive than non-governmental organisations (NGOs). While most of the organisations included in this study could be

Europe (Howard 2003). Hence, post-communist civil society is generally depicted as weak compared not only to civil societies in established democracies but also to post-authoritarian civil societies in Latin America and parts of Asia and Africa (Salamon *et al.* 2004, p. 52). In this article I aim to provide a more nuanced picture of the weaknesses of post-communist civil society by means of a case study of civil society in Latvia. I will explore the question of in what respect post-communist civil society can be depicted as weak and how the weaknesses can be explained.

Latvia shares the experience of communist rule with other post-communist countries and the experience of Soviet occupation with several other post-Soviet republics. Like in the other Baltic states, there was a relatively strong civil society in the interwar period, which was crushed under communist rule. However, in the late 1980s and early 1990s independent organisations re-emerged and the reinvention of civil society culminated in the popular movement for independence. By the end of the 1980s about 250,000 people were active in the Latvian Popular Front (*Latvijas Tautas Fronte*) (Pabriks & Purs 2002, p. 45). After independence, Latvia, like other new democracies emerging after communist rule, experienced a demobilisation of civil society. To a large extent the leaders of the independence movement left politics and there was an alienation of the masses from the ruling elite when politics became dominated by members of the former Soviet nomenclature (Pabriks & Purs 2002, pp. 67–68). New CSOs emerged, often as a result of foreign funding, but the number of people engaged in civil society activities decreased. There was an 'NGOisation' of civil society (Uhlin 2006, p. 56–60).

The developments of Latvian civil society during the first decade after independence has been reasonably well documented (Karatnycky *et al.* 1997; Ostrowska 1997; Smith-Sivertsen 2000; Zepa 1999; Karklins & Zepa 2001). However, more recent developments have been less thoroughly analysed. In particular, there is a lack of systematic analysis of empirical developments within the Latvian NGO-sector in relation to civil society theory, and there is even less research trying to broaden the perspective beyond NGOs. The aim of the present article is to contribute to filling these gaps in previous research.

Drawing on unique survey data, the article provides an account of civil society in Latvia in the early 2000s, focusing on individual activities as well as the structure of CSOs and cultural aspects, such as norms and values prevalent in the civil society sector. In this way it offers a more comprehensive analysis of post-communist civil society than has previously been available. Although not comparative in its approach, the study presents an analytical framework that can be used for broader comparative studies and tries to relate the empirical findings from Latvia to previous research on post-communist civil society as well as more general civil society theory.

In the following section I outline an analytical framework for empirical civil society research. I then present the surveys that make up the empirical data for this study and make some methodological clarifications. Based on the analytical framework the empirical analysis is divided into three sections: structural aspects on the individual

---

labelled NGOs, there are others such as trade unions and sports clubs which are not usually seen as NGOs.

level; structural aspects on the organisational level; and cultural features of Latvian civil society. As a concluding remark, I put the findings of this study in a broader comparative perspective, discuss how the weaknesses found in post-communist civil society can be explained, and consider developments of civil society after Latvia's entrance into the EU in May 2004.

An analytical framework for empirical civil society research

Civil society has been defined as 'a slice of society, whose core is the web of voluntary associations that articulate interests and values, and their system of interaction, as long as these units are not under the control of the state' (Waisman 2006, p. 22). This definition nicely captures what is generally considered to be the most important characteristics of civil society. Hence, I view civil society as an arena in which different actors act. This arena is analytically distinct from, but in practice often closely related to, other arenas like the state, political and economic society. It is a public sphere, excluding organisations concerned with inward-looking or private ends. While civil society actors are often collectively organised it is also possible to conceive of individuals articulating interests of public concern on the civil society arena. Civil society activities may include both political activities and non-political, for example recreational activities, but it is important to distinguish between political and non-political CSOs as they are likely to play very different roles.

Mainstream Western liberal democratic conceptions of civil society have been criticised on a number of issues and their applicability in a post-communist context could indeed be questioned. A fundamental criticism focuses on the common assumption that the main function of civil society is to strengthen democracy in the state. Mainstream democratisation research makes an instrumentalist reading of civil society, stressing its functional benefits for a statist democracy. Critics have pointed out that there are alternative conceptions of civil society—not least manifested in the East European anti-communist dissident movements—which concentrate on democracy and democratisation within civil society (Baker 2002). This, in many ways more radical understanding of civil society, is almost invisible in the mainstream democratisation and civil society literature. However, as the question of democratisation—either of the state or civil society—goes beyond the main focus of this article, I will not discuss this criticism further.

Another kind of criticism, of more direct relevance for the present study, focuses on the tendency to equate civil society with NGOs. As argued by Howard (2005, p. 231) 'an NGO can set up a fax machine and a website, but without members, without a constituency, it has very little to do with civil society'. Following this line of reasoning, Fagan (2005) suggests that while there may be many NGOs in post-communist Europe, this does not necessarily mean that there are strong civil societies. Focusing on permanent, long-established organisations, much empirical research on civil society tends to neglect episodic protest activities (Kopecký 2003, p. 14). Moreover, much of the discussion of the weakness of post-communist civil society is misplaced because of a too limited conception of civil society and the use of misleading measurements of the vibrancy of associational life in terms of the numerical strength of membership or the organisational density of NGOs alone

(Kopecký 2003, p. 2). We can reach a more comprehensive understanding of civil society if we include not only formal organisations, but also more diffuse social movements and protest activities (Kopecký 2003; Welzel *et al.* 2005). Hence I analyse both the characteristics of formal CSOs and individuals' participation in more episodic informal protest activities.

Another kind of criticism against mainstream Western conceptions of civil society focuses on the underlying normative assumption of the inherent peaceful and pro-democratic character of civil society, which has led to a distinction between 'civil' and 'uncivil' society. 'Uncivil movements', however, are often more authentic representatives of civil society in post-communist Europe than are foreign funded NGOs (Mudde 2003, p. 164); and if undemocratic actors are by definition excluded from civil society, the common argument that civil society supports democracy is close to becoming an argument based on meaningless circular reasoning. Hence, empirical civil society studies should not use 'civility' and pro-democracy attitudes as defining characteristics of civil society. Rather, questions of the degree of internal democracy, as well as support for pro-democratic and anti-democratic values within CSOs, are open empirical questions that should be examined. This is the approach followed in the present study.

Furthermore, I distinguish between structural and cultural features of civil society (Heinrich 2005). Structure refers to the extent and form of collective citizen action whereas culture refers to norms guiding this action. Two civil societies can have a similar structure (including size and vibrancy), but very different cultures. Following (Heinrich 2005, p. 221), I focus on the structure of civil society on individual as well as organisational levels and on civil society culture (Table 1). In order to find empirical indicators of these civil society dimensions we need data on the activities and attitudes of individuals in the general public as well as more specific features of CSOs. More precisely, on the individual level the structure of civil society can be analysed in terms of political engagement outside as well as within formal CSOs, and also based on individuals' knowledge about CSOs. A public opinion survey was conducted to collect these data. On the organisational level, a survey directed to activists in CSOs provided data on the field of activity of CSOs, their size (in terms of members and employees), internal democracy, autonomy from the state, and finally the type of activities carried out by the CSO. Concerning the culture of civil society—core norms and values—I

TABLE 1
ANALYTICAL FRAMEWORK AND EMPIRICAL INDICATORS

Structure: Individual level	*Structure: Organisational level*	*Culture: Core norms and values*

Data set:
  Public survey
	Data set:
	  Activist survey
		Data set:
		  Activist and public survey

Indicators:
  Political engagement
  Activity in CSOs
  Public knowledge about CSOs
	Indicators:
	  Field of activity of CSOs
	  Size
	  Internal democracy
	  Autonomy
	  Type of activities
		Indicators:
		  Support for democratic values
		  Trust
		  Social tolerance

analysed support for democratic values, general trust in people and social tolerance. In this respect it is interesting to compare activists and non-activists. Hence, both the activist and public survey is useful. The theoretical underpinnings as well as the operationalisation of these indicators are presented in the following sections. First, however, the surveys will be described.

Designing activist and public surveys

For the empirical analysis I rely on two surveys conducted specifically for this study.[2] First, 500 respondents, each representing a different CSO in Latvia, responded to a questionnaire on structural and cultural aspects of CSOs. The selection of CSOs was made through a random sample procedure from a list of 4,000 CSOs, available at an NGO centre in Riga. It should be noted that there is no universal criteria for CSOs in Latvia and it is impossible to obtain completely accurate statistical data (Vilka & Strupiss 2004, p. 50). The list from the NGO centre was considered the most reliable source at the time the survey was prepared (in early 2004). Representing each organisation, a 'core activist' (Lindén 2008, p. 75), not necessarily the chairperson, was selected for interviews. The fact that the description of each organisation relied on the evaluation of one single person might be considered a problem. However, the intention of the study was not to describe specific organisations, but rather, to create aggregate data on characteristics of CSOs based on how civil society activists perceive their organisations. For this purpose it was considered more valuable to include as many CSOs as possible, than to interview several people representing the same organisation.

The second survey was directed to a representative sample of people living in Latvia. For this public opinion survey a multi-stage probability sample with random route procedure was used. The sample was stratified geographically into five administrative districts and 132 sampling points based on community size. Quotas were set to achieve correct representation of the respondents' age and sex.

All interviews for both surveys were conducted by interviewers from Latvian Facts, a Riga based company with extensive experience in conducting public opinion polls and survey research. First versions of the questionnaires were tested on a sample of respondents in January and February 2004. Face-to-face interviews using questionnaires translated into both Latvian and Russian were carried out between 10 March and 20 May 2004 for the survey of activists, and from 10 March to 26 March for the public survey. Out of 653 contacts, 502 interviews were conducted for the activist survey. A total of 48 contacted respondents were not active in the organisation anymore and therefore were replaced by other respondents; 103 contacted interviewees refused to participate (mainly because of lack of spare time). In the public survey 1,283 contacts were made resulting in 1,000 interviews. A total of 129 contacted persons were not suitable because the sex or age quota was full and 154 persons refused to participate (mainly due to a lack of spare time).

In order to test reliability, 103 questionnaires in the activist survey and 157 in the public survey were submitted to verification procedures, including verification of the

---

[2]See also the work by Lindén (2008) and Uhlin (2009).

TABLE 2

POLITICAL ENGAGEMENT IN LATVIA (%, ABSOLUTE NUMBERS WITHIN PARENTHESES)

	Have done	Might do	Would never do
Signing a petition	19 (185)	53 (528)	28 (272)
Joining in boycotts	8 (76)	52 (512)	40 (396)
Attending lawful demonstrations	12 (114)	50 (498)	38 (373)

Note: The question was: 'Here are some different forms of political action that people can take, and I'd like you to tell me, for each one, whether you have actually done any of these things, whether you might do it, or would never, under any circumstances, do it' (*N* = 989).

Source: Civil Society Activism in Latvia—public (CSALSp) 2004, see footnote 2.

fact that the interview took place, date of interview, approximate duration and a general evaluation of the interviewer by the respondent. All 103 interviews in the activist survey and all 157 in the public survey were affirmed in this quality control. The reliability of two of the 502 completed interviews in the activist survey and 11 of the 1,000 completed interviews in the public survey were considered not entirely satisfactory by the interviewer and these interviews were deleted from the dataset, resulting in a total of 500 activist interviews and 989 public interviews. The results from the surveys were entered into SPSS data files.[3] In the following sections these data are analysed using descriptive statistics and regression analysis.

The structure of civil society: the individual level

Individuals' civic engagement is conventionally measured as a combination of membership in CSOs and other types of less formalised political engagement. The latter is the most difficult to measure, but several scholars have used questions in the World Values Surveys on individuals' political activities such as signing petitions, joining in boycotts and attending lawful demonstrations. I used the same questions in the Latvian survey conducted for the present study. The results show that political engagement in contemporary Latvia is rather limited (Table 2). In total, 19% had signed a petition and only 12% said they had attended a lawful demonstration. Even fewer (8%) had joined a boycott. However, about 50%, while not having done any of these things, said they might do it. Hence there is at least a potential for greater civil society activism. Nevertheless, as many as about 40% said they would never, under any circumstances, join a boycott or attend a lawful demonstration. This negative attitude towards relatively moderate forms of civic and political engagement among a relatively large group of people in contemporary Latvia is somewhat surprising given the rather recent history of mass demonstrations for independence.

In order to find out something about the characteristics of people who tended to be more prepared for political engagement, compared to those who were not active at all, I constructed an index of political engagement combining the three variables of signing

[3]The databases are referred to as Civil Society Activism in Latvia—activists (CSALSa) and Civil Society Activism in Latvia—public (CSALSp).

TABLE 3
THE EFFECT OF DIFFERENT INDIVIDUAL CHARACTERISTICS (CONTROLLING FOR REGION) ON POLITICAL
ENGAGEMENT IN LATVIA

	Political engagement
Constant	2.392***
Age	−0.963***
Female	
Male	0.250**
Latvian language	
Russian language	−0.145
Other language	−0.309
Latvian citizen	
Permanent resident	0.157
Russian citizen	0.522
No secondary education	−0.173
Secondary education	
Higher education	0.369***
Graduate education	Error
Much worse financially	−0.055
Somewhat worse financially	0.193
Neither better nor worse	
Somewhat better financially	0.050
Much better financially	−0.526
Riga	
Vidzeme	0.138
Kurzeme	−0.009
Zemgale	0.300*
Latgale	0.671***
R^2	0.071
R^2adj	0.055
N	980

Notes: OLS regression. Unstandardised beta coefficients are given.
Two tailed significance tests. *$p < 0.1$; **$p < 0.05$; ***$p < 0.01$.
The index of political engagement was created based on three forms of activities: signing a petition, joining in boycotts and attending lawful demonstrations. The answer 'Have done' was given the value 2, 'Might do' 1 and 'Would never do' 0. Adding the values for the three variables an index ranging from 0 to 6 was created. Independent variables are dummy variables.
Source: Civil Society Activism in Latvia—public (CSALSp) 2004, see footnote 2.

petitions, joining in boycotts and attending lawful demonstrations,[4] and made a regression analysis using different individual characteristics as independent variables (Table 3).

The analysis shows that age was a significant predictor of political engagement. Young people were more active than older people; men were more active than women; and higher education was associated with greater political engagement. All this is in line with what could be expected based on experiences from other societies.

It is interesting to note that there is no statistically significant relationship between citizenship or mother tongue and political engagement. Those having Latvian as their mother tongue tended to be somewhat more politically engaged compared to Russian speakers and people with other mother tongues, but this pattern was not statistically

[4]For discussion of this approach, see Armony (2004, p. 182).

significant. Surprisingly, permanent residents (and especially Russian citizens) scored higher on the political engagement index than Latvian citizens but, once again, this was not a statistically significant pattern. What we can conclude is that there is no indication that Latvians were more politically engaged (as measured here) than Russian speakers and non-citizens. This is somewhat surprising given ethnic tensions in post-Soviet Latvia and claims about the marginalisation of the Russian-speaking population. One possible explanation for this finding is that Russians in Latvia, despite the problematic citizenship question, are not a marginalised group. This would be consistent with the work of Aasland (2002), which found no indication that non-citizens were more at risk of social exclusion than were citizens in Latvia, when controlling for other variables like income and education. The finding that political engagement was not significantly higher among Latvians compared to Russian-speakers and non-citizens makes sense if there is no general social exclusion of non-citizens in contemporary Latvia. However, an alternative explanation might be that Russian-speaking non-citizens are no less engaged in these informal political activities than are the majority population, precisely because signing petitions, participating in boycotts and attending demonstrations are informal avenues for influencing politics, which might be the most important form of political engagement open to non-citizens who have limited access to the formal political system.

Surprisingly, political engagement was not more widespread in the capital Riga than elsewhere. On the contrary people living in Riga demonstrated less political engagement than in other regions, with people in Latgale in particular, but also in Zemgale, scoring much higher on political engagement. This difference cannot be explained by the different ethnic compositions of the regions as those variables are not significant in the regression model. A possible explanation might be that formal structures for political engagement (like NGOs and political parties) are stronger in Riga. In other regions where more formalised opportunities for civil society activism are fewer, people have to rely to a greater extent on less formalised types of political engagement.

Having examined less formalised political engagement in contemporary Latvia, I now turn to the second aspect of civic engagement: membership in CSOs. Previous research shows that organisational membership is substantially lower in post-communist countries than in most other contexts and, even within this group of countries, Latvia is below average for most types of CSOs (Howard 2003, pp. 65–66). However, compared to Russia and the other Baltic states organisational membership in general is somewhat higher in Latvia, according to data from the World Values Survey (Howard 2003, p. 69). The survey for this study (Table 4) indicates that only 6% of Latvia's residents were active in CSOs. This level of civil society activity is the same as has been found in other studies (Vilka & Strupiss 2004, p. 20). Only 17% said they had relatives or friends who were active in CSOs and less than 40% say that they knew about any CSO in their city, town or village.[5] The fact that more than 60% claimed that they did not even know of a CSO is a strong indication of the weak impact of CSOs in

---

[5]Among those who knew about CSOs in their city, town or village, political parties and social assistance organisations were most commonly mentioned, further emphasising the marginal impact of other types of CSOs.

contemporary Latvia. For most individuals CSOs did not seem to have any significance at all and only a small minority of about 6% was really active in CSOs.

Many of those who were active in a CSO were active in more than one organisation; 42% of the 500 civil society activists interviewed for this study were active in more than one organisation. Hence, it may be suggested that there is a rather small group of people that is responsible for most of the formalised civil society activities found in contemporary Latvia.

What then were the characteristics of civil society activists in Latvia? Table 5 gives some indications. Women are slightly overrepresented (6.4% compared to 5.9% for men) indicating that the gender-based exclusion found in the formal political sphere, as well as within the business community, is not replicated within civil society.

TABLE 4
Activity in, and Knowledge about, CSOs in Latvia (%)

Active[a] in social and/or political organisation/group	6.2
Relatives or friends active in social and/or political organisation	17.0
Know any social and/or political organisation active in own city/town/village	38.7

Notes: N = 989.
[a]Being active is here understood in a broad sense and might include just being a member of the organisation/group.
Source: Civil Society Activism in Latvia—public (CSALSp) 2004, see footnote 2.

TABLE 5
Activity in CSOs among Different Categories of People in Latvia (%)

Category	
Women ($N = 532$)	6.4
Men ($N = 457$)	5.9
Youth (15–25 years) ($N = 187$)	5.9
Middle aged (26–64 years) ($N = 620$)	5.3
Old (65–) ($N = 182$)	9.3
No secondary education ($N = 269$)	4.7
Higher education ($N = 216$)	9.4
Graduate education ($N = 9$)	22.2
Much better off than the average household ($N = 17$)	17.6
Much worse off than the average household ($N = 205$)	3.9
Latvian citizen ($N = 738$)	7.2
Permanent resident ($N = 238$)	2.1
Russian citizen ($N = 11$)	27.3
Latvian as mother tongue ($N = 571$)	8.8
Russian as mother tongue ($N = 374$)	2.9
Other mother tongue ($N = 44$)	0
Riga ($N = 326$)	5.2
Vidzeme ($N = 229$)	5.2
Kurzeme ($N = 134$)	8.2
Zemgale ($N = 142$)	11.3
Latgale ($N = 158$)	3.2

Note: Total $N = 989$.
Source: Civil Society Activism in Latvia—public (CSALSp) 2004, see footnote 2.

However, the fact that women were more likely than men to be civil society activists might be seen as an indication of the relative lack of power of CSOs. In a society characterised by structural discrimination against women, men tend to dominate the more powerful institutions whereas women are found in what are considered less significant and influential social groups.[6]

Older people (above 65) were overrepresented among those active in CSOs whereas younger people tended to dominate in less formalised types of political engagement (as shown in Table 3). The average age of activists in CSOs was somewhat higher (47 years) than for all respondents (45 years). This means that the same trend is found in Latvia as in most of the Western world where young people tend to be less active in formal organisations.

As could be expected, education was a strong predictor of activism in CSOs. People with higher education were overrepresented among the activists. Likewise, the pattern concerning socio-economic status is also very clear: people belonging to households much better off than average were highly overrepresented whereas those from households much worse off than average were underrepresented among activists in CSOs.

As shown above (Table 3) citizenship status and mother tongue did not have any statistically significant effect on less formalised political engagement. When it comes to activity in CSOs, however, the situation is different. Latvian citizens (and more surprisingly the small group of Russian citizens) were overrepresented among the activists whereas permanent residents were much less likely to be active in CSOs. People with Latvian as their mother tongue were overrepresented whereas those with Russian as their mother tongue (including almost all of those with permanent resident status) were much less likely to be active, and people with any other mother tongue were completely absent among the activists in CSOs. Based on these data we can conclude that non-citizens and those who did not have Latvian as their mother tongue were much less likely to be active in CSOs. This finding confirms previous research (Aasland 2002, p. 67; Ijabs 2006).[7] It underlines the importance of the distinction between informal political engagement and more formalised civil society activities. Whereas there is no significant difference between Latvians and Russian non-citizens in the first respect, Russian non-citizens were clearly underrepresented in the more formalised civil society sector. This might be explained by the policies on citizenship and language which created obstacles for political participation, but also the tendency of foreign donors supporting civil society in Latvia to concentrate mainly on ethnic Latvian NGOs (Ijabs 2006, p. 74).

Comparing the different regions of the country we find that people in Zemgale were more likely to be active in CSOs, whereas those living in Latgale are less active. Zemgale also had a higher degree of non-organised political engagement and thus stands out as a region with somewhat more civic engagement than the rest of Latvia.

---

[6]See Lindén (2008, pp. 88–98) for a more extensive analysis of the gender composition of Latvian civil society.

[7]Trade union membership was equally common among non-citizens and citizens, but most other types of organisational memberships were much more common among Latvian citizens (Aasland 2002, p. 67).

By contrast, Latgale had a lower degree of activism in formal CSOs, but a higher degree of political engagement than the rest of the country. This is a region where civic engagement is less likely to be organised through formal CSOs.

In conclusion, the structure of Latvian civil society, when measured on the individual level appears to be rather weak. Civic engagement—both measured as activity in CSOs and less formalised political engagement—was relatively low. A very large majority of people in Latvia were not at all active in any form of civil society activity. Among the small minority who were active we find some interesting characteristics. Young people were more likely to turn to less formalised types of political engagement whereas old people were overrepresented among those active in CSOs. Women were slightly overrepresented among those active in CSOs whereas men scored somewhat higher on political engagement. Education was a relatively strong predictor for both forms of civic engagement. The financial situation of one's household did not seem to be significantly related to political engagement, but it was a strong predictor of activity in CSOs, with activity being more likely the better one's financial situation. Citizenship status and mother tongue did not influence political engagement in a statistically significant way, but non-citizens and Russian-speakers were clearly underrepresented among activists in CSOs. There were also some interesting regional differences, with civic engagement (both in its organised and less formal forms) being higher in Zemgale and a pattern of more political engagement, but less activism within CSOs in Latgale.

The structure of civil society: organisational level

On 1 January 2004, there were 7,704 'social organisations' in Latvia according to data from the Latvian information technology company Lursoft (Vilka & Strupiss 2004, p. 18). There has been a steady increase in the number of CSOs since independence. Today no legal barriers to establish CSOs exist. However, bureaucratic hindrances and lack of information and education could still constitute obstacles (Vilka & Strupiss 2004, p. 24).

Let us now examine characteristics of CSOs in Latvia, starting with an overview of different fields of activity (Table 6). In the sample for this study, a quarter of the organisations are charity groups dealing with social welfare issues. The economic transformation following independence led to socio-economic hardship for many people as the role of the state as a provider of social welfare services drastically declined. The significance of social welfare organisations within Latvian civil society is a reflection of this privatisation of social welfare, which has also been supported by donor agencies providing funding for this type of CSO.

The second largest category of CSOs deals with issues related to democracy and human rights. These organisations represent a more explicitly political section of civil society. By contrast, the third largest category is made up of non-political recreational groups such as sports clubs and various cultural organisations. It is worth noting that environmental organisations which played such an important role in the struggle for independence only make up 4% of the CSOs in this sample. This is due to a general depoliticisation of environmentalism in Latvia related to tensions of economic, political and social transition (Galbreath & Auers 2009).

The size of CSOs can be measured in terms of membership as well as the number of employees. About one third of organisations were very small, with less than 20 members, and another 34% had between 21 and 100 members (Table 7). It is quite clear therefore that organised civil society in contemporary Latvia is predominantly made up of small NGOs with few members. Youth organisations in particular, but also recreational, educational and social welfare organisations, tend to have few members. Political organisations tend to have a larger membership. More than half of the organisations in the sample had no employees at all; and more than five employees were found in 13% of the CSOs. Hence, a majority of CSOs were small also in this

TABLE 6

FIELD OF ACTIVITY AMONG CSOs IN LATVIA (%, ABSOLUTE NUMBERS WITHIN PARENTHESES)

Field of activity	
Social welfare/charity	25 (125)
Democracy and human rights	14 (67)
Recreation (sport and culture)	12 (58)
Labour	8 (42)
Politics in general	8 (40)
Youth	7 (34)
Women	6 (32)
Education	6 (30)
National identity/ethnic issues	5 (27)
Other	5 (23)
Environment	4 (22)
Total	100 (500)

Source: Civil Society Activism in Latvia—activists (CSALSa) 2004, see footnote 2.

TABLE 7

MEMBERSHIP OF DIFFERENT TYPES OF CSOs (%)

	No membership (0–20)	*Small (21–100)*	*Medium (101–1,000)*	*Large (1,001–10,000)*	*Very large (more than 10,000)*
Politics	8 (3)	45 (18)	40 (16)	5 (2)	2 (1)
Human rights	22 (14)	40 (27)	31 (21)	4 (3)	3 (2)
Women	35 (11)	31 (10)	31 (10)	3 (1)	0
Labour	22 (9)	45 (19)	26 (11)	7 (3)	0
National identity	34 (9)	41 (11)	18 (5)	7 (2)	0
Environment	27 (6)	46 (10)	23 (5)	4 (1)	0
Social welfare	40 (50)	23 (29)	29 (36)	6 (7)	2 (3)
Youth	50 (17)	20 (7)	18 (6)	9 (3)	3 (1)
Recreation	42 (24)	36 (21)	17 (10)	3 (2)	2 (1)
Education	40 (12)	37 (11)	23 (7)	0	0
Other	30 (7)	35 (8)	35 (8)	0	0
Total	32 (162)	34 (171)	27 (135)	5 (24)	2 (8)

Note: The question was: 'What is the approximate number of members of the organisation/group?' Answers have been classified.

$N = 500$. (Absolute numbers within parentheses.)

Source: Civil Society Activism in Latvia—activists (CSALSa) 2004, see footnote 2.

TABLE 8

INTERNAL DEMOCRACY BY CATEGORY OF CSO (MEAN ON AN INDEX FROM 0 = NO INTERNAL
DEMOCRACY TO 100 = HIGH INTERNAL DEMOCRACY)

Field of activity	
Women	75
Other	72
Environment	69
Human rights	68
Labour	66
Education	65
Politics in general	65
Recreation (sport, culture, etc.)	64
Social welfare/charity	63
Youth	63
National identity/ethnic issues	62
Total	66

Note: The internal democracy of the organisation/group is measured through a combination of two questions: (1) 'How easy is it for an ordinary member of your organisation/group to influence decisions within the organisation/group?'; and (2) 'If members of your organisation/group are not satisfied with the leadership of the organisation/group, how easy is it to replace the leadership?' Alternatives given for both questions were: Impossible = 0, Very difficult = 25, Rather difficult = 50, Rather easy = 75, Very easy = 100. The two indicators were combined (by calculating the mean) to an index ranging from 0 = no internal democracy to 100 = high internal democracy.
$N = 500$.
Source: Civil Society Activism in Latvia—activists (CSALSa) 2004, see footnote 2.

sense, but as many as 46% had at least one employee. Thus, despite the low number of members in Latvian CSOs a substantial portion of these organisations had some salaried staff.

Internal democracy in CSOs is difficult to measure. Here I rely on the judgment of activists within each organisation, with the obvious risk that they tend to overestimate the democratic qualities of their organisation. Nevertheless, there is enough variation in the responses to the two survey questions associated with internal democracy to assume a certain degree of validity of this variable, although the results should be treated with some caution. Table 8 indicates that women's organisations had the highest degree of internal democracy of all CSOs in Latvia (scoring 75 on the index shown in Table 8) whereas CSOs focusing on national identity and ethnic issues were perceived to have least internal democracy (62 on the index shown in Table 8).

At least some degree of autonomy from the state is typically seen as a defining characteristic of CSOs (Hydén 1997, pp. 31–32). Autonomy, however, is hardly absolute. Activities within civil society depend on a legal framework that the state provides and in most countries many CSOs, at least to some extent, rely on state funding. Despite such state dependency, CSOs should ideally have a degree of political autonomy, being able to make independent decisions about their activities. Among the respondents 65% considered their organisations to be autonomous from the state, 17% said that they were financially dependent on state subsidies, whereas another 18% admitted that the organisation was politically dependent on the state (Table 9). Variation across categories of CSOs was significant. Almost all CSOs within the field

TABLE 9
DEGREE OF AUTONOMY FROM THE STATE BY CATEGORY OF CSO (%)

	State dependent	State funded	State autonomous
Education	3 (1)	3 (1)	94 (28)
Other	4 (1)	9 (2)	87 (20)
Women	6 (2)	19 (6)	75 (24)
Politics	15 (6)	10 (4)	75 (30)
Environment	14 (3)	14 (3)	72 (16)
Labour	12 (5)	19 (8)	69 (30)
Human rights	18 (12)	16 (11)	66 (44)
Youth	21 (7)	15 (5)	64 (22)
National identity	18 (5)	22 (6)	60 (16)
Social welfare	21 (26)	22 (27)	57 (72)
Recreation	36 (21)	19 (11)	45 (25)
Total	18 (89)	17 (84)	65 (327)

Note: The question was: 'How would you assess your organisation's/group's autonomy in relation to state authorities?' Respondents selected one of the following alternatives: (0) Highly dependent on state authorities for financial as well as political matters; (1) Dependent on some state subsidies and some political dependency; (2) Autonomous in most respects, but relies on some state subsidies; (3) Autonomous in most respects; (4) Completely autonomous. Answers have been classified as 'State dependent' (0 and 1), 'State funded' (2), and 'State autonomous' (3 and 4).
$N = 500$. (Absolute numbers within parentheses.)
Source: Civil Society Activism in Latvia – activists (CSALSa) 2004, see footnote 2.

of education (94%) claimed to be autonomous from the state whereas less than half of the recreational organisations said they were autonomous. State dependency is arguably less problematic for recreational CSOs than for more politically oriented groups.

Concerning the activities of Latvian CSOs, when representatives were asked how often their organisations or groups were involved in different activities, interest articulation, information gathering and public education turned out to be the most common, scoring 76, 75 and 74, respectively, on an index from 0 to 100 (Table 10). These are typical NGO activities, as are networking with similar organisations (which scored 69), fund seeking (66) and mobilisation of new members or supporters (65). Less common, but still carried out by a substantial part of Latvian CSOs, was transnational networking (55). On average Latvian CSOs scored much lower on more explicitly political activities such as writing petitions (30), lobbying political decision makers (29) and investigating and criticising abuse of state power (25). Such activities which are arguably most essential for civil society's role in strengthening democracy are seldom carried out by CSOs in Latvia. Almost non-existent were the more confrontational activities of organising demonstrations (7) and boycotts or strikes (3). The pattern is quite clear. Contemporary Latvian CSOs can be described as largely non-political and not at all confrontational. In this respect Latvia is similar to the other Baltic states and Russia (Uhlin 2006, pp. 74–76).

CSOs dealing with politics and human rights were somewhat less unlikely to organise demonstrations and boycotts, but also among those CSOs such confrontational activities were very rare. Political and human rights organisations also stand out

TABLE 10

ACTIVITIES OF CSOs PER CATEGORY (INDEX FROM 0 TO 100)

	Mobilisation	Articulating	Lobbying	State	Fund	Information	Education	Petition	Demonstration	Boycott	Networking own country	Networking other countries
Politics	72	80	52	54	65	82	79	46	16	7	74	56
Human rights	63	82	42	42	74	82	76	39	14	9	78	66
Women	76	76	31	14	69	79	77	19	3	0	77	55
Labour	65	73	26	16	53	75	72	33	4	2	62	59
National identity	64	77	12	16	66	72	70	20	3	0	73	55
Environment	64	68	31	30	65	75	77	33	5	1	71	50
Social welfare	62	75	26	23	70	72	72	34	8	1	65	49
Youth	68	78	18	18	71	67	76	18	2	5	66	54
Recreation	60	68	16	12	68	72	68	16	2	0	60	49
Education	65	74	21	10	52	79	82	23	0	0	63	42
Other	69	81	43	34	52	72	77	44	4	1	79	73
Total	65	76	29	25	66	75	74	30	7	3	69	55

Note: The question was: 'How often is the organisation/group involved in the following activities?'

Mobilisation = Mobilisation of new members/supporters; Articulating = Articulating and representing the interests of members/constituencies; Lobbying = Lobbying political decision makers; State = Investigating and criticising abuse of state power; Fund = Fund seeking; Information = Information gathering; Education = Public education; Petition = Writing petitions; Demonstration = Organising demonstrations; Boycott = Organising boycotts or strikes; Networking own country = Networking with similar organisations/groups in own country; Networking other countries = Networking with similar organisations/groups in other countries. Alternatives given were: Never = 0, Almost never = 20, Seldom = 40, Sometimes = 60, Often = 80, Very often = 100. The mean for each category of CSO is presented in the table. N = 495–500 depending on question.

Source: Civil Society Activism in Latvia—activists (CSALSa) 2004, see footnote 2.

as more likely to be engaged in lobbying, writing petitions and criticising the abuse of state power. Such explicitly political activities were naturally very uncommon among recreational CSOs, but also organisations dealing with national identity issues seemed to be surprisingly non-political in their activities.

In conclusion, the assessment of the structure of Latvian civil society, when measured on the organisational level, provides a more mixed picture than on the individual level. There was a relatively large number of CSOs and there had been a steady growth since independence. Nine out of 10 CSOs in this sample were established after independence. CSOs providing various kinds of social welfare services played an important role in Latvian civil society. Recreational organisations and more explicitly political CSOs focusing on democracy and human rights were also quite common. The typical Latvian CSO is a small organisation with few members. About two thirds of the CSOs included in the survey had less than 100 members and many were not membership-based at all. Despite the small size in terms of membership almost half of the organisations had some salaried staff. Hence the general picture is that CSOs in Latvia tend to be rather professional but mobilise few people.

Latvian CSOs have characteristics that to some extent put their democracy strengthening capacity into question. The measurement of internal democracy demonstrated shortcomings in a substantial portion of Latvian CSOs. Whereas internal democracy in women's groups was seen as reasonably good, CSOs working in the field of national identity and ethnic issues tended to have less internal democracy. A large majority of CSOs were judged by their representatives as autonomous in relation to the state. Less politically oriented sections of civil society, like social welfare and (especially) recreational CSOs tended to have considerably less autonomy than other CSOs. While the degree of autonomy of CSOs (as measured here) does not seem to be particularly problematic from a democratic perspective, an analysis of their activities indicates quite limited democratic functions. Most CSOs (not only recreational organisations) tended to be highly non-political in their activities. Activities like writing petitions, lobbying political decision-makers and investigating and criticising abuse of state power were rather uncommon, and more confrontational activities like organising demonstrations, boycotts and strikes were extremely rare. CSOs in contemporary Latvia can hardly be said to fulfil the democratic function of being a check against state power. Nor do they try to influence politics to any great extent.

The culture of civil society

Having presented an analysis of the structure of contemporary Latvian civil society, I now turn to cultural aspects. What norms and values characterise civil society in Latvia? First of all I examine support for democratic values. The survey (Table 11) indicated rather weak public support for democratic values in Latvia. A mean of about 60 on a scale between 0 and 100 reflected the fact that a large number of people living in Latvia were rather indifferent to, if not sceptical about democracy. However, when examining the different components of the index of support for democratic values, we find there was strong support for the principle of political equality and the protection of minority rights (a score of 80 or above) and relatively strong support for

TABLE 11
SUPPORT FOR DEMOCRATIC VALUES AMONG NON-ACTIVISTS AND CIVIL SOCIETY ACTIVISTS IN LATVIA
(INDEX FROM 0 = NO SUPPORT TO 100 = COMPLETE SUPPORT)

	Non-activists	Civil society activists
Democratic values	59	62
Political equality	83	85
Protection of minorities	80	82
Right to organise opposition	69	76
Political participation	41	44
Against strong-man rule	21	21

Note: The questions were: 'Below follows a set of thermometer questions where you get a chance to indicate in greater detail where you stand on each of the issues. The thermometer runs from 0 through 100. If you are in complete agreement with one of the statements below, you should give it 100. And if there is a statement you are in complete disagreement with, you should give it zero. (Give a number between 0 and 100 for each of the statements below.)'.
'Every citizen should have an equal chance to influence government policy'; 'The government has the responsibility to see to it that rights of all minorities are protected'; 'Any individual or an organisation has the right to organise opposition'; 'Widespread participation in decision-making often leads to undesirable conflicts'; 'It will always be necessary to have a few strong, able people actually running everything'. The first three statements represent democratic values whereas the last two statements indicate a lack of support for democracy. Hence, the results for the last two statements have been turned around in order to make comparisons easier. (For example, the mean for non-activists' agreement with the statement 'Widespread participation in decision-making often leads to undesirable conflicts' was 59. This results in a score of 41 in support of political participation.) The five statements are combined to an index of support for democratic values by adding the five components and dividing by five. Zero would mean a complete lack of support for democratic values and 100 complete support for democratic values.
$N = 498$–500 (depending on question) for activists and 908–924 (depending on question) for non-activists.
Source: Civil Society Activism in Latvia—activists (CSALSa) 2004 and Civil Society Activism in Latvia—public (CSALSp) 2004, see footnote 2.

the right to organise opposition. There was, however, a widespread scepticism against popular participation in political decision making and a strong desire for strong-man rule. This demonstrated support for an elitist version of democracy, in which basic democratic principles are respected, but with very limited popular participation.

When comparing the views of activists and non-activists there was no dramatic difference, although there was slightly more support for democratic values among activists than non-activists. While the margin was small, the pattern was consistent for all democratic values (with the interesting exception of the question of strong-man rule on which activists and non-activists held equally elitist views). The biggest difference between activists and non-activists concerned the right to organise opposition: hardly surprisingly activists were more supportive of this democratic right, which many of them relied on to form their organisations. The general pattern, however, was that Latvian civil society—as well as Latvian society at large—was characterised by support for core values associated with a limited form of elite democracy, with rather low support for political participation and a tendency to support strong-man rule.

Turning to a second indicator of the culture of civil society, generalised trust, we find that activists had considerably more trust in people than non-activists. Respondents were asked to indicate how strongly on a scale from 0 to 100 they agreed with the statement: 'Generally speaking, most people can be trusted'. The mean

TABLE 12

TRUST DEPENDING ON FIELD OF ACTIVITY FOR CIVIL SOCIETY ACTIVISM IN LATVIA (MEAN ON AN INDEX
FROM 0 = NO TRUST TO 100 = COMPLETE TRUST)

Field of activity	
Politics in general	70
Education	67
Women	67
National identity/ethnic issues	66
Democracy and human rights	63
Other	63
Labour	63
Social welfare/charity	60
Recreation (sport, culture, etc.)	59
Youth	56
Environment	42
Total	62

Note: Respondents were asked to indicate on a scale from 0 (completely against) to 100 (completely for) to what extent they agreed with the statement 'Generally speaking, most people can be trusted'.
$N = 499$.
Source: Civil Society Activism in Latvia—activists (CSALSa) 2004, see footnote 2.

for non-activists was 44 whereas the mean for activists was 62.[8] This cannot be interpreted as a very high level of trust for either group, but the difference is significant. Those who were active in CSOs in Latvia were more trusting than non-activists. Whether they acquired their trust through civil society activities or they became active in CSOs because they had a higher level of trust to begin with is impossible to judge from the data available here.

Trust varied considerably between different fields of civil society activity (Table 12). Those active in political CSOs, and also in educational and women's groups, were more trusting but, interestingly, activists in environmental CSOs tended to be considerably less trusting than other civil society activists. They even had less trust than non-activists (with a score of 42 compared to 44 on the trust index). This might be related to peculiarities of environmentalism in Latvia where many environmental organisations had a distinctly nationalist agenda and there were many quasi-environmental NGOs, for example created by the oil transit industry (Galbreath & Auers 2009).

As a third indicator of the culture of civil society I examined social tolerance among civil society activists compared with non-activists. Asked to indicate which categories of people they did not want to have as neighbours, civil society activists turned out to be much more tolerant than non-activists (Table 13). This applied for all categories of people except for the ideological categories of left-wing and right-wing extremists. Activists and non-activists were equally (in)tolerant of right-wing extremists (35% did not want them as neighbours) and activists were less tolerant than non-activists towards left-wing extremists (48% as compared to 43% did not want them as

[8]Non-activists: $N = 923$, standard deviation 25. Activists: $N = 499$, standard deviation 25. Source: Civil Society Activism in Latvia—public (CSALSp) 2004 and Civil Society Activism in Latvia—activists (CSALSa) 2004.

TABLE 13

SOCIAL TOLERANCE AMONG CIVIL SOCIETY ACTIVISTS AND NON-ACTIVISTS (% NOT WANTING CERTAIN PEOPLE AS NEIGHBOURS)

Would not like as neighbours	Civil society activists	Non-activists	Difference
Drug addicts	72 (358)	92 (857)	−20
Heavy drinkers	64 (322)	79 (737)	−15
Left-wing extremists	48 (239)	43 (402)	5
People with a criminal record	45 (224)	72 (665)	−27
Emotionally unstable people	37 (183)	63 (588)	−26
Right-wing extremists	35 (174)	35 (328)	0
Homosexuals	28 (140)	52 (481)	−24
People who have AIDS	20 (102)	53 (488)	−33
Roma	17 (83)	44 (412)	−27
Muslims	13 (64)	32 (300)	−19
Immigrants/foreign workers	12 (61)	21 (197)	−9
People of different race	6 (30)	10 (96)	−4
People with large families	3 (16)	9 (84)	−6
Jews	3 (14)	10 (98)	−7

Note: The question was: 'On this list are various groups of people. Could you please sort out any that you would not like to have as neighbours?' (Absolute numbers within parentheses.)

$N = 500$ for activists and 928 for non-activists. (Absolute numbers within parentheses.)

Source: Civil Society Activism in Latvia—activists (CSALSa) 2004 and Civil Society Activism in Latvia—public (CSALSp) 2004, see footnote 2.

neighbours). Compared to non-activists, civil society activists were considerably more tolerant (a difference of 20 percentage points or more) towards people who had AIDS, people with a criminal record, Roma, emotionally unstable people, homosexuals and drug addicts. Only two categories of people were not wanted as neighbours by a majority of civil society activists in the sample: drug addicts and heavy drinkers. There was little indication of racism or prejudices against immigrants or ethnic or religious minorities such as Jews, Muslims and the Roma population.

Thus, the norms and values prevailing in Latvian civil society were related to an elitist version of liberal democracy, with low support for political participation and a tendency to support strong-man rule. Civil society activists were not considerably more supportive of democratic values than non-activists. However, civil society activists had much more trust in people than non-activists and they tended to be much more tolerant against different minorities and marginalised groups than non-activists. Norms of social tolerance and trust were hence associated with contemporary Latvian civil society. These conclusions were in line with the broader analysis by CIVICUS, in which values tended to appear as the least problematic dimension of post-communist civil societies. In all post-communist civil societies covered by the CIVICUS index values like tolerance, solidarity with marginalised groups, respect for human rights and environmental protection were present (Heinrich & Fioramonti 2008).

Conclusion

Post-communist civil society is generally depicted as weak in international comparison. Through an analysis of civil society in Latvia, this study has tried to provide a more nuanced view, examining in which ways it can correctly be said to be weak, and also finding some stronger aspects of civil society development. Post-communist civil society in Latvia is weak when measured on the individual level. Only a small minority of people living in Latvia is active in CSOs or takes part in less formalised civil society activities. Civic and political engagement is low by any standards. This, however, is not unique to Latvia. On the contrary, the demobilisation of civil society following a transition to democracy is typical, not only for post-communist civil societies, but also for post-authoritarian countries in general.

When examining the structure of Latvian civil society on the organisational level, a more mixed picture emerges. There is a relatively large number of CSOs covering a broad spectrum of issue areas. While most of these groups are small in terms of membership, many are quite professional and have some salaried staff. There are shortcomings concerning internal democracy. Most CSOs are perceived as relatively autonomous in relation to the state, but financial dependence on local governments is likely to increase as foreign funding of CSOs has decreased since Latvia's entrance into the European Union in 2004. The most striking feature of contemporary civil society in Latvia is arguably its non-political character. A large majority of CSOs do not try to influence political decision-making or act as a check against the abuse of state power. More confrontational political activities like demonstrations and boycotts are extremely rare. Overall Latvian CSOs could not be said to perform the most common democracy-strengthening functions. Again, this is not unique to Latvia. Similar tendencies can be seen in other post-communist countries, including the other Baltic states as well as Russia. However, the lack of politicisation of civil society appears to be even more pronounced in Latvia. Civil society activists in Latvia believe they have less political influence compared to activists in Estonia, Lithuania and Russia (Uhlin 2006, pp. 110–11). Furthermore, while trust in political parties is generally rather low in the post-Soviet context, civil society activists in Latvia tend to have almost no trust at all in political parties. In this respect too, Latvia stands out when compared to the other Baltic states and Russia (Uhlin 2006, pp. 125–26).

The most positive evaluation, arguably, results from the analysis of the cultural dimension of civil society in Latvia. Norms and values prevalent in contemporary Latvian civil society are associated with a relatively high degree of trust and social tolerance, at least compared to the general public. There is also widespread support for important democratic values although support for participatory aspects of democracy is low and (like in many other post-communist countries) there is a tendency to support strong-man rule. Hence, the political culture of post-communist civil society in Latvia can be described as trusting, tolerant and pro-democratic, but rather elitist.

The relative weakness of post-communist civil society is a puzzle considering the strong civil society mobilisation in the overthrow of communist regimes (Dvorakova 2008). How can these weaknesses be explained given the massive civil society mobilisation at the end of the 1980s, manifested in the popular movement for independence in Latvia? Marc Howard, in his influential work (2003) emphasises three factors: firstly, there is a lack of trust in public organisations as a heritage from the communist regime; secondly, informal social networks between friends which developed under communist rule and are still in place lessen the need for more public social networks in the form of CSOs; and thirdly, there is a general disappointment with the post-communist regimes. The first two factors are related to the history of communist rule. It is very reasonable that decades of more or less totalitarian rule have shaped conditions for the development of post-communist societies. There were indeed many mass organisations under the communist regime, but these organisations did not act in a civil society arena. They were part of the party–state structure and membership was typically not voluntary. It is hardly surprising that people who have experienced such enforced state-controlled associational life are suspicious of public organisations. The second factor, the survival of friendship networks, concerns strategies to manage everyday life under communist rule. Informal social networks, for instance among relatives, neighbours and colleagues at the workplace, gave access to certain goods and services which were otherwise not available and led to the development of some kind of societal trust outside the control of the party–state. If such networks are still important in the post-communist context, there is less need to engage in formal public social networks, like the new CSOs. The question, however, is to what extent such informal networks really prevail in post-communist Europe. There is insufficient evidence from Latvia and other parts of the post-communist world to allow any firm conclusion on this issue.

Howard's third explanation to the weakness of post-communist civil society, a general disappointment with the performance of the post-communist regimes, also makes sense and it is certainly relevant in the case of Latvia. Severe economic and social problems, corruption and an unstable party system resulting in frequent changes of government have led to a widespread distrust in political and economic elites. However, it is not clear why this general distrust should include CSOs. One could in fact expect the dissatisfaction with political and economic elites to lead to increased support for advocacy CSOs criticising the established system.

Hence, a more significant factor behind the weakness of post-communist civil society—in Latvia as well as more generally—is probably the elitist character of many CSOs themselves. Most new CSOs have not emerged from below, but instead have been set up in order to receive foreign funding and carry out specific projects (Fioramonti & Heinrich 2007, p. 15). Many Latvian CSOs have been heavily dependent on foreign funding, especially from the Soros Foundation, until 2004 (Vilka & Strupiss 2004, p. 50). While foreign funding has been necessary for the establishment and survival of many CSOs, given the lack of locally available economic resources from public or private actors, it has also shaped the activities of these new organisations. With foreign funding there are fewer incentives to mobilise local citizens. Many civil society activists have been forced to prioritise the tasks of writing applications, carrying out donor-initiated projects and reporting these activities. There has simply been less time and need for public outreach activities. Hence, most people are ignorant about CSOs or find their activities irrelevant.

A modification of the prevalent scholarly conclusions about the weakness of post-communist civil society has been suggested by Petrova and Tarrow (2007). They differentiate between individual and relational dimensions of civic participation and argue that post-communist civil society is indeed weak on the individual dimension. There is little political participation through CSOs, which tend to have few if any grassroots connections. Nevertheless, a broad spectrum of CSOs has emerged since the breakdown of communist regimes and vertical relations between different CSOs, as well as between these groups and state officials, are developing. Hence, post-communist civil society is characterised by weak participatory activism, but relatively strong 'transactional activism', focusing on the ties among organised non-state actors and between them and political parties and state actors (Petrova & Tarrow 2007). This implies an elitist civil society, but not necessarily a weak one. To some extent the present study supports this view. The weakness of the individual dimension of post-communist civil society is confirmed in the Latvian case. In some respects civil society in Latvia is stronger on the organisational dimension. There is indeed a broad spectrum of CSOs in contemporary Latvia. The non-political character of their activities, however, makes it questionable to speak about a relatively strong 'transactional activism', which Petrova and Tarrow have found in other post-communist countries.

The data for this study were collected just before Latvia became a member of the EU in 2004. Since then the development of civil society in the country has shown contrasting trajectories: while there is an increasing number of NGOs—slightly more than 10,000 were registered in November 2008 (USAID 2009, p. 142)—a trend towards less citizen participation in voluntary associations between 2005 and 2007 has been reported (Miezaine & Simane 2007). Less formalised civil society activities have also been relatively rare. Social movements are far from prominent in contemporary Latvia (Miezaine & Simane 2007, p. 85). Nevertheless, there have been a number of protests against the government, most notably related to the minority education reform policy in spring and autumn 2004 (Miezaine & Simane 2005, p. 150; Ijabs 2006, p. 81), and against Prime Minister Kalvitis' decision to dismiss the Head of the Anti-corruption Bureau in the autumn of 2007 (Ikstens 2008), as well as violent riots in Riga in January 2009 in reaction to the severe economic crisis (Pridham 2009, p. 485). The economic crisis has had a negative effect on Latvian civil society and further aggravated problems of funding which arose when the main foreign donors left Latvia following EU membership. Private donors in Latvia tend to focus on recreational NGOs like sports clubs and cultural organisations. This makes it very hard for advocacy NGOs to secure funding (USAID 2008, p. 141). Moreover, the public image of NGOs is generally characterised by ignorance, if not hostility (USAID 2009, p. 148).

There are, however, more positive trends as well. Pridham (2009) argues that there have been some improvements in civil society development after EU membership. New funding has been made available through the EU Structural Funds and the fact that EU institutions recognise NGOs as partners has led to improved state–civil society relations in Latvia. Funding for NGO activities has also been made available through the 'National Program for Strengthening Civil Society 2004–2009' administered by the Ministry of Special Assignment for Social Integration (USAID 2009, p. 144).

To sum up the findings of this study, post-communist civil society in Latvia is weak when it comes to its capacity to mobilise people for civil society activities and recruit new members for CSOs. The non-political character of Latvia's civil society is also striking. The reasons for these weaknesses are partly related to the experiences of communist rule and partly an effect of the specific conditions under which new CSOs were set up with the support of foreign funding agencies. Concerning cultural aspects, some less negative assessments of Latvia's civil society can be made, as values of trust, tolerance and support for democracy (albeit in an elitist version) are relatively strong.

Future research could fruitfully examine such cultural dimensions of post-communist civil society development in more detail and also provide more systematic cross-country data on these issues.

Lund University

References

Aasland, A. (2002) 'Citizenship Status and Social Exclusion in Estonia and Latvia', *Journal of Baltic Studies*, 33, 1.

Anheier, H. K. (2004) *Civil Society: Measurement, Evaluation, Policy* (London, Earthscan).

Armony, A. C. (2004) *The Dubious Link: Civic Engagement and Democratization* (Stanford, CA, Stanford University Press).

Baker, G. (2002) *Civil Society and Democratic Theory: Alternative Voices* (London & New York, Routledge).

Celichowski, J. (2008) 'Civil Societies in Post-Communist Europe: The Challenges Posed by Social Isolation', in Heinrich, V. F. & Fioramonti, L. (eds) (2008).

CIVICUS (1997) *The New Civic Atlas: Profiles of Civil Society in 60 Countries* (Washington, DC, CIVICUS).

Dvorakova, V. (2008) 'Civil Society in Latin America and Eastern Europe: Reinvention or Imposition?', *International Political Science Review*, 29, 5.

Fagan, A. (2005) 'Taking Stock of Civil-Society Development in Post-communist Europe: Evidence from the Czech Republic', *Democratization*, 12, 4.

Fioramonti, L. & Heinrich, V. F. (2007) *How Civil Society Influences Policy: A Comparative Analysis of the CIVICUS Civil Society Index in Post-Communist Europe* (Washington, DC & London, CIVICUS/ODI Research Report).

Galbreath, D. J. & Auers, D. (2009) 'Green, Black and Brown: Uncovering Latvia's Environmental Politics', *Journal of Baltic Studies*, 40, 3.

Heinrich, V. F. (2005) 'Studying Civil Society across the World: Exploring the Thorny Issues of Conceptualization and Measurement', *Journal of Civil Society*, 1, 3.

Heinrich, V. F. & Fioramonti, L. (eds) (2008) *CIVICUS Global Survey of the State of Civil Society, Volume 2: Comparative Perspectives* (Bloomfield, IN, Kumarian Press).

Howard, M. M. (2003) *The Weakness of Civil Society in Post-Communist Europe* (Cambridge, Cambridge University Press).

Howard, M. M. (2005) 'Conceptual and Methodological Suggestions for Improving Cross-National Measures of Civil Society: Commentary on Heinrich', *Journal of Civil Society*, 1, 3.

Hydén, G. (1997) 'Building Civil Society at the Turn of the Millennium', in Burbidge, J. (ed.) (1997) *Beyond Prince and Merchant. Citizen Participation and the Rise of Civil Society* (New York, Pact Publications).

Ijabs, I. (2006) 'Russians and Civil Society', in Muiznieks, N. (ed.) (2006) *Latvian–Russian Relations: Domestic and International Dimensions* (Riga, LU Akademiskais Apgads).

Ikstens, J. (2008) 'Latvia', *European Journal of Political Research*, 47.

Karatnycky, A., Motyl, A. & Shor, B. (eds) (1997) *Nations in Transit 1997. Civil Society, Democracy and Markets in East Central Europe and the Newly Independent States* (New Brunswick & London, Transaction Publishers).

Karklins, R. & Zepa, B. (2001) 'Political Participation in Latvia 1987–2001', *Journal of Baltic Studies*, 32, 4.

Kopecký, P. (2003) 'Civil Society, Uncivil Society and Contentious Politics in Post-Communist Europe', in Kopecký, P. & Mudde, C. (eds) (2003).

Kopecký, P. & Mudde, C. (eds) (2003) *Uncivil Society? Contentious Politics in Post-Communist Europe* (London & New York, Routledge).

Lindén, T. (2008) *Explaining Civil Society Core Activism in Post-Soviet Latvia*, Stockholm Studies in Politics 123 (Stockholm, Stockholm University and Södertörns högskola).

Miezaine, Z. & Simane, M. (2005) 'Political Participation', in Commission on Strategic Analysis (2005) *How Democratic is Latvia? Audit of Democracy* (Riga, LU Akademiskais Apgads), available at: http://www.szf.lu.lv/files/petnieciba/publikacijas/Demokrat_en.pdf, accessed 22 March 2010.

Miezaine, Z. & Simane, M. (2007) 'Political Participation', in Commission on Strategic Analysis (2010) *How Democratic is Latvia? Monitoring of Democracy 2005–2007* (Riga, Zinatne), available at: http://www.szf.lu.lv/files/petnieciba/publikacijas/Demokratijas_monitorings_anglu_16.pdf, accessed 22 March 2010.

Mudde, C. (2003) 'Civil Society in Post-Communist Europe: Lessons from the "Dark Side"', in Kopecký, P. & Mudde, C. (eds) (2003).

Ostrowska, I. (1997) 'The Developing Civil Society: Peculiarities in Latvia', in Hjerppe, R., Kanninnen, T., Patomäki, H. & Sehm, K. (eds) (1997) *Democracy, Economy and Civil Society in Transition: The Cases of Russia and the Baltic States* (Helsinki, The Finnish Institute of International Affairs, UPI, and the National Research and Development Center of Welfare and Health, STAKES).

Pabriks, A. & Purs, A. (2002) *Latvia: The Challenges of Change* (London & New York, Routledge).

Petrova, T. & Tarrow, S. (2007) 'Transactional and Participatory Activism in the Emerging European Polity: The Puzzle of East-Central Europe', *Comparative Political Studies*, 40, 1.

Pridham, G. (2009) 'Post-Soviet Latvia: A Consolidated or Defective Democracy? The Interaction between Domestic and European Trajectories', *Journal of Baltic Studies*, 40, 4.

Salamon, L. M., Sokolowski, S. W. & Associates (eds) (2004) *Global Civil Society, Volume 2: Dimensions of the Nonprofit Sector* (Bloomfield, IN, Kumarian Press).

Salamon, L. M., Sokolowski, S. W. & List, R. (2004) 'Global Civil Society: An Overview', in Salamon, L. M., Sokolowski, S. W. & Associates (eds) (2004).

Smith-Sivertsen, H. (2000) 'Civil Society in the Baltic States: Participation and NGOs', in Aarebrot, F. & Knutsen, T. (eds) (2000) *Politics and Citizenship on the Eastern Baltic Seaboard: The Structuring of Democratic Politics from North-West Russia to Poland* (Kristiansand, Höyskoleforlaget).

Uhlin, A. (2006) *Post-Soviet Civil Society: Democratization in Russia and the Baltic States* (London & New York, Routledge).

Uhlin, A. (2009) 'Which Characteristics of Civil Society Organizations Support What Aspects of Democracy? Evidence from Post-Communist Latvia', *International Political Science Review*, 30, 3.

USAID (2008) *The 2007 NGO Sustainability Index for Central and Eastern Europe and Eurasia*, available at: http://www.usaid.gov/locations/europe_eurasia/dem_gov/ngoindex/2007/complete_document.pdf, accessed 22 March 2010.

USAID (2009) *The 2008 NGO Sustainability Index for Central and Eastern Europe and Eurasia*, available at: http://www.usaid.gov/locations/europe_eurasia/dem_gov/ngoindex/2008/complete_document.pdf, accessed 22 March 2010.

Vilka, I. & Strupiss, A. (2004) *The Development of Civil Society in Latvia: An Analysis* (Riga, Secretariat of the Minister for Special Assignments for Society Integration Affairs).

Waisman, C. H. (2006) 'Autonomy, Self-Regulation, and Democracy: Tocquevillean–Gellnerian Perspectives on Civil Society and the Bifurcated State in Latin America', in Feinberg, R., Waisman, C. H. & Zamosc, L. (eds) (2006) *Civil Society and Democracy in Latin America* (Houndmills, Basingstoke, Palgrave Macmillan).

Welzel, C., Inglehart, R. & Franziska, D. (2005) 'Social Capital, Voluntary Associations and Collective Action: Which Aspects of Social Capital Have the Greatest "Civic" Payoff?', *Journal of Civil Society*, 1, 2.

Zepa, B. (ed.) (1999) *Conditions of Enhancement of Civic Participation* (Riga, Baltic Data House).

The Development of Pensioners' Interest Organisations in Central and Eastern Europe: A Comparison of the Czech and Slovene Cases

SEÁN HANLEY

Abstract

Studies of organised interests in Central and Eastern Europe have overlooked constituencies shaped by the welfare state such as retired people. The article compares the development, structure and strategies of pensioners' interest organisations in the Czech Republic and Slovenia. It finds that sizeable, if poorly resourced, membership-based pensioners' interest organisations have emerged, largely independently of trade unions, and integrated into interest representation systems. Although lack of resources and organisational problems hamper lobbying capacity, these groups retain mobilisation potential. Comparison suggests that legacies and modes of transition still shape pensioners' interest organisations more than institutional structures or new population ageing strategies.

THE EXISTENCE OF DISTINCT AUTONOMOUS ORGANISED interests is central to the notion of a liberal-democratic polity (Schmitter 1992; Ost 1993, pp. 454–57; Baumgartner & Leech 1998). Indeed, Schmitter (2008, p. 199) goes so far as to suggest that interest groups are now the 'effective "citizens" of their respective democracies'. Unsurprisingly, therefore, studies of socio-economic interests and their representation and their linkage to policy makers have been a key strand of research on the development of the newer democracies in Central and Eastern Europe (Ost 1993; Padgett 1999; Pérez-Solórzano Borragán 2006; Cox 2007). Such research has, however, so far been curiously uneven. There is an extensive literature on organised labour (Pollert 1999; Crowley & Ost 2001; Kubicek 2004; Ost 2009; Myant 2010) and, to a lesser extent, employers' organisations (Myant 2000; Duvanova 2007) and other producer groups (Blažek 2002; Yakova 2004). However, while the importance of such groups in Central and Eastern European societies is undeniable, research on economic interest groups in Western democracies has long extended beyond those rooted in

The author gratefully acknowledges the support of the Nuffield Foundation Social Science Small Grants Scheme for the fieldwork for this research. I would also like to thank Dr Alenka Krašovec for her generous help in facilitating interviews in Slovenia and the then Czech Deputy Minister of Labour and Social Affairs Marian Hošek and Petr Wija of the ministry's Social Inclusion Section for discussing the Czech Preparation for Ageing programme with me.

employment relationships or the production process, with welfare states, in particular, increasingly recognised as powerful shapers of interests, capable of generating powerful and distinct social constituencies. One such constituency, whose potential organised influence has attracted growing scholarly attention, is the large and growing proportion of older and retired citizens in contemporary European democracies (Walker 1998; Lynch 2006; Goerres & Vanhyusse 2011).

Although the literature on post-communist pension and welfare reform has often noted the existence of pensioners' associations (Müller 1999, 2002; Orenstein 2000), there has so far been little or no direct examination of the ways in which retired people in the region have been organised as an interest constituency. This is potentially a significant lacuna. As shown in Figure 1, older and retired people in Central and Eastern Europe, as elsewhere in the developed world, make up a large and increasing proportion of citizens, with population ageing driven by the same underlying factors of longer life expectancy and declining fertility (Mukesh et al. 2007). At the same time Central and Eastern Europe has a number of regional peculiarities which may shape the development of retired people in the region as an organised interest in distinct ways. In addition to communist regimes' destruction or nationalisation of historically evolved social organisations and their legacy of stunting subsequent civil society development (Howard 2003), Central and Eastern Europe also possesses a distinct conjuncture of demographic, economic and institutional factors, which merit a specific study of the regional patterns of age-related interest group development. As relatively poor societies with extensive welfare and pension systems they face twin challenges of adaptation to a market economy and reform as a consequence of demographic change and fiscal austerity.

In this article I seek to address this gap through comparative case studies of the development of older and retired people's interest organisations in two Central and Eastern European democracies: the Czech Republic and Slovenia. Although touching on the politics of pension and welfare reform, rather than seeking specifically to quantify their influence in particular policy processes, the article seeks to assess the development of Central and Eastern European pensioners' organisations more broadly as a distinct and under-researched interest group sector, examining and explaining how their organisational development and strategies of influence have been configured in particular ways. The main empirical focus of the article is thus on national self-advocacy organisations which represent the group interests of older and retired people without themselves becoming party-political actors. Although taking in developments since 1989–1990, the article deals mainly with structures and strategies of pensioners' interest organisations in the period 2001–2010, a time of rapid organisational and policy development, when wider European contexts had the scope to make themselves felt alongside the impact of transition and historical factors.

The article proceeds as follows. First, it discusses propositions regarding older and retired people in Central and Eastern Europe as an interest group found—or implied—in work on post-communist social policy reform and civil society development and in studies of Western seniors' groupings, reviewing key reasons for pensioners' (generally assumed) weakness as an organised interest in Central and Eastern Europe. It then presents the Czech Republic and Slovenia as particular cases before

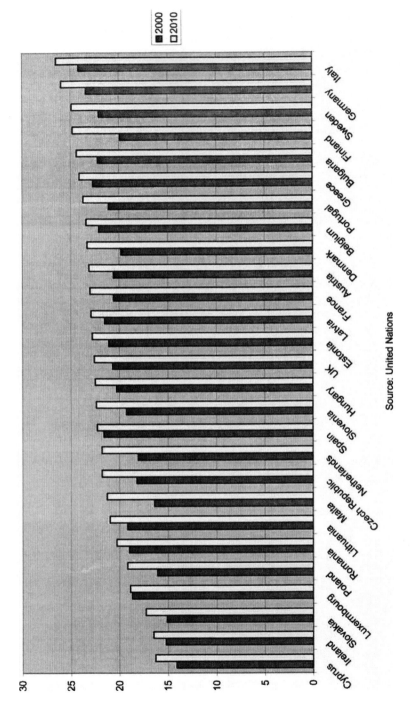

FIGURE 1. PERCENTAGE OF POPULATION AGED 60 OR OVER IN EU STATES. *Source:* compiled by the author from online data (specifically http://data.un.org/ Data.aspx?q=age+60&d=PopDiv&f=variableID%3a33#PopDiv. accessed 20 August 2012) (United Nations 2011).

making a structured, focused comparison of the development of pensioners' interest organisations and their strategies across the two cases. Next, it assesses the historical, institutional and contextual factors that shaped these configurations, testing certain assumptions in the literature and highlighting and explaining differences and commonalities between the two states. The article concludes by considering the implications of the case studies for wider research on retired and older people's interest organisations in post-communist Europe and their likely prospects.

Pensioners as an organised interest in post-communist Europe

Pensioners in post-communist Europe are often depicted as an archetypically disempowered and impoverished group of 'transition losers'. However, while this is undoubtedly true for some states and sub-groups, the general picture is more complex. Although welfare systems were cut back in much of Central and Eastern Europe, retired people enjoyed relative stability and continuity in pension provision as the systematic reform of pensions was initially postponed (Müller 1999; Orenstein 2000; Vanhuysse 2006a; Orenstein 2008a; Bohle & Greskovits 2009). Indeed, Vanhuysse (2006a) argues that pensioners were among key groups of potential 'transition losers' that were deliberately cushioned by Central and Eastern European policy makers through 'strategic social policy' intended to 'divide and pacify' anti-reform constituencies and pre-empt mass social protest. Moreover, as the state remained the main provider of pensions and income for most retired people through public pension systems dating from the socialist period (Večerník 2006; Vanhuysse 2006a), and pensioners in the region were a large and relatively homogeneous group in terms of income and lifestyle, they faced, in the post-communist state, a stable, single and clearly defined interlocutor.

While size, homogeneity and a high shared interest in welfare and pension outcomes potentially facilitated interest aggregation and group organisation, at the same time retired people in the region faced a number of obstacles and disincentives to collective action and organisation. These were often more sharply posed forms of those facing retired citizens in many democracies: geographical dispersal; less extensive social networks; lower material resources in comparison with other citizens; higher turnover of members and leaders; lower capacity to disrupt social and economic life; and difficulty in framing a strong socio-political identity based on withdrawal from economic activity or entering the final stage of the life course (Pratt 1993; Walker 1998; Vanhuysse 2008; Wang 1999). Reviewing retired people's potential for collective action in Central and Eastern Europe compared with that of other groups, Vanhuysse (2008) concluded that pensioners' lack of material and network resources, lower physical strength and lack of prior organisation would hamstring their capacity for group action, inclining them towards 'peaceful voice' rather than contentious protest. Vanhuysse (2008) saw such 'peaceful voice' primarily in terms of older people's electoral participation, discounting interest group politics as likely to be impeded by many (but not all) of the constraints blocking disruptive protest, and likely to be further undermined by the weak levels of civic participation characteristic of economically inactive 'outsider' groups. Available empirical evidence and theoretical reasoning thus suggested that, while not wholly lacking incentives for collective action, pensioners in post-communist Central and Eastern Europe would struggle to organise collectively to pressurise governments.

The Czech Republic and Slovenia as case studies

The Czech Republic and Slovenia are selected as 'most likely cases' (Eckstein 1975) in Central and Eastern Europe for the development of relatively strong retired people's interest organisations. Both made relatively early demographic transitions and, as Figure 1 shows, have high (but stable) proportions of older and retired citizens at the mid-range relative both to other Central and Eastern European states and EU members generally. Both also possess relatively high living standards and extensive and well-administered welfare states, which exemplify the distinct Central European pattern of post-communist social policy noted above (Večerník 2004, 2006; Vanhuysse 2006a). As illustrated in Figure 2 they thus have broadly maintained, while gradually reducing, the value of old age pensions relative to average wages. Both are established democracies with stable institutions which offer a predictable set of formal opportunity structures for the development of organised interest groups and, until the most recent elections (2010 in the Czech Republic, 2011 in Slovenia), had stable party systems with patterns of party competition centring on distributional conflicts, which are likely to facilitate and legitimise the development of economic interest groups, although the class nature of left–right divisions is more muted in Slovenia (Deegan-Krause 2006; Jou 2011).

The Czech Republic and Slovenia are, however, distinct within the Central and Eastern European region in having delayed—until recently—the adoption of systematic pension reforms in favour of parametric and incremental changes (Müller 1999, 2002; Guardiancich 2012). This reflects the stronger fiscal position of the Czech and Slovene public pension systems, the absence of strong majority coalitions committed to pension reform and, to a more limited extent, the ability of trade unions to mobilise public opinion against raising the retirement age (Müller 1999, 2002; Orenstein 2000; Guardiancich 2004, 2012). Despite the recent passing of legislation for systemic pension reform by governments driven by the imperatives of fiscal austerity, at the time this article was completed the fate of pension reform in both states was still uncertain.[1] What is certain, however, is that in both cases social policy areas of central concern to pensioners' organisations enjoyed continued and high political salience, potentially favouring their development. At the same time the historical and institutional contexts in Slovenia and the Czech Republic—such as the nature of the outgoing communist regime; the transition from communism; patterns of formal consultation and representation of interest groups; and levels of polarisation and fragmentation of the party system—vary in potentially important ways enabling cross-case comparison.

---

[1]Legislation for systemic pension reform was passed by the Slovene National Assembly in December 2010, but subsequently negated by a referendum six months later. Meanwhile, in the Czech Republic, pension reform legislation to create a compulsory second pillar was introduced by the majority centre-right government of Petr Nečas and was passed by the parliament in November 2011. However, the government's loss of a reliable majority following splits in the small Public Affairs Party (*Věci veřejné*), make implementation of the reforms uncertain.

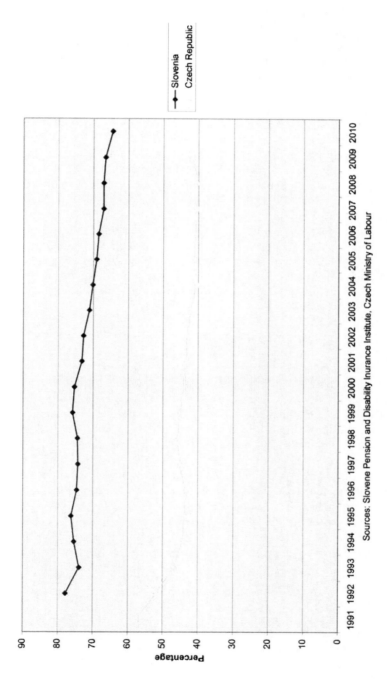

FIGURE 2. MEAN OLD AGE PENSION RELATIVE TO MEAN NET SALARY, 1991–2010. *Sources*: for Slovenia: complied by the author from Zavod za pokojninsko in invalidsko zavarovanje Slovenije (2011, Table XI, p. 7); Zavod za pokojninsko in invalidsko zavarovanje Slovenije (2006, Table X, p. 4); http://www.zpiz.si wps wcm connect c4e1798046562600 9db0fff b319e11ce Monthly+Statistics+Overview-2010 9db0fff b319e11ce. accessed 20 August 2012; http://www.zpiz.si/wps/wcm/connect/8e19fd804409134ba97af9745e837060/en_msp_2005.pdf?MOD=AJPERES&CACHEID=c4e1798046562600 9db0fff b319e11ce, accessed 20 August 2012. Zavod za pokojninsko in invalidsko zavarovanje Slovenije (ZPIZ) is the Pension and Disability Insurance Institute of Slovenia. For the Czech Republic: *Výzkumný ústav práce a sociálních věcí* (Research Institute for Labour and Social Affairs) (2012, Table II, p. 19); http://praha.vupsv.cz Fulltext bullNo27.pdf, accessed 20 August 2012. This institute is an agency of the Czech Ministry of Labour and Social Affairs which is the original source/complier of the data.

Structures and strategies

In both the Czech Republic and Slovenia a range of interest organisations seeking to represent retired and older people developed rapidly after the fall of communism. Although there are no systematic comparative typologies of seniors' organisations, the forms of organisation which emerged in both states broadly paralleled the two most prevalent types of pensioners' self-organisation found in Western Europe: trade-union sponsored groupings and independent, territorially based associations (Evers & Wolf 1999). Umbrella organisations coordinating the activities of smaller pensioners' and seniors' groups were also identified as a relevant organisational form, especially in the Czech Republic. As in some Western European states, 'pro-senior' charitable organisations and NGOs providing services and advocacy for older people, but not seeking to represent them, were also present. The strategies of influence deployed by pensioners' interest organisations in the two cases broadly fit within the comparative typologies identified in the interest group literature on Western democracies. Most, to use the terminology of Binderkrantz (2005), were 'direct' strategies of contacting and consulting with officials and office-holders and lobbying legislators and parties, rather than 'indirect' strategies of mobilising members and supporters in campaigns and protests, or working to influence public and elite opinion through the media. The following sections compare and examine the principal pensioners' groups in the two cases in closer and more systematic detail.

Trade-union sponsored pensioners' groupings

Given their size, resources and ageing memberships, trade unions have often been seen as the most forceful advocates of the interests of pensioners in Central and Eastern Europe (Müller 1999, 2002; Orenstein 2000). Moreover, in much of the region, including the Czech Republic and Slovenia, trade unions' access to policy makers is specifically institutionalised through national tripartite bodies created in the early 1990s, whose remits include both economic and labour market issues and broader social policy questions (Myant et al. 2000; Fink-Hafner 1998; Lukšič 2003; Guardiancich 2012).[2] Of the two case studies examined here, Slovenia's tripartite institutions have usually been considered to be more strongly neo-corporatist (Bohle & Greskovits 2007; Guardiancich 2012); however, in both countries they have a role in reviewing draft legislation, and the Czech tripartite council's importance has arguably often been underestimated (Valterová 2006). Trade unions in both the Czech Republic and Slovenia have also possessed the organisational and mobilisational capacity to stage mass demonstrations and occasional strikes, protesting aspects of social and economic policy, including pension issues, a trend which has become more marked and widespread since 2008–2009 as governments

---

[2]The Czech Council of Economic and Social Agreement (*Rada hospodářské a sociální dohody*, RHSD) was created in 1990 while Slovenia's Economic and Social Council (*Ekonomsko-socialni svet*, ESS) was established in April 1994.

have imposed austerity measures and prioritised social policy reforms, often bypassing mechanisms for social dialogue (Guardiancich 2012).[3]

In both the Czech Republic and Slovenia the principal trade-union federations made an early strategic choice in the 1990s to seek to organise and represent pensioners. This was partly a response to membership decline stemming from economic restructuring—and, in particular, to large numbers of older workers leaving employment for retirement—and partly an aspect of broader adjustment strategies intended to extend unions' representative role to economically inactive, socially vulnerable groups. In the Czech Republic, for example, the principal union federation, the Bohemian–Moravian Confederation of Trade Unions (*Českomoravská konfederace odborových svazů*, ČMKOS), successor to the communist-era Revolutionary Trade Union Movement (*Revoluční odborové hnutí*, ROH), formally included the goal of 'influenc[ing] the formation and implementation of social policy including care for pensioners' in its statutes.[4] The early activism of independent pensioners' associations (discussed below), which seem to have emerged very rapidly after the fall of communism, may also have played a role in alerting trade unions to the potential importance of pensioners as a constituency.

Central to this strategy in both cases was the creation of trade-union sponsored groupings to organise and coordinate retired members. However, the Czech and Slovene cases exhibit contrasting organisational strategies. In the Czech Republic in 1991 ČMKOS established the Association of Retired Trade Unionists (*Asociace důchodců odborářů při ČMKOS*, ADO) as a national advisory body for the '. . . defence of the rights, interests and needs of pensioners organised in trade unions' (ADO 2001, p. 2), who numbered an estimated 20% of the ČMKOS membership in 2009 (Myant 2010). The Association of Retired Trade Unionists thus represents some 90,000 retired trade unionists, a figure which, although much like the overall ČMKOS membership, falling in recent years. As a result ADO is now formally the largest representative organisation of pensioners in the Czech Republic.

In contrast to their Czech counterparts, Slovene trade unions did not (and do not) allow members to continue membership after retirement. Instead, in partial imitation of the model in neighbouring Italy, Slovene trade-union confederations have created distinct pensioners' unions. The Union of Free Trade Unions of Slovenia (*Zveza svobodnih sindikatov Slovenije*, ZSSS)—the largest Slovene trade-union federation which, like the ČMKOS, is the successor of the official communist-era union federation—formed the Trade Union of Pensioners of Slovenia (*Sindikat upokojencev*

---

[3] In 1994–1995 Czech trade unions organised mass petitions, a 15-minute symbolic strike and protest demonstrations against proposed increases in the retirement age. Large Czech trade union demonstrations opposing austerity measures and fiscal and social reforms also took place in November 1997, June 1998, May 2009, May 2011 and April 2012 (Myant 2010; *MF Dnes*, 23 April 2012). In November 2005 Slovene trade unions organised peaceful mass demonstrations against proposed flat tax reforms and in 2011 they were instrumental in gathering sufficient signatures to trigger a referendum on pension reform laws and changes to the retirement age. They also organised a general strike of public sector workers in April 2012 (*Slovenian Times*, 18 April 2012).

[4] 'Statut Českomoravské konfederace odborových svazů', available at: http://www.cmkos.cz/data/articles/down_2055.pdf, accessed 1 October 2010. Earlier drafts of the statutes include the same commitment.

Slovenije, SUS) in 1992 in anticipation of the negative social impacts of market reform on pensioners and older people. In 2008 SUS had an estimated 12,000 members, organised into nine regional organisations. This represents about 4% of ZSSS's total membership, a much lower proportion than in the Czech Republic or, indeed, in most other European states (Carley 2004). This is largely explained by the fact that members of industrial branch unions must choose to join SUS on retirement, rather than being automatically enrolled.[5]

Pensioner voice in trade unions

Such contrasting patterns of organisation translate into contrasting patterns of influence within the wider union movement. Despite formally representing almost one in five ČMKOS members, in practice the Czech Republic's ADO is a weak body. Czech trade unions' general practice of organising retired members in local level clubs linked to workplace branches means that ADO has no individual or collective membership. It also has minimal resources.[6] Although the Association's statutes envisage a wide-ranging public role, including input into tripartite negotiations, it in fact plays a more limited role and functions largely as a source of advice and information to the ČMKOS leadership and as a coordinator of retired members across member unions, subordinating external lobbying to the Council of Seniors of the Czech Republic (*Rada seniorů České republiky*, RSČR) umbrella grouping (discussed below) of which it is also an affiliate.

The Association seems to have little or no direct input into ČMKOS's work in the Council of Economic and Social Agreement (RHSD), whose meetings ADO representatives do not attend even in a backroom capacity. The Association thus largely depends for influence on personal access to ČMKOS leaders and, to a lesser extent, on links to social democrat politicians with a background in the trade unions. While such access was reportedly good and provided a channel for influence, ADO's limited role and resources, its leaders felt, could sometimes lead ČMKOS to overlook pensioners when formulating its responses to policy proposals, a view echoed by polling conducted for ADO in 2003–2004 which showed widespread scepticism among pensioners towards the trade unions' role as defenders of their interests.[7]

Slovenia's SUS, by contrast, is a fully fledged member union of ZSSS and is represented accordingly at ZSSS congresses and in its governing bodies. It also enjoys greater institutional access to tripartite structures than its Czech counterpart: SUS leaders reported that they were able to represent their organisation's views and interests through involvement with the trade union delegation on Slovenia's Economic and Social Council (ESS). As with other individual unions, SUS leaders were on

[5]Interview with Konrad Breznik, President of SUS, and Miloš Mikolič, Secretary General of SUS, Ljubljana, 9 December 2008. Breznik estimated that about 10% of those leaving other unions through retirement chose to join SUS.

[6]ADO is based in a small suite of offices in ČMKOS's Prague headquarters, shared with the Council of Seniors of the Czech Republic; it has no permanent administrative staff. In 2008 its annual budget—allocated directly by ČMKOS—was 96,000 Czech crowns (approximately €3,800).

[7]Asociace důchodců odborářů, 'Pruzkům o sociální situaci důchodců prosinec 2003–leden 2004', unpublished document in the author's possession.

occasion invited to join the wider ZSSS delegation and to participate in the formulation of its negotiating stance.[8] However, the influence afforded by SUS's more independently constituted structure was arguably offset by its relatively small membership, which left it overshadowed both as a formal representative of pensioners and as a social force by Slovenia's extensively organised Federation of Pensioners' Associations of Slovenia (*Zveza društev upokojencev Slovenije*, ZDUS) discussed below.[9]

Pensioners' associations

Territorially organised membership associations with elected leaderships are among the oldest and most enduring form of retired people's self-organisation in Western democracies (Pratt 1993). Pensioners' organisations of this type can be found in both the Czech Republic and in Slovenia and, perhaps surprisingly, have a depth of grassroots organisation and a degree of importance in interest representation, which generally exceeds those of trade-union sponsored pensioners' groupings.

The principal such association in the Czech Republic is the Union of Pensioners of the Czech Republic (*Svaz důchodců České republiky*, SDČR) formed in January 1990 as one of the first new interest groupings in post-communist Czechoslovakia. The Union's precise origins are unclear, as its founders are no longer alive and organisational records have been lost.[10] However, its formation seems to have been prompted by fears over the possible social impact of the change of regime on retired and older people and it seems to have been loosely patterned on the type of official social organisation characteristic of the socialist period.[11] Originally a Prague-based initiative, the Union quickly developed branches in other localities and grew throughout the 1990s, in part by absorbing existing pensioners' clubs.[12] Although its membership declined from a peak of 30,000 in the mid-1990s, its current 93 local branches and 22,500 members, grouped into regional and sub-regional structures (Solich 2008), make the SDČR one of the larger individual membership organisations founded in the Czech Republic after 1989. It is the only Czech retired people's interest grouping with a nationwide grassroots organisation.

SDČR publications stress the voluntary and public spirited nature of its members' and officials' activism and emphasise the organisation's distinct status as a body run

---

[8]Interview with Konrad Breznik and Miloš Mikolič, Ljubljana, 9 December 2008.

[9]SUS was unrepresented on the boards of public corporations managing the health and welfare systems. In 2009 four of the five pensioner representatives on the Council of the Pensions and Social Insurance Institute (*Zavod za pokojninsko in invalidsko zavarovanje Slovenije*, ZPIZ) and all seven in the Assembly of the Health Institute (*Zavod za zdravstveno zavarovanje Slovenije*, ZZZS) were from ZDUS.

[10]A 70-member preparatory committee met in mid-January 1990 and the Union was formally registered at the end of that month, holding its first national congress in December 1990.

[11]The Union of Pensioners of the Czech Republic (*Svaz důchodců České republiky*) is one of a handful of national civil society organisations founded after 1989 to use the title '*svaz*' ('union'), characteristic of communist-era social organisations.

[12]Interviews with Jan Solich, outgoing President of the Union of Pensioners of the Czech Republic, Hradec Králové, 13 November 2008 and Zdeněk Pernes, President of the Council of Seniors of the Czech Republic, Prague, 27 November 2008.

by pensioners for pensioners, sometimes referring to it as a self-organising 'pensioner community' (*důchodcký obec*) rather than simply an organisation. However, while this claim is not inaccurate, as with many Czech civil society organisations, the scope and autonomy of the Union are limited. With a membership of no more than 2% of Czech old age pensioners, the Union's claim to representativeness was limited and its grassroots base was sometimes overshadowed at the local level by the large elderly mass memberships of the Czech Republic's two biggest historic parties, the Communists (*Komunistická strana Čech a Moravy*, KSČM) and the Christian Democrats (*Křesťanská a demokratická unie–Československá strana lidová*, KDU–ČSL), which in 2005–2006 together comprised some 105,000 retired people (KSČM 2005, p. 54; Linek & Pecháček 2006, pp. 18, 32).

In contrast to ADO, the Union is heavily dependent on public funding, principally grants from the Czech Ministry of Labour and Social Affairs and, at the local level, from municipalities. The effectiveness of the Union as a national interest organisation was, paradoxically, further undermined by its locally-based grassroots character. Websites and local news reports suggest that—unusually for a Czech civil society organisation—the SDČR's local and regional groups were often better organised and more active than the Union's national leadership structures, which were extremely weakly resourced: in 2008, for example, the income of SDČR nationally was a mere 1.1 million crowns (approximately €45,000) of which 20% came from membership fees and 80% came from grants and state subsidies (Solich 2008). Local branches, combining interest representation with the provision of socio-cultural activities, often enjoyed relatively easy access to direct municipal funding reinforcing their autonomy and leading to wide variation in the nature of their activities, including relationships with political parties and local authorities. The Union's long-term inability to develop into a larger, more integrated national interest organisation contributed to the creation of the Council of Seniors of the Czech Republic umbrella grouping discussed below into which the Union, like ADO, largely subsumed national-level lobbying after 2005.

The principal independent pensioners' association in Slovenia is the Union of Pensioners' Associations of Slovenia (*Zveza društev upokojencev Slovenije*, ZDUS). Like the Czech SDČR, ZDUS is a national grassroots membership organisation, combining interest representation with educational and socio-cultural activities and delivery of social services. However, having existed as an official organisation under socialism, it is a mass organisation which operates on a markedly different scale from its Czech counterpart. Although membership has declined since the 1990s when it reached over 300,000 (ZDUS 2001, p. 38), at the end of 2007, the last year for which exact data are available, ZDUS had 472 local branches and 238,132 members (ZDUS 2008), making it the largest single civil society organisation in Slovenia with a membership comparable to the ZSSS trade-union federation (which has 300,000 members). Approximately 50% of retired people in Slovenia are members of ZDUS.

ZDUS has, moreover, retained property and resources accumulated during the communist period, principally the profitable Delfin hotel complex in Izola, the proceeds of which cover the running costs of the organisation's national headquarters (ZDUS 2009, pp. 4–5). However, despite the introduction in 2008 of an annual levy of one euro per member to develop its central structures, ZDUS still requires external sources of income to sustain itself (ZDUS 2009, pp. 4–5). In 2008, for example, it received at least half its income of around €1 million from state and EU grants, with much of such external funding directed to support educational and welfare projects that ZDUS was contracted to deliver.[13]

Despite being a much longer established organisation than the Union of Pensioners of the Czech Republic, ZDUS has experienced very similar problems of organisational coordination: the federation's local associations had a high degree of *de facto* autonomy, resulting in widely varying concerns and capacities, making it sometimes difficult for ZDUS leaders to coordinate and mobilise their huge organisation behind cohesive national policies and priorities. ZDUS's status as an expansive but weakly led mass social organisation with an active grassroots also helps explain a peculiarity of Slovene politics: the existence of a small successful pensioners' interest party, the Democratic Party of Pensioners of Slovenia (*Demokratična stranka upokojencev Slovenije*, DeSUS), which has been represented in parliament since 1992 and is a regular participant in governing coalitions of left and right since 1998, (including the centre-right administration of Janez Janša formed in January 2012).[14] DeSUS originally emerged as a local electoral grouping in February 1990 based on the Maribor branch of ZDUS, one of a number of such grassroots seniors' initiatives to develop during the political ferment of Slovenia's transition to democracy and independence in 1988–1991.

Umbrella bodies

In both states, the multiplicity of pensioners' and seniors' groups has led to the creation of umbrella bodies to coordinate their activities and to provide a stronger and more legitimate interlocutor for the state. This pattern has however, been particularly marked in the Czech Republic, where the fragmented and chaotic early development of new interest organisations representing vulnerable welfare state client groups—and uncertainties over their representativeness and legitimacy—led to the early formation in February 1991 of the Coordinating Committee of Organisations of Pensioners and Disabled People (*Koordinační výbor organizací duchodců a zdravotně postižených*, KVOD) of which the Union of Pensioners and (later) ADO were members. Although formally recognised for consultation as an interlocutor by the Ministries of Health and Labour, KVOD's effectiveness was limited by the looseness of its organisation and the diverging interests and views of its members. Such differences led to the departure of new Western-style NGOs, which viewed a focus on lobbying to maintain levels of state-administered welfare and pension benefits as too narrow, as well as the exit of

---

[13]In 2008 ZDUS received approximately €320,000 from Slovene government institutions such as the Pension Insurance Institute (ZPIZ) and the Ministry of Labour (MDDSZ); €293,000 was from EU funding and €130,000 in income came from the Hotel Delfin (interview with Bogdan Urbar, then General Secretary of ZDUS, Ljubljana, 10 December 2008).

[14]DeSUS was initially part of the United List of Social Democrats (*Združena lista socialnih demokratov*, ZLSD) created by Slovenia's reformed Communists. It first entered parliament independently in 1996.

many disabled people's organisations, which sought (successfully) to develop their own distinct interest group sector.[15]

The transformation of KVOD into an umbrella group for pensioners and seniors was, however, spurred only some years later by competition from the NGO sector and, indirectly, by the emergence of a distinct Czech public policy agenda relating to older people and population ageing. In 2002, to its leaders' considerable surprise, KVOD failed in a bid to win funding under the EU's PHARE programme from the Civil Society Development Fund (*Združena lista socialnih demokratov*, NROS) to coordinate the creation of new Seniors' Councils, envisaged by NROS as a forum on seniors' issues for civil society groups and healthcare professionals.[16] Instead, a relatively small human rights NGO with roots in the dissident movement the Czech Helsinki Committee (*Český helsinský výbor*, ČHV) won the grant. Although the ČHV initiative was overtaken by the creation of the Czech government's advisory Council on Seniors and Population Ageing (discussed below), and the lack of long-term funding meant the projects had limited impact, the decision was seen by KVOD leaders as humiliating for their more broadly based organisation, prompting them in May 2005 to create the Council of Seniors of the Czech Republic (RSČR) as a more structured umbrella body focused on the needs of retired people which would be organised on recognisably 'European' lines.[17]

The RSČR proved considerably more successful than KVOD, steadily expanding from 12 member organisations in 2005 to 43 members in 2010 (Rada seniorů České republiky 2009, 2010), and claiming to represent some 320,000 'organised seniors' (Rada seniorů České republiky 2010, p. 2).[18] The Council, however, centres around the two largest nationwide seniors' groupings affiliated to KVOD, the Union of Pensioners (SDČR) and ADO, with the bulk of other member organisations consisting of small locally or regionally based pensioners' groups or associations of retired members of trade unions and professional bodies outside the main ČMKOS federation. The leaders of SDČR and ADO, together with the Council's founder and president Zdeněk Pernes, have always played key leadership roles. The Council sees its role very strongly in terms of national interest representation and intermediation, regarding its legitimacy to represent the Czech Republic's 1.93 million old age pensioners as stemming not only from membership size, but also from its status as a 'united pensioners' movement'.[19] Although a confederal body based on collective membership, the Council has thus focused considerable effort on creating its own structures distinct from those of member organisations, including regional branches, rather than being a loose alliance or forum as is commonly the case with 'seniors councils' in Western Europe (Evers & Wolf 1999).

[15]Interviews with Jan Solich, 13 November 2008, Zdeněk Pernes, 27 November 2008, and Jan Lorman, Director of Life '90 NGO, Prague, 20 November 2008.

[16]'PHARE 2002—Podpora aktivního života seniorů', undated, available at: http://www.nros.cz/cilove-skupiny/prijemci/seznamy-prijemcu, accessed 1 November 2010.

[17]Interview with Zdeněk Pernes, Prague, 27 November 2008.

[18]As the Council's members typically lack detailed or accessible membership records, assessment of the precise numbers it represents is difficult.

[19]'O třetí generaci se Zdeňkem Pernesem', 21 May 2008, available at: http://respekt.ihned.cz/rozhovory/c1-35753860-o-treti-generaci-se-zdenkem-pernesem, accessed 1 November 2010.

However, partly in order to facilitate organisational development and access resources, the RSČR also plays a direct role as a grant-based service provider of help and support to older people, running telephone helplines and four professionally staffed regional advice centres. Such projects are financed by grants from the Ministry of Labour and Social Affairs and the Ministry of Local Development and from charitable donations from companies which make up the bulk of the Council's income. In 2009 RSČR had an annual income of just under four million Czech crowns (approximately €160,000), of which 2.9 million consisted of state subsidies, the bulk coming from the Ministry of Labour and Social Affairs (Rada seniorů České republiky 2010).[20] Such modest sums, which are roughly equivalent to levels of state funding received by a successful extra-parliamentary political party in the Czech Republic, are—allowing for differences in country size—a fraction of those annually available to Slovenia's ZDUS. Nevertheless they give the Council greater resources than its larger member organisations. The RSČR thus effectively functions as the sole national pensioners' interest organisation in the Czech Republic.

In Slovenia, by contrast, the dominant position and mass membership of ZDUS generated much weaker incentives to create umbrella structures. Although there is an equivalent body to the RSČR, the Coordinating Committee of Seniors' Organisations of Slovenia (*Koordinacijski odbor Seniorskih organizacij Slovenije*, KOSOS), it is a weak *ad hoc* body lacking any separate organisational existence of its own which has functioned only sporadically since its creation in 2005, acting mainly as a vehicle for cooperation between ZDUS and the Pensioners' Trade Union (*Sindikat upokojencev Slovenije*, SUS) and as an occasional platform for negotiations with government.

Strategies of influence

While the influence strategies of trade-union sponsored pensioners' groupings are to a large extent determined by their position within union structures, independent pensioners' organisations have a range of potential options. Although, when interviewed in 2008–2009 leaders of pensioners' associations allowed the possibility that they might organise independent grassroots mobilisation,[21] the focus of both the Council of Seniors of the Czech Republic and Slovenia's ZDUS has largely been on 'direct' strategies of influence (Binderkrantz 2005): consulting with policy makers and lobbying to influence government programmes and legislation. In the Czech Republic the Council of Seniors makes use of the main formal institutional access points for interest groups: consultation with parliamentary committees (Kopecký 2001) and the longstanding practice (formalised in 2002) of ministries consulting designated stakeholders (*připomínkové místa*) on draft government legislation. Both the Union of Pensioners and the Council of Seniors of the Czech Republic (RSČR) have long been designated by the Ministries of Labour and Social Affairs and Health as such

---

[20]The remainder of the Council's income is derived from sales of its monthly magazine *Doba seniorů*, which has a circulation of 6,000–10,000. Membership fees typically account for around 1% of annual income (Rada seniorů České republiky 2007, 2010).

[21]Interview with Zdeněk Pernes, Prague, 27 November 2008 and telephone interview with Mateja Kožuh Novak, President of ZDUS, 19 February 2009.

stakeholder and regularly make formal responses to proposed legislation, focusing on laws on social benefits and pensions (particularly their annual uprating), healthcare and housing. They are also regularly invited to parliamentary committees on health and social affairs.

However, while well-established and formally open, the Czech consultation system has a high level of official discretion; as with many *připomínkové místo* groups in civil society (Kunc 2006), the Czech RSČR appeared to be consulted at a relatively late stage, with their submissions typically confined to brief, highly specific responses to draft legislation. This, however also reflected the organisation's limited resources and the limitations of the public subsidy it receives, which is earmarked for the delivery of advice and support services to older people, rather than legislative monitoring or policy research: while the RSČR reportedly had small expert teams of qualified volunteers to analyse proposed legislation numbering some 25 people,[22] it clearly lacked the capacity for broader, sustained research. Indeed, as with other Czech interest organisations (Kunc 2006), the consultation process thus appears to serve more as a source of information than as a channel for influence.

In contrast to the Czech Republic, Slovenia historically lacked a procedure for pre-legislative consultation: only in January 2009 in response to pressure from ZDUS did Slovenia's Labour, Family and Social Affairs Ministry create four *ad hoc* joint consultation committees allowing seniors' organisations to comment on draft legislation affecting them, although more general consultation standards were passed later in the same year.[23] This was to some extent compensated for by the greater openness of Slovene parliamentary committees to interest groups, including pensioners' organisations (Fink-Hafner & Krašovec 2005). However, one unusual feature of Slovenia's legislative and parliamentary system normally empowering interest organisations—the fact that the upper chamber of parliament, the National Council (*Državni svet*), represents functional and territorial interests (Fink-Hafner 1998)—was closed to ZDUS: National Council representatives are nominated only by professional and producer groups and local government, excluding groups defined by age or welfare status. Interestingly, despite being a far larger, better resourced organisation, like the Czech RSČR, Slovenia's ZDUS also seems to have been impeded in playing an effective role in the legislative process by inadequate structures for tracking and engaging with policy making and law making. Notwithstanding its huge mass membership, for many years the organisation lacked a professionalised national headquarters, only establishing a structure of policy-oriented commissions capable of shadowing government ministries' legislative work in 2008 following leadership change.[24]

---

[22]Interview with Zdeněk Pernes, Prague, 27 November 2008.

[23]'Dogovor med Ministrstvom za delo, družino in socialne zadeve in Zvezo društev upokojencu Slovenije', 16 February 2009, available at: http://www.mddsz.gov.si/fileadmin/mddsz.gov.si/pageup loads/dokumenti__pdf/mddsz_zdus_dogovor.pdf, accessed 1 February 2011; and 'Resolution on Legislative Resolution', available at: www.mju.gov.si/.../RESOLUCIJA_zadnja_verzija_ENG_19nov 09.doc, accessed 1 February 2010.

[24]Telephone interview with Mateja Kožuh Novak, 19 February 2009.

Interest group–party relations

For interest groups in both states political parties play a key role as gatekeepers to political power and the legislative process (Fink-Hafner 2006; Kopecký 2006). Pensioners' interest organisations in both states have thus sought, broadly successfully, to maintain regular contacts with parties and party politicians, reporting regular bi-lateral meetings with politicians in elected office of both left and right, often initiated at the interest groups' request (Rada seniorů České republiky 2007, 2010; ZDUS 2008, 2009, 2010). Both ZDUS and the RSČR (and its affiliates) emphasise that they are non-partisan organisations open to all seniors and are careful to avoid acts of overt partisanship, formally recommending, for example, at election times only that their members should vote but not making explicit endorsements. However, in both the Czech Republic and Slovenia at the time this research was conducted, pensioners' interest organisations had much closer and better developed, if ambiguous, relationships with parties of the left and centre-left: the Slovene Social Democrats (*Socialni demokrati*, SD) and Liberal Democracy of Slovenia (*Liberalna demokracija Slovenije*, LDS)[25] and, in the Czech Republic, the Czech Social Democrats (ČSSD) and the Communist Party of Bohemia and Moravia (KSČM).

Such affinities reflect overlapping commitments to a relatively expansive welfare state, the political and career background of interest group leaders,[26] and, in some instances, the greater concern of left-wing parties to work with pensioners' interest groups and organised interests generally. In the Czech Republic, Social Democrat and Communist politicians are thus frequent interviewees in publications of the Council of Seniors (RSČR) and regularly attend congresses of RSČR and its affiliates, while individual social democrat and communist deputies with whom the RSČR has developed contacts have sometimes acted as an additional channel of influence by presenting legislative amendments drawn up by the Council to parliament. In 2010 the Union of Pensioners of the Czech Republic (SDČR) went one step further by signing formal cooperation agreements with three left-wing parties: the Social Democrats, the Communists and the non-parliamentary populist grouping, Sovereignty (*Suverenita*).[27]

In Slovenia, the greater difficulty of legislative amendment by individual deputies, the greater bargaining weight afforded by its mass membership and the more fragmented nature of the centre-left have led ZDUS to focus more on influencing government programmes and coalition making. In December 2008, for example, a ZDUS-led delegation presented a memorandum of demands to the newly formed centre-left administration of Borut Pahor, which seemingly resulted in the inclusion of a commitment to create a new Office for Older People in the new government's

---

[25]LDS dropped out of the Slovene parliament in the December 2011 elections.

[26]Mateja Kožuh Novak, the President of Slovenia's ZDUS, for example, served as a parliamentary deputy for the post-communist Social Democrats in 1992–1996, while Zdeněk Pernes, chair of the Czech RSČR, is a former member of the Communist Party of Bohemia and Moravia and was elected to Prague city council on the party's list in 1998.

[27]'Komunisté budou spolupracovat se Svazem důchodců', *Parlamentní listy*, 15 July 2010, available at: http://www.parlamentnilisty.cz/kraje/ustecky/170266.aspx, accessed 1 December 2010. Centrist and centre-right parties were also reportedly approached but rebuffed or ignored the offer.

programme.[28] Similarly, in January 2012 following indecisive parliamentary elections, ZDUS's leaders pressed deputies in centre-left parties (unsuccessfully) to support the prime ministerial candidacy of Zoran Janković, whose new left-liberal Positive Slovenia (*Lista Zorana Jankovića–Pozitivna Slovenija*, LZJ–PS) grouping had emerged as the largest party (STA 2012).

Interestingly, ZDUS's relationship with the Democratic Party of Pensioners of Slovenia (DeSUS) has generally been a detached one, with strong elements of rivalry. Despite brief periods of cooperation, as in 2010 over shared opposition to pension reform proposals, ZDUS—which later accepted a revised version of the proposals— became highly critical of the DeSUS, attacking the party for withdrawing from the (2008–2011) centre-left Pahor government as well as its later willingness in January 2012 to join a centre-right administration, claiming that the party was unrepresentative and opportunistic.[29] Such tension between pensioners' interest groups and pensioners' parties, when they have emerged, is common, given overlapping claims to represent the same constituency (Hanley 2011).

New agendas, new opportunities?

Pensioners' interest organisations in both states appear to have gained an additional channel for contact and consultation through official reframing of population ageing as a distinct new policy challenge requiring distinct new responses and the creation of new consultative *cum* representative institutions. Although linked to a growing international movement for pension reform (Orenstein 2008b), such new policy agendas saw population ageing as a broader challenge with ramifications stretching across health and social care; education and civil society development, requiring a coordinated response to foster intergenerational solidarity and non-discrimination; promote the dignity and autonomy of older people; and enhance older people's participation in society and the economy. In Central and Eastern Europe such new agendas emerged partly through European and international contexts and partly through the influence of domestic NGOs.

Despite an imperfect legal framework, Slovenia and the Czech Republic both saw rapid growth in the NGO sector, including age-related 'pro-senior' NGOs (Green 1999; Havlič *et al.* 2001). The origins, agendas and organisational forms of such NGOs offered a distinct alternative to those of pensioners' interest groups and, to some extent, a rival model. The largest pro-senior NGO across the two cases, Life '90 (*Život '90*) in the Czech Republic, for example, was formed in 1990 by middle-aged social activists with backgrounds in the arts, drawing inspiration from foreign models such as Abbé Pierre's Emmanaus community and Austrian seniors' initiatives. Accordingly,

---

[28]The breakdown of social dialogue in 2009–2010 following the imposition of austerity measures saw the Pahor government back out of this commitment ('Pahor: Urada za starejše ne bo', 19 April 2010, available at: http://zlataleta.com/urad-za-starejse/, accessed 11 March 2011).

[29]In 2011 DeSUS polled 76,853 votes (6.97%) and had a stated membership of 13,690. Analysts generally agree that, as a pivotal party, DeSUS had a narrow but real leverage over aspects of pension and social policy (Guardiancich 2012). However, the 2008–2012 Minister of Labour and Social Affairs, Ivan Svetlik, a DeSUS nominee, was an independent technocrat and the party exercised no real control over the Ministry itself.

its vision stressed the gradual re-locating of social and care services for older people in communities and civil society, rather than in the state (Život '90 2001, p. 5). After a spell of voluntary activism, the group quickly professionalised into a Western-style advocacy and service NGO without members, which was administered 'like an enterprise' by its founders, with employees or volunteers having a contractual relationship with the organisation.[30] However, unlike pensioners' interest organisations, despite higher levels of funding, Life '90 eschewed the development of a nationwide organisation, seeking instead to be a catalyst for change in public policy and public opinion through its projects and media work.

However, the main impetus for change came from Central and Eastern European states' 'downloading' of policy agendas stemming from external commitments such as the EU's Open Method of Coordination Social Protection *acquis* and the 2002 UN International Plan of Action on Ageing (United Nations 2002; European Commission 2005). Such commitments led states across Central and Eastern Europe, including the Czech Republic and Slovenia, to adopt coordinated, multi-agency population-aging strategies.

New modes of consultation

As is characteristic of newly defined policy fields (Meyer & Imig 1993, p. 258), such programmes led to the opening up of new political space for interest organisations: in both states policy makers quickly gave way to objections from pensioners' organisations that, while the programmes spoke of engagement and partnership with civil society, they had been formulated in a technocratic fashion by officials and contained no concrete provision for participation by civil society groups. This led directly to the creation of new consultative councils on ageing in which pensioners' groups were represented.

The Czech Republic adopted its first five-year National Programme of Preparation for Ageing in 2003, and following a positive response to demands from pensioners' organisations, Zdeněk Škromach, then Social Democrat Minister of Labour and Social Affairs, created the Government Council for Seniors and Population Ageing (*Rada vlády pro seniory a stárnutí populace*, RVSSP) in 2005. The Council's mission was initially defined as one of promoting active ageing and the engagement of older people and evaluating the 2003–2007 National Programme of Preparation for Ageing, but it was later extended to become a vehicle for strategic partnership between government and civil society enabling 'the participation of older people in decision-making on issues that significantly affect their lives' (Ministerstvo práce a sociálních věcí 2008, p. 51).

The RVSSP, which usually meets three times a year, is composed of 28 members. Of these, 12 are from central government—including the minister and deputy minister (*náměstek*) of the Ministry of Labour and Social Affairs (who chair the Council); deputy ministers from six other government departments; and representatives of the two parliamentary committees on social affairs. There were additionally four representatives of seniors' organisations—of which three were from the RSČR and

---

[30]Interview with Jan Lorman, Prague, 20 November 2008.

its affiliates—and two representatives from old-age oriented NGOs, with the remaining members drawn from professional and civil society groups including employers, trade unions, regional and local government, health insurance companies and the medical profession.

In 2006 Slovenia adopted the Strategy for Care of Older People Until 2010 (Ministry of Labour, Family and Social Affairs 2008) and in the autumn created the Council for Solidarity in the Co-existence of Generations and Quality of Population Ageing (*Svet za solidarno sožitje generacij in za kakovostno staranje prebivalstva*), an advisory body for population ageing and seniors' issues similar to that already established in the Czech Republic. As in the Czech Republic its formation stemmed partly from pressure from the ZDUS pensioners' union and objections that the Strategy had been prepared by ministerial experts with little input from outside organisations or representatives of older people (Helpage International 2007). Although governmental advisory bodies are uncommon in Slovenia and their status less formalised than in the Czech Republic, the Council was similar in composition and status to that of the Czech RVSSP, having been formed under the auspices of the Ministry of Labour to coordinate and monitor ministries' implementation of the Strategy of Care. The 24-member Council meets five or six times a year and, as in the Czech Republic, brings together representatives of ministries, pensioners' organisa- tions and NGOs, service providers and gerontologists, with membership evenly divided between central government and non-governmental bodies.[31] However, while the government side on the Czech RVSSP is represented by elected politicians at ministerial or deputy ministerial level and senior civil servants, the government side on Slovenia's Council for Solidarity is represented only by mid-ranking officials below the level of ministerial directorate head.

The creation of advisory bodies to address the growing importance of retired people as a social group, institutionalising their representation, was a potentially important innovation. However, for a number of reasons the scope of consultation they opened up to pensioners' interest organisations in both states appears to have been a limited extension to traditional practices. In both states such bodies were poorly resourced and lacked both a formal role in the legislative process or any influence in policy formula- tion and were largely confined to oversight and scrutiny. In the Czech Republic, for example, the second (2008–2012) National Programme of Preparation for Ageing was initially wholly drafted by an inter-ministerial experts' group and then submitted to the Council for comment.[32] Both bodies also lacked budgets or administrative resources of their own leaving them reliant on information supplied by other agencies, and they were often hampered by poor or patchy coordination between ministries.

Close comparison of the two cases, however, highlights important differences in the underlying relationships between state and social actors in the two bodies. Although both Councils were organised around norms of consensus, the influence of pensioners' organisations within them varied. In the case of the Czech Government Council for

[31]Interview with Davor Dominkuš, Head of Social Affairs Directorate of the Slovene Ministry of Labour, Family and Social Affairs and mid-level ministerial officials, Ljubljana, 18 February 2009.

[33]'Jednací řád Rady vlády pro seniory a stárnutí populace', available at: http://www.mpsv.cz/cs/ 2859, accessed 1 November 2010.

Seniors and Population Ageing, the Labour Ministry's ability to set its agenda,[33] led its discussions to be often heavily focused on social services and healthcare issues, paying less attention to the principal concerns of seniors' organisations grouped in the RSČR: pensions and living standards. Requests by pensioners' representatives that the Council discuss issues such the 2005 'Bezděk Report' on options for pension reforms were thus rejected on the grounds that pensions were an issue affecting the whole of society and would thus be more appropriately discussed by political parties.[34] In Slovenia ZDUS had greater influence on representation in the Council for Solidarity and Co-existence of Generations whose proceedings it chaired. However, this was offset by the fact that, in contrast to the Czech RSVVP, it was attended on the government side by only middle-ranking officials, leaving ZDUS representatives dissatisfied with the level of influence and access afforded.[35]

Assessing and explaining patterns of interest group development

Although they parallel familiar organisational forms found in Western Europe, the retired people's interest organisations that have developed in the Czech Republic and Slovenia call for some degree of reassessment of earlier assumptions. Despite their generally assumed weakness, in both cases pensioners' interest organisations emerge as quite sizeable membership organisations with significant elements of local grassroots organisation. Czech pensioners' organisations grouped in the Council of Seniors organise some 17% of pensioners, a figure which, even allowing for a degree of overestimation, compares favourably with the density of Czech trade-union membership among employees, which Myant (2010, p. 7) estimates as being as low as 10%. Moreover, Slovenia's ZDUS, which organises approximately 50% of the country's pensioners, has an organisational density rivalling the largest national seniors' associations in Western Europe (in Sweden and Austria) (Evers & Wolf 1999; Feltenius 2007).

In both cases such grassroots structures were maintained through the provision of local level socio-cultural facilities to members as 'selective incentives' combined with otherwise low demands, both financially and in terms of participation, and through significant external funding from state and European bodies for the delivery of welfare and socio-cultural programmes, which were instrumentalised by interest group leaders to maintain and develop their organisations. Despite this, given the range of collective action problems noted by Vanhuysse (2008), the formation and emergence of such relatively large organisations is still puzzling. Moreover, somewhat contrary to expectations, in both cases independent pensioners' associations represent a more significant force in terms of membership, resources and, arguably, political influence than trade-union sponsored pensioners' groupings. Finally, given their greater than

[33]'Jednací řád Rady vlády pro seniory a stárnutí populace', available at: http://www.mpsv.cz/cs/ 2859, accessed 1 November 2010.
[34]'Záznam z 11. zasedání Rady', 4 December 2009, available at HYPERLINK http://www.mpsv.cz/ cs/8621 accessed 20 November 2010 and 'Záznam z 12. zasedání Rady', 28 April 2010, available at http://www.mpsv.cz/cs/8923 accessed 20 November 2010.
[35]Interviews with officials in the Slovene Ministry of Labour, Ljubljana, 18 February 2009 and telephone interview with Mateja Kožuh Novak, 19 February 2009.

anticipated organisational capacities, the choice of 'direct' strategies of lobbying, contact and consultation by pensioners' interest organisations in both states may also need re-examination.

Regime legacies

Contrary to blanket assumptions about Central and Eastern European pensioners' lack of pre-existing organisation and capacity (Vanhyusse 2008, p. 13), the Czech and Slovene cases clearly highlight the importance of legacies from outgoing communist regimes relevant to their development as organised interests. In the first instance straightforward organisational inheritances—the ability to draw upon, recoup and re-organise pre-existing structures—seem highly relevant to the development of viable pensioners' interest organisations in both cases, albeit to different degrees. In Slovenia this is clearly visible in ZDUS's status as the direct successor to an official communist-era mass social organisation, having been formed in 1945–1946 as a welfare organisation to cope with post-war austerity. ZDUS—alongside national equivalents in other republics—was quickly integrated into the Yugoslav communist regime's institutional structures, operating (with varying degrees of autonomy) as part of the official trade-union federation before finally becoming a separate body in the 1960s (ZDUS 2001, pp. 31–32).

In communist Czechoslovakia, by contrast, although as in other Soviet-type regimes a range of social groups were formally represented through mass organisations, there were no official organisations representing pensioners or older citizens. Instead older and retired people were organised at a purely local level in social clubs or associations of retired former colleagues run by local authorities and state enterprises. This absence of an official communist-era organisation for older people explains why Czech pensioners' organisations have failed to match the membership density of ZDUS. At the same time, however, the relative success of the Czech Union of Pensioners (SDČR) in early organisation-building compared to other post-1989 membership organisations suggests it benefited from an ability to incorporate pre-existing local clubs and groups.[36]

Czech–Slovene comparison also suggests that communist regime type may matter for the durability of communist-era social organisations. Slovenia, as a constituent part of Tito's model of Yugoslav 'self-managed' socialism, developed a complex, decentralised web of overlapping socio-political institutions (Cohen 1989). In the case of ZDUS, as 'self-managed socialism' was implemented across Yugoslavia from the 1950s, both the Union itself and the local pensioners' associations that formed its basic units became more autonomous (ZDUS 2001, pp. 9–38), a trend which accelerated after 1974 when Yugoslavia's new constitution and associated legal reform gave explicit recognition to 'self-managing interest groups' (Havlič *et al.* 2001; ZDUS 2001, pp. 31–32). While its relatively decentralised autonomous grassroots later made ZDUS an unwieldy organisation, it also arguably generated legitimacy and embeddedness that contributed to ZDUS's survival as a mass organisation after the fall of communism.

---

[36]Interview with Jan Solich, Hradec Králové, 13 November 2008.

In Czechoslovakia after 1968, the regime reverted to a rigid 'bureaucratic authoritarian' form of communism (Kitschelt *et al.* 1999). Accordingly, official mass organisations in communist Czechoslovakia were highly centralised, bureaucratic shells with formalistic membership and participation, lacking elements of grassroots engagement and legitimacy, which typically led to the collapse of mass membership organisations after the fall of communism. The Czech Union of Women (*Český svaz žen*, ČSŽ), for example, had an estimated membership of half a million in 1989, which plummeted to 40,000 by the mid-1990s (Havelková 2008), declining to 18,000 by 2009.[37] Even if an official mass seniors' organisation had existed, given the nature of Czechoslovakia's regime it might therefore have suffered similar contraction, rather than the smooth continuity achieved by ZDUS.

Despite a broad literature on the legacies of communist rule for the development of civil society organisations in Central and Eastern Europe generally (Howard 2003; Pérez-Solórzano Borragán 2006)—including more focused work on Central and East European trade unions (Crowley 2004; Ost 2009)—there is seemingly little research on the impact of national forms of communism on the subsequent configuration of particular interest group sectors. The patterns highlighted above are, however, broadly in accordance with the findings of Grzymała-Busse (2001, 2002) in her work on former ruling communist parties. Grzymała-Busse found that outgoing communist regimes' varying levels of internal pluralism and openness to society affected subsequent patterns of national organisational development.

However, this research suggests that such regime legacies may work differently for social organisations; while for communist successor parties, regime pluralism and openness facilitated the dismantling of mass memberships, for a social organisation like ZDUS they may have promoted its preservation as a mass membership organisation. However, it seems difficult to draw any straightforward causal connection between communist regime type and the existence (or non-existence) of official mass organisations for older people: East Germany for example, possessed a 'bureaucratic-authoritarian' regime but accommodated the *Volkssolidarität*, a national organisation providing voluntary self-help and social services to older people (Chamberlayne 1995). Moreover, while ZDUS's position in the 'self-managed' system of the Slovene Socialist Republic may have facilitated organisational continuity, in other ways it left it ill-equipped to operate in the more pluralised political and policy-making environment that emerged with democratisation. Unlike official mass social organisations of youth and women, ZDUS was not formally represented in the communist-era Socialist Alliance of Working People of Slovenia (*Socialistična zveza delovnega ljudstva Slovenije*, SZDLS) which offered representation and a degree of influence in the multi-tiered, multi-cameral legislative structures characteristic of Yugoslav socialism, relegating it to a largely socio-cultural role. While individual ZDUS officials sometimes gained political office at the local level,[38] at the national level its leaders did not develop the 'portable skills' of negotiation and coalition-making usually associated with *nomenklatura* elites in liberal communist regimes

---

[37] 'O Českém svazu žen', undated, available at: http://www.csz.cz/view.php?cisloclanku=2008100 004, accessed 1 March 2012.

[38] Interview with Bogdan Urbar, Ljubljana, 10 December 2008.

(Grzymała-Busse 2001, 2002), resulting in ZDUS's subsequently slow process of organisational learning, adaptation and modernisation.

Patterns of transition and the regime-based divisions

In both states it also appears that the transition from communism, and the politically fluid period that immediately followed, was a critical juncture for the development of pensioners' interest organisations. Firstly, notwithstanding the existence of 'strategic social policy' intended to insulate retired voters from the harshest consequences of transition (Vanhuysse 2006a, 2006b), early uncertainty over the impacts of market reforms on older people acted as a crucial impetus to the formation of pensioners' organisations, allowing collective action problems to be overcome as well as spurring trade unions into creating their own pensioners' groupings.

Contrasting regime types, however, also conditioned contrasting patterns of transition from communism, which can further explain variation between the Czech and Slovene cases. By the late 1980s Slovenia had developed a liberal reformist communist regime of 'national accommodation' which presided over—and sought to manage—growing social and political pluralism, ultimately working with opposition forces to achieve national independence and a transition to multi-party democracy in 1990–1991 (Bebler 2002). This smooth and consensual transition—and the institutional choices associated with it—facilitated a consensual pattern of party politics in the 1990s centring on moderate parties of the left with roots in the former ruling party and reformist *nomenklatura* (Guardiancich 2012). Such a climate not only allowed ZDUS, like other former official mass organisations, to emerge with resources intact, but reduced potential conflict with both government policy makers and activists seeking to develop Western-style NGOs working with older people. ZDUS was structured as a traditional mass interest organisation, strongly oriented towards pensions and social citizenship and it was sometimes critical of new agendas on ageing, as over-medicalised and too focused on vulnerable sub-groups (Helpage International 2007). However, although occasionally awkward in its relationships with NGOs,[39] its dominant and well-established position made it an inevitable but acceptable partner for both government and the NGO sector. Correspondingly, without seeking to emulate them wholesale, ZDUS's leaders sought to learn from NGOs, including European NGO alliances such as AGE Platform (which it joined in 2008), as a means to modernise and professionalise its lobbying and communications.[40]

In contrast, the rapid collapse of the Czechoslovakian regime in November–December 1989's 'Velvet Revolution' saw the overnight introduction of pluralism in the context of unreformed socialist-era institutions and practices. The sudden and polarising nature of the Czech transition led to a sharp and contentious demarcation of 'communist' organisational and political forms and new, 'democratic' alternatives derived from the West or from the thinking of the dissident opposition. As well as generating a polarising effect in politics, such a 'regime divide', as Grzymała-Busse

[39]See for example 'Diversity is the Treasure of Society—Final Activity Report', available at: http://ec.europa.eu/social/BlobServlet?docId=2083&langId=en, accessed 1 February 2011.
[40]Telephone interview with Mateja Kožuh Novak, 19 February 2009.

(2001) terms it, also bisected the emerging older people's interest sector, generating a very sharp divide between the NGO model typified by Life '90 and that of organisations in the Council of Seniors of the Czech Republic.[41] This was paralleled by a sharp ideological and policy divide in understandings of the needs and interests of retired and older people: while Life '90 focused, broadly in line with European agendas, on the empowerment, autonomy, inclusion and rights of older people, the groups in the RSČR were more concerned with levels of state welfare, health and pension provision, seeing NGO preoccupations as secondary issues, and expressing scepticism about the relevance of EU agendas for a post-communist country such as the Czech Republic. Although there is limited cooperation, relations between Life '90 and the Council of Seniors are distant, with each quietly critical of the other's agendas and strategies, and aware that they reflect underlying political differences.[42] This divide can also be seen in a similar wariness towards Czech pensioners' interest organisations on the part of Labour Ministry officials, which contrasts markedly with the generally positive attitudes expressed towards ZDUS by Slovene officials.

Trade unions and pensioners' organisations

In both the Czech Republic and Slovenia there is a close relationship between pensioners' organisations and trade unions: in addition to the existence of trade-union sponsored pensioners' groupings, independent pensioners' interest organisations in both states have been closely aligned with the main trade-union federation, and they share its ambiguous political position of combining formal non-alignment with informal links with parties of the left (Avdagic 2004). Despite their size and the resources of their sponsors, trade-union based seniors' groupings in both states play a surprisingly secondary role in organising pensioners as an interest constituency. In Slovenia this is in part explicable by the large pre-existing structure of ZDUS. However, it is also evident in the Czech Republic where national pensioners' associations were organisationally much weaker, and where in formal terms, the trade-union backed ADO was a very large organisation.

Although Czech and Slovene trade unions seem to have been initially slow to recognise the potential importance of pensioners as a constituency, such attitudes seem to lie in trade unions' difficulties in reconciling the representation of a growing retired population with their core role of representing (declining) numbers of employee members, whose interests and priorities may diverge and, potentially, even conflict with those of current pensioners. While it is perhaps an exaggeration to suggest in these two cases that 'the elderly were among very first constituencies to be shaken off the radar of union elites' (Vanhuysse 2008, p. 21), it is striking that the (very different) institutional vehicles created for the representation of their retired members by the principal trade-union federations in each state have the effect of limiting the

---

[41]Havelková (2008) notes similar tensions between the Czech Union of Women (ČSŽ), a former official mass organisation, and newer feminist NGOs.

[42]Life '90's director Jan Lorman acknowledged that its stress on non-state provision put it 'more towards the right' (interview, Prague, 20 November 2008).

pensioners' voice within the wider movement, either through the absence of national representative structures (as in the Czech Republic) or by the requirement for re-registration in a separate organisation (in Slovenia). While the two cases provide limited evidence of political divergence between organised labour and pensioners' groups, given broadly shared views on social and economic policy, tensions are identifiable, especially in relation to issues of intergenerational justice. In Slovenia for example, having accepted revised pension reform laws, ZDUS did not join trade unions in campaigning for a referendum to nullify them and recommended that its members vote for the reforms (Kristan 2011; Kožuh Novak 2011).[43] Such findings suggest that, notwithstanding the post-communist context, relationships between retired and employed workers with trade unions are broadly consistent with patterns found in Western Europe (Anderson & Lynch 2007)

Strategies

As anticipated by Vanhuysse (2006a, 2008), mobilisation strategies played a very limited role in the repertoire of pensioners' interest organisations. This, however, cannot wholly be explained by the collective action problems he discusses were solved on a sufficient scale to create and maintain relatively large membership organisations. Interviewed in 2008 and 2009, interest group leaders in both states were confident that they could organise protests,[44] and an organisation such as Slovenia's ZDUS clearly has ample ability to mobilise members *en masse*, having organised large regional festivals and successful one-off national initiatives such as the 2010 petition campaign to replace the management of the Vzajemna health insurance cooperative, of which many pensioners were members (Zupanič 2010).

As interest group leaders themselves suggested, the orientation towards direct strategies of lobbying and engagement with policy makers and legislators thus seems to represent a deliberate strategic choice reflecting the greater perceived long-term efficacy of directly seeking to influence political and legislative outcomes. This is consistent with broader patterns among interest groups, which represent a well-defined sectional constituency and focus on a limited number of policy areas (Binderkrantz 2005).[45]

However, while there is no automatic or exclusive correspondence between organisational forms and strategies of influence deployed (Binderkrantz 2005), there has arguably been a mismatch between Central and Eastern European pensioners' organisations' grassroots membership structures, low levels of professionalisation and limited concentration of resources at national level, characteristic of pensioners' organisations in both states, and the requirements of effective legislative monitoring and lobbying. Among organisations seeking to engage with and influence policy makers in both Central and Eastern Europe and elsewhere, there has been a

[43]The referendum held in June 2011 overwhelmingly rejected the reformed pension system.
[44]Interviews with Jiří Pernes, Prague, 27 November 2008 and Mateja Kožuh Novak, 19 February 2009 (telephone interview).
[45]Interviews with Jiří Pernes, Prague, 27 November 2008 and Mateja Kožuh Novak, 19 February 2009 (telephone interview).

discernable trend away from participatory structures (Tarrow & Petrova 2007, p. 15; Skocpol 2003). This pattern of organisational mismatch among pensioners' organisations—and the slow pace of their organisational modernisation—contrasts markedly with the development of an NGO like Life '90, which made a rapid transition from volunteer activism to professionalism without nationwide grassroots structures, which closely fitted its dual strategy of engaging with policy makers and influencing public opinion through the media. The mismatch between pensioners' interest organisations' chosen structures and chosen strategies seems path-dependent, carrying over from an earlier model of mass social organisation as a means of establishing legitimacy and representativeness—and hence claiming access to policy makers.

Conclusions

Despite the widely perceived weakness of pensioners as an organised social group, the Czech and Slovene cases highlight that sizeable membership-based pensioners' interest organisations integrated into national interest representation systems can emerge in Central and Eastern Europe—and that they can do so independently of trade unions. Relative success in organisation building and maintenance was, however, combined with resource weakness characteristic of many non-producer civil society groups in the region: even under the 'best case' conditions of Slovenia, ZDUS's extraordinarily high organisational density still left a significant dependence on external funding.

The emergence, somewhat against expectations, of viable and broad, but resource-poor, pensioners' interest organisations was shaped by a mixture of impulses, some previously little known: the survival of forms of social organisation for older and retired people developed under communism; the galvanising effect of early fears over the social impact of transition; post-communist governments' need for interlocutors to legitimise and inform their policies; and the diffusion of new paradigms of population ageing as new policy sectors requiring stakeholder consultation and participation.

In comparative terms, the two cases suggest that the nature of the outgoing communist regime and the nature of transition are of particular importance in laying down distinct legacies, which affected both the availability of organisational resources to emerging pensioners' interest organisations and, more indirectly, their relationship with NGOs and policy makers. Future research would, however, need to theorise such legacies more widely and systematically, taking into account the distinct legacies of patronage-based communist regimes (Kitschelt *et al.* 1999) and the diverse structure of social and welfare organisations under communist regimes, which may not be reducible to existing typologies of communist regimes.

Cross-national variations in formal institutional opportunities, by contrast, seem from the Czech–Slovene comparison to have been of more limited relevance. The greater openness of the Slovene political system to the representation of social interests seem to have been offset by a traditional conceptualisation of corporate socio-economic interests, which excluded even a broad organisation such as ZDUS from the National Council and Social and Economic Council. Consultation structures created to give civil society groups a voice in new population ageing strategies, the two cases suggest, have so far had limited impact as these have been *ad hoc* bodies lacking real power with sometimes restricted agendas, excluding high-profile issues like pension reform, which political parties, officials and traditional social partners have reserved to themselves. Wider comparative research on the configuration of pensioners' interest organisations in Central and Eastern Europe would, however, have to allow for the greater institutional instability of party systems and, in particular, the greater fluidity of left parties in some Central and Eastern European democracies.

Despite lacking appropriate resources or concentrations of expertise, in the period reviewed pensioners' interest organisations in both cases opted to focus heavily on strategies of elite-level engagement with legislators and policy makers. Their retention of broad membership structures, however, suggests a greater than assumed mobilisation capacity, suggesting that, like economic interest groups such as trade unions—and perhaps in coordination with them—they could also deploy protest strategies if social dialogue and consultation mechanisms are eroded by the politics of austerity.

University College London

References

ADO (2001) *Minulost, přitomnost, budoucnost* (Prague, ČMKOS).

Anderson, K. M. & Lynch, J. (2007) 'Reconsidering Seniority Bias: Aging, Internal Institutions, and Union Support for Pension Reform', *Comparative Politics*, 39, 2, January.

Avdagic, S. (2004) *Loyalty and Power in Union–Party Alliances*, Discussion Paper 0/47 (Cologne, Max Planck Institute for the Study of Societies).

Baumgartner, F. R. & Leech, B. L. (1998) *Basic Interests: The Importance of Groups in Politics and in Political Science* (Princeton, NJ, Princeton University Press).

Bebler, A. (2002) 'Slovenia's Smooth Transition', *Journal of Democracy*, 13, 1, January.

Binderkrantz, A. (2005) 'Interest Group Strategies: Navigating Between Privileged Access and Strategies of Pressure', *Political Studies*, 53, 4, December.

Blažek, P. (2002) 'Reprezentace zěmědelských zajmů v politickém systému České republiky: ekonomické (profesní) zájmové skupiny', *Politologicka revue*, 8, 1, January.

Bohle, D. & Greskovits, B. (2007) 'Neoliberalism, embedded neoliberalism and neocorporatism: Towards transnational capitalism in Central-Eastern Europe', *West European Politics*, 30, 3, May.

Bohle, D. & Greskovits, B. (2009) 'Poverty, Inequality, and Democracy: East-Central Europe's Quandary', *Journal of Democracy*, 20, 4, October.

Campbell, A. L. (2003) *How Policies Make Citizens: Senior Political Activism in the American Welfare State* (Princeton, NJ, Harvard University Press).

Carley, M. (2004) 'Trade Union Membership 1993–2003', available at: http://www.eurofound.europa. eu/eiro/2004/03/update/TN0403105U.htm, accessed 15 October 2008.

Chamberlayne, P. (1995) 'Self-Organization and Older People in Eastern Germany', in Craig, G. & Mayo, M. (eds) (1995) *Community Empowerment: A Reader in Participation and Development* (London, Zed Books).

Cohen, L. J. (1989) *The Socialist Pyramid: Elites and Power in Yugoslavia* (London, Mosaic Press).

Cox, T. (2007) 'Democratization and State–Society Relations in East Central Europe: The Case of Hungary', *Journal of Communist Studies and Transition Politics*, 23, 2, June.

Crowley, S. (2004) 'Explaining Labor Weakness in Post-Communist Europe: Historical Legacies and Comparative Perspective', *East European Politics and Societies*, 18, 3, August.

Crowley, S. & Ost, D. (eds) (2001) *Workers after Workers' States: Labor and Politics in Postcommunist Eastern Europe* (Lanham, MD, Rowman and Littlefield).

Deegan-Krause, K. (2006) *Elected Affinities: Democracy and Party Competition in Slovakia and the Czech Republic* (Stanford, CA, Stanford University Press).

Duvanova, D. S. (2007) 'Bureaucratic Corruption and Collective Action: Business Associations in the Post-Communist Transition', *Comparative Politics*, 39, 4, July.

Eckstein, H. (1975) 'Case Study and Theory in Political Science', in Greenstein, F. I. & Polsby, N. W. (eds) (1975) *The Handbook of Political Science* (Reading, MA, Addison-Wesley).

European Commission (2005) *Confronting Demographic Change: A New Solidarity Between the Generations* (Brussels, European Commission).

Evers, A. & Wolf, J. (1999) 'Political Organization and Participation of Older People: Traditions and Changes in Five European Countries', in Walker, A. & Naegele, G. (eds) (1999) *The Politics of Old Age in Europe* (Buckingham, Open University Press).

Feltenius, D. (2007) 'Client Organizations in a Corporatist Country: Pensioners' Organizations and Pensions Policy in Sweden', *Journal of European Social Policy*, 17, 2, May.

Fink-Hafner, D. (1998) 'Organized Interests in the Policy-Making Process in Slovenia', *Journal of European Public Policy*, 5, 2, June.

Fink-Hafner, D. (2006) 'Slovenia: Between Bipolarity and Coalition Building', in Jungerstam-Mulders, S. (ed.) (2006).

Fink-Hafner, D. & Krašovec, A. (2005) 'Is Consultation Everything? The Influence of Interest Groups on Parliamentary Working Bodies in Slovenia', *Czech Sociological Review*, 41, 3, June.

Goerres, A. & Vanhuysse, P. (2011) 'Mapping the Field: The Comparative Study of Generational Politics and Policies', in Goerres, A. & Vanhuysse, P. (eds) (2011) *Ageing Populations in Post-industrial Democracies: Comparative Studies of Policies and Politics* (Basingstoke, Routledge).

Green, A. T. (1999) 'Nonprofits and Democratic Development: Lessons from the Czech Republic', *Voluntas*, 10, 3, September.

Grzymala-Busse, A. (2001) 'Coalition Formation and the Regime Divide in East Central Europe', *Comparative Politics*, 34, 1, October.

Grzymala-Busse, A. (2002) *Redeeming the Communist Past: The Regeneration of Communist Parties in East Central Europe* (Cambridge, Cambridge University Press).

Guardiancich, I. (2004) 'Welfare State Retrenchment: The Case of Pension Reforms in Poland and Slovenia', *Managing Global Transitions*, 2, 1, Spring.

Guardiancich, I. (2012) 'The Uncertain Future of Slovenian Exceptionalism', *East European Politics & Societies*, 26, 2, May.

Hanley, S. (2011) 'The Emergence of Pensioners' Parties in Contemporary Europe', in Tremmel, J. (ed.) (2011) *A Young Generation Under Pressure? The Financial Situation and the 'Rush Hour' of the Cohorts 1970–1985 in a Generational Comparison* (Berlin, Springer Verlag).

Havelková, H. (2008) 'Otázniky českého ženského hnutí po roce 1989', in Gjuričová, A. & Kopeček, M. (eds) (2008) *Kapitoly z dějin české demokracie po roce 1989* (Prague, Paseka).

Havlič, S., Ramovš, J. & Ramovš Ksenija (2001) 'National Report the Third Sector in Slovenia', available at: www.ceis.it/euroset/products/pdf/Third_Sector_in_Slovenia.PDF, accessed 15 October 2008.

Helpage International (2007) 'Age Demands Action in Slovenia', September, available at: http://helpage.bluefountain.com/es/Site/Resources/AgeDemandsActionbriefings/main_content/B9iW/mipaa_slovenia_for_web.pdf, accessed 4 April 2011.

Howard, M. M. (2003) *The Weakness of Civil Society in Post-Communist Europe* (Cambridge, Cambridge University Press).

Jou, W. (2011) 'Left–Right Orientations and Ideological Voting in New Democracies: A Case Study of Slovenia', *Europe-Asia Studies*, 63, 1, January.

Jungerstam-Mulders, S. (ed.) (2006) *Post-Communist EU Member States—Parties and Party Systems* (Aldershot, Ashgate).

Kitschelt, H., Mansfeldová, Z., Markowski, R. & Tóka, G. (1999) *Post-Communist Party Systems: Competition, Representation, and Inter-Party Cooperation* (Cambridge, Cambridge University Press).

Kopecký, P. (2001) *Parliaments in the Czech and Slovak Republics: Party Competition and Parliamentary Institutionalization* (Aldershot, Ashgate).

Kopecký, P. (2006) 'The Rise of the Power Monopoly: Political Parties in the Czech Republic', in Jungerstam-Mulders, S. (ed.) (2006).

Kožuh Novak, M. (2011) 'Komu naj verjamem?', *ZDUS Plus*, 4, 6.

Kristan, T. (2011) 'Društva upokojencev še bolj odločno za pokojninsko reformo', *Delo*, 22 April.

KSČM (2005) *Obsahové materiály VI. sjezdu KSČM* (Prague, KSČM).

Kubicek, P. (2004) *Organized Labor in Postcommunist States: From Solidarity to Infirmity* (Pittsburgh, PA, University of Pittsburgh Press).

Kunc, S. (2006) 'Zájmové skupiny jako politický aktér', in Mansfeldová, Z. & Kroupa, A. (eds) (2006) *Proměny reprezentace zájmů po vstupu do Evropské unie* (Prague, SLON).

Linek, L. & Pecháček, S. (2006) *Základní charakteristiky členské základny KDU-ČSL, Sociologické studie 6:06* (Prague, Sociologický ústav AV ČR).

Lukšič, I. (2003) 'Corporatism Packaged in Pluralist Ideology—The Case of Slovenia', *Communist and Post-communist Studies*, 36, 4, December.

Lynch, J. (2006) *Age in the Welfare State: The Origins of Social Spending on Pensioners, Workers and Children* (Cambridge, Cambridge University Press).

Meyer, D. S. & Imig, D. R. (1993) 'Political Opportunity and the Rise and Decline of Interest Group Sectors', *Social Science Journal*, 30, 3, September.

Ministerstvo práce a sociálních věcí (2008) *National Programme of Preparation for Ageing for 2008–2012 of the Czech Republic* (Prague, MPSV).

Ministry of Labour Family and Social Affairs (2008) *The Strategy of Care for the Elderly Till 2010* (Ljubljana, Ministry of Labour Family and Social Affairs).

Mukesh, C., Betcherman, G. & Banerji, A. (2007) *From Red to Gray: The 'Third Transition' of Ageing Populations in Eastern Europe and the Former Soviet Union* (Washington, DC, World Bank).

Müller, K. (1999) *The Political Economy of Pension Reform in Central-Eastern Europe* (Cheltenham & Northampton, MA, Edward Elgar).

Müller, K. (2002) 'Beyond Privatization: Pension Reform in the Czech Republic and Slovenia', *Journal of European Social Policy*, 12, 4, November.

Myant, M. (2000) 'Employers' Interest Representation in the Czech Republic', *Journal of Communist Studies and Transition Politics*, 16, 4, September.

Myant, M. (2010) *Trade Unions in the Czech Republic* (Brussels, ETUI).

Myant, M., Slocock, B. & Smith, S. (2000) 'Tripartism in the Czech and Slovak Republics', *Europe-Asia Studies*, 52, 4, June.

Orenstein, M. A. (2000) *How Politics and Institutions Affect Pension Reform in Three Postcommunist Countries*, World Bank Research Working Paper 2310 (Washington, DC, World Bank).

Orenstein, M. A. (2008a) 'Postcommunist Welfare States', *Journal of Democracy*, 19, 4, October.

Orenstein, M. A. (2008b) *Privatizing Pensions: The Transnational Campaign for Social Security Reform* (Princeton, NJ, Princeton University Press).

Ost, D. (1993) 'The Politics of Interest in Post-Communist East Europe', *Theory and Society*, 22, 4, August.

Ost, D. (2009) 'The Consequences of Postcommunism: Trade Unions in Eastern Europe's Future', *East European Politics & Societies*, 23, 1, February.

Padgett, S. (1999) *Organizing Democracy in Eastern Germany: Interest Groups in Post-Communist Society* (Cambridge, Cambridge University Press).

Pérez-Solórzano Borragán, N. (2006) 'Post-Communist Interest Politics: A Research Agenda', *Perspectives on European Politics and Society*, 7, 2, June.

Pollert, A. (1999) 'Trade Unionism in Transition in Central and Eastern Europe', *European Journal of Industrial Relations*, 5, 2, July.

Pospišil, O. & Němcová, H. (2010) '20. výročí záložení SDČR', *Zpravodaj Svazu důchodců České republiky*, 4/2010.

Pratt, H. J. (1993) *Gray Agendas: Interest Groups and Public Pensions in Canada, Britain and the United States* (Ann Arbor, MI, University of Michigan Press).

Rada seniorů České republiky (2007) *Výroční zpráva za rok 2006* (Prague, RSČR).

Rada seniorů České republiky (2009) 'Programové priority a další úkoly Rady seniorů České republiky na období let 2009–2013', 15 May, available at: http://www.rscr.cz/prispevky/ukolyrady.pdf, accessed 1 May 2011.

Rada seniorů České republiky (2010) *Výroční zpráva za rok 2009* (Prague, RSČR).

Schmitter, P. C. (1992) 'The Consolidation of Democracy and the Representation of Social Groups', *American Behavioral Scientist*, 35, 4–5, March.

Schmitter, P. C. (2008) 'The Changing Politics of Organised Interests', *West European Politics*, 31, 1–2, January–March.

Skocpol, T. (2003) *Diminished Democracy: From Membership to Management in American Civic Life* (Norman, OK, University of Oklahoma Press).

Solich, J. (2008) 'Činnost Svaz důchodců České republiky 2005–2008 (od 6. sjezdu)', *Zpravodaj SD ČR*, 4/2008.

Tarrow, S. (1998) *Power in Movement* (Cambridge, Cambridge University Press).

Tarrow, S. & Petrova, T. (2007) 'Transactional and Participatory Activism in the Emerging European Polity: The Puzzle of East-Central Europe', *Comparative Political Studies*, 40, 1, January.

United Nations (2002) *Madrid International Plan of Action on Ageing*, available at: http://www.un.org/ageing/madrid_intlplanaction.html, accessed 3 January 2010.

United Nations (2011) *World Population Prospects: The 2010 Revision*, Department of Economic and Social Affairs, Population Division (New York, United Nations).

Valterová, A. (2006) 'Česká tripartita v evropském kontextu', *Středoevropské politické studie*, 4, 8, Autumn.

Vanhuysse, P. (2006a) *Divide and Pacify: Strategic Social Policies and Political Protests in Post-Communist Democracies* (Budapest, Central European University Press).

Vanhuysse, P. (2006b) 'Czech Exceptionalism? A Comparative Political Economy Interpretation of Post-Communist Policy Pathways, 1989–2004', *Sociologický časopis/Czech Sociological Review*, 42, 6, December.

Vanhuysse, P. (2008) 'Creating Outsiders: Silent Non-Exit, Broken Voice, and Political Anomie through Post-Communist Social Policy', unpublished paper, available at: http://papers.ssrn.com/sol3/papers.cfm?abstract_id=1212652, accessed 1 January 2011.

Večerník, J. (2004) 'Who Is Poor in the Czech Republic? The Changing Structure and Faces of Poverty after 1989', *Czech Sociological Review*, 40, 6, December.

Večerník, J. (2006) *The Changing Social Status of Pensioners and the Prospects of Pension Reform*, Prague Economic Papers 3/2006 (Prague, University of Economics).

Výzkumný ústav práce a sociálních věci (Research Institute for Labour and Social Affairs) (2012) 'Main Economic and Social Indicators of the Czech Republic 1990–2011', *Bulletin*, 27.

Walker, A. (1998) 'Speaking for Themselves: The New Politics of Old Age in Europe', *Education and Ageing*, 13, 1, January.

Wang, F. T. Y. (1999) 'Resistance and Old Age: The Subject Behind the American Seniors' Movement', in Chambon, A., Irving, A. & Epstein, L. (eds) (1999) *Foucault Reader for Social Work* (New York, Columbia University Press).

Yakova, I. (2004) 'Représentation des intérêts professionnels dans le secteur agricole en République Tchèque et en Bulgarie: quelle européanisation de l'action?', *Politique européenne*, 1, 12, Winter.

Zavod za pokojninsko in invalidsko zavarovanje Slovenije (2006) *Monthly Statistics Overview—Year 2005* (Ljubljana, Zavod za pokojninsko in invalidsko zavarovanje Slovenije).

Zavod za pokojninsko in invalidsko zavarovanje Slovenije (2011) *Monthly Statistics Overview—Year 2010* (Ljubljana, Zavod za pokojninsko in invalidsko zavarovanje Slovenije).

ZDUS (2001) *Upokojenci Slovenje 1946–2001* (Ljubljana, ZDUS).

ZDUS (2008) *Pokročilo o delu Zveze društev upokojencu Slovenije za leto 2007* (Ljubljana, ZDUS).

ZDUS (2009) *Poročilo o opravljenem delu v letu 2008* (Ljubljana, ZDUS).

ZDUS (2010) *Poročilo o delu v letu 2009 in predlogi za delo v letu 2010* (Ljubljana, ZDUS).

Život '90 (2001) *Výroční zpráva za rok 2000* (Prague, Život '90).

Zupanič, M. (2010) 'Vzajemna v rokah upokojencev', *Delo*, 26 July.

Civil Society, Trade Unions and Post-Soviet Democratisation: Evidence from Russia and Ukraine

PAUL KUBICEK

CIVIL SOCIETY IS A DOMINANT THEME in post-communist politics. It was a prominent discourse in much of the anti-communist dissident literature, and in the past decade scores of works have been produced celebrating civil society's role both in bringing down communist regimes and in serving as a foundation for a new democratic order.[1] This work is often based on the Tocquevillian principle that civil society—defined as a social sphere distinct from the family, market and the state, and composed of independent, voluntary associations and networks of citizens—plays a central role in democratic consolidation by fostering values of citizenship, community and political participation among the population and by creating structures to prevent the emergence of authoritarian state power. Carothers notes: 'civil society is the connective tissue that transitional countries need to join the forms of democracy with their intended substance, to ensure that new democratic institutions and processes do not remain hollow boxes and empty rituals'.[2] Causal arguments about the strength or weakness of civil society can be invoked to explain the relative success (Poland) or failure (Russia) of democratic consolidation in a number of post-communist countries.

Whereas civil society is ubiquitous in academic and political discourse, trade unions are far less popular as subjects for analysis. This, however, is puzzling on several grounds. First, in all post-communist states trade unions are by far the largest organisations in civil society, with membership in the millions. Yet, for all the attention lavished on civil society in general, this sizeable component of civil society has not been given concerted attention. Second, trade unions and working-class movements historically have been identified as crucial forces for democracy.[3] One would therefore think that their role in post-communist politics and in democratisation efforts would be worth examination. Third, given the twin demands of democratisation and marketisation in post-communist states and the position of unions as potentially important actors in both political and economic arenas, one would think they would be important players in the political economy of post-communist reform. Indeed, some in the immediate post-communist period did make mention of the need to either convince, co-opt or even coerce unions in order to push forward economic reform.[4]

However, any hopes or fears associated with organised labour in the post-communist period never materialised, even in Poland, where Solidarity was *the* central political actor for many years. True, on occasion, as in Poland and Ukraine in 1993 and in Russia in 1998, worker mobilisation can generate a political crisis. But much of this worker radicalism has occurred outside the framework of trade unions, and, overall, unions' role has been nothing like one might have thought, given their previous role in helping bring down communist governments, their sheer size, and the socioeconomic disaster that has accompanied the move to the market. Unions' relative silence is thus a puzzle;[5] they have been, to borrow from a Sherlock Holmes story, dogs that *should have* barked. This, of course, also explains their relative absence from much academic work. However, I would contend that workers' organisations should not be overlooked, for even dogs that do not (or perhaps cannot) bark may shed clues about what has transpired in the post-communist era.

This article will focus on trade unions in Russia and Ukraine, the two largest post-communist countries, where economic conditions have also been particularly dire and elites' commitment to democracy has been questionable at best. It has three modest aims. First, it will attempt to 'unpack' the notion of civil society and highlight why trade unions do not fit neatly into civil society as the term is often used. Second, it aims to briefly document and explain organised labour's marginalisation in these states. One important argument is that organised labour is weak in these states not only because of its past, subservient role, but also because economic reform in these states has hampered trade union development. Finally, what union weakness means in terms of democratisation will be discussed. A key notion guiding this article is that an examination of trade unions forces us to broaden our understanding of democracy to include how a distorted political economy belies claims about democracy based solely on the holding of competitive elections.

Trade unions and civil society: an uneasy relationship

It is worthwhile to subject some of the claims and assumptions surrounding the term 'civil society' to closer scrutiny. One issue is the relationship between civil society and democracy. While prevailing wisdom posits a positive relationship between the two, not all accept this as a given. Carothers notes that there is a certain 'romanticisation of civil society' by many in the West, insofar as it is viewed as 'town hall politics writ large' and composed of 'legions of well-mannered activists who play by the rules, settle conflicts peacefully, and do not break any windows'.[6] In part, this is attributable to a mythologised conception of American democracy, but it is also a reflection of the fact that the visible face of civil society in Eastern Europe—in the leaders of Solidarity, Civic Forum, Sajudis and other liberally oriented, anti-communist groups—was democratic. These examples, however, miss the point that in certain cases—in which political participation precedes political institutionalisation, to use Huntington's terminology—a vibrant civil society can undermine democracy. The classic case is Weimar Germany, and in comparing Weimar with present-day Russia one set of scholars noted that democracy in Russia survives in part because civil society is so *weak*.[7] One might also note that groups in civil society need not be 'civil', and can include radical nationalists, fascists, communists or others that do 'break windows' or do not wholly embrace democratic or liberal values. The *quality*, not *quantity*, of civil society therefore is central to any debate.

Another problem, one perhaps less immediately obvious, revolves around the arguments of Madison that creep into the civil society literature. Madison famously maintained in *Federalist X* that pluralism was beneficial because it mitigated the pernicious effects of factions, since a multiplicity of groups would prevent any one faction from becoming a majority and create (in the modern political science lexicon) 'cross-cutting cleavages'.[8] Competition among several groups—with no single group constituting a majority—would safeguard democracy and the rights of minorities. This pluralist assumption is implicit in the civil society literature, as the focus is on the benefits of general popular activism and organisation and not on the democratic credentials (or lack thereof) of any particular group. Put another way, much of the literature on civil society tends to make it an abstract notion and assume that its activities, *in toto* at least, are directed to the common good. Rarely is concerted attention given to the different components that comprise it, or the various and often antagonistic interests they espouse.

These digressions are important, because once one begins to move beyond civil society as a catch-phrase and discuss specific parts of civil society such as trade unions, one can see how trade unions may not fit neatly into many of the above arguments. One problem is that unions (and for that matter many other groups) are not entirely 'civic', if, as is often the case, 'civic' is taken to mean 'civic-minded' or being oriented towards positions that seek to benefit the polity or the citizenry as a whole. Unions are not universal organisations; they are particularistic.[9] They must, first and foremost, serve the interests of their members. These may or may not coincide with the greater good, and it is this notion of 'interest' that is lacking or is downplayed in much of the discussion surrounding civil society.[10] Moreover, one should also note that not all unions or union members will have similar interests. In part because of debates over the proper course of reform, there has been a splintering of the labour movement in most post-communist countries, in which some unions (usually the communist successor unions) have taken a more sceptical view of free market reforms and newer, 'non-traditional' unions have embraced some aspects of change and have tended to align with more liberal political parties. Thus, treating unions as an undifferentiated whole would be as mistaken as analysing civil society without paying attention to the particular features of its major components.

This discussion provides a link to another issue: the relationship between trade unions and democracy. Although unions have, of late, fallen into some disrepute, most analysts, taking a longer view, would posit a positive correlation between working-class mobilisation and democratisation. Workers, being the plurality, if not the majority, in most countries, see democracy as a means of empowering themselves, and working-class organisations and parties have pushed for democratisation and generally have been willing to play by democratic rules once democracy has been established. However, in post-communist conditions, given the communist heritage of the post-communist trade unions, one can wonder whether all unions in these countries are fully-fledged democratic organisations. For example, insofar as one of their goals would be self-preservation, they may try to preserve elements of the old system and stifle the emergence of new organisations that would challenge their position. They may also continue to have ties with (reformed?) communist parties. Capturing this notion of unions' possible ambivalence towards democracy, one Russian labour sociologist gave his work on trade unions the title *Hope or Threat*.[11]

More serious, however, is the problem unions may pose for democratic politicians interested in free market reforms. Insofar as unions may have the power and interest to undermine these reforms, they are the 'enemy', and indeed have been treated with suspicion by many post-communist leaders, including Leszek Balcerowicz in Poland, Vaclav Klaus in the Czech Republic and Boris El'tsin in Russia.[12] The contrast is all too evident. Civil society as a whole, with all its normative assumptions included, is lauded: unions are, to put it mildly, another matter, groups that need to be beaten or subdued if democratic consolidation and marketisation are to have a chance.[13]

Of course, this discussion points to a central tension between democracy and the market, one that can be overblown (e.g. several countries have weathered the storm of the 'dual transition') but one that nonetheless merits attention. At the risk of invoking a bit of Marxism, it is difficult to understand the pathologies of democratic transition in several states, notably Russia and Ukraine, without taking into account how marketisation and the resulting economic dislocation have affected political processes. Specifically, the issue hinges on the distribution of property, an issue that was absent in the earlier transitions to democracy in Southern Europe and Latin America and hence ignored as well in 'transitology'.[14] However, this issue has been of central concern to workers and trade unions, and privatisation (or, as Russians are wont to say, *prikhvatizatsiya* (grabbing) has fundamentally altered the political economy of these states, upon which it may or may not be possible to build a democratic system. These considerations of political economy (e.g. property distribution, class relations, creation of a 'ruling class') take one far beyond both the purely 'electoral' understandings of democracy and the ground trod by most studies of 'civil society', and compel one to ask the more difficult, more value-laden, and hence more interesting questions of who rules and/or for whom policies are adopted.[15]

The point of this discussion is that one can profit by 'unpacking' the notion of civil society and looking more carefully at its constituent parts. Using civil society exclusively in some normative or Madisonian sense may obscure more than it reveals, and arguably may be only a chimera. Tangible groups and interests must be taken into account. The multifarious components within civil society will differ, and even trade unions themselves will not be homogeneous entities. However, once one accepts the need to subject the various parts of civil society to scrutiny, the consideration of trade unions becomes obvious, particularly when one takes into account the importance of political economy in post-communist transformation. It is to the cases of Russian and Ukrainian unions that we now turn.

Trade unions in Russia and Ukraine

The communist heritage

Before jumping ahead, it is worth briefly discussing trade unions during Soviet times, as today's unions are not built on a *tabula rasa*. By far the largest union confederations in both countries are the direct successors to the All-Union Central Committee of Trade Unions (VTsSPS) and the corresponding republic-level organisation in Ukraine. Post-Soviet unions continue to be shaped by this heritage. Unfortunately, however, their communist-era experience is not particularly auspicious for construction of a democratically oriented, powerful trade union movement.

The reasons for this are not hard to find.[16] Despite the rhetoric of 'dictatorship of the proletariat' and de facto mandatory trade union membership (which made unions the largest organisations in the country), organised labour did not exercise a leading role in communist society. This was reserved exclusively for the vanguard of the working class, the Communist Party, and labour organisations, like all other groups in society, were subjugated to the party. In the particular case of unions, however, they were the lowest ranking members of a troika of party/director/union at individual enterprises, and were expected to play what many observers have called a 'dual role', although more properly one could say it was a 'triple role'. One role was to serve the party as a 'transmission belt' from above to below and function, in Lenin's formulation, as 'schools of communism'. In this case priority would be on order, discipline and fulfilment of the plan. Their second role was as a subsidiary and ally of management, working in a paternalistic manner with directors to distribute social insurance funds and various work-related social benefits (daycare, subsidised vacations, apartments, recreation and cultural facilities) and lobbying ministries jointly with directors for more support for their branch or enterprise. Managers, it is worth noting, were members of the union as well (they qualified as 'hired workers') and in fact they exercised much power in the union. Workers were thus integrated into the system not only at the macro-level (e.g. loyalty to the Soviet state or the party) but they and their unions were also integrated into the enterprise, the *kollektiv*, and depended heavily upon management for their well-being.[17] The third, and by far the least pronounced, role was to defend workers against arbitrary actions of managers, such as unjustified dismissals, violations of safety codes or capricious changes in work norms. While some have argued that labour shortages in the USSR gave workers some power at the shop-floor level,[18] the fact is that the unions, as organisations, never enjoyed significant power at any level of Soviet society and did nothing to encourage autonomous worker mobilisation. They were 'paper trade unions'.[19] While one could maintain that there was some sort of 'Soviet social contract',[20] this 'contract' was built upon a bargain in which workers forfeited any right to independent political or social activity. The ultimate enforcement mechanism would also be the tanks of the party-state, as the workers who launched a strike in Novocherkassk discovered in 1962.

Under Gorbachev there was an effort to reform industrial relations and the role of workers.[21] In the 1987 law on state enterprises, workers' councils (first created in 1983) were empowered to elect managers and given a role in the governance of the enterprise. At the same time Gorbachev attempted to increase the autonomy of enterprise directors by decentralising and introducing self-financing. The results of Gorbachev's *perestroika* are rather well known: confusion, drops in production and the beginnings of 'spontaneous privatisation'. Despite his arguably good intentions, Gorbachev's reforms did not lead to worker empowerment, and in 1990 new laws stripped worker's councils of many of their rights.

As the system moved toward its ultimate denouement, however, there was some autonomous mobilisation of workers from below. In July 1989 a wave of strikes among coal miners in Russia and Ukraine offered a stiff challenge to Gorbachev and the Soviet trade unions. This strike was the result of the failures of both the macro and enterprise level reforms to live up to the aspirations of the workers. It also was a repudiation of the existing trade unions, which were rejected by the workers as tools of management.[22] These strikes, however, were not just a local phenomenon: they demanded (in addition to lower prices and more consumer goods) more political and economic reform. Some concessions were given to the miners, but the lasting legacy of this wave of strikes was the formation in autumn 1990 of an Independent Miners' Union (NPG), which would lead strikes again in 1991 in support of privatisation and for El'tsin in his battle with Gorbachev. While the NPG was the most visible new union in the twilight of the USSR, there were others (e.g. air traffic controllers, pilots, train drivers, dockworkers), and these associations posed a major challenge to both the Soviet trade unions and the party that stood behind them. With the collapse of the party in 1991 one might have hoped that these new, still small (most numbered only a few thousand members) trade unions, espousing the rhetoric of democracy and genuine worker representation, would help spearhead the creation of a new trade union association in the former Soviet Union.

Post-Soviet Russian trade unions

This however was not to be. While these unions still exist, the trade union movement, such as it is, is dominated by the Federation of Independent Trade Unions of Russia (FNPR), the successor body to the VTsSPS. While its membership has fallen from a self-declared 66 million in 1991 to 38 million 10 years later, its unions (43 branch and 89 territorial bodies) represent 95% of the unionised workers in Russia. It has also held onto property (sanatoria, health clinics, sports facilities, childrens' camps, apartments, offices) held by the VTsSPS which is valued at some $6 billion and generates an annual income of $300 million.[23] This property is, by the FNPR's own admission, crucial to keeping and attracting members, and it has been a major topic of dispute between the FNPR and its rivals.[24]

While the FNPR has been successful in keeping the bulk of its resources, it has arguably been less successful in re-shaping itself into a genuine representative of the workers. True, the FNPR claims a vast number of members, but critics of the FNPR (and some within the FNPR) concede that membership for most is perfunctory, not a conscious choice of a worker but a result of inertia, habit or even perhaps threats to the worker. There is little doubt that the FNPR is not perceived in a favourable light, which raises additional questions about the motivations for union membership. Survey after survey reports that trade unions are not trusted by the public and are not seen as an effective institution.[25] The FNPR has also been unable—unwilling may be more accurate—to mobilise the bulk of its members to protest at economic conditions and policies that have been catastrophic to millions of workers.[26] Much of the FNPR's activity—in protests, lobbying and political campaigning—has been in concert with managers of enterprises and employers' organisations, and this can cast doubt on how far the unions have succeeded in becoming a voice of *workers*.[27] This behaviour is reinforced by ties at the enterprise level, where managers are often still members of the unions and have the resources to co-opt or coerce union leaders. Thus what one sees in Russia is an immense but 'toothless and tame' organisation—one that is inherently conservative, one that cannot act autonomously and one that cannot mobilise its membership.[28]

While some of these problems can be directly attributed to the FNPR's heritage and slack labour markets that inhibit worker mobilisation, difficulties also arise from the FNPR's troubled and often ambiguous relationship with the political authorities. In 1991 the FNPR declared its political independence, breaking from the Communist Party, but it quickly emerged as a critic of the El'tsin government. It lobbied together with enterprise directors for credits to industry, wage increases and provisions for 'insider privatisation' through buy-outs by managers and workers. Such moves helped undermine the 'shock therapy' reforms, but ultimately they brought little to workers, as real wages plunged and worker self-ownership was a chimera, undermined by the *prikhvatizatsiya* of the directors themselves. Empowered by these 'victories', the FNPR pushed further, openly declaring its support for the Supreme Soviet in the latter's stand-off with El'tsin and calling for mass action on behalf of the Khasbulatov-Rutskoi faction. When this failed to materialise and El'tsin prevailed with the help of Russian tanks, the FNPR was left extremely vulnerable. Although reports indicate that El'tsin considered banning the FNPR entirely, he backed away from this radical move, although it did remain a possibility.[29] Instead, he forced a leadership change of the FNPR and took the right of legislative initiative and control of social funds away from unions.[30] The unions, as well as other groups in Russian society, were clearly on the defensive as El'tsin began to concentrate power in his hands. A Social Accord was duly signed in 1994, and since then the FNPR has tried to avoid playing an explicitly political role. Mikhail Shmakov, the head of the FNPR, maintained that open confrontation with the regime would 'throw our trade unions onto the backwaters of public life' and would be a 'threat to the existence of the FNPR'.[31] True, the FNPR has not been entirely silent, but its protests are restricted to purely economic demands, 'social partnership' remains its dominant discourse even as its ostensible 'partners' continually show bad faith to workers (i.e. the wage arrears crisis), and some speculate that its days of protest are held only to fend off complaints from local unions that the FNPR is not doing enough. Certainly, the FNPR has not been leading the most radical protests or demanding the resignation of the government, as miners did in 1998 when they by-passed all the unions and blockaded railways to draw attention to the fact that some workers had not been paid for over nine months.

The FNPR, fearing government action against it (e.g. nationalisation of its property) has been declawed. It has eschewed radicalism, forging electoral alignments with the Russian Union of Industrialists and Entrepreneurs in 1993 and 1995 and with Fatherland-All Russia (OVR) in 1999. These 'safe' choices, however, have not been very successful.[32] For its part, the government found an ability to work with the FNPR, particularly under Prime Minister Viktor Chernomyrdin, formerly a leader in the industrialist lobby. At the same time, it began to distance itself from its erstwhile allies, the 'independents' such as the NPG, which were also hamstrung by a number of organisational problems. Though a presence in the mining and transport sectors, they have not developed any new niches or greater organisational strength since 1991.[33] By 1998 the NPG had even come full circle, demanding the resignation of a President whom it had steadfastly supported scarcely a decade before and even named an honorary member.

Thus in Russia what has emerged is a strange and distorted 'social partnership', supported by tripartite commissions and other less formal forms of government-union interaction. While the unions can claim some victories, i.e. a fairly liberal law on trade unions, many are rather hollow. General and collective agreements have been routinely abrogated, as was witnessed most clearly in the case of the wage arrears crisis, which reached a peak in 1998 when over $10 billion was owed to over 20 million workers.[34] Tripartite bodies have an insufficient legal basis, and they have become a 'disorganised sideshow', 'a ritual', 'only a device for letting off steam'.[35] The problems are many, but boil down to a couple of crucial points: 'partnership' is impossible given the inequality in power between the state and the unions, and the ability of workers to press their claims is severely hampered by fears of unemployment or loss of work-based benefits. The farce of Russian 'social partnership' was revealed most clearly in 2000, when the state, worried about debt payments, passed a 'unified social tax' that placed all social insurance monies under the exclusive authority of the Tax Ministry. Unions protested, but to no avail.

One interesting development has been the attempt to adopt a new Labour Code in Russia. A much-amended Soviet-era one has been in force, and in 1998 the government (with IMF support) put forward a new code that would have stripped the unions and workers of many of the rights they enjoyed, on paper at least, under Soviet law. All unions protested, the national tripartite commission refused to approve it, but the government went ahead and introduced its measure into parliament, where the unions managed in autumn 2000 to convince parliamentarians to block it. However, in spring 2001 the FNPR and the government agreed on a compromise version that passed a first reading in the Duma in July. While the bill does grant workers protections in a variety of areas (on issues such as vacations, overtime, mandatory collective agreements, although opponents argue that these protections are rather weak), it has generated controversy because some of its provisions could be harmful, even fatal, to the newer, smaller unions.[36] According to the proposal, employers would be obligated to negotiate only with the union representing the majority of workers (almost always an FNPR union), employers could also negotiate with 'other representatives of workers' (which could create an opening for employers to create their own 'pocket' unions), and the question of strikes would be determined by the entire work collective, not trade unions (the latter would take the potential bite out of the still-active 'independents'). This draft has bitterly divided the union movement, and ironically put communists and the erstwhile reformist, new unions on the same side. Many construe it as an assault by the government on freedom of association. As Anatolii Ivanov, a Duma member and vice-president of the non-FNPR All-Russian Confederation of Labour, asked a fellow Duma member from the FNPR, 'If you are free to organise but *de facto* the law will refuse to recognise you to negotiate with the employer, what kind of freedom is that?'.[37]

In various ways, then, one can note how unions in Russia are constrained because of the political environment. In this, unions share much with other groups in civil society. However, as noted, unions are important players in the economic arena as well. What can be said about unions in the new political economy of Russia?

Here we shall focus on perhaps the most fundamental reform in the post-Soviet period: privatisation. Over 80% of Russian workers work in the private (non-state) sphere, and, following Marx, one would expect the change in ownership would produce significant repercussions, including on trade unions and the general sphere of labour relations. While privatisation would no doubt present some new obstacles for unions, one might at minimum suspect that it would break the troika of state–director–union that had constrained autonomous union activity in the past, and that post-Soviet unions would begin to behave more like Western trade unions.

For the most part, however, this has not been the case, even as privatisation gave way to massive corruption and the swindling of workers.[38] Here it is worth noting how privatisation of large enterprises took place in Russia. The initial plan of Anatolii Chubais, the privatisation 'tsar', was to have open auctions. This was amended, under pressure from directors and unions, to allow the work collective (comprising both workers and management) to decide the form of privatisation, with one option to purchase 51% of the shares of their firms. This 'insider privatisation' was the choice of 73% of large Russian enterprises,[39] and it promised—in theory—to make genuine worker self-management a reality. Certainly, some excitement was generated by the prospect of true, legal ownership in the firm. However, as is well known, all did not work out as planned. Workers lacked information about their enterprises, generally deferred to management, and gradually began to sell their shares, as they did not receive any dividends, they needed money to make up for non-payment of wages, and they succumbed in some cases to coercion from management. The directors, with minimal outlay of capital, became the owners of the firms, and the workers, who were promised much, were left with nothing.[40]

Since privatisation was rushed through and preceded restructuring, workers in the privatised Russian economy have suffered from low wages, wage delays, dismissals and periods of forced administrative leave. Union leaders, to be sure, lament the results of privatisation, but they have distanced themselves from the question of property. One leader of a non-FNPR union maintained that 'questions of property, of ownership, these are not questions for trade unions, they have no bearing on labour relations'.[41] The desire is for effective, competent ownership—ironically an echo of Chubais—but the unions themselves largely eschew any role in management of the enterprise. Instead, even in well-known cases of labour militancy such as the literal battles over ownership at Norilsk Nickel, the Kuznetsk Metallurgical Plant and the Vyborg Paper Mill, the workers have mobilised against managers and owners whom they view as incompetent and allied with a rival ownership group.[42] Out of desperation, they are compelled to 'sell' their support at a very low price. In general, however, organised labour has stood on the sidelines when major questions of property or macroeconomic reforms are considered, thus belying claims about Russian 'corporatism' or 'social partnership'.

Let us now turn to the effects of privatisation. One clear effect has been a decline in union membership. Overall, trade union membership has dropped by almost half, and has fallen more rapidly since large-scale privatisation was launched in 1993–94. In addition to workers who have retired or lost their jobs, there has certainly been significant movement to new enterprises and jobs in the private sector, as traditional 'working-class' jobs have far less attraction than in the past. These new jobs—including those in banking, marketing, retail, petty trade and sweatshops—are almost entirely non-unionised, and many of them (estimates are about 10 million workers) are in small enterprises employing fewer than 50 workers.[43] Galina Strela of the Social-Economic Department of the FNPR acknowledged that the FNPR unions had made virtually no headway in this 'new economy', and Tat'yana Sosnina, head of the Union of Textile and Light Industry workers, conceded that it was 'pointless' to pursue unionisation in such enterprises, as work stability is low, employers are hostile, and workers themselves express little demand for unionisation.[44] Boris Golovkin, vice-chairman of the Nizhny Novgorod FNPR, observed: 'We have yet to create mechanisms to attract people from small, private, mainly service enterprises to the unions. This has to become a priority, but we will have to find some way of attracting these people in order to preserve our strength'.[45]

In large industrial enterprises unionisation rates remain high—upwards of 80–90%, although again this may be more out of inertia than enthusiasm or confidence in the union. Unions continue to function where they did in Soviet times, and privatisation has not been accompanied by union busting *en masse*, although several leaders would note that some new non-state owners do display a hostile attitude toward trade unions and that new unions are difficult to form.[46] However, one does not see, as a rule, a significant change in the functions or actions of many trade unions. As before, much union activity is done in conjunction with management, and there has been shockingly little union-management antagonism in many sectors, even as conditions for workers have deteriorated. There is joint activity in both political alliances and in lobbying efforts toward the state to extract credits and subsidies for particular branches or enterprises, the latter commonplace in Soviet times too. This is true in the motor industry, the aviation industry, the military-industrial complex, electricity, metallurgy, coal mining, textiles and the budget sector (teachers, doctors etc.). Despite privatisation in many of these sectors, state orders, state protection from foreign competition or state investment is still desperately needed, and thus unions and directors lobby together. Moreover, in cases such as the Lomonosovsky Porcelain Factory in St Petersburg and the Krasnoe Sormovo plant in Nizhny Novgorod, workers have mobilised in support of existing management who are threatened with dismissal or replacement by new owners.[47] Some might explain this joint union-management action as a holdover from the collective mentality of Soviet times ('*eto nash zavod*') or a residue of promises of worker self-ownership. However, it is not simply a cultural artifact. In many ways it makes sense, as the state must play a supportive role if many sectors are to survive and profitability means wages and jobs. Unions need not be adversarial toward management all the time. However, as Gordon argues, 'often joint action with the directors ends up with the factual loss of independence', as unions lose sight of workers' interests and become a tool of management, both in political lobbying and in ensuring discipline and worker acquiescence on the shop floor.[48]

What this adds up to, of course, is that the unions have not substantially changed at the enterprise level, even in privatised companies. The party-state may be out of the enterprise, but all this has done is to leave unions subordinate 'partners' in a bi-lateral relationship with management. The result, a product of the past heritage, desperate economic conditions and the new form of ownership, is union passivity and worker alienation from the unions. Surveys conducted among workers in eight sectors in summer 1997 are exceptionally telling. The results found that 33% of workers thought unions did not do anything, 18% credited them with supplying some social services, and fewer than 10% thought they defended workers interests on questions of wages, working conditions and resolution of work conflicts. On overall satisfaction, only 5% thought unions defended workers well, with more (12%) saying unions only supported directors. Lastly, when asked who defended their interests, the answers no one (54%), immediate bosses (24%) and directors of the enterprise (11%) ranked higher than trade unions (9%). Only coal miners were more likely to name unions (23%) than their bosses (16%) as their defenders.[49] This not only reinforces points about the lack of internal reform but demonstrates that privatisation has not fundamentally changed labour relations in Russia.

Of course it is unfair to make blanket statements. One can find examples of active unions, both 'non-traditional' ones and those in the FNPR. One such case of the latter would be the union at Tulachermet, a metallurgical factory in Tula, south of Moscow. Here the union has been involved in many long-standing battles with management over wages, working conditions and enterprise management. What stands out at this enterprise, as opposed to a neighbouring one where the union leader asserted that 'in principle there can be no conflict between the directors and the workers', is that Tulachermet has divested itself of many of its social resources (stadia, clinics, sanatoria) and that it was taken over by an 'outside' owner intent on cutting costs and not cosy with the existing trade union.[50] Notably, the 'non-traditional' unions also lack such social resources, and thus they do not play the passive role of the enterprise's social department. However, leaders of most of the existing unions have a corporate interest in maintaining this property and their services, for without them their position at the enterprise would be far less assured. The result, however, is that 'state paternalism' has been replaced by 'private paternalism', administered by unions in concert with management.[51] Ironically, the future of the unions, therefore, will in large part depend upon whether management wants to sacrifice some profitability and pay for the social institutions of the 'collective' in order to preserve union dependence and docility. In the long run it might be more rational to continue to 'buy off' the union and let it have its social sphere. The result, as Gordon foresees it, will be not the disappearance of unions but the preservation of 'pseudo-unions' engaged exclusively in social service functions and unable and unwilling to press claims against management vigorously.[52]

One additional consequence of the 'new economy' is worth mentioning: the breakdown in union solidarity. True, worker unity may have always been a bit of a myth, but the construction of a post-Soviet workers' movement is complicated by the emerging economic system. One sees this in numerous ways. Income inequality has markedly increased,[53] and many unions are in a competitive struggle over state funds. Additionally, some of the largest companies (Gazprom, Lukoil, Yukos, Norilsk Nickel) have their own company-based unions, and one can argue as well whether these structures are little more than creatures of management. Certainly, however, if these unions—which could easily form the vanguard of a workers' movement—are bought off, occupied exclusively with narrow, enterprise-specific concerns, or form their own association outside the FNPR (which is rumoured to be under discussion), this will harm union solidarity.[54] Finally, one sees that worker activism itself is also more focused on more specific problems. Writing about the coal miners, Borisov finds that their earlier (1989–92) general societal demands have been replaced with concerns in a gradually narrowing perspective, from their branch, to their enterprise, to only those workers who are engaged in protest activity.[55] This is indicative of a more general decentralisation and fragmentation of organised labour, and it is a crucial point if one is interested in a worker or union *movement* and not just individual unions. In short, at best, 'acting locally' may become the norm, particularly as collective bargaining continues to be decentralised. However, the other half of the slogan—'think globally'—may well be forgotten.

Post-Soviet Ukrainian trade unions

Ukrainian trade unions share many features with their Russian counterparts. It could hardly be otherwise. In addition to a common Soviet past, both sets of trade unions confront the problems of making a transition to a new system in conditions characterised by economic deprivation of workers, corruption and centralisation of presidential power. What stands out in the Ukrainian case, however, is the slower pace of economic reform, the greater union detachment from political questions and, until the end of 2000, the absence of such acute political crises and battles as have gripped Russia.

The Ukrainian Federation of Trade Unions (FPU), formed in 1990, is the dominant trade union body in the country. The successor to the Soviet-era unions, it unites 40 branch and 26 regional unions and in 2001 claimed 14.4 million members, down from 26 million at its creation. Current figures represent 94% of workers employed at enterprises with an FPU union and about 75% of the Ukrainian workforce, although these numbers are belied by some survey work showing significantly lower rates of unionisation.[56] Like the FNPR, the FPU inherited the Soviet-era union property, and until 2001 administered state social insurance funds, which critics charge gave it a coercive means to retain members.[57]

The FPU, however, is beset by numerous troubles. The first is that of public confidence in trade unions, which has remained low throughout the post-Soviet period and is significantly lower than in Russia.[58] While one could note that Ukrainians' confidence in virtually all institutions is low, unions rank among the bottom of various socio-political institutions. Second, the FPU has been beset by a series of internal schisms based on regional and branch interests. Many of these are over property, but also reflect resentment by some over the lack of reform in the central FPU structure. One regional leader lamented that 'the FPU is the most conservative institution in society'.[59] In February 2000 many regional unions did not heed the FPU's call for a national day of protest, which can be interpreted either as an act of rebellion, an indication that these unions are incapable of mobilising members, or that they are 'reconciled to the lack of fulfilment of the government's obligations'.[60] The FPU is worried about its organisational capacity, prompting some, including the leader of the once recalcitrant coalminers' union, to say that without re-establishing democratic centralism it will be impossible to strengthen the union movement.[61] More serious, perhaps, are questions of breaking with the past, particularly dependence upon the employer. Employers still belong to many FPU unions, and some FPU leaders will concede that they have yet to really understand their role in the market economy, finding it more convenient to ally with employers. This, however, has been the refrain for many years, but one sees little reform impulse within the FPU. Again, as in Russia, common interests are in part facilitated by economic conditions. For many union leaders the FPU continues to have a dual role: protecting workers and boosting production and profitability.[62] However, the FPU has been successful on neither front. Despite a decade of severe economic problems, the FPU has refrained from calling a national strike, and its occasional protests have not been as intense or sustained as those of non-FPU unions. Hence critics charge that it is a 'state union', loyal to the 'party of power'.

The FPU's limitations are highlighted by its forays into the political realm. It had limited success in its support for candidates in the 1994 parliamentary elections (24 of 242 won, including five union leaders) and in 1998 it conducted an ill-fated experiment, serving as the basis for the Ukrainian Workers' Party, which received a mere 0.79% of the vote.[63] Seven union leaders were elected in plurality districts or on other party lists, and they have allied with centrist, pro-presidential factions. Despite the government's inability to fulfil its promises mandated by the Constitution itself, FPU MPs and the organisation as a whole are not part of any opposition movement. The FPU was unable to settle on a candidate in the first round of the 1999 presidential election, but in the second round backed the incumbent, Leonid Kuchma, despite the fact that under his tutelage living standards had declined and corruption flourished. The FPU's silence during the protests in 2000–01 surrounding 'Kuchma-gate' was deafening, with some branch unions calling off strikes so as not to encourage 'radical elements' demanding the resignation of the president.[64] In a sense, the FPU is powerless to act, even if it wanted to. The FPU chief adviser on political questions explained: 'In order for us to enter into political action, we must see concrete results. If Stoyan (FPU head and an MP) joins the opposition, what will this bring? Who stands behind Stoyan? In truth, no one. People are passive, and thus opposition serves no purpose'.[65] As in Russia, one might also note that the FPU cannot afford to disturb the reigning authorities, for fear that they would move against the union, e.g. confiscating its property. One FPU leader conceded that 'unions still exist because they disturb no one'.[66]

Like the FNPR, the FPU puts a high premium on social partnership, which it upholds as a model for state-employer-union relations. Tripartism exists at the local, regional and national level, the latter primarily through the National Committee for Social Partnership, established in 1993. Unfortunately, 'social partnership' has yielded Ukrainian workers very little: the average wage (about $55 per month) is below the government-defined living minimum, the government has been unable to prevent illegal wage arrears, growth in GDP in 2000 did not lead to growth in real wages, and the FPU itself reports over 2 000 000 (!) cases of violations of laws on labour in 2000.[67] The most important provisions—jobs, wages, wage arrears—in yearly General Agreements are not fulfilled, yet the FPU leadership duly signs a new one for the following year. Obviously, the system is flawed: tripartite agreements are not adequately funded, there is a lack of legal basis (from 1991 to 1999 there was no law on trade unions, employers or social partnership; the third is still lacking) and the state cannot be held accountable for its failures. Noting all these problems, one FPU official asked: 'What can we do? Strikes are not successful and only create instability. We could do absolutely nothing and suffer in silence, but this would be the end of us as well. Social partnership is the only path available to us in present circumstances'.[68] This is a perfect illustration of what one writer described as the 'Ukrainian way' of post-communist development: a 'bad peace' is preferable to a 'good war'.[69] The result, of course, is stagnation and continued popular alienation.

In addition to the FPU, there are some smaller, new trade unions in Ukraine. For the most part, they are in the same sectors—mining and transport—as in Russia. They have been plagued by many problems: lack of resources, pressure from management, the FPU and political authorities, and internal divisions. An initial attempt to establish a confederation in 1994–95 floundered on personal disputes, and the reconstituted Confederation of Free Ukrainian Trade Unions (KVPU) was established only in 1997. Its largest member by far is the NPG, which claims 52 000 members, but it counts dockers, train drivers and others among its ranks. Perhaps the biggest difference between these unions and their Russian counterparts is a diminished political role. The NPG was active in a major 1993 strikewave in eastern Ukraine, but this action yielded little, economically or politically, except, ironically, to local officials and mine directors, who did gain various subsidies for their industry.[70] Later efforts to forge political alliances with reform-oriented leaders floundered. The then NPG leader Oleksandr Mril' noted that Ukrainian parties were more inclined toward *diktat* than true cooperation, and the leader of the Independent Railway Unions contended that political parties wanted to play the role of pimp and transform the unions into 'prostitutes'.[71] Not much has changed since then. Many trade union leaders insist that political parties have sold out to the authorities, and one put a colorful spin on the classic collective action problem:

> If there was a likely concrete result, a light at the end of the tunnel, then political action would be possible. However, I see none, and I am afraid that it is dangerous to move forward in the dark ... Politics is a dirty business, and for us, now, it is a waste of time.[72]

True, the NPG, though not the KVPU, has been active more recently, especially in the wake of 'Kuchmagate'. Again, however, political protests brought no results, and amid all the protests it was Viktor Yushchenko, the reform-oriented prime minister supported by the NPG, not Kuchma, who was forced from office. One NPG leader attributes their failures to enterprise managers, who bused their own, pro-Kuchma supporters to meetings, thereby hindering the movement to collect signatures for a referendum to remove the President.[73] This point is an important one, as it reveals a connection between trade unions, enterprise level politics and the weakness of democratic opposition in Ukraine. This puts another spin on recent death threats from Ukrainian special security forces against NPG leaders engaged in worker activism.[74]

These unions could claim a small victory in 2000 when the Constitutional Court overturned sections of the 1999 Ukrainian law on trade unions. This law envisioned a registration process for unions as well as limitations on the number of nationally recognised unions in each sector of the economy. It thus shared some features with the new Russian Labour Code but, thanks to the efforts of several MPs, the Human Rights Ombudsman and the ILO, these provisions were annulled.[75] However, a final revision of the law has yet to be passed, and some leaders would call this at best a Pyrrhic victory:

> That decision was made for Europe, for you. It is just a piece of paper. In the localities, nothing has changed ... The year that the law was in force was a disaster for independent unions, and many have been forced to start from scratch. One might say that we have the best laws in the world, but in reality they mean nothing at all. For example, the law says you cannot fire a union leader. Yet this happens all the time. Anytime any individual begins to act too independently, he is served with some sort of lawsuit. It's illegal, of course, but it makes the work of independent trade unions next to impossible.[76]

What of unions and the new political economy? First, one should realise that reform has proceeded much more slowly and with much more difficulty in Ukraine than in Russia. President Leonid Kravchuk (1991–94) put forth no genuine reform plan, and his successor's reform programmes have not lived up to their promises. Privatisation began in earnest in 1994–95, and by 1999 the private sector's share of GDP reached 55%, although large-scale privatisation had not progressed far since 1995.[77] A small number of shares—typically under 10% at each enterprise—were purchased through privatisation certificates distributed to the population, and many enterprises were privatised through renting mechanisms that were open to all sorts of corruption. Directors received privileges to buy shares on the market, but workers were unable to use similar privileges because hyperinflation had eaten away their savings. Despite their efforts, trade unions 'from the beginning of privatisation were pushed away from participation in the process'.[78] They had no legally defined role, and most decisions on the subject were made by state edict, with nominal participation of the work collective. In 2000–01 under Yushchenko the government did push through more privatisation programmes, but by this stage there was even less worker involvement and no privileges as in the past.

Unions have been hurt during this process. Employment in the industrial sectors of the economy has fallen precipitously, with many unions reporting a drop in membership of at least half. Many of these workers, of course, have found jobs in small, privatised companies. Unions, however, have not prospered in new enterprises in the private sector, and the leading 'union' in this sector functions more as a lobby for employers. Its leader claims that there is no conflict of interest between employers and workers, that in present circumstances workers are thankful to have any job, and that if there is exploitation by employers, well, '*C'est la vie*. That is the reality of the transition period'.[79] Other unions offer at least rhetorical support for workers. However, they are in little position to offer much real assistance. One union leader explained:

> What can we do? People come to us. They say, 'Help us. We want our wages. They are not paying us'. [Metallurgical] companies request work, and then refuse to pay. So we go to the state, and the state says we have no money, and besides, it is not our business. We do not manage the firm. So we go to the managers, and they also say we have no money. Sure, we can take them to court, but this takes time and in the end, there is not a legal base in the country to enforce any decision. If the choice is between paying workers or bankruptcy, the

state is not going to force a big company to go out of business. In the end, the worker sees how powerless we are, and of course we suffer for this.[80]

There are a variety of other problems, many similar to those in Russia. Most unions report pressure against them from the new owners, who try to run the enterprise as their own fiefdom and see little role for unions. While most organisations have withstood this pressure, they have not found a new, independent role in the enterprise. One union leader, aware of how Western unions work, bemoaned the fact that most Ukrainian unions were merely social welfare departments, handing out vacation vouchers or administering children's camps. His comments were surprisingly frank, and in sharp contrast to those leaders who have fought tooth and nail to control these provisions:

> When I went to Austria, I talked to union leaders about cooperation and exchanges, and proposed to arrange sports competitions or send our children to each other's camps. They had no idea what I was talking about. 'We have nothing to do with such things', they said … Then I saw the attention they gave to details of collective agreements, and how they were able to gain advantages for their workers. Now I wonder, what the hell are we doing with these childrens' camps when we can't even get decent wages for our workers?[81]

In addition, the drop-off in union membership has hampered the financial status of unions. The union can no longer support many enterprise union leaders. They have to work in the enterprise as well, which limits their time for union work as well as creating dependency upon the owners.[82] One does not yet see in Ukraine the formation of 'company unions' at giant firms but, as in Russia, it is difficult to speak of union solidarity. The head of the Education and Science Workers' Union acknowledges that the formation of the state budget is a free-for-all, with unions attempting to 'pull the blanket over themselves' and win benefits for their own members.[83] Thus unions are limited in their ability to articulate a coherent strategy to deal with many of the common problems they face.

Trade unions and post-Soviet democratisation

Does it matter that trade unions are so enfeebled? What does this say about post-Soviet democratisation? How does consideration of trade unions add to our understanding of processes of democratisation and civil society?

As to the question of whether it matters or not, let us consider a counter-factual scenario. Let us suppose that unions were strong, trusted by their members, mobilising workers against abuses by management, lobbying the government on socioeconomic policies and courted by political parties. Instead of worker passivity in the face of severe economic crisis, one would see worker activism. If the government failed to live up to its promises to workers, it would be held accountable. Reform measures would have to take into account the position of organised labour. Winners of elections would be beholden to trade unions, not the oligarchs.

How different Russia and Ukraine would look! Of course, one could say this would be impossible—a social-democratic fantasy—and one might even add that 'if the unions were effective in defending their members, the regime would try to repress them'.[84] This, of course, speaks volumes about the existing political economy in these states if labour activism is written off as impossible. However, the point is that a strong labour movement could have forced the government to pay more attention to social issues, implement a more 'civilised' form of privatisation, uphold the rule of law and take action on problems such as the wage arrears crisis. While some economic problems were unavoidable, governments did have choices. In the Russian case, reform was rushed through despite public opposition to many policies and the lack of institutional development to ensure its success. In Ukraine, from 1992 to 1994 reform was minimal, despite the cost of economic depression on living standards. 'Reform', when it came, lacked both a well-developed social dimension and basic standards of transparency, producing generally the same results as in Russia. Despite rhetoric of 'social partnership', labour was excluded from policy making. All of this could have been done differently.

Of course, while conceding that it *could* have been done differently, one could argue that strong organised labour would only have made matters worse. For example, following Aslund, one could contend that Russia's problem was that it abandoned 'shock therapy' too soon,[85] and that, given labour's opposition to El'tsin's programme, a strong labour movement would have made adoption of many 'necessary reforms' impossible. Moreover, one could argue that a strong labour movement would have precipitated greater political instability. Arguments of this type, of course, reveal the disjuncture between the rhetoric of the importance of civil society and the consideration of real players in civil society. Taken to its logical conclusion, one would argue that marketisation and democratisation were incompatible, and that only authoritarian systems could push through wide-ranging reforms. This, of course, lacks empirical support.[86] However, it is true that labour in the post-Soviet context, while not necessarily wholly anti-reform, would have wanted to preserve many elements of the old system, particularly social guarantees. This need not mean, though, that the demands of marketisation should have been or should be privileged over the demands of democratisation. If one takes democratisation seriously, one may be forced to abandon purely economic considerations of efficiency or sticking to a certain theoretically informed blueprint. While achieving social consensus on a reform programme would have been difficult, it need not have been impossible, particularly if international financial agencies were not beholden to neo-liberal dogmatism. The fact is, of course, that the reforms as adopted, with the political marginalisation of labour, served the interests of only a few, creating a political economy that is now the primary barrier to democratic consolidation.

Moreover, to argue that it could have been worse downplays precisely how bad it has been, both from the standpoint of economic consequences and democratic progress. Neither Russian nor Ukrainian 'democracy' is built upon popular participation, and 'social partnership' has been impossible given the fact that capital and labour do not meet as anything close to equals in current circumstances. In Russia what one has witnessed is a 'revolution from above' (backed by international financial institutions), designed to create a rudimentary bourgeois capitalist order, which has resulted in an 'oligarchic corporatism' or 'dependent democratisation'.[87] In Ukraine the residual authoritarian corporatist structures of the Soviet era have barely been transformed, although it is now clear that the state has become little more than a kleptocracy.[88] Strong groups in civil society such as trade unions could mitigate the main problems in both states—overcentralisation of authority and lack of checks on both political and economic power. However, the state and the new economic elite have not respected them, and this attitude has been facilitated in many cases by the unions themselves, who refrain from taking an independent position on many important political and economic questions. In any event, to argue that democracy can be built by effectively excluding and undermining large groups in civil society flies in the face of most understandings of democracy. The imposition of the post-Soviet order in both Russia and Ukraine has thus been far removed from the recommendations of transitologists about social pacts. Again, given questions of economic reform and particularly property redistribution, it might have been difficult to forge such a pact, but the fact is that there was no real effort to do so. Post-Soviet politics is defined by *lack* of popular participation and input. Both Russia and Ukraine are examples par excellence of elite-dominated polities, and they show the limits of elites' ability to craft a democracy, given the marginalisation of popular representatives. Trade union weakness, far from serving any project of marketisation or democratisation, reveals the shallowness of the democratic transition, as formally democratic institutions are not supported by democratic practice. Christensen notes:

> The problem of disjuncture between the formal rules of democracy and the actual power relations within a state is no more evident than in Russia, precisely because the struggles over property, control of resources, social (dis)empowerment, and state (non)responsiveness are so acute.[89]

This point leads to consideration of the importance of political economy and its role in facilitating or constraining groups in civil society. The economic reforms in Russia and Ukraine, particularly privatisation, were adopted without popular input. They have resulted in a distorted economic system that further limits the ability of actors such as trade unions to exercise political or economic influence. Ostensibly designed to create a new bourgeoisie, these reforms have created an oligarchy. One does not have to be a Marxist to wonder how a system of political economy based upon an oligarchy—where wealth and power are highly concentrated and the masses lack meaningful political and economic resources—can be transformed into a consolidated, liberal democracy. The result is laced with irony: reforms designed to lay the groundwork for democracy were carried out in a very undemocratic manner for fears that some popular elements would undermine them. The results of these 'reforms', however, severely limit prospects for democratic consolidation. The window of opportunity for democratisation today may be less open than before the 'reforms' were launched, as witnessed by Ukrainian society's weakness in the face of growing authoritarianism and by popular support for, or at least acquiescence in, Putin's strong-arm tendencies in Russia.

In addition, one should note that marketisation has undermined prospects for union solidarity. If before, in both Russia and Ukraine, incipient independent labour unions attempted to mobilise support around general social demands, they now have a much narrower focus, often eschewing any political involvement. Each struggles to 'pull the blanket over itself' and the result is that the trade union movement as a whole is left in the cold. One might conclude that this is perfectly natural, but it again exposes the difference between civil society in the abstract—lauded in the fight against the party-state—and interest associations, whose narrower, self-concerned pursuits may do little to counter a still heavy-handed state that often practices a divide and rule strategy or co-opts leaders of public associations. Divisions within civil society in turn facilitate the ability of the ruling elite to preserve itself and use its power to pursue its own narrow interest. The result, of course, is that society as a whole has scarcely benefited from years of 'reform'.

The weakness of civil society and the rise of an oligarchy in both countries, bemoaned by would-be democratisers, is in part the very result of policies pursued by yesterday's 'reformers'. Despite rhetoric about the importance of civil society, one can see that many of the most basic policies in the post-Soviet period have helped undermine a key actor in civil society, trade unions. Now that civil society is severely impaired and vast inequalities in wealth have been created, it is difficult to envision how one moves the process of democratisation forward. Given the lack of any strong societal force—and here trade unions are one group that logically comes to mind—to dislodge the oligarchs and push for fundamental changes, it is hard to be sanguine about democratic prospects in either country.

Oakland University

[1] A search in July 2001 in Wilson Social Science Abstracts produced 109 articles with the key words Eastern Europe or Russia and civil society since 1991.

[2] Thomas Carothers, *Aiding Democracy Abroad* (Washington DC, Carnegie Endowment for International Peace, 1999), p. 248.

[3] David Collier & Ruth B. Collier, *Shaping the Political Arena: Critical Junctures, The Labor Movement, and Regime Dynamics in Latin America* (Princeton, Princeton University Press, 1991); and Dietrich Rueschemeyer, Evelyne Huber & John D. Stephens, *Capitalist Development and Democracy* (Chicago, University of Chicago Press, 1992).

[4] In particular see Adam Przeworski, *Democracy and the Market* (Cambridge, Cambridge University Press, 1991), pp. 181–182.

[5] Answers are provided, albeit in various ways, in Stephen Crowley, *Hot Coal, Cold Steel* (Ann Arbor, University of Michigan Press, 1997); Sarah Ashwin, *Anatomy of Patience* (Manchester, Manchester University Press, 1999); and Debra Javeline, *Protest and Passivity: How Russians Respond to Not Getting Paid* (Ann Arbor, University of Michigan Press, 2002)

[6] Carothers, *Aiding Democracy*, p. 248.

[7] Samuel Huntington, *Political Order in Changing Societies* (New Haven, Yale University Press, 1968); Stephen Hanson & Jeffrey Kopstein, 'The Weimar/Russia Comparison', *Post-Soviet Affairs*, 13, 3, 1997, pp. 252–283.

[8] James Madison, 'Federalist X', *The Federalist Papers* (New York, Penguin, 1987 [first published 1788]).

[9] Corporatist theory would argue that the larger unions are and the more inclusive their membership, the more unions will have to take responsibility for the general good of society. This may be true in the sense that one over-arching union federation will be more universal than particular branch or local unions, but it does not entirely remove the notion of a particular interest from that federation's *raison d'être*.

[10] See David Ost, 'The Politics of Interest in Post-Communist Europe', *Theory and Society*, 22, 4, 1993, pp. 453–485.

[11] Leonid Gordon, *Nadezhda ili ugroza* (Moscow, IMEMO, 1995).

[12] For basic points of view of Balcerowicz and Klaus see their interviews in Mario Blejer & Fabrizio Corriceli (eds), *The Making of Economic Reform in Eastern Europe* (Aldershot, Edward Elgar, 1995).

[13] Such are the arguments made in Samuel Valenzuela, 'Labor Movements in Transitions to Democracy: A Framework for Analysis', *Comparative Politics*, 21, 4, July 1989, pp. 445–472; Przeworski, 1991; Stephan Haggard & Robert Kaufman, *The Political Economy of Democratic*

Transitions (Princeton, Princeton University Press, 1995); and Barbara Geddes, 'Challenging the Conventional Wisdom', in Larry Diamond & Marc Plattner (eds), *Economic Reform and Democracy* (Baltimore, Johns Hopkins University Press, 1995).

[14] For an excellent critique of 'transitology' with an eye toward post-Soviet trade unions see Paul Christensen, *Russia's Workers in Transition* (DeKalb, Northern Illinois University Press, 1999), Chapter 1.

[15] For discussion of 'electoral democracy' see Larry Diamond, 'Is the Third Wave Over?', *Journal of Democracy*, 7, 3, July 1996, pp. 20–37. For recent consideration of Ukraine in these terms see Paul Kubicek, 'The Limits of Electoral Democracy in Ukraine', *Democratization*, 8, 2, Summer 2001, pp. 117–139.

[16] Numerous works give extensive coverage to trade unions and the working class under communism. See Arcadius Kahan & Blair Ruble (eds), *Industrial Labor in the USSR* (New York, Pergamon Press, 1979); Blair Ruble, *Soviet Trade Unions: Their Development in the 1970s* (Cambridge, Cambridge University Press, 1981); Walter Connor, *The Accidental Proletariat: Workers, Politics, and Crisis in Gorbachev's Russia* (Princeton, Princeton University Press, 1991); and Simon Clarke *et al.*, *What About the Workers? Workers and the Transition to Capitalism in Russia* (London, Verso, 1993), Chapter 4.

[17] This explanation is integral to the analysis in Ashwin, *Anatomy of Patience*.

[18] See Donald Filtzer, *Soviet Workers and De-Stalinization* (Cambridge, Cambridge University Press, 1992).

[19] Ashwin, p. 27. Some have argued for the existence of corporatism in the USSR, but at best this was authoritarian 'state corporatism', and unions never had independence from political authorities. See Valerie Bunce & John Echols, 'Soviet Politics in the Brezhnev Era: Pluralism or Corporatism?', in Donald Kelley (ed), *Soviet Politics in the Brezhnev Era* (New York, Praeger, 1980).

[20] For a critical review of this thesis see Linda Cook, *The Soviet Social Contract and Why It Failed: Welfare Policy and Workers' Politics from Brezhnev to Yeltsin* (Cambridge, Harvard University Press, 1993).

[21] The best works on this period are Connor, *The Accidental Proletariat*; Christensen, *Russia's Workers*; and David Mandel, *Rabotyagi: Perestroika and After Viewed from Below* (New York, Monthly Review Press, 1994).

[22] Surveys reported by Clarke *et al.* indicate that in 1989 only 4% of workers respected their unions, and 1990 surveys in the strike regions of the Kuzbass and Donbass found small fractions of workers (14% and 6% respectively) satisfied with their unions. See Clarke *et al.*, *What About the Workers?*, pp. 94–95 and pp. 114–115. See also Vadim Borisov, *Zabastovki v ugol'noi promyshlennosti* (Moscow, Centre for Comparative Labour Studies, 2001).

[23] *Kommersant*, 24 May 2001, p. 2.

[24] Aleksandr Dolgorybin, head of FNPR organisational department, interview, Moscow, 24 May 2001. Surveys of workers also show many find these benefits important spheres of union activity. See V. Naumov & S. Tatarnikova, *Motivatsiya profsoyuznogo chlenstva* (Moscow, Moscow Federation of Trade Unions, 1996).

[25] The All-Russia Centre for the Study of Public Opinion (VTsIOM) routinely asks about confidence in trade unions. In September 2000 only 11.4% expressed complete confidence and 28.3% said they had some, which is actually a bit higher than most results from 1994 to 1999. Still, unions ranked second to last (above only political parties) of all social institutions in terms of public confidence, behind the militia, courts, government and lawyers! See *Monitoring obshchestvennogo mneniya*, 2000, 6(50), November–December.

[26] For lack of public involvement in protests see Javeline, *Protest and Passivity*. Many of the most visible—and effective—worker actions since 1993 have been spontaneous, occurring with no union oversight. See Petr Bizyukov, 'Al'ternativnye profsoyuzy na puti osvoeniya sotsial'nogo prostranstva', *Sotsiologicheskie issledovaniya*, 2001, 5, pp. 34–36, and Borisov, *Zabastovki*.

[27] For links between FNPR and employers see Gordon, *Nadezhda*; Walter Connor, *Tattered Banners: Labor, Conflict, and Corporatism in Postcommunist Russia* (Boulder, Westview, 1996); and Linda Cook, *Labor and Liberalization* (New York, Twentieth Century Fund, 1997).

[28] *Nezavisimaya gazeta*, 28 April 1998, p. 3.

[29] David Mandel, 'Russia: The Labour Movement and Politics', *Labor Focus on Eastern Europe*, 52, Winter 1996, p. 46.

[30] These funds—health, social insurance, pension and employment—were to be placed in state custody and be managed 'with the participation of all-Russian associations of trade unions'. De facto, unions retained some control over these funds at the enterprise level until 2001 when a new, unified social tax went into effect.

[31] Quoted in Mandel, 'Russia', pp. 58–59.

[32] In 1993 the alliance garnered 0.93%, and 1.59% in 1995. OVR did better, and the FNPR now has 15 of its own in parliament, although only four were elected on the OVR ticket (three from the Communists, one from Unity and seven independents).

[33] Bizyukov, 'Al'ternativnye profsoyuzy'.

[34] Javeline, *Protest and Passivity*.

[35] Connor, *Tattered Banners*, pp. 166–167; Vadim Borisov, 'Sotsial'noe partnerstvo v Rossii: spetsifika ili podmena ponyatii?', *Sotsiologicheskie issledovaniya*, 2001, 5, pp. 56–66 at p. 63; and interview with Valentin Presnyakov, main legal inspector for Union of Flying Staff, Moscow, 4 June 2001.

[36] *Kommersant*, 6 June 2001, p. 2; and *Nevavisimaya gazeta*, 7 June 2001, p. 3.

[37] Discussion of Ivanov with Andrei Isasev at Round Table at the ILO-co-sponsored Conference on Freedom of Association, Moscow, 27 May 2001.

[38] For a critical view see Chrystia Freeland, *Sale of the Century: Russia's Wild Ride from Communism to Capitalism* (New York, Crown, 2000).

[39] Christensen, *Russia's Workers*, p. 107.

[40] This story was repeated in over 40 interviews with union leaders in May–June 2001. Only in 1 sector—textiles, one of the least profitable ones—did the union official note that some firms continued to be owned by the workers.

[41] Petr Sudakov, head of Nizhny Novgorod Sotsprof affiliate, interview, 8 June 2001.

[42] See Christensen, *Russia's Workers*, pp. 137–138; B. I. Maksimov, 'Klasovyi konflikt na Vyborgskom TBK: nablyudeniya i analiz', *Sotsiologicheskie issledovaniya*, 2001, 1, pp. 35–47; Mikhail Tarasenko, Chairman of the Union of Miners and Metallurgy Workers, interview, Moscow, 18 May 2001.

[43] 'Unions' such as the Union of Workers in Small and Medium Business were created at the initiative of the employers. They were designed primarily to defend the interests of the non-state sector as a whole. See interview with Aleksandr Popov, head of this union, in *Profsoyuzy i ekonomka*, 1999, 7, pp. 8–16.

[44] Interviews, Moscow, 16 and 29 May 2001.

[45] Interview, Nizhny Novgorod, 8 June 2001.

[46] Union-employer conflicts were a prominent theme at the aforementioned ILO Conference, May 2001.

[47] Interview with Oleg Lvov, international department of Sotsprof, Moscow, 23 May 2001.

[48] Gordon, *Nadezhda*, p. 46.

[49] Sample of 1442 workers, results published in Natalya Kovaleva, 'Konflikty, profsoyuzy, sotsial'-naya zashchita: otsenki rabotnikov i rukovoditelei predpriyatii', *Monitoring obshchestvennogo mneniya*, 1997, 5(31), September–October, pp. 26–32.

[50] For *Tulachermet* the source is Vasilii Filinov, head of union committee, interview, Tula, 31 May 2001. Other comment is by Evgenii Akimov, head of union committee at Tula Combine Factory, Tula, 1 June 2001.

[51] Gordon, *Nadezhda*, p. 46. At the Gorky Automobile Factory (GAZ) the union leader bragged about numerous social services, including subsidised food, noting, however, that these 'amenities' did necessitate lower salaries. Interview, Nikolai Kamanev, vice-chairman of GAZ union, Nizhny Novgorod, 7 June 2001.

[52] Gordon, *Nadezhda*, p. 46.

[53] By sector, in 2001, agricultural workers earned on average 863 rubles, cultural workers 1226, light industry 1252, ferrous metals 6163 and energy 7375 (28 RR = $1) (*Izvestiya*, 24 May 2001, p. 1).

[54] For concerns on Lukoil see Andrei Mrost, 'Praktika raboty mezhdunarodnykh profsoyuznykh organizatsii i TNK', in *Profsoyuzy Moskvy v usloviyakh globalizatsii ekonomiki* (Moscow, Moscow Federation of Unions, 1999).

[55] Borisov, *Zabastovki*, pp. 389–390.

[56] A survey of over 6000 active workers, conducted in autumn 2000 by the National Statistics Office, found about 50% of manufacturing workers claiming union membership, 35% of service workers, and about 55% in the public sector. See Guy Standing & Laszlo Zsoldos, *Coping with Insecurity: The Ukrainian People's Security Survey* (Geneva, ILO, 2001), p. 26.

[57] From 1 October 2001 a tripartite board of unions, state officials and employers will administer five different social insurance funds. The FPU lobbied hard against this change.

[58] Surveys from 1994 to 2000 conducted by the Sociological Institute of the Academy of Sciences find, consistently, 12–15% claiming total or some confidence in unions. In contrast, 47–53% express little or no confidence in them. Lack of confidence in new trade unions is about the same (*Personal and Economic Safety: Measurement Problems and Solutions* (Kyiv, ILO, 2001), p. 49).

[59] Yaroslav Kendizor, head of the L'viv FPU unions, *Mist* (Kyiv), 11 July 1994, p. 13.

[60] Petr Shvets, 'Narushitelei konstitutsii—k otvetu', *Profsoyuzy* (Moscow), 2000, 5, p. 17.

[61] Viktor Turmanev, *Profspilkovi Visti*, 20 April 2001.

[62] Svetlana Rodina, socio-economic bureau of Union of Agro-Industrial Complex, interview, Kyiv, 4 July 2001.

[63] D. Balan, 'Uchast' Federatsiyi profesiyskykh spilok Ukrainy u vyborchykh kampaniyakh 1994 ta 1998 rokiv', in *Suchasnyi profspilkovyi rukh v Ukrainy* (Kyiv, Academy of Labour and Social Relations, 2000), pp. 26–40.

[64] 'Kuchmagate' refers to the alleged recordings of the president, Leonid Kuchma, engaging in all sorts of illegal activities, ranging from embezzlement and harassment of judges to ordering the disappearance of an opposition journalist, Georgii Gongadze, later found dead. These were made public in November 2000 but Kuchma squashed a full investigation into the matter.

[65] Mykola Dvirnyi, interview, Kyiv, 11 July 2001.

[66] Yuri Krivenko, head of L'viv Auto Transport and Road Workers, *Profspilkovyi visti*, 6 April 2001, p. 2.

[67] *Profspilkovyi visti*, 20 April 2001, p. 1, and 8 June 2001, p. 1.

[68] Serhei Kondryuk, expert on protection of workers' economic interests, interview, Kyiv, 11 July 2001.

[69] Evgen Golovakha, 'Suchasnapolitychna sytuatsiya y perspektyva derzhavno-politychnoho ta ekonomichnoho rozvytku Ukrainy', *Politychny portret Ukrainy*, 1993, 4, p. 5.

[70] Most were the same ones that they had been pressing for prior to the strike, and many speculate that they encouraged the strike to make fulfilment of their demands more likely. See Borisov, *Zabastovki*, 2001, Chapter 4; and Rick Simon, *Labour and Political Transformation in Russia and Ukraine* (Aldershot, Ashgate, 2000), pp. 150–159.

[71] *Mist* (Kyiv), 16 May 1994; and Semen Karikov, interview, Kyiv, 24 July 1994.

[72] Vyacheslav Brudovsky, vice-chairman of Volyn regional branch of 'Capital-Regions', interview, Kyiv, 8 July 2001.

[73] Nikolai Mitrov, president of NPG at Dobropoleugol, Donetsk region, interview, Kyiv, 8 July 2001.

[74] Mikhail Volynets, President of NPG, *Aspekt* (Kyiv), 2001, 7, July, p. 2.

[75] Vasyl Kostrytsya, ILO representative in Kyiv, interview, 5 July 2001.

[76] Brudovsky, interview.

[77] European Bank for Reconstruction and Development (EBRD), *Transition Report 2000* (London, EBRD, 2000).

[78] Inna Styrnyk, 'Profspilky ta pryvatizatsiya', in *Suchasnyi profspilkovyi rukh*, p. 184.

[79] Vladmir Bondarenko, President of Union of Workers in Innovative and Small Businesses, interview, Kyiv, 10 July 2001.

[80] Vasil Yan'shyn, chairman of Construction Workers Union, interview, Kyiv, 9 July 2001.

[81] *Ibid.*

[82] Vasyl Levchenko, vice-chairman of Union of Machine and Instrument-Building Workers, interview, Kyiv, 13 July 2001. He estimates that this is the case in over half of the enterprises in his sector.

[83] Leonid Sachkov, interview, Kyiv, 6 July 2001.

[84] Mandel, 'Russia', p. 59.

[85] Anders Aslund, 'Lessons of the First Four Years of Systematic Change in Eastern Europe', *Journal of Comparative Economics*, 19, 1994, pp. 22–38.

[86] In particular see Haggard & Kaufman, *The Political Economy*; and Geddes, 'Challenging the Conventional Wisdom'.

[87] Sergei P. Peregudov, *Gruppy interesov i Rossiiskoe gosudarstvo* (Moscow, Editorial URSS, 1999); and Simon, *Labour and Political Transformation*.

[88] Paul Kubicek, *Unbroken Ties: The State, Interest Associations, and Corporatism in Post-Soviet Ukraine* (Ann Arbor, University of Michigan Press, 2000).

[89] Christensen, *Russia's Workers*, p. 6.

Driving at Democracy in Russia: Protest Activities of St Petersburg Car Drivers' Associations

MARKKU LONKILA

Abstract

This article investigates two strongly opposing modes of organisational activity among Russian car drivers in St Petersburg: Freedom of Choice (*Svoboda Vybora*) is a contentious grassroots association whereas the city district chapter of the All-Russian Society of Car Drivers (*Vserossiiskoe Obshchestvo Avtomobilistov*) is part of a nationwide Soviet-era organisation collaborating closely with the authorities. The article describes the history, goals and adversaries, organisation and contact networks, and membership and repertoires of action of the two organisations. In the final section, they are compared in order to spell out the variety and specific features of joint action in Russia.

DESPITE THE PUTIN–MEDVEDEV GOVERNMENTS' ATTEMPTS at control, a wide variety of civic initiatives critical of the authorities surfaced throughout the Russian Federation during the latter half of the first decade of the 2000s. These initiatives included protests, movements and strikes by pensioners, car drivers, workers, environmentalists, housing activists, soldiers' mothers, antifascists and youth movements, political opposition, and other groups.[1]

Some of the recent and well known forms of protest in Russia have been organised by car drivers, whose activities are the focus of this article. These activities are studied

I am obliged to Risto Alapuro, Ursa Dykstra, Boris Gladarev, Laura Henry, Olga Koveneva, Nikolai Likhodedov, Eeva Luhtakallio, Philip Torchinsky, Anastasia Tsygankov, Anna Zaitseva, Tuomas Ylä-Anttila and the two anonymous reviewers of *Europe-Asia Studies* for their help and comments. My research assistant Sylvi Nikitenkov deserves special thanks for her invaluable help in all phases of the research. This study has been financed by the Academy of Finland.

[1]Weekly reviews of protests are available through the internet at www.ikd.ru (last accessed 3 January 2010), and they were at the focus of the colloquium 'Engagements, solidarités, lien social: penser les mobilisations collectives en Russie' organised at the Ecole des Hautes Etudes en Sciences Sociales in Paris in 2008. (See also Clément 2008.) Although only 6% of Russians in 2008 reported taking part in a lawful public demonstration in the previous 12 months, this proportion exceeded the corresponding figure in Finland (2.5%), the Netherlands (3.3%), the UK (3.8%) and was not lagging far behind Sweden (6.4%) or Belgium (7.4%), to take only few examples (European Social Survey 2008).

on the local level, through a detailed investigation of two car drivers' associations in St Petersburg: Freedom of Choice (*Svoboda Vybora*, SV) and a city district chapter of the All-Russian Society of Car Drivers (*Vserossiiskoe Obshchestvo Avtomobilistov*, VOA). SV is a recently established grassroots organisation based on voluntary work, employing contentious rhetoric with a stress on the political rights of citizens, and functioning with negligible financial means.[2] The city district chapter of the St Petersburg VOA, on the other hand, is part of a traditional, nationwide organisation that originated in the Soviet era. It has a salaried staff and significant financial and material resources.[3] Both organisations were involved in disputes in 2007 and 2008. SV emerged to begin with as a contentious organisation, fighting against the malpractices of the authorities, notably the notoriously corrupt Russian traffic police. The VOA, on the other hand, began as a bureaucratic and non-contentious organisation which was drawn into the so-called 'garage war' that has been waged in St Petersburg since 2006 against the expropriation of VOA-administered garage parking areas.

The case of car drivers was selected for this study for several reasons. First, car driving has become a major problem of daily life in big Russian cities. A dramatic increase in the number of cars, without corresponding investment in public transport, street repair and maintenance or parking facilities, has resulted in catastrophic traffic jams, particularly during rush hours. Second, in their daily lives, many if not most Russian car drivers have to struggle constantly with the state in the form of the traffic police.[4] Third, car drivers' struggles have been among the most visible forms of Russian protest in recent years.

[2]The data for this article come from a larger comparative project conducted at the Department of Sociology, University of Helsinki in collaboration with Professor Risto Alapuro. In the framework of the project information about four types of civic association, including car drivers' associations, was collected in Russia, Finland, Estonia and France. The data comprises interviews with the associations' leadership, structured questionnaires mapping the associations' contact networks, as well as annual reports and by-laws of the associations. Unless otherwise mentioned, the section 'Svodoba Vybora—A contentious, "Western" mode of civic organising in Russia' is based on an interview with the chairman of *Svoboda Vybora* of St Petersburg on 4 December 2007, and the section titled 'All-Russian Society of Car Drivers (VOA)—A hybrid model of organising in Russia' is based on an interview with the chairman of one of the VOA's St Petersburg city district chapters conducted on 28 January 2008. Both interviews were conducted by Anastasia Tsygankova.

[3]Besides the two organisations examined in this article, there are several other Russian organisations or movements of car drivers such as *Komitet po Zashchite Prav Avtomobilistov* (the Committee for the Defence of Car Drivers' Rights, KZPA, http://kzpa.ru/, http://spb.kzpa.ru/, last accessed 23 June 2009), and movements protecting garage owners' rights against expropriation in St Petersburg such as *Andreevskii Strazh* (Andreev's guard, www.parking.nw.ru, last accessed 7 January 2011). The latest Russian car drivers' movement TIGR (in Russian 'tiger', abbreviated from *Tovarishchestvo Initsiativnykh Grazhdan Rossii*—Association of Enterprising Russian Citizens) was organised in the Russian Far East and recently received much public and media attention for its demonstrations against the government's decision to raise the customs rate on imported cars. See http://tigru.org/, accessed 23 June 2009.

[4]The struggles concern, among other things, arbitrary fines for speeding or parking. A car parked in the wrong place in St Petersburg can be confiscated by the police and then be collected from a special place in exchange for money. According to the chairman of *Svoboda Vybora*, 90% of the confiscations are illegal and in some city districts the police, court and public prosecutor work together to extort money from car owners. The magnitude of the cat-and-mouse game between car drivers and traffic police in St Petersburg is illustrated by the results of a survey conducted by the insurance company

Studying two different modes of organising of car drivers contributes to the debate regarding the development of Russian civil society.[5] One recurring feature of this debate has been the question of the applicability of Western concepts and models, formed in a different social and historical context, to present-day Russia. Measuring Russia only with the yardstick of Western models runs the risk of leading to 'deficit studies' of Russia which often end up describing Russia mostly in terms of what it is lacking in comparison to the 'West' (Alapuro & Lonkila 2000). If the state of Russian civil society is measured by the rate of membership in voluntary associations, for example, as in the well-known work by Marc Morjé Howard (2002a, 2002b), the weakness of Russian civil society is confirmed time and again.

A more balanced approach also pays attention to the particular features of Russian forms of joint action and organising. These kinds of studies have investigated, among other things, the variety of organisational forms and the conception of rights in Russia (Henry 2006, 2009), searched for a 'third way' between the liberal and statist models of civil society (Johnson 2006), analysed the 'civil society substitutes' (Kurilla 2002) and described Russian activists' oscillation between personal and public engagements (Koveneva 2008, 2009). They have also revealed the complexity of the notion of the 'Soviet legacy' and turned it from an independent variable in causal explanation into a fruitful question for study.

An important topic closely related to the development of civil society concerns the existence and functioning of public forums in which citizens can freely articulate their interests, deliberate and mobilise for joint action. The existence of such forums in the Russian mass media is far from certain. The main Russian television channels, the most significant media in terms of audience size, do not, for example, as a rule broadcast views critical of the government. According to a study of the Russian media by the Centre for Journalism in Extreme Situations in 2006, most of the television channels studied did not offer the opposition significant airtime or opportunities to challenge the political establishment. Instead, all the monitored state-funded media showed a heavy bias in favour of the state administration, government, and particularly the president. Especially biased was the broadcasting of the nationwide, state-funded channels TV Russia and First Channel, the most popular Russian TV channel:

> In the two months of the monitoring, the state-funded First Channel provided 93% of its political news coverage to the ruling powers, 99% of which was assessed as either positive or neutral in tone. In the same period, the opponents of the current establishment (KPRF [*Kommunisticheskaya Partiya Rossiiskoi Federatsii*], the Union of Right Forces (*Soyuz Pravykh Sil*), *Yabloko*, the Republican Party (*Respublikanskaya partiya*) and others) received a combined total of some 1% of mostly negative or neutral coverage. (Centre for Journalism in Extreme Situations 2006)

Rossgosstrakh in June 2008. A total of 44% of all St Petersburg drivers surveyed claimed to have bribed the traffic police at least once during the previous year, thus placing the city at the top of the list for bribery on the Russian roads (*St Petersburg Times*, 10 June 2008).

[5]For more comprehensive reviews of the abounding literature on civil society development in Russia see, for example, Crotty (2009) and Evans *et al.* (2006).

Although the study found deviation from this pattern especially in print media, and also in regional media and private TV broadcasting, the authors concluded that 'Russian media generally lacks investigative and critical reporting that would offer the public an in-depth analysis and assessment of political subjects or State officials' (Centre for Journalism in Extreme Situations 2006).

Maria Lipman's (2009) account of the Russian media supports these conclusions. In her opinion, the media does not promote political competition or hold the government to account on the people's behalf. Instead, the major national TV channels are used as tools of state propaganda; the critical voices are marginalised and tolerated both as a safety valve for critically minded Russians and as a show card for the foreigners worried about the freedom of speech in Russia. This state of affairs in the Russian media has important consequences for civic activism. One of them is the increasing role of the Russian-language section of the internet in contentious joint action (a topic which will be addressed below).[6]

This study makes a contribution to the research on Russian civil society by investigating some particular features and varying forms of civic action. In order to meet this goal, the two selected associations and their activities will be examined with the help of justification theory as developed by Luc Boltanski and Laurent Thévenot (1991, 2006)[7] and the theory of 'regimes of engagement' developed by Laurent Thévenot (2006, 2007). These theories help to make sense of the moral principles used by associations to justify their activities, and the tension between the personal attachments and the public action of the activists. Justification theory focuses on ways of solving public disputes by referring to moral principles or moral 'orders of worth' shared by the disputing parties. Though the number of these moral orders is not prescribed, Boltanski and Thévenot discuss six examples: the market order, the industrial order, domestic order, civic order, fame-based order and inspiration-based order. The first four are relevant to this study and will be described briefly below.

First, in the market order, the greatness (*grandeur*) of an actor is defined by wealth and ultimately measured by markets. To take the example of a physician, greatness in this order could be measured by her commercial success in running a medical business. In the industrial order, to continue our example, the same physician may be valued—irrespective of her commercial success—by her efficiency and measured in concrete terms by the number of patients handled per day. In the domestic order, the greatness of the physician is evaluated by her position in the system of mutual dependency, as in the case of a trusted family doctor who has been treating all the members of the family for years and from whom one can expect favourable treatment as a result. Finally, in the civic order, a doctor is evaluated by her willingness to treat all patients equally as citizens.[8]

Justification theory stresses the multiple and situational nature of action. Depending on the particular situation, the same actor may refer to different orders of worth and

---

[6]See also Lonkila (2008).

[7]See also Boltanski and Thévenot (1999) and Wagner (1999).

[8]The other two of the original orders of worth are the orders of fame and inspiration. In our medical example, in the order of fame a great or worthy physician would be someone well-known in the media, whereas in the order of inspiration such a person would be someone who is a genius as a surgeon.

thus make it possible to construct compromises between different orders to temporarily suspend disagreements. To some extent justification theory resembles the framing approach commonly used in social movement research but is not identical to it. The three main differences are first, that justifications are always related to moral issues, whereas framing draws on more general cultural resources; secondly that justification analysis takes into account the material world of objects as proof for the justifications; and thirdly that, unlike framing in social movement theory, justification is not always considered as intentional, strategic action (Ylä-Anttila 2009). However, the framing approach coincides with justification theory in several ways: both take the situation as their point of departure; frames—just as worlds of justification—are tools people used to navigate in daily life situations; and both are fragile and constantly vulnerable to criticism and denunciation (Luhtakallio 2009, 2010).

In his later work Laurent Thévenot (2006, 2007) has linked justification theory to his model of 'regimes of engagement', that is, to the various modes of actors' engagement with their environment. Particularly interesting in this model from the viewpoint of this article is the relation between the 'familiar regime' of local and personal attachments and the 'public regime' of political action as illustrated in Olga Koveneva's comparative study of environmental movements in France and Russia. According to Koveneva, in the French context a credible involvement in public action requires activists to detach themselves from the particularities of and personal attachments to the local context and ties, whereas in Russia staying attached to them serves as the basis of credible public action (Koveneva 2008, 2009; Alapuro & Lonkila forthcoming).

The next two sections describe briefly the history, goals and adversaries, organisation and contact networks, and membership and repertoires of action of the two organisations. In the final section, the cases are compared in the light of justification theory to spell out the specificity of the two modes of Russian joint action.

Svoboda Vybora—*A contentious, 'Western' mode of civic organising in Russia*

History

Svoboda Vybora of St Petersburg is a contentious non-governmental organisation (NGO) emphasising the importance of defending the political rights of citizens. The history of the organisation can be traced back to May 2005 when rumours about the prohibition of cars with right-hand drive steering wheels started spreading through the internet. The right-hand-side drivers managed to mobilise nationwide and organise drive-by demonstrations (*avtoprobegi*) in the streets of several large Russian cities on 19 May. The demonstrations were well covered in the media and the new addition of motorised demonstrations to the Russian protest repertoire took the authorities by surprise. When street-cleaning lorries with powerful water sprayers were brought into action against the demonstrations 'everyone got into their cars which got washed and that's all'.

The internet, particularly the common movement discussion forum (www.19may.ru) played an important part in organising and mobilising these demonstrations (Greene 2007). To begin with, Vyacheslav Lysakov, the Moscow-based founder of the forum, declared himself to be the head of the emerging Interregional Social Organisation of Car Drivers 'Freedom of Choice' (*Mezhregional'naya Obshchestvennaya Organizatsiya Avtomobilistov Svoboda Vybora*). However, this met with opposition from activists in several localities in Russia and on 19 May 2006 they established a competing network of local organisations, the Russian Car Owners' Federation (*Federatsiya Avtovladel'tsev Rossii*).[9] The particular catalyst of the division of the movement was the 'Oleg Shcherbinskii affair'. Oleg Shcherbinskii was a Russian car driver arrested and falsely accused of the death of the governor of the Altai region in a car accident, but later released due to protests organised by means of the internet.

This study focuses on the local *Svoboda Vybora* of St Petersburg which is a member of the Russian Car Owners' Federation (*Federatsiya Avtovladel'tsev Rossii*), and which somewhat confusingly bears the same name as the Lysakov-led movement. The St Petersburg *Svoboda Vybora* decided to register as an official non-governmental organisation in 2006 in accordance with the new law on NGOs, but it ran into difficulties. The registration was first declined and was finally accepted eight months later, on 17 October 2006.

Goals and adversaries

The rhetoric on the organisation's website is openly and explicitly contentious.[10] SV declares as its mission 'defending the rights and interests of the organisation's members, car drivers and the citizens of St Petersburg':

> Can car drivers defend their rights by focusing only on the questions of car owners?
>
> Of course not!
>
> Because car drivers' rights are related not only to driving (traffic regulations) but also to the rights of the owner, his political and social rights.
>
> One has to use all means (methods) for protection of one's rights and interests: all constitutional means, for the time being. Enough of putting your trust in the tsar and sitting in the kitchen! Wake up and join us! We will work together so as to transform ourselves from slaves into human beings!

In the interview, the chairman of the St Petersburg *Svoboda Vybora* noted that many Russians take the abstract goal of 'defence of rights' to mean offering services of legal defence free of charge. People turned to *Svoboda Vybora* expecting it to offer the same kind of free and ubiquitous care which the Soviet state used to offer to its citizens in most spheres of life (Zdravomyslova 2004; Alapuro 2010; Colin Lebedev 2009). This attitude led to problems in daily encounters between the Svoboda Vybora activists and citizens.

> [people] come to us thinking that we are a similar legal firm, only free of charge. But you have free cheese only in a mouse trap. We try to explain that ... that in general we are not

[9]http://www.autofed.ru/about.html, accessed 23 June 2009.
[10]http://www.svspb.ru, accessed 9 January 2010.

lawyers … We are common car drivers, one works as a bookkeeper, another as locksmith. This does not matter because we simply decided that the most important thing is to solve common problems together.

The actions of SV are aimed at the Russian 'power vertical'—the hierarchical and centralised system of organising political and administrative power. The sharp and contentious rhetoric represents a clear choice differentiating SV from the associations collaborating with state power, such as the Moscow-based *Svoboda Vybora* led by Lysakov. Unlike Lysakov, who works in close collaboration with legislators and is well connected with state administration,[11] SV clearly tries to fulfil the critical watchdog function of civic organisations by holding the authorities in check and protecting individual citizens against the arbitrary practices of power holders.

Organisation and contact network

The formal structure of SV is democratic to the extent that, according to its chairman, it has led to ineffectiveness. All decisions are made at the general meetings of the members, and between the meetings by the coordinating committee, whereas the chairman and vice-chairman hold only nominal power.[12] This kind of structure is ineffective, for example, when quick decisions have to be made:

We discussed for one and a half weeks whether we should organise one protest or should we not. So, there is no capacity for quick action. But everything is very democratic.

The internet was central for the founding of the all-Russian SV, and continues to play an important part in the activities of the St Petersburg SV which runs its own website with a forum especially for the problems of car drivers.[13] The internet allows for SV and its members to deliberate, mobilise for action, disseminate information, and even run the organisation's day-to-day operations, for example through virtual meetings.[14] The chairman considers SV's web presence extremely important because through the web successful court cases against authorities can be made public and consequently they can encourage and empower the members of the public struggling with similar problems:

[11]Author's interview with Vyacheslav Lysakov, Moscow, 17 June 2008. According to Lysakov, despite these connections and the 8,500–9,000 registered members in the nationwide forum, the movement had neither office nor any salaried personnel in the summer of 2008. There was not much money coming in from membership fees or individual donations. Lysakov's mobile phone bill, for example, was paid by a donor, and he himself made a living writing columns in various papers. Lysakov was a well-known national figure who was continuously being contacted by the Russian media. In his own words, he had good contacts with the presidential administration, and in the interview he openly reflected upon the possibility of running for election to the state *duma*.

[12]In the case of equal votes, however, the chairman has the decisive vote.

[13]See Lonkila (2008) on the importance of the internet for Russian civic activism.

[14]The meetings of the coordinating committee were usually related to the preparation of action. When there were no actions, there was thus no need for regular meetings. In line with the infrequent activities it was finally decided that the committee could also officially meet virtually in the forum or make decisions by phone.

> Demonstrations help people to feel that they are not alone. Even if only 50 people show up you can see that though there are only a few people around, you're not alone. And the website is good particularly because people may visit it, read, and look for a model of how other people have acted: 'Well he wrote an application and sent it to that court' ... I consider the website to contain another level of action ... for some people it may even give more than going out in the street.

The only monetary revenues of SV are membership fees (R300—less than €10) which, however, were paid by only two persons during 2007. SV had discussed applying for grants but, lacking plans for fund-raising action, the organisation did not submit any applications.

SV's contact network include St Petersburg's Committee for Lawfulness and Order (*Komitet po zakonnosti i pravoporyadku*) although it had had a difficult relationship with the association. SV and the Committee had sued each other in the past but, more recently, they have managed to negotiate a truce. More generally SV's collaboration partners include the Committee for the Defence of Car Drivers' Rights (*Komitet po Zashchite Prav Avtomobilistov*, KZPA), *Yabloko* and the Centre for Development of Non-commercial Organisations (*Tsentr Razvitiya Nekommercheskikh Organizatsii*). SV and KZPA have been in communication and have given each other assistance, though KZPA has specialised in questions of legal defence and refrained from street actions.[15] In all, the association's partner network is comprised of civic organisations, many of them critical of the present-day Russian power structures.

Membership and repertoires of action

The association had 20 registered members at the end of 2007, of whom less than 15 participated periodically in preparations of actions and only three were permanent activists. The majority of the members were men (and only three were women), their ages ranging between 20 and 40 years. Although the number of people sympathising with SV actions was most likely much bigger than its meagre membership or participant figures, there seemed to be little prospect of recruiting more members. To the question 'Why do people join SV?' the chairman replied laconically: 'In general, they don't. They prefer to stand aside'. When asked about hindrances to SV's activity, the chairman emphasised people's passivity:

> How to name it [Russians' reluctance to act] ... probably a wish that someone else would do things for you; would act physically or just would think on your behalf. [This is] a kind of attempt to put the heaviest weight on someone else.

---

[15]In addition, the newspaper *Delovoi Peterburg* and the TV channel 'Fifth Channel' (*Pyatyi kanal*) were mentioned among SV's important contacts in 2007. The chairman seemed to be astonished by the coverage given to SV actions by the St Petersburg branch of the Fifth Channel during 2007 because he had thought of it as an 'instrument completely controlled by the governor', and because the channel had been present since 2005 at all actions of SV but had not broadcasted the reports. National channels (NTV, TNT, First Channel, and RTR) had also been present at the actions.

Public drive-by demonstrations formed the most important part of SV activities but, at best, the number of participants in such SV actions was around 200, as in the protest for Oleg Shcherbinskii. At its lowest, as in a demonstration for cheaper petrol prices, only five cars showed up. Moreover, the demonstrations were organised infrequently: altogether there were five actions between 19 May 2005 and the end of 2007. In addition to demonstrations, SV had also planned other actions, but these were not implemented.

SV's mode of action was thus based on the idea that NGOs should fight for individual freedoms and human rights against the increasingly authoritarian Russian state. Regrettably, SV's kind of civic action did not seem to enjoy much success among St Petersburg's inhabitants. The number of activists in late 2007 was negligible and the organisation functioned practically without resources. The chairman was disappointed with the citizens' passivity and the whole organisation seemed to be on the edge of fading out.

The All-Russian Society of Car Drivers (VOA)—A hybrid model of organising in Russia

History

The origins of the VOA were as part of the Soviet state apparatus. The organisation, originally called All-Russian Voluntary Society of Car and Motorcycle Amateurs (*Vserossiiskoe Dobrovol'noe Obshchestvo Avtomotolyubitelei*, VDOAM), was established during the Soviet era in 1973 to deal with problems such as road safety and parking caused by the rapid increase in the number of cars at that time. In the Soviet Union almost everything related to cars, such as tyres, oil, spare parts and repair and maintenance services at state-run garages were in short supply. Obtaining a standard *Zhiguli*—the Soviet version of a Fiat 124—required either years of waiting or jumping the queue through connections or bribes. Membership of VDOAM was helpful both in terms of acquiring scarce products as well as gaining access to the services of state-run garages.

In the post-Soviet era VOA still controls important and scarce resources, and in particular the garage parking places in big Russian cities, the administration of which it inherited from VDOAM. In St Petersburg VOA rents the land allocated for garage parking lots from the city, while the individual garages are built by the garage owners (*garazhniki*). Because of the great number of these parking places in St Petersburg[16] their yearly rents yield significant revenues, not to speak of the money earned from car wash and repair facilities located in many parking areas. As the city grew in size in the wake of the economic boom of the early 2000s the value of the garage parking areas multiplied. This created the context for the events that became known as the 'garage war' in which the garage owners were threatened with the expropriation and demolition of their garages.[17]

---

[16]According to Streltsova (2008), VOA administered roughly 300 parking areas in St Petersburg in 2008.

[17]'Garage war' is often used in the Russian media to describe this struggle. In the Russian language, 'garage war' (*garazhnaya voina*) is phonetically close to 'civil war' (*grazhdanskaya voina*).

The St Petersburg VOA played an important role in this war where the control of immense garage parking lots in the city centre was at stake. The murder of Dmitry Troyan, the chairman of the St Petersburg VOA on 26 November 2007 was related by some commentators to his activities in defending the garage owners against the building of a new bypass road (*Zapadnyi Skorostnoi Diameter*) in St Petersburg (Skrodenis *et al.* 2007). However, some local commentators such as German and Strel'nikova (2007) related the murder rather to the commercial activities conducted under the aegis of the VOA—aided by its status as a social organisation (*obscshestvennaya organizatsiya*) inherited from the Soviet era.[18]

Whatever the reasons for the murder, Troyan had been a visible chairman, opposing the demolition of the garages publicly and assisting the garage owners in filing court cases. His follower in the chairman post, probably warned by the example, has kept a much lower profile and declined open confrontations with the Russian 'power vertical'.[19]

Organisation and contact networks

According to the city district chairman, VOA is, along with the Communist Party (*Kommunisticheskaya Partiya Rossiiskoi Federatsii*), 'among the very few Soviet organisations whose structure and directions of activity have not essentially changed since the Soviet era'.[20] The basic cell of VOA is the 'primary organisation' (*pervichnaya organizatsiya*, PO) which number 13,500 in over 1,000 Russian cities and in 74 of 89 sub-federal regions of the Russian Federation. In St Petersburg the POs run garage parking areas (*garazhnye stoyanki*) in each city district. The total number of the individual garages in the city is said to exceed 370,000 (Balueva 2007) of which 180,000 are estimated to be administered by VOA (Alexandrov 2008); their areas cover an estimated 1,000 hectares of land.[21]

In these parking areas the members of the PO may keep their cars in small structures built of metal sheets, concrete or bricks, often surrounded by barbed wire and guarded around the clock. The parking areas usually have electricity and running water and may contain car repair and washing services. According to one journalist's account at least part of the charges for car repair services is paid 'under the table' and their total annual sum may allegedly amount to tens of millions of euros (Streltsova 2008).[22]

[18]In a similar manner (Streltsova 2008) related the murder to 'money' and Zeya (2007) to the 'financial wealth of the association'. Troyan's murder had been preceded by other violent assaults on VOA functionaries (German & Strel'nikova 2007).

[19]In this context, arranging an interview with the VOA in St Petersburg was not easy. Our Russian research assistant tried first to make appointments with Troyan and then, following his death, she contacted all the city district offices of the VOA, one of which directed her to the new temporary chairman of the St Petersburg VOA. However, the new chairman refused to give an interview and told the interviewer to contact the VOA chairman of one of the St Petersburg city districts, who finally agreed to the interview request.

[20]Here one is tempted to disagree with the chairman at least in terms of the development of the Communist Party.

[21]A native Leningrader, Vladimir Putin also owns a VOA garage in a PO in the Kirov district (Rogozin 2007).

[22]When we asked about the financing of the organisation the district chairman mentioned membership fees and, when probed, 'small-scale commercial activity' (*nebol'shaya kommercheskaya*

The city district headed by our respondent—one of St Petersburg's 18 city districts—alone contained 36 POs with 16,000 individual garages employing altogether 340 salaried workers:

> In every PO, that is, garage parking lot, there is the elected chairman, bookkeeper, guards, janitors and mechanics, that is, exactly the kind of workforce you'll find at any small factory, any small *sovkhoz* or any small or big organisation.

The PO is governed by a general assembly of the members which approves the annual accounts (checked by a revision committee) and the budget for the next year. Between the general assemblies, the PO is run by a council and the chairman of the PO, who are elected every five years. POs in each city district elect the highest decision-making body for their district (*konferentsiya mestnoi organizatsii*); the city districts elect the decision-making body of St Petersburg and the Leningrad region (*konferentsiya regiona'lnogo otdeleniya*) and, finally, Russian regions elect the all-Russian congress (*s'ezd*) of the VOA at the head of the whole organisation. This hierarchical nature of the organisation was clearly evident in the following words of the district chairman:

> The chairmen of the POs are under my command, I am under the command of the city council [*gorodskoi sovet*] and the city council is under the command of Moscow. As in the Communist Party.

Goals and adversaries: participating in the 'garage war'

According to its by-laws, the objectives of the VOA are to 'unite citizens for solving together the problems of safe use, maintenance and exploitation of the means of automobile transportation, and also the protection of the rights and legal interests of association members'. Although the by-laws also mention defence of car drivers' rights as one of the VOA's goals, its activities have not been focused on struggling with the malpractices of state officials, such as the police. Rather, the VOA has collaborated with the police and the authorities and its activities have revolved around traffic safety issues, and most importantly around parking, maintenance and servicing of the VOA members' cars in the local garage parking areas. The VOA also runs four driving schools in the city and negotiates discounts for its members with insurance and petrol companies.

In our interview the district chairman listed the main goals of the organisation as to help in conserving the means of transportation, to campaign for lower parking fees for citizens with low income in the case of the destruction of their garages, and to maintain the unity of the organisation. Reflected in this list is the ongoing theme of the garage war and attempts to appropriate land used for garaging, to which the chairman referred in the interview:

deyatel'nost'), referring to car repair activities and fees from the open-air parking lots without garages. However, dissatisfaction concerning the money transfers within the organisation has been published in the press. See for example, Rutman (2001) and Pisarenko (2007).

[T]he city grew and these areas became very useful for any person with a lot of money. He can come to Valentina Ivanovna [Matvienko, the governor of St Petersburg] and say, for example: 'Valentina Ivanovna, I want to build a shopping mall here. Let us evict 1,500 garage owners. You will take care of these cars; let them keep their cars in their own yards'.

As noted above, one of the main reasons for the demolition of the garages was the building of the *Zapadnyi Skorostnoi Diameter*—the new bypass road planned to ease the immense traffic jams of the city centre.[23] The chairman recognised the needs of city planning and growth but countered this argument by emphasising social equality:

We understand perfectly that the garages [VOA garage parking lots] belong to the last century, that one has to build [new] parking places, but there is no need to run people over with bulldozers ... We need a programme of the St Petersburg government. [Think about] a person who gave his whole life to this city, worked here honestly, paid taxes, who is not only a taxpayer but a citizen, who works, lives, raises kids—everything for the well-being of the city. This person has a 15–20 year-old car worth $300 on the market. And they want to sell him a garage parking space which costs between $15,000– and $20,000. Of course he will keep his car in the yard, below his window [instead of in the expensive parking area]. And he cannot sleep during the night because he'll be watching his car. In what condition will he leave for work in the morning, this fireman, welder, dental technician, teacher? ... In our garage parking areas we charge up to R5,000 yearly, not monthly.

According to an announcement by Governor Matvienko in 2009, in the preceding five years 9,759 individual garages had been demolished and 3,460 more were planned to be demolished during 2009.[24] Some of the garage owners were warned of the evictions only a couple of days before they took place and the garages of some resisters were bulldozed down (Skryabikov & Kholopova 2006). In addition to the social injustice at stake in the garage war there is the question of the legal status and market value of the individual garages built by the *garazhniki*. Should the garages be considered real estate property, the demolition of which requires a court decision? What is the just amount of compensation for a demolished garage? The adversaries of the VOA in the garage war remained largely anonymous, but in the chairman's opinion they seemed to consist of a combination of local civil servants of the city administration working in accordance with unknown businessmen. The organisation tried to find allies by supporting the United Russia (*Edinaya Rossiya*) party both in municipal and national elections:

At the moment we have concluded an agreement with United Russia, our ruling party. We supported United Russia in the city council elections and before the *Gosduma* elections we arranged an assembly of all our organisations asking our *garazhniki* to support United Russia in the elections. We fully supported United Russia.

In response to an increase in the number of demolitions and either the lack or the small amount of monetary compensation received by *garazhniki* for their demolished

---

[23]Streltsova (2008) also refers to the city plans in early 2008 to sell garage parking areas for the construction of shopping centres.

[24]http://www.vposelok.ru/news/areanews/2658/, accessed 5 October 2010.

garages, the dissatisfaction among the rank and file members of the VOA grew. Local POs started to leave the VOA and establish independent garage parking areas (Pisarenko 2007) and other political entrepreneurs appeared in the arena. Under the leadership of a former city council member, Sergei Andreev, presently working for the *Spravedlivaya Rossiiya* party, part of the *garazhniki* organised into *Andreevskii Strazh* (Andreev's guard), 'a social movement defending the rights of garage owners'.[25]

According to Andreev, the VOA's leadership in St Petersburg was working in cooperation with the Governor Matvienko, and the organisation continued to collect rents even for the garages whose lease with the city has already expired. Furthermore, instead of paying *garazhniki* the market price for garages that were appropriated by the authorities, the owners were offered only a small percentage of it, or nothing at all. In the garage parking area *Parnas* for example, containing spaces for 12,000 cars, the owners 'were not paid a single kopek'. Recently also more violent means of eviction, such as setting fire to garages, have been used. In sum, the VOA's contract with United Russia had not benefited the garage owners, since the demolitions continued. Andreev's guard therefore called for decent compensation for the garages and a construction programme for new parking areas. In 2009 the movement claimed to have collected 15,000 signatures in a petition for the dismissal of governor Matvienko and aimed at collecting 100,000.[26]

Membership and repertoires of action

As noted above, in the VOA being a member meant paying membership fees for which one received benefits such as parking, repair and maintenance services, and discounts for gas and traffic insurance. This client-based membership was clearly different from the 'civic' model of SV, and one may ask if there is a real difference between VOA and a commercial organisation selling parking, repair and maintenance services (Rutman 2001).[27] As with commercial enterprises, a VOA member did not receive any services from the organisation without paying, whereas in SV paying a membership fee was neither emphasised nor controlled. Unlike in SV, there was also a distinction between the salaried staff (including the service providers and the administration) and the member-clients.

Under the leadership of Troyan, the organisation had actively and publicly resisted the demolitions of garages (Kholopova 2006). After Troyan's murder however, the VOA adopted a low profile and instead of continuing an open campaign, it counted on achieving its goals through alliances with the city administration power holders.[28] In general, the administration of POs seemed to form the most important, time consuming and profitable type of activity by the VOA. Also, since the POs needed electricity and water and often provided washing, repair and maintenance services,

---

[25]*Obshchestvennoe dvizhenie v zashchitu prav vladel'tsev ploskostnykh garazhei*, see http://parking.nw.ru, accessed 7 January 2011.

[26]The information in this paragraph is based on a telephone interview with Sergei Andreev, 26 June 2009, conducted by Sylvi Nikitenkov.

[27]The same question may be asked, of course, of many organisations in Western countries.

[28]The website of the St Petersburg VOA, available at: http://spbgoovoa.ru/news.php?readmore=10, accessed 8 January 2010.

their administration required specialised staff, such as mechanics, electricians, and round-the-clock guards. In addition to these partly commercialised activities, the organisation also continued the Soviet era tradition of citizens' patrols (*narodnaya druzhina*), whose voluntary workers, *druzhinniki*, monitor traffic in collaboration with the traffic police and give lectures on traffic regulations and safety at local schools. For example:

> On 1 September [the beginning of the school year] our *agitavtobus* drives around distributing brochures which inform children of traffic regulations. We also organise contests at schools or even kindergartens with the GIBDD [*Gosudarstvennaya Inspektsiya Bezopasnosti Dorozhnogo Dvizheniya*, Russian Federal Road Safety Service]. In addition, every one of my 36 primary organisations, that is, garage parking areas [in this city district] supports a school [*podshefnaya shkola*] … We work in close cooperation with schools and in the meetings with the [city] administration I've heard warm words about our organisation more than once.[29]

Thus, VOA seems to form an example of a 'hybrid' organisation combining commercial, civic and social activities in its repertoire (*cf.* Johnson 2006). The chairman expressed the wish that, because of this socially useful work, the city administration would understand 'at least the needs of the retired and low-income citizens' in the negotiations concerning the expropriation of garages. This would indeed be easy were the decisions made in the city district where VOA has already established trustful social ties with the local administration:

> I want to say that the head of the [city district administration] N.N. is a very attentive and sensitive person, and we have normal relations with her, but she is not the head of the city and there are things she cannot allow. … As they say, you cannot beat the wind.

The network of VOA's most important partners included, according to the chairman, the city parliament (*Zakonodatel'noe Sobranie*), one insurance company and one petrol company. In addition, the interviews reveal cooperation with local schools and police—most probably based on old Soviet-era connections—and, significantly, United Russia as the most important ally in the garage war.

In sum, its history, current activities and contact networks would suggest locating VOA rather in the sphere of state structures or commercial enterprises than in civil society (Henry 2006). However, the *druzhinniki* of the organisation also carry out civic activities at the local level in close collaboration with police, much as in Soviet times. This suggests that focusing only on contentious, Western types of organising may neglect a distinct part of the Russian reality. It also reminds us of the complex nature of 'the Soviet legacy'. Phenomena which at first glance appear to be part of the legacy of the communist era—as the VOA chairman himself likes to see his organisation—may under closer scrutiny have gained new meanings and functions in the post-Soviet context (Burawoy & Verdery 1999).

---

[29] See also Mezentsev (2009) for a more detailed description of the work by VOA patrols.

Forms of public justifications and local attachments of Svoboda Vybora and VOA

The cases presented above illustrate two modes of organising in Russia. This section will address the differences between the two cases both in terms of the moral justifications used in public by SV and VOA and their attachments to the accustomed local milieus and traditions, as well as their movement between the public and familiar 'regimes of engagement'. In order to conduct a public campaign successfully, the local, familiar and sometimes intimate experiences of both car drivers and *garazhniki* had to be 'translated' into more general and public vocabulary. These 'translations' were conducted differently by SV and VOA and they brought to light the tensions arising from the efforts to integrate the plurality of engagements (Thévenot 2007).

Justifications and the local anchorage of Svoboda Vybora

From the justification perspective, SV's 'Western' mode of watchdog-style civic activism seems to be justifying its action solely by the civic order of worth with a stress on the political rights of car driver-citizens against unjust or corrupt authorities (Henry 2009). Ultimately, these rights do not concern only the St Petersburg car drivers but all Russian citizens. SV's contentious rhetoric would require Russians to accept and adhere to a world of citizens, unknown to each other, united only by their inalienable rights, and represented by the vanguards of civic organisations or movements.

Despite its status as a St Petersburg-based organisation, the local attachments of *Svoboda Vybora* are not of primary importance. The association emerged as a part of a nationwide movement organised through the internet rather than as a local group built on an existing network of friends. As a result, the association is open for anyone to join, and the repertoire of action consists mostly of public demonstrations aimed at gaining followers. Since the contentious rhetoric mostly excludes access to nationwide established mass media, recruiting and mobilisation rely on internet-based communication.

Even though the movement is organised around cars they seem to be a somewhat contingent means to the ultimate goal of democratisation and could be replaced by other objects, since the essence of the action rests on the world of abstract democratic ideals. It is as if cars give up their materiality and are transformed into objects loaded with civic qualities (Koveneva 2008; Alapuro & Lonkila 2010).

Judging by the decline in the activities of SV, many Russians do not seem to adhere to democratic ideals, which are neither supported by the tangible world of objects, nor by the logic of Russian society's mode of functioning which is still largely based on the importance of personal contact networks (Ledeneva 1998; Lonkila 1998, 1999; Alapuro & Lonkila 2000; Alapuro 2001). Moreover, as is implied in the confusion of the defence of human rights with free legal services in the activities of SV described above, SV's call for individuals to stand up in defence of their civic rights may be interpreted among many Russians as an offer to distribute free services, to which they became accustomed during the Soviet era. It seems as if the process of defining and qualifying Russian democracy could be open to several different interpretations, and that social rights were given priority in this process (Henry 2009).

Justifications and local anchorage of the VOA

In contrast to SV's focus on political rights, and in accordance with the 'hybrid' nature of the VOA, the city district chairman we interviewed used various moral justifications to support the VOA's activities. They varied from 'industrial order' principles of city planning, arguing that the planned construction of the new car parking houses could not solve the problems created by the removal of VOA garage parking areas; to 'civic order' principles, arguing that demolishing garages causes social injustice; to 'domestic order' principles, based on the value of the trusted ties at the garage parking areas; and to 'market order' principles, arguing that the *garazhniki* should receive the market price for their demolished garages. All these registers and their combinations were evoked in different contexts against various adversaries: in the struggle against the threat of expropriation social injustice arguments were useful, but in seeking compensation for the already demolished garages, civic principles were combined with market principles for seeking the 'going price' for a removed garage.

Also unlike *Svoboda Vybora*, the VOA is tightly anchored in local traditions, networks and material objects in the garage parking areas and the city districts. The local nature of the association and its involvement in the garage war did not encourage nationwide mobilisation: the VOA does not claim to represent all Russian car drivers or garage owners but only its members, to whom it provides very concrete and tangible services. Moreover, the organisation's deal with the powerful elites resulted in the alienation of part of the members, creating a niche for competing, more contentious *garazhniki* movements.

Thus, one of the main differences between the Western-oriented *Svoboda Vybora* and the VOA with its roots in the Soviet period, may be summarised as follows: on the one hand, *Svoboda Vybora* leans on the 'horizontal' virtual ties of the internet without traditional attachments to local and material reality, and its political, moral and highly contentious call does not resonate with the citizens; on the other hand the *garazhniki*, have both material objects and 'vertical' local networks to which to attach their activities, as well as social causes understood by the citizens, but their grassroots uprisings seem to have been stopped short by their own bureaucracy.[30]

The success of both organisations could thus be questioned. In a larger context, however, the former actually has been successful as part of a nationwide wave of protest which has managed to force the Russian power holders to back off—at least temporarily. Moreover, as is shown by the protests organised by the new car drivers' movement TIGR (*Tovarishchestvo initsiativnykh grazhdan Rossii*) in several parts of Russia including St Petersburg, the Russian-language segment of the internet continues to function as an important arena for emerging new movements and for cooperation between local civic groups. Its role is even likely to grow if the new law of NGO registration causes new movements to avoid official registration and to channel their activities instead into various 'projects', 'campaigns' and 'networks' organised through the internet. The ties thus created may stay dormant for the time being but prove vital in the case of future mobilisations (Lonkila 2008).

---

[30]On 'horizontal' and 'vertical' attachments of civic organisations, see Alapuro and Lonkila (2000).

The VOA could not stop the demolition of garages, though at least for the time being it succeeded in maintaining its organisation. Critics have reproached VOA for having exchanged its civic goals for money in a deal with power holders and for having become a commercial organisation more interested in its own survival than in the protection of its rank-and-file members. However, in the event of a new construction boom the pressures for the removals would be likely to mount again, and the continuation of the garage war with both new and already organised competitors might endanger the unity of the organisation.

An open question and important topic for future studies is the possibility of combining the 'horizontal' (*Svoboda Vybora*) and 'vertical' (VOA) modes of joint action in Russia. This kind of organising—seeds of which seem to be already emerging—necessarily implies a central role for the internet in functioning as a coordinating device, 'bridging' the trusted networks and facilitating movement between the public and familiar regimes. The increasing popularity of Russian social network sites such as *Zhivoi Zhurnal*, *Odnoklassniki* and *Vkontakte* might indicate a first step in this direction. The next step, crucial for this kind of organising, would be to find ways to create trust in the bridges between the individual groups to increase their potential for creating change.

University of Helsinki

References

Alapuro, R. (2001) 'Reflections on Social Networks and Collective Action in Russia', in Webber, S. & Liikanen I. (eds) (2001).

Alapuro, R. (2010) 'Diabetes Associations and Political Culture in St. Petersburg and Helsinki', in Huttunen, T. & Ylikangas, M. (eds) (2010).

Alapuro, R. & Lonkila, M. (2000) 'Networks, Identity, and (In)Action. A Comparison between Russian and Finnish Teachers', *European Societies*, 2, 1.

Alapuro, R. & Lonkila, M. (2010) 'Political Culture in Russia in a Local Perspective', Alapuro, R., Mustajoki, A. & Pesonen, P. (eds) (forthcoming).

Alapuro, R., Liikanen, I. & Lonkila, M. (eds) (2004) *Beyond Post-Soviet Transition. Micro Perspectives on Challenge and Survival in Russia and Estonia* (Helsinki, Kikimora Publications).

Alexandrov, A. (2008) 'Otkat ot parkinga', *Delo*, 4 February, available at: http://www.idelo.ru/496/18.html, accessed 23 June 2009.

Balueva (2007) 'Garazhe—uzhe ne vash!', *Delo*, 5 March, available at: http://www.idelo.ru/454/9.html, accessed 30 June 2009.

Boltanski, L. & Thevénot, L. (1991) *De la justification. Les économies de la grandeur* (Paris, Éditions Gallimard).

Boltanski, L. & Thevénot, L. (1999) 'The Sociology of Critical Capacity', *European Journal of Social Theory*, 2, 3.

Boltanski, L. & Thevénot, L. (2006) *On Justification. Economies of Worth* (Princeton & Oxford, Princeton University Press).

Burawoy, M. & Verdery, K. (1999) 'Introduction', in Burawoy, M. & Verdery, K. (eds) (1999).

Burawoy, M. & Verdery, K. (eds) (1999) *Uncertain Transition. Ethnographies of Change in the Postsocialist World* (Lanham, MD, Rowman & Littlefield).

Centre for Journalism in Extreme Situations (2006) *Russian political scene in the media*, 2nd report, 6 July 2006, available at: http://www.memo98.sk/en/data/_media/russia_2nd_report_final.pdf, accessed 28 January 2010.

Clément, K. (2008) 'New Social Movements in Russia: A Challenge to the Dominant Model of Power Relationships?', *Journal of Communist Studies and Transition Politics*, 24, 1, March.

Colin Lebedev, A. (2009) *Du souci maternel à l'action en commun. Le Comité des mères de soldats de Russie et ses requérants (1989–2001)*, Doctoral dissertation (Paris, Insitut d'Etudes Politiques de Paris).

Crotty, J. (2009) 'Making a Difference? NGOs and Civil Society Development in Russia', *Europe-Asia Studies*, 61, 1.

European Social Survey (2008) *European Social Survey Round 4 Data*, Data file edition 1.0, Norwegian Social Science Data Services, Norway, Data Archive and distributor of ESS data, available at: http://www.europeansocialsurvey.org/, accessed 5 October 2010.

Evans, A. B. Jr., Henry, L. A. & McIntosh Sundstrom, L. (eds) (2006) *Russian Civil Society. A Critical Assessment* (London, M. E. Sharpe).

German, P. & Strel'nikova, S. (2007) 'V garazhnoi voine poyavilsya trup', *Vash tainyi sovetnik*, 24 December.

Gofman, A. B. (ed.) (2008) *Traditsii i innovatsii v sovremennoi Rossii. Sotsiologicheskii analiz vzaimodeistviya i dinamiki* (Moscow, Rossiiskaya politicheskaya entsiklopediya ROSSPEN).

Greene, S. (2007) 'Road Rage: Svoboda Vybora and the Russian Automotive Rebellion', Annual meeting of the American Sociological Association, New York, 11 August.

Henry, L. (2006) 'Shaping Social Activism in Post-Soviet Russia: Leadership, Organizational Diversity, and Innovation', *Post-Soviet Affairs*, 22, 2.

Henry, L. (2009) 'Redefining Citizenship in Russia. Political and Social Rights', *Problems of Post-Communism*, 56, 6.

Howard, M. (2002a) *The Weakness of Civil Society in Post-Communist Europe* (Cambridge, Cambridge University Press).

Howard, M. (2002b) 'Postcommunist Civil Society in Comparative Perspective', *Demokratizatsiya*, 10, 3.

Huttunen, T. & Ylikangas, M. (eds) (2010) *Witnessing Change in Contemporary Russia* (Helsinki, Kikimora Publications).

Johnson, J. E. (2006) 'Public–Private Permutations. Domestic Violence Crisis Centers in Barnaul', in Evans, A. B., Jr., Henry, L. A. & McIntosh Sundstrom, L. (eds) (2006).

Kholopova, L. (2006) 'Peterburzhtsy zashchishchayut svoi garazhi s kokteilim Molotova', *Komsomol'skaya Pravda*, 30 October.

Koveneva, O. (2008) 'O starom i novom v praktikakh grazhdanskogo uchastiya: dinamika mitinga nashikh dnei', in Gofman, A. B. (ed.) (2008).

Koveneva, O. (2009) 'Considering the Principles of Living Together in Human Communities: comparative Franco-Russian Research', Paper presented at the conference *On Russianness*, University of Helsinki, 3–4 December.

Kurilla, I. (2002) 'Civil Activism without NGOs: The Communist Party as a Civil Society Substitute', *Demokratizatsiya*, 10, 3.

Ledeneva, A. (1998) *Russia's Economy of Favours: Blat, Networking and Informal Exchange* (Cambridge, Cambridge University Press).

Lipman, M. (2009) 'Media Manipulation and Political Control in Russia', available at: http://www.carnegieendowment.org/publications/index.cfm?fa=view&id=37199, accessed 7 January 2011.

Lonkila, M. (1998) 'Social meaning of work. Aspects of teacher's profession in post-Soviet Russia', *Europe-Asia Studies*, 50, 4.

Lonkila, M. (1999) *Social Networks in Post-Soviet Russia: Continuity and Change in the Everyday Life of St. Petersburg Teachers* (Helsinki, Kikimora Publications).

Lonkila, M. (2008) 'The Internet and Anti-military Activism in Russia', *Europe-Asia Studies*, 60, 7.

Luhtakallio, E. (2009) 'Justifying in the Local Public Sphere: Newspaper Representations of Encounters between Citizens and Cities in Helsinki and Lyon', Paper presented at the 9th conference of the European Sociological Associations, Lisbon, Portugal, 2–5 September.

Luhtakallio, E. (2010) *Local Politicizations. A Comparison of Finns and French Practicing Democracy*, Doctoral dissertation manuscript (Helsinki, University of Helsinki).

Mezentsev, F. (2009) 'Rabote po BDD—shirokii razmakh i effektivnost'', *Vesti (Sankt-Peterburg)*, 16 June.

Pisarenko, A. (2007) 'Garazhdanskaya voina. Vladel'tsy garazhei vykhodyat iz sostava VOA. I sozdayut svoi kooperativy', *Novaya Gazeta*, 26–28 March, available at: http://www.novayagazeta.spb.ru/2007/21/10, accessed 22 June 2009.

Rogozin, O. (2007) 'Garazhye voini', *Izvestiya*, 27 February, available at: http://www.izvestia.ru/spb/article3101563/?print, accessed 21 June 2009.

Rutman, M. (2001) 'Vremya revolutsii ne proshlo?', *Sankt-Peterburgskie Vedomosti*, 14 February, available at: http://www.pressa.spb.ru/newspapers/spbved/2001/arts/spbved-2419-art-52.html, accessed 23 June 2009.

Skrodenis, T., Ponomareva, V. & Druzhininsky, M. (2007) 'Murder of St. Petersburg Activist Casts Shadow Over Western High Speed Diameter Project', *CEE Bankwatch Network*, 19 December, available at: http://www.bankwatch.org/newsroom/release.shtml?x=2064405, accessed 20 April 2010.

Skryabikov, A. & Kholopova, L. (2006) 'Lyuboi garazh: byl vash, stal nash!', *Komsomol'skaya Pravda*, 3 November.
Streltsova, S. (2008) 'B garazhnoi voine pribavilos' polkovodtsev i deneg', *Tainyi sovetnik*, 15, 293, 21 April, available at: http://www.fontanka.ru/2008/04/21/048/, accessed 23 June 2009.
Thévenot, L. (2006) *L'action au pluriel. Sociologie des régimes d'engagement* (Paris, Éditions La Découverte).
Thévenot, L. (2007) 'The Plurality of Cognitive Formats and Engagements: Moving between the Familiar and the Public', *European Journal of Social Theory*, 10, 3, pp. 409–23.
Wagner, P. (1999) 'After Justification. Repertoires of Evaluation and the Sociology of Modernity', *European Journal of Social Theory*, 2, 3.
Webber, S. & Liikanen, I. (eds) (2001) *Education and Civic Culture in Post-communist Countries* (New York, Palgrave).
Ylä-Anttila, T. (2009) 'The Globalization Debate: A Public Justifications Analysis', Paper presented at the 9th conference of the *European Sociological Associations*, Lisbon, Portugal, 2–5 September.
Zdravomyslova, E. (2004) 'Self-identity Frames in the Soldiers' Mothers Movement in Russia', in Alapuro, R., Liikanen, I. & Lonkila, M. (eds) (2004).
Zeya, N. (2007) 'Segodnya snesli garazh, zavtra otnimut zhizn'', *Gazeta.ru*, 19 December, available at: http://www.gazeta.ru/auto/2007/12/18_a_2444099.shtml, accessed 8 January 2010.

Making a Difference? NGOs and Civil Society Development in Russia

JO CROTTY

Abstract

The role of non-governmental organisations (NGOs) in the development of Russia's civil society has been the focus of academic study since the collapse of the Soviet Union in 1991. In light of this literature, this article aims to assess the impact of the movement that has most often been seen as very promising for Russia's future civil society development—the environmental movement—by utilising research undertaken in Samara *Oblast'* of the Russian Federation. While the results do reveal some positive contributions to civil society development in Russia, they also exhibit many similarities with other studies in the extant literature, illustrating the relative weakness of Russia's social movements in the area of civil society development.

SINCE THE COLLAPSE OF THE SOVIET UNION, MANY studies have examined the activity of social movements across the Russian Federation, from women's groups (Sperling 1999; Sundstrom 2002, 2005) and trade unions (Baglione & Clark 1998), to human rights and law enforcement (Taylor 2006; Holland 2004). Scholars have observed the behaviour and activity of such groups from a multiplicity of angles including their scope, type and structure (Cook & Vinogradova 2006; Henry 2006; Salmenniemi 2005; Yanitsky 1996), and the impact of overseas donor funding (Crotty 2003; Sundstrom 2005), in order to assess their contribution to the development of Russian civil society (Knox *et al.* 2006; Murphy 2003; Holland 2004). In so doing, they have found that the structure of many NGOs is inappropriate for civil society building (Cook & Vinogradova 2006; Henry 2006); that overseas funding has been inadequate or insufficiently grounded in the Russian context to contribute to civil society building (Crotty 2003; Sundstrom 2005); and that the groups themselves often lack the will or ability—irrespective of their structure or endowment of overseas funding—to actively participate in civil society (Cook & Vinogradova 2006; Henry 2006; Salmenniemi 2005; Knox *et al.* 2006; Murphy 2003; Holland 2004). In the light of this literature, this article aims to examine the capacity of the social movement most often hailed as Russia's most 'promising agent of civil society development' (Henry 2002, p. 2), namely the environmental movement, and its impact on the development of civil society within one region of the Russian Federation.

Definitions of civil society abound in the literature (Jensen 2006), but for the purposes of this article civil society will be defined as 'the sphere ... situated between the state and the market which can serve as a promoter of democratic values, provide models of active citizenship and temper the power of the state' (Kuchukeeva & O'Loughlin 2003, pp. 557–58). This sphere is made up of 'autonomous, freely chosen, intermediary organisations' (Neace 1999, p. 150) that bridge the space between the individual and the state. Advocacy groups or social movements therefore pluralise the democratic arena (Mercer 2002) and provide 'opportunities for individuals to practice citizenship' (Salmenniemi 2005, p. 737). They facilitate a vibrant and functioning civil society that is necessary to make democracy work (Hale 2002) by bridging the gap between the individual and the state (Knoke 1999; Portes 1998).

Given this, Taylor (2006) breaks down the democratic functions of civil society in facilitating civic engagement and the participation therein, into three aspects: first, drawing from Putnam (1993), he contends that civil society should teach citizens 'norms and values' synonymous with democracy; second, that 'autonomous voluntary associations' should act as a counterweight to the state and thereby hold it to account; and third, that 'autonomous voluntary associations' should be capable of working in a partnership arrangement, serving not only as a 'watchdog to the state, but also as a resource' in developing democracy (Taylor 2006, p. 196). Consistent with this approach, in a study of environmental movements across a range of countries Doherty and Doyle (2006) have identified a number of key characteristics of social movements that contribute to their effectiveness in fulfilling their democratic functions. They note that to be effective they must embody a public political dimension, with a goal of achieving political or social change. In order to achieve this, movements must be based on a common identity developed over time by participants in collective action, and regularly interact with others outside of their organisation.

In operationalising this approach to civil society, we are drawing largely on a 'Western' model to observe the contribution made by Russian environmental groups to its development. In so doing, we follow other scholars in transposing this Western model into studies of other parts of the world (Mendelson & Gerber 2007; Kennedy et al. 1998; Gibson 2001). That said, it has been stated by some scholars that Russia is 'different' or a 'special case' and that Western models cannot be easily transposed (Golenkova 1999; Vorontsova & Filatov 1997). While noting this, we draw on the experience of other scholars attempting to use a Western model of civil society within their work in non-Western settings, such as Lewis (2002) who notes that while there may be specific differences in the practices adopted by NGOs and pressure groups in non-Western settings, the Western model remains a useful tool as it has the capacity to 'inspire' action vis-à-vis the building of democratic structures.

Evidence within the extant literature of Russian social movements fulfilling the three roles described by Taylor, as set out within this Western model of civil society, are scant at best. Many factors are cited to explain this, including the Soviet legacy (Smolar 1996; Mishler & Rose 1997); an absence of trust in new democratic structures (Shlapentokh 2006; Sapsford & Abbott 2006; Ahl 1999); nostalgia for the past (Munroe 2006; Sil & Chen 2004) arising from disappointment with the outcomes of the transition process (Dowley & Silver 2002; Luong & Weinthal 1999); and more recently, state-sponsored attempts to curtail the activity of social movements (Machleder 2006).

It is against this background that this article utilises longitudinal data collected between 2002 and 2006 in Samara *Oblast'* on the Samara Environmental Movement (SEM). It sets out to compare the experiences and contribution to civil society by the SEM to those of other groups and movements across the Russian Federation. By assessing the SEM's activity within Taylor's (2006) framework, it exposes some fledgling shoots of Russian civil society development, capable of bridging the gap between the individual and the state, but it also reveals many similarities with studies of other cases across the former Soviet Union (FSU), illustrating a common pattern of behaviour and relative weakness in the area of civil society building from NGOs and social movements. Before these findings are discussed however, an overview of both Russian civil society development and the experiences of other social movements across the Russian Federation are examined.

Russian civil society development

Knox *et al.* (2006, p. 12) have described the situation of Russian civil society as in a 'holding pattern'. After more than 15 years, despite 'kernels' of civic activism (Gellner 1994) that were present at the time of the collapse of the Soviet Union, Russian civil society remains weak and ineffective in the face of an ever strengthening state.

The Soviet legacy and the transition process

The legacy of the Soviet Union still casts a shadow over the development of Russian civil society. It continues to shape the structure of Russian society and the propensity of individuals to engage with social movements and other civic organisations. In this context the Soviet Union's approach to civic activity remains a topic of debate within the literature, with some scholars viewing Soviet civil society as 'historically weak' or 'oppressed' and actively removed from society (Nichols 1996; Osgood & Ong 2001; Woolcock 1998; Kennedy *et al.* 1998). Others contend that Soviet civil society was not weak, but 'institutionalised' (Rose 1995; Mishler & Rose 1997; Hartner 1998). As the state provided institutions where individuals could interact outside the home—such as sports clubs, social clubs and crèches—the membership of these state-sponsored organisations was not voluntary, but assumed. This assumed membership represented an institutionalisation of Soviet civil space rather than its outright removal. The institutionalised civil space, alongside the active state suppression of spontaneous, autonomous voluntary associations, led individuals to rely on their network of friends, family and individual connections inside the home (Howard 2002). These networks nurtured a mistrust of elites and so put distance between the individual and the state.

Whether viewed as 'weak' or institutionalised however, the outcome in the post-Soviet present is seen as the same. The forced volunteering and assumed membership of state run organisations of the past has fostered a rejection of such in the present. Smolar sees such a rejection

> as a natural reaction to years of forced participation and mobilisation. Everyday life under socialism taught people to survive as individuals and to fear any association with independent collective action … [Today] the shakiness of independent organisations, including political parities, suggests that lack of a culture for free collective activity. (Smolar 1996, p. 33)

Given this history of 'forced' volunteering and its consequences, alongside the propensity for the individual to rest on personal contacts, it was not surprising that autonomous voluntary organisations in the post-communist environment found it difficult to engage the public and thus perform any civil society role in bridging the gap between the individual and the state.

The inability of pressure groups to engage with the public was further compromised as the Russian population underwent what Sapsford and Abbott (2006) have termed a 'fundamental demoralisation' in response to the outcomes of the transition process. Delight at the collapse of the Soviet regime quickly turned to disillusionment and disappointment (Howard 2002) as individuals experienced rising crime and law-lessness, unemployment, spiralling costs for health care and education, and increasing uncertainty within their day-to-day lives (Dowley & Silver 2002; Luong & Weinthal 1999; Zaslavskaya 2006). Simultaneously, the old distrusted elites enriched themselves through illegitimate means (Hanson 1997; Linz & Krueger 1996) facilitating a sense of both distance and distrust of what were now 'new' elites. As a result individuals were more likely to rely on their network of friends and family rather than turn to an outside body—state or otherwise—for assistance. Therefore Russian civil society has remained weak, a fact which both Presidents Boris Yel'tsin and Vladimir Putin attempted to exploit.

State-sponsored curtailment of social movement activity

During the Yelt'sin era, the law 'On Public Associations', passed in 1999, required all public organisations which had registered under a previous 1995 act of the same name, to re-register. This requirement led to many NGOs disappearing from the list of 'official' groups. They either failed to re-register or had their re-registration denied. Others had their re-registration held up as a result of deficiencies in paperwork or other administrative issues (Squier 2002). While this presented a problem for some active NGOs, many inactive or 'paper' NGOs were also removed from the official list, thus making the extant list a more accurate reflection of the number and scope of active organisations within the Russian Federation. Moreover, the impact of this requirement for re-registration was limited when compared to actions taken under Putin to curtail civil society activity.

Even before his re-election in 2004, Putin had been more proactive than Yel'tsin in seeking to control the activity of NGOs and Russian civil society. His first attempt was to use his 'civic forum'. Although hailed by some as a positive step towards a process of reciprocity between the government and civil society (Hudson 2003), this approach was in fact 'statist' in its orientation (Sil & Chen 2004, p. 359; Knox *et al.* 2006). Although NGOs and social movements were asked to participate in forums with the federal government, it was the government that drove both the agenda and the associated outcomes. Moreover, the civic forum initiative was accompanied by an alteration of the tax code, which imposed a single social tax on non-profit organisations regardless of purpose or status (Sil & Chen 2004). Although designed to curb the activity of trade unions, it simultaneously discouraged the formation of new civic organisations (Sil & Chen 2004) and impeded the activity of many existing organisations, thus curtailing their participation in the civil forum process.

Following his re-election in 2004, Putin sought to bring Russia's 'independent civil society organisations under the wing of the state' (Hale *et al.* 2004, p. 315). Attempts were made to tarnish the reputations of some organisations by describing them as traitors or treasonous as a result of their association with overseas donors (Hale *et al.* 2004). This was followed by Putin's decision to formulate legislation to contain the activity of NGOs and social movements in response to the role played by international NGOs in the so-called 'Colour Revolutions' of other former Soviet States (Chaulia 2006).

By means of a new 'NGO Law',[1] Putin sought to restrict the activity of advocacy groups that 'threaten[ed] the sovereignty of Russia, its national independence, territorial integrity, unity or originality, its cultural heritage or national interests' (Machleder 2006). The law also placed restrictions on donations from foreign NGOs to Russian groups and stepped up the administrative burden placed upon Russian-based groups. Not surprisingly, this legislation drew much criticism from the international community *vis-à-vis* the development of civil society and democracy in Russia. In particular, it was argued that the financial and registration requirements of this law place a disproportionate burden on smaller groups, leading them to curtail their activity, and thereby weakening an already weak civic arena (BBC 2006). (The direct impact of this legislation has yet to be explored within the literature however, as its medium and long-term impact has yet to be established.)

Thus, a combination of increased regulation, the Soviet legacy and an absence of generalised trust in Russia's democratic and social institutions has made the operating environment extremely difficult for Russia's NGOs and social movements.

Russian NGOs in transition

According to some authors, the mass protest movements that assisted in precipitating the collapse of the Soviet Union and regimes across the Eastern Bloc were based on a 'common heritage', embodied a public political dimension and had social change as their goal (Perepjolkin & Figatner 1997; Bernard 1996). These social movements—for the most part those attached to the environmental movement—were focused on achieving widespread social and political change by drawing ordinary citizens into their activities. However when the Soviet Union collapsed, these movements splintered and imploded as their *raison d'etre*—regime change—evaporated. These groups had developed quickly, bypassing the development of a 'common identity', and so as the Soviet Union collapsed, so did their widespread support. Other priorities, and a lack of embedded common heritage amongst its participants led to the aforementioned 'splintering' of the movement into a myriad of small, locally focused movements, NGOs and grass roots organisations. A review of the activities and configuration of Russian NGOs and social movements following the collapse of the Soviet Union shows that unlike their *Glasnost'* counterparts, they exemplify few of the characteristics described by Doherty and Doyle (2006).

[1]The law's official title is 'On Introducing Amendments into Certain Legislative Acts of the Russian Federation', however in common parlance this is often referred to as the 'Russian NGO Law'. For more information see Machleder (2006).

Russian NGOs and civil society development

Recently, a number of scholars have reviewed the type, structure and scope of Russia's NGOs (Cook & Vinogradova 2006; Henry 2006). Despite using different labels, their characterisations are very similar, with each identifying three specific types of organisational form.[2] These are reviewed below alongside an assessment of their ability to contribute to Russia's civil society development.

The first group identified by both Henry (2006) and Cook and Vinogradova (2006), were Grass Roots Organisations or GROs. Both studies found that GROs focused their campaigning activity almost exclusively on local or single issues. These issues were either concerned with the demands of the membership, for example, veterans' affairs, or a specific group or issue outside the membership, for example, animal welfare or ecology (Cook & Vinogradova 2006). GRO membership was usually drawn from academics or educators working in a specific field and as a result such organisations tended to be hierarchical, dominated by an individual or core group with specifically related qualifications or by particular professions (Murphy 2003). The membership tended to be parochial, based on pre-existing relationships and though sometimes nominally 'open' to all, it rarely expanded beyond the core group. GROs did not strive for mass mobilisation or reach out to the wider Russian population through their campaigning activities (Tynkkynen 2006; Sundstrom 2002). Few groups therefore had a strategy for expanding their membership or their resources (Evans 2002; Salmenniemi 2006). Some went further, and actively discouraged the inclusion of new members (Henry 2006). These limits put on membership or membership aspirations therefore restricted the awareness of the groups' existence within the ordinary population (Sundstrom 2002). Such groups tended to be rather 'cliquish' and parochial, drawing membership from pre-existing networks; and as they did not act to counter the anti-volunteering mindset left over from the Soviet Union, their ability to contribute to civil society development was therefore limited (Smolar 1996).

GROs also tended to approach campaigning through non-combative means, using round tables, publications and consultations to influence policy, although their parochial nature tended to keep them small, usually with a deficit of skilled personnel. In addition, most groups operated on limited or no funding, and relied on personal donations or small one-off grants from overseas organisations for basic campaigning items such as a computer (Sperling 1999; Crotty & Crane 2004). The majority of GROs were also apolitical, actively resisting confrontation with the state (Tynkkynen 2006). As a result they were 'invisible' to government (Cook & Vinogradova 2006) and so lacked any direct influence over policy making (Knox *et al.* 2006). They therefore failed to act as either a counterweight to the state, or a resource in civil society building (Taylor 2006). This, in combination with their parochial nature also limited their 'bridging' capacity between the individual and the state (Knoke 1999; Portes 1998).

The second group to be identified by Henry (2006) and Cook and Vinogradova (2006) were 'professional' policy or advocacy organisations (POs). These organisations had a broad national or international focus with membership drawn from the Russian intelligentsia (Cook & Vinogradova 2006). They were almost entirely reliant on

[2] A detailed overview can be found in Appendix 1 of this article.

overseas funding for their operations and long-term survival. Members of these organisations were drawn further into the international NGO circuit through conferences and training overseas. Most of their activity was focused on practical action such as pollution prevention projects and human rights advocacy. While these groups were politically adversarial their contribution to Russian civil society development was limited due to their reliance on overseas donor funding (Cook & Vinogradova 2006).

Since the collapse of the former Soviet Union, many scholars have noted that reliance on overseas donor funding has had the opposite effect to what was intended (Klose 2000; Henry 2001; Mendelson 2001; Henderson 2002; Richter 2000, 2002; Weinthal 2002; Crotty 2003; Murphy 2003; Sundstrom 2005). Rather than bolstering its development, overseas funding has created a class of NGO that is distanced from Russian society and thus it has 'widened the gap between activists and the rest of society' (Henderson 2002, p. 75). This is because, the foreign assistance offered has not been sufficiently grounded in the norms of the society within which the NGO operates (Crotty 2003). The consequences of a donor-driven agenda have been examined in a number of studies across the Russian Federation (Henry 2001; Henderson 2002; Richter 2000, 2002; Crotty 2003; Murphy 2003; Sundstrom 2005). A minority of studies have illustrated the potential benefits of donor funding, including democracy building and the development of civil society (Weinthal 2002), the fostering of more democratic NGOs (Mendelson 2001), and the assisting of NGOs in achieving their goals through grant-assisted projects and actions (Klose 2000). The majority however, (Henry 2001; Henderson 2002; Richter 2000, 2002; Crotty 2003; Murphy 2003; Sundstrom 2005) have indicated that inappropriate administration often facilitates little more than 'maintaining their [NGO's] continued existence' (Henry 2001, p. 11).

The presence of overseas funding often leads groups to cut themselves off from their immediate surroundings and to adopt the agendas of the overseas organisation. As a result, they fail to reach out to ordinary Russians *vis-à-vis* participation and membership. Sundstrom's (2005) study of overseas assistance to soldiers' and women's rights NGOs is a case in point: where overseas donors worked directly with groups campaigning against domestic violence, or for the humane and lawful treatment of soldiers, there were some positive outcomes. This was because the overseas donors were working within an area that had resonance with the Russian population. In so doing, the assistance offered did allow NGOs to successfully lobby for legislative and policy improvements. However, where assistance had been offered to women's rights organisations—concerning the general empowerment of women—donors adopted a 'Western issue' with a 'Western' agenda, and thus lacked sufficient grounding to make the same level of policy or regulatory impact (Sundstrom 2005; Crotty 2003). In addition, Sundstrom (2005) also noted that neither recipient groups used the donor funding received to 'reach out' to the Russian public. Thus, while the funding had allowed some to act as a 'counterweight' to the state (Taylor 2006), it did not facilitate bridging between the individual and the state (Richter 2002).

The third group identified by Henry (2006) and Cook and Vinogradova (2006) were government affiliates or 'marionette' organisations (MOs), closely linked to the operations of the state. Such groups were either allied to, formed part of, or performed consultancy work for a regulatory or state body. They were usually endowed with office space and other resources either directly or indirectly by the state. Membership of these organisations was limited to those with the 'right credentials' and was usually drawn from the ranking official's circle of associates (Murphy 2003). The primary aim of these organisations was to support the state in its activities, but they were also recognised as official NGOs and represented civil society organisations in this capacity at round tables and other meetings. These groups, by their very nature, were politically subservient, and yet at the same time, they were the most successful in terms of size of membership and revenue generated (Murphy 2003). MOs took two distinct forms. A relatively small number were GROs that had transformed themselves into MOs as a result of the 'monetarisation of Russian society' (Salmenniemi 2005, p. 742). The majority however, embodied an extension of the state-sponsored curtailment of civil society noted above.

In the absence of overseas funding, Russian social or third sector organisations have become dependent on donations and volunteers to ensure their survival. Most GROs lack access to both, and are thus forced to engage in 'survival strategies' (Henry 2002). Some chase small one-off grants from overseas donors, but are usually put off by the complex application procedures demanded for relatively small sums (Crotty 2003). Thus they rely on funds emanating from their own community or within their own membership. As a result, they work with miniscule budgets or without any financial assistance at all and their contribution to either policy making or civil society is limited.

Recognising this, some GROs, particularly those situated within the academic community, started to offer their services as consultants to the state in their area of expertise as a way to finance their research and activity (Henry 2006). In so doing, however, these GROs have made themselves subservient to the state. The state has become their only source of income, thereby weakening their ability to act as a counterweight to it. This type of organisation reflects the 'working together' approach illustrated by Lewis (2002) in his study of civil society and NGO activity in Africa. Here NGOs and other groups were much less 'autonomous' than the traditional 'Western' model of civil society would advocate, yet these organisations whilst working in partnership with the state were still independent organisations. As a result such organisations still had the capacity, despite their lack of autonomy, to contribute to civil society development. However, in Samara and in Russia as a whole, the number of GROs ensuring their survival in this way was small when compared either to the number of directly state-sponsored NGOs, or to genuine marionette or government affiliated organisations that were adjuncts of the state.

The government affiliates or MOs are the most 'institutionalised' of all the three NGO types characterised in this article. As noted, most have paid staff, office space, and are legally registered as NGOs (Squier 2002). Despite this, as organisations they stand outside Russia's civil space. Most are formed by bureaucrats within the state administration and draw their memberships from within that state function or from other elite groups, such as business leaders, with an interest in their subject area. Most MOs also have membership restrictions, limiting those who can join to those with certain credentials or with official invitations (Crotty 2006). This helps protect their identity and also ensures that they are supportive of the state's regulatory agenda and often fulfil a public participation function in policy making (Henry 2006). They are therefore not part of Russia's civil society, but participate as what Cook and Vinogradova have called 'putative' representatives of it (2006, p. 35). Rather than being independent of the state, they are extensions of it. Thus they do not teach citizens the 'norms and values' synonymous with democracy nor do they act as a counterweight to the state. However, they do work in a partnership arrangement with the state, but as a 'resource', furthering its agenda, rather than in fulfilling the role described by Taylor as 'developing democracy' (2006, p. 196). They therefore perform no civil society function.

Thus, returning to Doherty and Doyle's (2006) key characteristics for social movements, both GROs and POs appear to have a goal of achieving political or social change. All three, GROs, POs and MOs, are based on a common identity developed over time by participants in collective action, though the identities developed by the GROs and MOs are inward looking. Both GROs and MOs restrict their membership, officially or unofficially, and are not 'open' to all. None of the three however have regular contact or interaction with others outside their organisations. Overseas donors appear to limit the contact that POs have with those beyond the international NGO community. The GROs are parochial and deliberately stand back from engaging with the public. The MOs, as part of the state apparatus, have no incentive to extend their reach beyond their remit of supporting the state's regulatory agenda. Thus, on the whole, the extant literature indicates that Russian NGOs embody few of the characteristics of an active and effective social movement and as a result have little opportunity to contribute to civil society development.

The environmental movement in Samara Oblast'

In the light of the previous discussion the following section of this article describes the author's research on the environmental movement in Samara, examining the capacity of this social movement in the development of civil society within one region of the Russian Federation. As noted above, the environmental movement has been identified by a number of authors as the most promising of Russia's social movements for the promotion of civil society development.

The research study

Samara *Oblast'* was chosen as the site for this study as it exhibits a typical profile of many 'industrialised' *oblasts* outside of Moscow and St Petersburg (Hanson 1997) and contains a conservation area, the Samara Luka National Park, within which are situated the Zhiguli Mountains. In the transition era, Samara *Oblast'* has become a centre of relative prosperity and development following progressive policies towards ownership transfer, reconstruction and development (Hanson 1997). It also has an environmental movement (SEM) consisting of 15 separate organisations.

Informants were first identified through a web-based database of Russian environmental groups published jointly by EcoLOGIA (Ecologists Linked for Organizing Grassroots Initiatives and Action)—a US organisation providing support for grass roots environmental initiatives across the former communist bloc—and the

Sacred Earth Network.[3] Registering 1,471 entries for the Russian Federation as a whole, this database included nine entries for Samara *Oblast'*. With the assistance of project partners, the Samara State University, another six organisations were located and identified.[4] A 'snowball' approach was then used to identify a cross section of citizens across Samara *Oblast'* who would be willing to participate in the project. Again, Samara State University provided the first access points.

Given the developmental nature of Russian democracy, an inductive approach to the research design was taken. Case studies were conducted at 15 environmental groups in Samara *Oblast'*. The analysis was based on both formal and informal approaches to data gathering and research participation within the case study environment (Stake 1995). The activity of the SEM was observed during three discrete fieldwork periods between 2002 and 2006. Personal, semi-structured interviews[5] were also conducted with a leader of each individual NGO, and with other active members at each visit to obtain a picture of their activity and behaviour during a period of increasing economic prosperity, but of declining freedoms *vis-à-vis* NGO activities. Questions dealt specifically with their activities and attitudes towards civil society development and the role each individual NGO had to play in that development; they were directed at group leaders and key members on three separate occasions in order to identify changes or consistency in activity. Each interview was recorded and transcribed *in situ*. These interviews were then coded for key themes, which were then compared between visits to identify behavioural patterns, changes or consistency in their approach to civil society development, and their role therein. The analysis revealed many similarities with other NGOs described within the extant literature. However, some fledgling shoots of civil society development were also identified. It is to these research findings that we now turn.

Findings

The first key difference observed between the SEM and the situation in Russia more widely was the absence in Samara of POs. Professional Organisations as they have been described in the extant literature did not exist within the SEM. Outside Moscow and St Petersburg the opportunities for such organisations to have contact with international movements and organisations is considerably less. Moreover, Samara *Oblast'* did not exemplify an ongoing international issue, such as, for example, human rights abuse in Chechnya (Holland 2004) which could attract international NGO attention. As a result, the SEM did not contain any group that could be characterised as a PO, although one GRO was in receipt of sustained overseas donor funding over the period of this study. Moreover, the SEM also contained one group that could be described as 'alternative' as it used combative and anarchic methods to achieve campaigning objectives. Thus the research presented below details the activity of 11 GROs, although it should be noted that three groups—The Samara Bird Society, the

---

[3]See http://www.ecologia.org/SENdb and http://www.sacredearthnetwork.org/, accessed June 2006.
[4]Profiles of all the NGOs in this study can be found in Appendix 2.
[5]In order to meet commitments given to respondents to ensure confidentiality, only their position and an English description of their organisation are given in this article.

Samara Branch of the Socio-Ecological Union and the alternative group The Rainbow Keepers—all ceased to exist during the course of this study. The study also included three MOs. The findings relating to the GROs, including the alternative group, will be described first, followed by discussion of the three MOs.

The GROs. By their very nature, the majority of the groups in this study, both GRO and MO, are concerned with an issue outside their membership—the natural environment. Five of the 11 GRO groups focused exclusively on single issues which were exclusively local. For example, the Cottage People campaigned to stop the dumping of municipal waste within the vicinity of their *dachas*, the Samara Bird Society was focused on the protection of local species, and the Friends of Samaraskaya Luka National Park (Friends) were concerned with the protection of the national park. The remaining six organisations campaigned on a broader range of issues, but again these issues were local to Samara *Oblast'*. None of the GROs campaigned on broader national or international issues, indicating that their campaigning agenda was very similar to that of GROs identified elsewhere in the literature (Cook & Vinogradova 2006).

Also in common with findings elsewhere in Russia (Henry 2006; Murphy 2003), the membership of five GROs was drawn from the academic community, with all five being dominated by one key academic or core group guiding the direction of the organisation. For example, the Novo-Kuibyshevsk Socio-Ecological Union (NSKEU) membership was made up entirely of academics in the field of ecology, chemistry and pollution measurement, with three key individuals taking all the major decisions for the organisation. At the Samara Regional Ecological Society (SRES), an ecology professor led the organisation, with much of the membership being drawn from graduate students and other faculty members in related fields.

These groups had an ambivalent attitude to membership recruitment. In their view, their role was to 'raise the ecological culture of the population' (Leader, Samara Society of Humanities and Aesthetics) through their activity, but not to draw the public into their organisation. They perceived ordinary people to be indifferent to environmental problems, uncaring about the natural environment, and uninterested in volunteering for advocacy groups like their own. They only wanted to work with people who were already 'active' (Leader, SREC). If an individual or group already engaged in campaigning was observed, then they would approach them, but they did not seek to draw ordinary Russians into their organisations, stating that such activity was a 'waste of time' or 'useless' (Leader, SREC). Thus, reflecting Henry's (2006) characterisation of NGOs elsewhere in Russia, these groups were parochial and inward looking, and exhibited little desire to reach out to the wider Russian population. As a consequence, none of these groups reported an increase in membership during the course of this study.

The campaigning approach of these organisations was also similar to that noted by writers such as Henry (2006). These groups 'campaigned' by engaging in 'round-table' discussions where they would invite panels of experts to discuss a particular issue and publish articles and pamphlets on ecological topics. Access to these round-tables was by invitation only, and their publications, while available directly from these groups, were not in the public domain. Some, particularly the SRES, would also use the local media, writing to newspapers and appearing on local television to communicate various environmental problems, but they stood back from confronting the state and regulatory authorities directly. As none of these groups had any direct funding, much of their activity was an extension of the academic work of their members, and thus by its nature, limited in its reach to the wider population of Samara. This and their parochial nature meant that this sub-set of GROs displayed characteristics similar to those found elsewhere in Russia (Cook & Vinogradova 2006; Knox *et al.* 2006) in that it was not visible to government, failed to have any influence on policy making, and thus failed to act either as a counterweight to the state or as a resource for building civil society. The campaigning activity and rejection of active recruitment of these groups also meant they engaged in no bridging activity between the individual and the state.

Of the other organisations, the Socio-Ecological Unions (Samara and Tol'yatti) and the Rainbow Keepers were the remnants left over from much bigger organisations created during the *perestroika* period (Perepjolkin & Figatner 1997; Bernard 1996). However, the membership of these organisations declined after the collapse of the Soviet Union, and declined further during the course of this study whilst the Samara Socio-Ecological Union (SSEU) and the Rainbow Keepers ceased to function entirely by the mid-point of this study. In interviewing the leaders of these two organisations, both cited a combination of economic and resource pressures for their declining activity and a perception that the public were not interested in the movement. The leader of the SSEU stated that members started drifting away as they found it increasingly difficult to find the time to actively participate. Economic demands upon them meant that they had little time to dedicate to the SSEU. He also expressed frustration that the campaigning activity of the SSEU appeared to have little impact or resonance with the public, and as a result, had become demotivated. The leader of the Rainbow Keepers stated that they needed a room and other resources to work, and as they had no way of obtaining such resources, they had decided to cease their activity. Neither cited state-led attempts to curtail their action as the reason for their decline. Thus, it was economic pressures, coupled with an absence of resources that led to the decline of these groups, rather than attempts by the state to reign in their activity.

The remaining three organisations were made up of members from the local community. The Cottage People drew its membership from the owners of *dachas* threatened by a municipal waste site. Initiative 2 (I2) drew its members from the small town of Chapaevsk to campaign against the construction of a factory to decommission chemical weapons on their territory. Both these organisations were initially successful because their campaigning issue had a direct impact on its membership, but they had difficulty in sustaining that membership beyond campaigning on a single issue.

I2 members were successful in preventing the construction of the plant on the territory of Chapaevsk. They achieved this by drawing the ordinary population of Chapaevsk into their activity, using contacts in schools and firms in the town to start a petition against the construction of the factory. They also used these contacts to hold a number of successful rallies at the proposed construction site. Following this success, the leadership attempted to re-orientate the organisation to focus on a broader set of environmental issues but they found it increasingly difficult to maintain the level of interest in issues that were not immediately relevant to the population. Despite their previous campaigning success, they still had a deficit of skills. The leadership appeared to have little understanding of how to alter the remit of the organisation successfully or seek out the participation of the ordinary population where the issues they would like to campaign on did not have an immediate impact upon them. This skills deficit also included a lack of know-how concerning fundraising. Funding for the initial campaign had come from the local community and participants but once this campaign was over, I2 had neither any sustainable sources of funding or resources, nor any knowledge of how to access such funding. As a result, their membership dwindled to less than 20 over the course of this study, with very little real campaigning activity being undertaken.

A similar story was told by the Cottage People. Initially the organisation had some key successes in recruiting individuals immediately affected by the threat of the waste site plans. The leader had also used her contacts to engage a lawyer to work for them *pro bono*. They planned successful demonstrations outside the regional administration building and generated positive press about their cause. However, their efforts were in vain as the waste site was located within the vicinity of the *dachas*. Despite this, the leader of the organisation attempted to use the skills she had acquired, to re-orientate the organisation to campaign on broader environmental themes. However, although they had around 100 members to begin with, they soon drifted away, along with the leader's access to campaigning resources, once their original campaigning remit disappeared. Over the course of this study, the activity of the remaining membership of the Cottage People became more intertwined with that of the SRES with whom the leader had strong connections.

The two cases above are of note as although the organisations have experienced decline over the period of this study, their initial success in engaging the population in their activity does indicate that groups are able to generate civic activity. Despite the Soviet legacy of forced volunteering (Smolar 1996), and the documented lack of trust in social institutions (Shlapentokh 2006), where the issue impacts on the individual directly, an NGO can provide a bridge between that individual and the state (Neace 1999). Moreover, despite Cook and Vinogradova's (2006) claims that such organisations are 'invisible' to the state, both I2 and the Cottage People illustrate that it is possible to influence state policy, in the case of I2, or at least appear on its radar, in the case of the Cottage People. The problem comes in sustaining that activity beyond a single issue. Moreover, there was little evidence from this study that individuals who participated in either the Cottage People's or I2's campaigns became longer-term activists. Thus such single issue groups appear able to generate small pockets of 'one off' civic activity, and briefly act as a counterweight to the state, but they are unable to make a lasting contribution to Russia's civil society development. Both organisations made attempts to create sustainable organisations, but failed due to both a skills deficit and an absence of resources.

The only group not to experience a decline or stalling of membership numbers during this study was the Friends of Samaraskaya Luka National Park. Moreover it was the only group to achieve clear campaigning success and attract sustainable sources of overseas and domestic funding. Although it was set up by an academic working within the National Park, Friends was very different from the other academic based GROs discussed above insofar as it was not dominated by academic activity, and was not closed to members without the requisite qualifications or association with an academic institution. In fact Friends was a deliberately open organisation with a remit to attract members from the wider population of Samara *Oblast'*. Friends' aim was to promote and protect the uniqueness of the National Park in the face of increasing industrial pressures. Within one year of its inception in 2001 it had signed up around 125 people from the surrounding towns and cities and this rose to more than 150 during the course of this study.

Friends charged a nominal membership fee of 20R per annum and placed a strong emphasis on promoting both the park and the organisation, actively encouraging its membership to participate in these activities. It produced booklets on the nature of the park using members' photographs, and it undertook promotion events such as an annual 'fun run' within the park attracting 3,000 participants annually. The fun run was also accompanied by educational material and volunteers staffed stalls promoting both Friends, and the uniqueness of the park. Members were also engaged in voluntary educational projects in local schools. A long-term goal was the building of a visitors' centre for the park. Friends also actively undertook their own fundraising, printing their own calendars, park currency and postcards and promoted their work on local television.

Friends also successfully engaged overseas organisations such as the World Wide Fund for Nature, UNESCO and the Charity Aid Foundation (CAF). These links, particularly with CAF, had allowed them to become acquainted with Western approaches to fundraising, promotion and campaigning. They had one paid member of staff and office space. As a result, Friends mobilised supporters to confront the continuing presence of mining companies within the National Park. They were also successful in challenging both the regional administration and the mining firm in achieving a commitment to halt mining in the park by the end of 2009. In so doing, they used their membership base and resources to act as a counterweight to the state. Moreover, it appeared that Friends' overseas funding was orientated towards their needs, and did not result in a distancing of it from the local population. They appear to have been able to use overseas assistance to achieve their own goals rather than Western goals.

Thus, by actively engaging the local population, Friends became a fledgling source of civil society development in the region. The group was able to teach local people the 'norms and values' synonymous with democracy through their participation within the organisation. Moreover, the leader himself stated at the end of this research project that he now saw Friends as a 'cushion between the administration and the park', protecting it from its industrial development and therefore acting as a counterweight (Leader, Friends) to the state. The example of Friends therefore illustrates that groups within the Russian Federation are capable of developing the right skills and sustaining resources both locally and from overseas, and to act as a bridge between the individual and the state. However, Friends is the only example of such a group in this study, and while it had a growing membership, it was still minute in comparison to the population of Samara *Oblast'* as a whole. Moreover, its success here is judged against specific, predominantly Western, criteria for civil society organisations as acknowledged above. Samara and Russia as a whole have a long way to go in developing more organisations that resemble Friends or developing their own model for an organisation which, while not conforming to a Western set of criteria, still facilitates civil society development and citizen participation therein.

MOs. Both types of MO were present in this study. One group, the Academy of Ecologists (AE) was previously a GRO, which had begun to offer consultancy services to the regional administration as a strategy to ensure its survival. The other two, the Samara Ecology Rights Centre (SERC) and the Samara Ecology Club (SEC) were both established as adjuncts to the Regional Committee for Natural Resources, whose remit includes environmental protection.[6]

The Academy of Ecologists was similar to some of the GROs in this study, in that their membership was made up entirely of those with PhDs in the area of ecology. They differed from the GROs however in actively restricting their membership to those with the right qualifications, and they ensured that this was maintained by making membership by invitation only. During this period, AE actively restricted its membership to no more than 50 members, and made no changes to its approach to recruitment. Although instituted in 1995, the group had already begun to carry out consultation practices for the regional administration by the beginning of this study. Initially they hoped to carry on their research work into pollution-control solutions, but by the end of the research period, their only source of income was state consultancy, and so this dominated their agenda. This consultancy work enabled them to maintain their organisation, and they certainly had a steady flow of income and resources far in excess of all the GROs in this study except for Friends. However, while AE was more successful at generating revenue and maintaining its membership than many of its GRO counterparts in Russia, as described by Murphy (2003), its proximity to the state and its consultancy activity meant that it was no longer an agent of civil society. Although technically registered as an NGO, it did not seek to bridge the gap between the individual and the state, and could no longer act as a counterweight to the state. It did provide resources to the state—but to further the state's agenda, not to help it build civic institutions. These factors and its implied political subservience meant that AE performed no civil society function.

SEC and SERC were examples of the more institutionalised form of MO now present across Russia. They had paid staff, office space, and although they were connected directly or indirectly to the state and regulatory authorities, they were registered as public institutions. Both organisations were connected to one key official within the regional ministry for national resources (which includes environmental protection). This official had set up SEC as an environmental interest group for key individuals within Samara *Oblast'*, including company leaders such as representatives from Russia's largest oil and gas companies and Russia's largest automobile manufacturer, AvtoVAZ Lada, leading academics, elected officials and other ranking members of Samara's regulatory bodies. Although their membership was growing during the period of this research, like AE above, it was also limited to those who had been recommended or invited. Their resources came from charging membership fees and donations from local companies. Their stated aim was the 'professional assessment of the environment in the Samara region' (Leader, SERC). Their activities included an annual prize for the 'greenest' company, and a monthly publication communicating the environmental achievements of its members. Again, although registered as a public institution, the

---

[6]The Regional Committee for Natural Resources is the regional/*oblast'* extension of the State Committee for Natural Resources, or *Minresursov*.

organisation existed to represent the interests of the membership, and not the interests of the natural environment. Moreover, their proximity to the state and their closed membership also meant that the SEC had no civil society function.

Finally, SERC was a public organisation set up within the state bureaucracy. It had paid staff, including lawyers and biologists, and worked directly for the regional administration. Although it had previously had a small grant from the Soros Foundation, its sole income source during the course of this study came from the state. Its role as a registered public organisation was to participate in public consultation exercises and round tables, thereby acting as what Cook and Vinogradova (2006, p. 35) have described as a 'putative' representative of civil society in these settings. It had no membership, only paid employees, and did not seek out volunteers or campaign on environmental issues; yet during the course of this study it had increased the number of its paid employees and moved to larger offices. Its sole remit was to act as a resource to the state in furthering and supporting its agenda. Thus, despite its relative success in terms of access to resources and increasing its paid staff, as with AE and SEC above, it performed no civil society function, and was instead an agent of the state.

In summary, the MOs in this study show similarities with those described in the extant literature in this area. These organisations were the most successful in this study at generating income, and acquiring paid staff and office space, yet at the same time they performed no civil society function despite being registered as public institutions; this is in sharp contrast to the majority of the GROs who experienced a decline in activity, resources and membership during this research.

Conclusion

The purpose of this study was to assess the contribution made by the SEM to the development of civil society within one Russian region, Samara *Oblast'*, by comparing the characteristics of Russian NGOs within the extant literature, to those within the SEM. In so doing, many of the characteristics described within the literature are replicated here. Save the absence of professional organisations, all but one of the NGOs that make up the SEM conformed to the description of Russian NGOs found elsewhere. The Samara GROs also displayed the following range of particular characteristics that have been found in other studies' Russian NGOs more widely: they focussed on single or local issues (Cook & Vinogradova 2006); more than half were dominated by academics and were hierarchical in nature (Crotty 2006; Murphy 2003); all but three—Cottage People, I2 and Friends—were parochial, failing to reach out to the ordinary population or strive for mass mobilisation (Tynkkynen 2006; Sundstrom 2002); with the exception of NKSEU, I2 and Friends, they mostly used apolitical methods of campaigning such as round tables and publications, and were devoid of regular or substantive funding sources (Henry 2006; Cook & Vinogradova 2006); and all had seen their membership and activity decline during the course of this study. As a result, all but three of the GROs were 'invisible' to government (Cook & Vinogradova 2006).

Similarly, the MOs in this study also conformed to type as revealed by studies from other parts of Russia: each either performed consultancy work for, or were an adjunct of the state (Henry 2006) and thus were 'putative' representatives of civil society rather than active participants (Cook & Vinogradova 2006, p. 35). Although they had increased their membership, paid staff and activity during this period, their proximity to the state meant that they performed no civil society function. In combination, these characteristics meant that the majority of the groups in this study, MO or GRO, contributed nothing to Russia's civil society development. Thus, they did not correspond to the characteristics described by Taylor (2006) of teaching citizens the 'norms and values' of democracy, acting as a counterweight to the state, or as a 'resource' in developing democracy.

The only active contributions to civil society development in Samara came from the three GROs, the Cottage People, I2 and Friends. Although initially successful at engaging the public and acting as a counterweight to the state, both the Cottage People and I2 failed to translate their single-issue groups into organisations with a broader remit. Only Friends succeeded in productively using endowments of overseas funding, thus proving an exception to the findings of the majority of extant literature in this area (Henry 2001; Henderson 2002; Richter 2000, 2002; Crotty 2003; Murphy 2003; Sundstrom 2005). In contrast to most other Russian NGOs they were able to build an organisation made up of volunteers, capable of generating its own funding, and thus effecting sustained and successful campaigning, in their case within the area of the National Park. Thus Friends was the only group in this study capable of conforming to the roles outlined by Taylor (2006) of teaching citizens the 'norms and values' of democracy and acting as a counterweight to the state, and by Neace (1999) of bridging the gap between the individual and the state in a sustainable way.

The results of this research allow a number of conclusions to be drawn, but these issues should be seen in light of this study's limitations. While this research has shown a strong relationship between the results presented here, and those collated from studies of Russian NGOs elsewhere, it should be noted that this article focuses only on one group of NGOs, the SEM, in one *Oblast'*. Results taken from a wider sample or from a different sub-set of NGOs may have demonstrated a different relationship with the extant literature. In addition, the article, following many other scholars in this area, for example Mendelson and Gerber (2007), explicitly uses a Western construct to examine the development of Russian civil society and the contribution of NGOs and pressure groups to it. Adopting an alternative framework may have yielded different results.

Returning to Doherty and Doyle's (2006) characterisation of social movements, it is clear that the SEM as a whole does not fulfil the criteria set out by these scholars. As the SEM was devoid of professional organisations, which are politically adversarial (Henry 2006), and was dominated by apolitical GROs and politically subservient MOs, the SEM failed to embody a public political dimension. Moreover, as the majority of the GROs were 'invisible' to government (Cook & Vinogradova 2006), and focused on single or specifically local issues, with no ambition for mass mobilisation (Tynkkynen 2006; Sundstrom 2002), few embodied a goal of achieving political or social change. Moreover, as the remit and make-up of the GROs and MOs were so distinct—one allied to the state, one with no influence over it—the SEM lacked a common identity developed over time by participants in collective action, and failed to regularly interact with others outside of it. Consequently, it could not be described as a 'social movement', and so, it had little impact overall on environmental policy in the region. It also failed to engage the public, and thus contributed little or nothing to Samara's civil society development. Evidence from Samara therefore seems to refute the notion that the environmental movement is 'the most promising agent of civil society development' (Henry 2001, p. 2) within the Russian Federation, as its pattern of development and contribution to civil society to date differs little from that of other social movements detailed within the literature.

The above notwithstanding, three groups—the most successful of which was Friends—did manage to fulfil Taylor's (2006) criteria for facilitating civic engagement, but this was on a minute scale. For the future, if NGOs in Russia are to be more successful, mechanisms must be found that can replicate the Friends model on a much larger scale across the Russian Federation. However, the groups that ceased to function during the course of this study illustrate the number of obstacles that must be overcome to achieve this, though it is of note that these groups cited the economic issues and disillusionment that have dominated Russian society since transition as the reason for their collapse.

In the future, groups will have to contend with Putin's NGO law and its restrictions and ramifications, in combination with the growing number of MOs dominating Russia's civil space. Both findings indicate moves to what some have termed a 'nationalisation' (Ljubownikow *et al.* 2008) of Russian civil society. This is likely to limit or curtail any efforts made to replicate the Friends model across the Russian Federation. Without such attempts however, Russian civil society is likely to remain in the same 'holding pattern' identified by Knox *et al.* (2006), with the prospect of under-development or worse for the foreseeable future.

Aston University Business School

References

Ahl, R. (1999) 'Society and Transition in Post-Soviet Russia', *Communist and Post-Communist Studies*, 32, 2, pp. 175–93.

Baglione, L.A. & Clark, C.L. (1998) 'The Challenge of Transforming Russian Unions: The Mining and Metallurgy Trade Union', *Problems in Post-Communism*, 45, 1, pp. 43–53.

BBC (2006) *Russian MPs Approve NGO Controls*, available at: http://news.bbc.co.uk/1/hi/world/ Europe/4554894.stm, accessed April 2006.

Bernard, M. (1996) 'Civil Society after the First Transition: Dilemmas of Post-Communist Democratisation in Poland and Beyond', *Communist and Post-Communist Studies*, 29, 3, pp. 309–30.

Chaulia, S. (2006) *Democratisation, NGOs and the Colour Revolutions*, Open Democracy Discussion Paper, available at: http://www.opendemocracy.net/xml/xhtml/articles/3196.html, accessed July 2006.

Cook, L.J. & Vinogradova, E. (2006) 'NGOs and Social Policy Making in Russia's Regions', *Problems of Post-Communism*, 53, 5, pp. 28–41.

Crotty, J. (2003) 'Managing Civil Society: Democratization and the Environmental Movement in a Russian Region', *Communist and Post Communist Studies*, 36, 4, pp. 489–508.

Crotty, J. (2006) 'Reshaping the Hourglass? The Environmental Movement and Civil Society Development in the Russian Federation', *Organisation Studies*, 27, 9, pp. 1319–38.

Crotty, J. & Crane, A. (2004) 'Transitions in Environmental Risk: Management Capability and Community Trust in Russia', *Journal of Risk Research*, 7, 4, pp. 413–29.

Doherty, B. & Doyle, T. (2006) 'Beyond Borders: Transitional Politics, Social Movements and Modern Enviromentalisms', *Environmental Politics*, 15, 4, pp. 697–712.

Dowley, K.M. & Silver, B.D. (2002) 'Social Capital, Ethnicity and Support for Democracy in the Post-Communist States', *Europe-Asia Studies*, 54, 4, pp. 505–27.

Evans, A.B. (2002) 'Recent Assessment of Social Organisations in Russia', *Demokratizatsiya*, 10, 2, pp. 322–41.

Gellner, E. (1994) *Conditions of Liberty: Civil Society and Its Rivals* (New York, Penguin).

Gibson, J. (2001) 'Social Networks, Civil Society, and the Prospects for Consolidating Russia's Democratic Transition', *American Journal of Political Science*, 45, 1, pp. 51–69.

Golenkova, Z.T. (1999) 'Civil Society in Russia', *Russian Social Science Review*, 40, 1, pp. 56–79.

Hale, H.E. (2002) 'Civil Society from Above? Statist and Liberal Models of State-building in Russia', *Demokratizatsiya*, 10, 3, pp. 313–17.

Hale, H.E., McFaul, M. & Colton, T. (2004) 'Putin and the "Delegative Democracy" Trap: Evidence from Russia's 2003–04 Elections', *Post-Soviet Affairs*, 20, 4, pp. 285–319.

Hanson, P. (1997) 'Samara: A Preliminary Profile of a Russian Region and its Adaptation to the Market', *Europe-Asia Studies*, 49, 3, pp. 407–29.

Hartner, S. (1998) 'Stretching the Concept of "Social Capital": Comment on Peter Kirkow, "Russia's Regional Puzzle: Institutional Change and Adaptation"', *Communist Economies and Economic Transformation*, 10, 2, pp. 271–77.

Henderson, S. (2002) 'Selling Civil Society: Western Aid and the Nongovernmental Organization Sector in Russia', *Comparative Political Studies*, 34, 2, March, pp. 71–80.

Henry, L. (2001) *The Greening of Grassroots Democracy? The Russian Environmental Movement, Foreign Aid and Democratisation*, Berkeley Program in Soviet and Post-Soviet Studies, Working Paper Series (Berkeley, CA, University of California).

Henry, L. (2002) 'Two Paths to a Greener Future: Environmentalism and Civil Society Development in Russia', *Demokratizatsiya*, 10, Spring, pp. 1–6.

Henry, L.A. (2006) 'Shaping Social Activism in Post-Soviet Russia: Leadership, Organisational Diversity and Innovation', *Post-Soviet Affairs*, 22, 2, pp. 99–124.

Holland, M. (2004) 'Chechnya's Internally Displaced and the Role of Russia's NGOs', *Journal of Refugee Studies*, 17, 3, pp. 334–46.

Howard, M.M. (2002) 'Postcommunist Civil Society in Comparative Perspective', *Demokratizatsiya*, 10, 1, pp. 285–305.

Hudson, G. (2003) *Civil Society in Russia: Russia's Democratic Development*, Center for Citizen Initiatives, available at: http://www.ccisf.org/home/articles/oct_2003/hudson_10.21.2003.htm, accessed May 2006.

Jensen, M.N. (2006) 'Concepts and Conceptions of Civil Society', *Journal of Civil Society*, 2, 1, pp. 39–56.

Kennedy, B.P., Kawachi, I. & Brainerd, E. (1998) 'The Role of Social Capital in the Russian Mortality Crisis', *World Development*, 26, 11, pp. 2029–43.

Klose, L. (2000) 'Lets Help the River: Volga NGO Builds Links with Local Government', *Give and Take: A Journal on Civil Society in Eurasia*, Fall.

Knoke, D. (1999) 'Organizational Networks and Corporate Social Capital', in Leanders, R. Th. A.J. & Gabbay, S.M. (eds) (1999) *Corporate Social Capital and Liability* (Boston, MA, Kluwer).

Knox, Z., Lentini, P. & Williams, B. (2006) 'Parties of Power and Russian Politics: A Victory of the State over Civil Society?', *Problems of Post-Communism*, 53, 1, pp. 3–14.

Kuchukeeva, A. & O'Loughlin, J. (2003) 'Civic Engagement and Democratic Consolidation in Kyrgystan', *Eurasian Geography and Economics*, 44, 8, pp. 557–87.

Lewis, D. (2002) 'Civil Society in African Contexts: Reflections on the Usefulness of a Concept', *Development and Change*, 33, 4, pp. 569–86.

Linz, S.J. & Krueger, G. (1996) 'Russia's Managers in Transition: Pilferers or Paladins?', *Post Soviet Geography and Economics*, 37, 7, pp. 97–425.

Ljubownikow, S., Crotty, J. & Rodgers, P.W. (2008) *Playing Catch: Can Grassroots Organisations and NGOs Substitute for the State in Russia?* BASEES Conference, Cambridge, March.

Luong, P.J. & Weinthal, E. (1999) 'The NGO Paradox: Democratic Goals and Non-democratic Outcomes in Kazakstan', *Europe-Asia Studies*, 51, 7, pp. 1267–84.

Machleder, J. (2006) *Contextual and Legislative Analysis of the Russian Law on NGOs*, Discussion Paper (Moscow, INDEM Foundation), available at: http://www.indem.ru/en/publicat/Russian_NGO_Law_03252006.pdf, accessed 3 Ocrober 2008.

Mendelson, S.E. (2001) 'Unfinished Business. Democracy Assistance and Political Transition in Eastern Europe and Eurasia', *Problems of Post-Communism*, 48, 3, pp. 17–27.

Mendelson, S.E. & Gerber, T.P. (2007) 'Activist Culture and Transnational Diffusion: Social Marketing and Human Rights Groups in Russia', *Post-Soviet Affairs*, 23, 1, pp. 50–75.

Mercer, C. (2002) 'NGOs, Civil Society and Democratisation: A Critical Review of the Literature', *Progress in Development Studies*, 2, 1, pp. 5–22.

Mishler, W. & Rose, R. (1997) 'Trust, Distrust and Skepticism: Popular Evaluations of Civil and Political Institutions in Post-Communist Societies', *The Journal of Politics*, 59, 2, pp. 418–51.

Munroe, N. (2006) 'Russia's Persistent Communist Legacy: Nostalgia, Reaction and Reactionary Expectations', *Post-Soviet Affairs*, 22, 4, pp. 289–313.

Murphy, J. (2003) 'Civil Society and Social Capital in the Post-Socialist Russian North', *Polar Geography*, 27, 2, pp. 174–96.

Nichols, T.M. (1996) 'Russian Democracy and Social Capital', *Social Science Information*, 35, 4, pp. 629–42.

Neace, M.B. (1999) 'Entrepreneurs in Emerging Economies: Creating Trust, Social Capital and Civil Society', *Annals, AAPSS*, 565, pp. 148–61.

Osgood, M. & Ong, B.N. (2002) 'Social Capital Formation and Development in Marginal Communities with Reference to Post-Soviet Societies', *Progress in Development Studies*, 1, 3, pp. 205–19.

Perepjolkin, L. & Figatner, Y. (1997) 'Environmental Movements in Moscow', in Lang-Pickvance, K., Manning, N. & Pickvance, C.G. (eds) (1997) *Environmental and Housing Movements: Grassroots Experience* (Aldershot, Avebury).

Portes, A. (1998) 'Social Capital: Its Origins and Applications in Modern Sociology', *Annual Review of Sociology*, 24, pp. 1–24.

Putnam, R.D. (1993) *Making Democracy Work: Civic Traditions in Modern Italy* (Princeton, NJ, Princeton University Press).

Richter, J. (2000) *Citizens or Professionals: Evaluating Western Assistance to Russian Women's Organisations*, manuscript, Carnegie Endowment for International Peace, 3 (Washington, DC, Carnegie Endowment for International Peace).

Richter, J. (2002) 'Promoting Civil Society: Democracy Assistance and Russian Women's Organisations', *Problems of Post-Communism*, 49, 1, pp. 30–41.

Rose, R. (1995) 'Russia as an Hourglass Society: A Constitution without Citizens', *East European Constitutional Review*, 4, 3, pp. 34–42.

Salmenniemi, S. (2005) 'Civic Activity—Feminine Activity? Gender, Civil Society and Citizenship in Post-Soviet Russia', *Sociology*, 39, 4, pp. 735–53.

Sapsford, R. & Abbott, P. (2006) 'Trust, Confidence and Social Environment in Post-Communist Societies', *Communist and Post Communist Studies*, 39, 1, pp. 59–71.

Shlapentokh, V. (2006) 'Trust in Public Institutions in Russia: The Lowest in the World', *Communist and Post-Communist Studies*, 39, 2, pp. 153–74.

Sil, R. & Chen, C. (2004) 'State Legitimacy and the (In)significance of Democracy in Post-Communist Russia', *Europe-Asia Studies*, 56, 3, pp. 347–68.

Smolar, A. (1996) 'Civil Society after Communism. From Opposition to Atomization', *Journal of Democracy*, 7, 1, pp. 24–38.

Sperling, V. (1999) *Organising Women in Contemporary Russia: Engendering Transition* (Cambridge, Cambridge University Press).

Squier, J. (2002) 'Civil Society and the Challenge of Russian Gosudarstvennost', *Demokratizatsiya*, Spring, pp. 23–31.

Stake, R. (1995) *The Art of Case Research* (Thousand Oaks, CA, Sage Publications).

Sundstrom, L.M. (2002) 'Women's NGOs in Russia: Struggling from the Margins', *Demokratizatsiya*, Spring, pp. 126–368.

Sundstrom, L.M. (2005) 'Foreign Assistance, International Norms and NGO Development: Lessons from the Russian Campaign', *International Organisation*, 59, Spring, pp. 419–49.

Taylor, B.D. (2006) 'Law Enforcement and Civil Society in Russia', *Europe-Asia Studies*, 58, 2, pp. 193–213.

Tynkkynen, N. (2006) 'Action Frames of Environmental Organisations in Post-Soviet St. Petersburg', *Environmental Politics*, 15, 4, pp. 639–49.

Vorontsova, L.M. & Filatov, S.B. (1997) 'The Russian Way and Civil Society', *Russian Social Science Review*, 38, 3, pp. 16–31.

Weinthal, E. (2002) *State Making and Environmental Co-operation. Linking Domestic and International Politics in Central Asia* (Cambridge, MA, MIT Press).

Woolcock, M. (1998) 'Social Capital and Economic Development: Toward a Theoretical Synthesis and Policy Framework', *Theory and Society*, 27, 2, pp. 151–208.

Yanitsky, O.N. (1996) 'The Ecological Movement in Post-Totalitarian Russia: Some Conceptual Issues', *Society and Natural Resources*, 9, 1, pp. 65–76.

Zaslavskaya, T.I. (2006) 'Contemporary Russian Society', *Sociological Research*, 45, 4, pp. 6–53.

Appendix 1. Categorisation of Russian NGOs

		Government Affiliates	Grass Roots Organisations	Professional Organisations
Henry (2006)	Characteristics	• Primary aim is to support the government in enforcing existing regulation • Receive government sponsorship • Have a large number of 'paper' members • Highly institutionalised with leaders often working for or having experience of working for the state administration	• Single issue and local focus • Strong orientation towards academic and scholarly participation • Leaders are drawn from education sphere • Limited or no resources • Limited or no overseas funding connections • Campaigning activity focused on educational projects and active participation. for example cleaning river banks • Apolitical	• Broad campaigning focus, national and international • Membership drawn from Russian intelligentsia • Reliance on overseas grants and connections for funding and continued existence • Campaigning activity focused on practical problem solving, for example pollution reduction studies • Drawn into the wider overseas network of NGO *vis-à-vis* Western sponsored conferences, training etc. • Politically adversarial
		Marionettes	Grass Roots Organisations	Policy/Advocacy Organisations
Cook and Vinogradova (2006)	Characteristics	• Created by the state or government officials • Support the agenda of the state • Membership and staff taken from the immediate circle of the official who created the organisation • Have NGO status and participate in consultations with the state as civil society representatives • Resources come directly or indirectly from the state	• Focused on satisfying the needs of its membership, for example, veterans or a specific group or cause for example social problems or environmental issues • Funding sources are limited to private contributions or overseas funding • Campaign through round tables. consultation. commissions • Many generate a good relationship with local officials • Apolitical	• Focus on policy or assisting the development of other NGOs • Politically adversarial • Broad campaigning focus • Resources from overseas donors predominate

Appendix 2. The Samara environmental movement

Classification	Name	Size, date established, membership	Main objectives	Sources of funding
GRO				
1.	Samara Society of Humanities and Aesthetics	• 1998 • 57 key members on board—stable throughout the course of the project • All academics	• Public education and betterment of peoples lives	• Small member donations only
2.	Cottage People	• 1999 • Up to 100, declining throughout project • Cottage Owners in coalition with other groups	• To stop the dumping of municipal waste in the vicinity of their *dachas*	• None
3.	Samara Branch Socio-Ecological Union	• Early 1990s • Previously up to 25 people, declined to three and then to zero throughout the course of the project	• Various environmental projects, information dissemination and education	• Two grants from Soros Foundation in the past • Now defunct
4.	Movement of Animal Protectors	• 1995 • 20–30 members—stable during the duration of the project	• Animal shelter for stray pets—particularly dogs and cats • Educating children and the public about animal protection • Changing Russian Law on Animal protection and cruelty to animals	• No external funding • Member donations
5.	Socio-Ecological Union—Tol'yatti Branch	• 1989—registered 1993 • 80 members in four branches, stable during the course of the project	• Improve the quality of the environment and health in Tol'yatti • Public education	• Little • Some for consultancy
6.	Initiative 2—Chapaevsk	• 1997 • 100+ declining to 17 during the course of the project	• To maintain the closure of a factory constructed for the decommissioning of Chemical Weapons in Chapayevsk	• One small historical grant for PC • Members donations

(continued)

Appendix 2. (Continued)

Classification	Name	Size, date established, membership	Main objectives	Sources of funding
7.	Socio-Ecological Union—Novo-Kuibyshevsk Branch	• 1992 • 10 core members with three on 'guiding' council, stable during course of project • Multiple links with other organisations in the city from which support is drawn for actions	• Improve the ecological situation in NK with particular focus on industrial pollution • Contribute to the improvement of the Volga and Volga region	• Limited but successful in obtaining a number of one off grants. No grants obtained during the course of this study
8.	Samara Regional Ecological Society	• 1998—Group of academics (friends) • 15 members on the board—academics. Membership stable during the course of this study	• To improve ecological culture and politics	• None
9.	Samara Bird Society	• 1984 • 10 members, various ages with scientific background or students at the beginning of the project. Now zero	• Protection of birds in the Samara Region • Establishing the protection of species listed in the Red Book • Prevention of hunting in spring and poaching	• No sources of funding, none sought • Now defunct
10.	Friends of the Samarskaya Luka National Park—Zhiguliovsk	• 2001 • 125 members increasing to 150 during the course of this study	• Education, protection and cleaning of the Samarskaya Luka National Park	• Small grants • UNESCO • World Wide Fund for Nature • Business subsidies
11.	Rainbow Keepers—Samara Branch	• 1989, seven active members with a further 50 associates. Reduced to zero during the course of this project	• Improve the consciousness of people and themselves	• Limited • Some assistance from national organisation • Now defunct

(continued)

Appendix 2. (Continued)

Classification	Name	Size, date established, membership	Main objectives	Sources of funding
MO				
1.	Samara Ecological Rights Centre	• 1996, 20 workers, increased to 30+ during the course of this study • Academics and students at the universities in Samara • Paid workers—lawyers and biologists	• Share intellectual and practical knowledge about the environment • Establish ecological legislation • Defend ecological rights of the population	• Charge for services • Grants from Soros Foundation and other grants from Administration
2.	Samara Ecology Club	• 1999 • 30 organisations and 100 individual members, increased to 150 individuals and 50 organisations during the course of this study	• Professional assessment of environmental situation in Samara	• Membership fees from organisations and individual members • Company sponsorship of events and awards
3.	Academy of Ecologists	• 1995 • 37 members—all academics, mostly professors. Membership stable during the course of this project	• To develop scientific solutions to environmental problems • Act as environmental consultants to companies and the administration in Samara	• Charge for consulting • Membership fee

Index

Note: Page numbers in **bold** type refer to figures
Page numbers in *italic* type refer to tables
Page numbers followed by 'n' refer to notes

Related titles from Routledge

Elites and Identities in Post-Soviet Space

Edited by David Lane

The dissolution of the communist system led to the creation of new states and the formation of new concepts of citizenship in the post-Soviet states of Central and Eastern Europe.

This book addresses how domestic elites (regional, political and economic) influenced the formation of national identities and the ways in which citizenship has been defined. A second component considers the external dimensions: the ways in which foreign elites influenced either directly or indirectly the concept of identity and the interaction with internal elites. The essays consider the role of the European Union in attempting to form a European identity. Moreover, the growing internationalisation of economies (privatisation, monetary harmonisation, dependence on trade) also had effects on the kind of 'national identity' sought by the new nation states as well as the defining by them of 'the other'.

This book was originally published as a special issue of *Europe-Asia Studies*.

April 2012: 246 x 174: 214pp
Hb: 978-0-415-50022-7
£85 / $145

Available from all good bookshops